EDUCATION 95/96

Twenty-Second Edition

Editor

Fred Schultz
University of Akron

Fred Schultz, professor of education at the University of Akron, attended Indiana University to earn a B.S. in social science education in 1962, an M.S. in the history and philosophy of education in 1966, and a Ph.D. in the history and philosophy of education and American studies in 1969. His B.A. in Spanish was conferred from the University of Akron in May 1985. He is actively involved in researching the development and history of American education with a primary focus on the history of ideas and social philosophy of education. He also likes to study languages.

SCHOOL OF EDUCATION
CURRICULUM LABORATORY
UM-DEARBORN

Cover illustration by Mike Eagle

Annual Editions
A Library of Information from the Public Press

The Dushkin Publishing Group, Inc.
Sluice Dock, Guilford, Connecticut 06437

The Annual Editions Series

Annual Editions is a series of over 65 volumes designed to provide the reader with convenient, low-cost access to a wide range of current, carefully selected articles from some of the most important magazines, newspapers, and journals published today. Annual Editions are updated on an annual basis through a continuous monitoring of over 300 periodical sources. All Annual Editions have a number of features designed to make them particularly useful, including topic guides, annotated tables of contents, unit overviews, and indexes. For the teacher using Annual Editions in the classroom, an Instructor's Resource Guide with test questions is available for each volume.

VOLUMES AVAILABLE

Africa
Aging
American Foreign Policy
American Government
American History, Pre-Civil War
American History, Post-Civil War
Anthropology
Archaeology
Biology
Biopsychology
Business Ethics
Canadian Politics
Child Growth and Development
China
Comparative Politics
Computers in Education
Computers in Business
Computers in Society
Criminal Justice
Developing World
Drugs, Society, and Behavior
Dying, Death, and Bereavement
Early Childhood Education
Economics
Educating Exceptional Children
Education
Educational Psychology
Environment
Geography
Global Issues
Health
Human Development
Human Resources
Human Sexuality
India and South Asia

International Business
Japan and the Pacific Rim
Latin America
Life Management
Macroeconomics
Management
Marketing
Marriage and Family
Mass Media
Microeconomics
Middle East and the Islamic World
Money and Banking
Multicultural Education
Nutrition
Personal Growth and Behavior
Physical Anthropology
Psychology
Public Administration
Race and Ethnic Relations
Russia, the Eurasian Republics, and Central/Eastern Europe
Social Problems
Sociology
State and Local Government
Urban Society
Violence and Terrorism
Western Civilization, Pre-Reformation
Western Civilization, Post-Reformation
Western Europe
World History, Pre-Modern
World History, Modern
World Politics

Cataloging in Publication Data
Main entry under title: Annual editions: Education, 1995/96.
   1. Education—Periodicals. I. Schultz, Fred, comp. II. Title: Education.
370'.5   73-78580   ISBN: 1-56134-353-6
LB41.A673

Twenty-Second Edition

Printed in the United States of America

Printed on Recycled Paper

Editors/ Advisory Board

EDITOR

Fred Schultz
University of Akron

ADVISORY BOARD

Members of the Advisory Board are instrumental in the final selection of articles for each edition of Annual Editions. Their review of articles for content, level, currentness, and appropriateness provides critical direction to the editor and staff. We think you'll find their careful consideration well reflected in this volume.

STAFF

To the Reader

In publishing ANNUAL EDITIONS we recognize the enormous role played by the magazines, newspapers, and journals of the *public press* in providing current, first-rate educational information in a broad spectrum of interest areas. Within the articles, the best scientists, practitioners, researchers, and commentators draw issues into new perspective as accepted theories and viewpoints are called into account by new events, recent discoveries change old facts, and fresh debate breaks out over important controversies.

Many of the articles resulting from this enormous editorial effort are appropriate for students, researchers, and professionals seeking accurate, current material to help bridge the gap between principles and theories and the real world. These articles, however, become more useful for study when those of lasting value are carefully *collected, organized, indexed,* and *reproduced* in a *low-cost format,* which provides easy and permanent access when the material is needed. That is the role played by *Annual Editions.* Under the direction of each volume's *Editor,* who is an expert in the subject area, and with the guidance of an *Advisory Board,* we seek each year to provide in each *ANNUAL EDITION* a current, well-balanced, carefully selected collection of the best of the public press for your study and enjoyment. We think you'll find this volume useful, and we hope you'll take a moment to let us know what you think.

Public policy debate on schooling continues to be intense. The past year has been one in which the debates over public policy regarding the use of public monies to educate our youth have intensified, as have the ongoing dialogues over school reform and equality of educational opportunity. There is a rich vein of journal literature regarding the quality of American education. The public schools have their firm defenders, and the school "choice" debate has increased. Further intensifying these concerns is the emergence of private corporate entities seeking to contract to provide educational services in public school systems. This attempt at privatization in Baltimore and a few other cities has generated intensive opposition from the American Federation of Teachers (AFT), the National Education Association (NEA), and others who defend the nation's traditional patterns of public schooling. There is also renewed concern about the safety of students in many metropolitan areas. Additionally, debate intensifies over what role schools should play in character development, and the dialogue is ongoing about what moral and cultural canons the public schools ought to champion. These and other important educational topics are addressed in this edition of *Annual Editions: Education 95/96.* The unit overview essays that I have written for this year's edition address all of the above canons as well as others.

American communities are intensely interested in local school politics and school funding issues. Not only the 26th Annual *Phi Delta Kappa*/Gallup poll of public attitudes toward the public schools but other essays in this edition reflect these interests and concerns as well. There continues to be healthy dialogue about and competition for the support of the various "publics" involved in public schooling.

The essays reflect spirited critique as well as spirited defense of our public schools. There are competing, and very differing, school reform agendas being discussed, as has been the case for years now. Democratic publics tend to debate and disagree on important issues affecting public institutions and resources. All of this occurs as the United States continues to experience fundamentally important demographic shifts in its cultural makeup. In 1993 the cultural composition of the United States indicated that 30 percent of all American school children were from cultural minority groups. By the year 2000, it is estimated that 43 percent of the overall student body will be comprised of students from minority cultural backgrounds. Minority student populations are growing at a much faster rate than traditional Caucasian populations. Many scholars argue that the distinction between majority and minority school populations is being steadily eroded and will become relatively meaningless by the year 2030; if demographic trends continue, Caucasian students will be the minority by 2030.

Dialogue and compromise continue to be the order of the day. The many interest groups within the educational field reflect a broad spectrum of viewpoints ranging from various behaviorist and cognitive developmental perspectives to humanistic ones. The agendas and interests of students, parents, state/provincial governments, and the corporate world continue to compose the many differing views on how people should learn.

In assembling this volume, we make every effort to stay in touch with movements in educational studies and with the social forces at work in schools. Members of the advisory board contribute valuable insights, and the production and editorial staffs at The Dushkin Publishing Group coordinate our efforts. Through this process we collect a wide range of articles on a variety of topics relevant to education in North America.

The readings in *Annual Editions: Education 95/96* explore the social and academic goals of education, the current condition of the nation's educational systems, the teaching profession, and the future of American education. In addition, these selections address the issues of change and the moral and ethical foundations of schooling.

As always, we would like you to help us improve this volume. Please rate the material in this edition on the form provided at the back of this book and send it to us. We care about what you think. Give us the public feedback that we need.

Fred Schultz

Fred Schultz
Editor

Unit
1

How Others See Us and How We See Ourselves

Five articles examine today's most significant educational issues: the debate over privatization, the quality of schools, and the current public opinion about U.S. schools.

The concepts in bold italics are developed in the article. For further expansion please refer to the Topic Guide and the Index.

Unit 2

Rethinking and Changing the Educative Effort

Five articles discuss the tension between ideals and socioeconomic reality at work in today's educational system.

Unit 3

Striving for Excellence: The Drive for Quality

Four selections examine the debate over achieving excellence in education by addressing issues relating to questions of how best to teach and how best to test.

The concepts in bold italics are developed in the article. For further expansion please refer to the Topic Guide and the Index.

Unit 4

Morality and Values in Education

Four articles examine the role of American schools in teaching morality and social values.

The concepts in bold italics are developed in the article. For further expansion please refer to the Topic Guide and the Index.

Unit 5

Managing Life in Classrooms

Four selections consider the importance of building effective teacher-student and student-student relationships in the classrooms.

Unit 6

Equality of Educational Opportunity

Six articles discuss issues relating to fairness and justice for students from all cultural backgrounds and how curricula should respond to culturally pluralistic student populations.

Unit 7

Serving Special Needs and Concerns

Seven articles examine some of the important aspects of special educational needs and building cooperative learning communities in the classroom setting.

The concepts in bold italics are developed in the article. For further expansion please refer to the Topic Guide and the Index.

Unit 8

The Profession of Teaching Today

Eight articles assess the current state of teaching in U.S. schools and how well today's teachers approach subject matter learning.

The concepts in bold italics are developed in the article. For further expansion please refer to the Topic Guide and the Index.

Unit 9

A Look to the Future

Three articles look at new forms of schooling that break from traditional conceptions of education in America.

The concepts in bold italics are developed in the article. For further expansion please refer to the Topic Guide and the Index.

Topic Guide

This topic guide suggests how the selections in this book relate to topics of traditional concern to students and professional educators involved with the study of education. It is useful for locating articles that relate to each other for reading and research. The guide is arranged alphabetically according to topic. Articles may, of course, treat topics that do not appear in the topic guide. In turn, entries in the topic guide do not necessarily constitute a comprehensive listing of all the contents of each selection.

TOPIC AREA	TREATED IN:	TOPIC AREA	TREATED IN:
American Association of University Women (AAUW)	28. How Schools Shortchange Girls	Equality of Educational Opportunity	23. Canon Debate 24. Investing in Our Children 25. Teaching Culturally Diverse Students 26. School Guides Students 27. Gender Machine 28. How Schools Shortchange Girls
American Federation of Teachers	9. Myths and Facts about Private School Choice 10. Precarious Politics of Privatizing Schools	Ethics and Education	15. Return of Character Education 16. Ethnic Studies and Ethics Studies 17. Why Johnny Can't Tell Right from Wrong 18. Ethical Communication in the Classroom
Censorship	40. Challenges to the Public School Curriculum	Ethnic Studies	16. Ethnic Studies and Ethics Studies 23. Canon Debate 25. Teaching Culturally Diverse Students
Change and Restructuring in Education	6. On to the Past 7. European Schools 8. Selling the Schools 9. Myths and Facts about Private School Choice 11. Redirecting Reform 14. Stop Expecting the Worst of Schools	Eurocentric Curriculum (The "Canon" Debate)	23. Canon Debate
Character Education	15. Return of Character Education	Excellence and Education	2. School Reform 4. International Report Card Shows U.S. Schools Work 11. Redirecting Reform 12. High Standards for All? 13. Blueprint for Renewal 14. Stop Expecting the Worst of Schools
Choice in Education	8. Selling the Schools 9. Myths and Facts about Private School Choice 10. Precarious Politics of Privatizing Schools		
Classroom Management	19. Pathways to Safer Schools 20. Middle Schoolers "Do Justice" 21. How to Create Discipline Problems 22. Lesson Plan Approach for Dealing with School Discipline	Future of Education	44. Searching for Terms 45. Plug-In School 46. American Schools
		Gallup Poll	5. *Phi Delta Kappa*/Gallup Poll
Community Service	24. Investing in Our Children	Gender and Schooling	27. Gender Machine 28. How Schools Shortchange Girls
Comparative and International Education	4. International Report Card 7. European Schools	Good Teaching	21. How to Create Discipline Problems 22. Lesson Plan Approach for Dealing with School Discipline
Critiques of Schooling	2. School Reform 3. What's Behind the Decline of Public Schools? 4. International Report Card 10. Precarious Politics of Privatizing Schools 14. Stop Expecting the Worst of Schools		36. How to Recognize Good Teaching 37. Needed: A New Literacy 38. Giving Their Best 39. Educating for Understanding 42. Exploring the Thinking of Thoughtful Teachers 43. Five Standards of Authentic Instruction
Discipline	19. Pathways to Safer Schools 20. Middle Schoolers "Do Justice" 21. How to Create Discipline Problems 22. Lesson Plan Approach for Dealing with School Discipline	Grading	38. Giving Their Best
		Home Schooling	29. Case for Home Schooling
		Literacy	37. Needed: A New Literacy 39. Educating for Understanding
Educational Decline	3. What's Behind the Decline of Public Schools? 6. On to the Past 11. Redirecting Reform 14. Stop Expecting the Worst of Schools	Moral Development	15. Return of Character Education 16. Ethnic Studies and Ethics Studies

TOPIC AREA	TREATED IN:	TOPIC AREA	TREATED IN:
Morality in Schooling	15. Return of Character Education 16. Ethnic Studies and Ethics Studies 17. Why Johnny Can't Tell Right from Wrong 18. Ethical Communication in the Classroom	**School-Community Relations**	24. Investing in Our Children 40. Challenges to the Public School Curriculum 41. Building School Communities
Multicultural Education	16. Ethnic Studies and Ethics Studies 23. Canon Debate 24. Investing in Our Children 25. Teaching Culturally Diverse Students 26. School Guides Students	**Self-Esteem**	26. School Guides Students 27. Gender Machine 28. How Schools Shortchange Girls
		Sex Education	34. Everyone Is an Exception
Peer Mediation	19. Pathways to Safer Schools 20. Middle Schoolers "Do Justice"	**Teaching**	21. How to Create Discipline Problems 22. Lesson Plan Approach for Dealing with School Discipline 21. How to Recognize Good Teaching 37. Needed: A New Literacy 38. Giving Their Best 39. Educating for Understanding 42. Exploring the Thinking of Thoughtful Teachers 43. Five Standards of Authentic Instruction
Politics of Local Schooling	13. Blueprint for Renewal		
Privatization and Schooling	8. Selling the Schools 9. Myths and Facts about Private School Choice 10. Precarious Politics of Privatizing Schools		
Public Perceptions of Schools	1. America Skips School 3. What's Behind the Decline of Public Schools? 5. *Phi Delta Kappa*/Gallup Poll	**Technology and Schools**	35. Building a Smart Work Force 44. Searching for Terms 45. Plug-in School
		Teenage Rape and Sex	32. Poverty, Rape, Adult/Teen Sex
Reflective Teaching	37. Needed: A New Literacy 39. Educating for Understanding 42. Exploring the Thinking of Thoughtful Teachers 43. Five Standards of Authentic Instruction	**Tracking**	33. Blowing up the Tracks
		Values and Teaching	15. Return of Character Education 16. Ethnic Studies and Ethics Studies 17. Why Johnny Can't Tell Right from Wrong 18. Ethical Communication in the Classroom
Renewal in Education	6. On to the Past 11. Redirecting Reform 12. High Standards for All? 13. Blueprint for Renewal 14. Stop Expecting the Worst of Schools	**Violence and Children**	30. Violence as a Public Health Issue for Children 31. Everyday School Violence 32. Poverty, Rape, Adult/Teen Sex
School Reform	2. School Reform 3. What's Behind the Decline of Public Schools? 6. On to the Past 7. European Schools 8. Selling the Schools 9. Myths and Facts about Private School Choice 10. Precarious Politics of Privatizing Schools 11. Redirecting Reform 12. High Standards for All? 13. Blueprint for Renewal 14. Stop Expecting the Worst of Schools		

How Others See Us and How We See Ourselves

Democratic societies have always enjoyed spirited dialogue and debate over the purposes of their public institutions. Aristotle noted in his *Politics* that citizens of Athens could not seem to agree as to the purposes of education. He noted further that many of the city's youth questioned traditional values. So has it been wherever people have been free. Yet this reality of democratic life in no way excuses us from our continuing civic duty to address directly, and with our best resources, the intellectual and social well-being of our youth. Young people "read" certain adult behaviors well; they see it as hypocrisy when the adult community wants certain standards and values to be taught in schools but rewards other, often opposite, behaviors in society. Dialogue regarding what it means to speak of "literacy" in democratic communities continues. Our students read much from our daily activities and our many information sources, and they form their own shrewd analyses of what social values actually do prevail in society. How to help young people develop their intellectual potential, as well as to become perceptive students of and participants in democratic traditions, are major public concerns. These have always been primary concerns to democratic educators.

Do Americans take the education of the nation's youth as seriously as they should? Do we really care about the well-being of the young?

Concerns regarding the quality of public schooling can also be seen in the social context of the dramatic demographic changes currently taking place in North America and especially in the United States, which is experiencing the second largest wave of immigration in its history. Cuts in federal government funding over the past 12 years of such important early educational programs as Head Start have created a situation in some areas of the nation (such as West Virginia) where only about one in three eligible children from poverty-level homes can have a place in Head Start programs. In addition, school dropout rates, adult and youth illiteracy, the increasing rate of teenage pregnancy, and several interrelated health and security issues in schools cause continued public concern.

The public's perception of the costs and the effectiveness of new school programs is vague at best because we are uncertain about the long-term success of certain models of innovation. For instance, some state departments of education are imposing 9th- and 12th-grade exit standards that are academically demanding, as well as "tiered diplomas" (qualitatively different exit credentials), for high school graduates. We are not sure what the overall public reactions to such policies will be, even though competency testing has been going on in several states and provinces for some time.

There is public uncertainty as well regarding whether or not state and provincial legislators will or should accept a greater state government role in funding needed changes in the schools. Intense controversy continues among citizens about the quality and adequacy of our schools. Meanwhile, the plight of many children is getting worse, not better. Some have estimated that a child is molested or neglected in the United States every 47 seconds; a student drops out of school every 8 seconds. More than a third of the children have no health insurance coverage. Our litany of tragedies affecting our nation's children and teenagers could be extended; however, the message is clear: there is grave, serious business yet to be attended to by the social service and educational agencies that try to serve American youth. People are impatient to see some fundamental efforts made to meet the basic educational needs of young people in the mid-1990s. The problems are the greatest in major cities and in more isolated rural areas. Public perceptions of the schools are affected by high levels of economic deprivation among large minority sectors of the population and by the economic pressures that our interdependent world economy produces as a result of international competition for the world's markets.

Studies conducted in the past few years, particularly the Carnegie Corporation's study of adolescents in the United States, document the plight of millions of young persons in North America. Some authors point out that although there was much talk about educational change in the 1990s, those changes were only marginal and cosmetic at best. States responded by demanding more course work and tougher exit standards from school. The underlying causes of poor academic achievement, however, received insufficient attention. With still more than 25 percent of school children in the United States living at or below the poverty level, and almost a third of them in more economically and socially vulnerable nontraditional family settings, the overall social situation for many young persons continues to be difficult. The public wants more effective governmental responses to public needs.

Alternative approaches to attracting new and talented teachers have received sympathetic support among some sectors of the public, but these alternative teacher certification approaches have met with stiff opposition from large segments of the incumbent school staff systems. Many states are exploring and experimenting with such programs at the urging of government and business leaders. Yet many of these alternative programs appear to be too superficial and are failing to teach the candidates in these programs the new knowledge base on teaching and learning that has been developed in recent years.

So, in the face of major demographic shifts and of the persistence of many long-term social problems, the public watches how schools respond to new as well as old challenges. In recent years, these challenges have aggravated rather than allayed much public concern about the efficacy of public schooling. Various political, cultural, corporate, and philanthropic interests continue to articulate alternative educational agendas. At the same time, the incumbents in the system respond with their own educational agendas, which are reflecting their views from the inside. Overall, it is surely the well-being and the academic progress of students that are the chief motivating forces behind the recommendations of all well-meaning interest groups in this dialogue.

Looking Ahead: Challenge Questions

What educational issues are of greatest concern to citizens today?

What ought to be the policy directions of national and state governments regarding educational reform?

What are the most important problems blocking efforts to improve educational standards? How can we best build a national public consensus regarding the structure and purposes of schooling?

What social factors encourage at-risk students to drop out of school early?

What are the differences between the myth and the reality of U.S. schooling? Have the schools done anything right?

How can we most accurately assess public perceptions of the educational system?

What is the functional effect of public opinion on national public policy regarding educational development?

What generalizations concerning public schools in the United States can be drawn from the *Phi Delta Kappa/ Gallup* poll data?

—F. S.

AMERICA SKIPS SCHOOL

Why we talk so much about education and do so little

Benjamin R. Barber

Benjamin R. Barber is Whitman Professor of Political Science and Director of the Whitman Center at Rutgers University and the author of many books including Strong Democracy *(1984),* An Aristocracy of Everyone *(1992), and* Jihad Versus McWorld *(Times Books, 1995).*

On September 8, the day most of the nation's children were scheduled to return to school, the Department of Education Statistics issued a report, commissioned by Congress, on adult literacy and numeracy in the United States. The results? More than 90 million adult Americans lacked simple literacy. Fewer than 20 percent of those surveyed could compare two metaphors in a poem; not 4 percent could calculate the cost of carpeting at a given price for a room of a given size, using a calculator. As the DOE report was being issued, as if to echo its findings, two of the nation's largest school systems had delayed their openings: in New York, to remove asbestos from aging buildings; in Chicago, because of a battle over the budget.

Inspired by the report and the delays, pundits once again began chanting the familiar litany of the education crisis. We've heard it all many times before: 130,000 children bring guns along with their pencils and books to school each morning; juvenile arrests for murder increased by 85 percent from 1987 to 1991; more than 3,000 youngsters will drop out today and every day for the rest of the school year, until about 600,000 are lost by June—in many urban schools, perhaps half the enrollment. A lot of the dropouts will end up in prison, which is a surer bet for young black males than college: one in four will pass through the correctional system, and at least two out of three of those will be dropouts.

In quiet counterpoint to those staggering facts is another set of statistics: teachers make less than accountants, architects, doctors, lawyers, engineers, judges, health professionals, auditors, and surveyors. They can earn higher

THE YOUNG, WITH THEIR KEEN NOSES FOR HYPOCRISY, ARE IN FACT ADEPT READERS—BUT NOT OF BOOKS. WHAT THEY READ SO ACUTELY ARE THE SOCIAL SIGNALS EMANATING FROM THE WORLD IN WHICH THEY WILL HAVE TO MAKE A LIVING

salaries teaching in Berlin, Tokyo, Ottawa, or Amsterdam than in New York or Chicago. American children are in school only about 180 days a year, as against 240 days or more for children in Europe or Japan. The richest school districts (school financing is local, not federal) spend twice as much per student as poorer ones do. The poorer ones seem almost beyond help: children with venereal disease or AIDS (2.5 million adolescents annually contract a sexually transmitted disease), gangs in the schoolyard, drugs in the classroom, children doing babies instead of homework, playground firefights featuring Uzis and Glocks.

Clearly, the social contract that obliges adults to pay taxes so that children can be educated is in imminent danger of collapse. Yet for all the astonishing statistics, more astonishing still is that no one seems to be listening. The education crisis is kind of like violence on television: the worse it gets the more inert we become, and the more of it we require to rekindle our attention. We've had a "crisis" every dozen years or so at least since the launch of *Sputnik*, in 1957, when American schools were accused of falling behind the world standard in science education. Just ten years ago, the National Commission on Excellence in Education warned that America's pedagogical inattention was putting America "at risk." What the commission called "a rising tide of mediocrity" was imperiling "our very future as a Nation and a people." What was happening to education was an "act of war."

Since then, countless reports have been issued decrying the condition of our educational system, the DOE report being only the most recent. They have come from every side, Republican as well as Democrat, from the private sector as well as the public. Yet for all the talk, little happens. At times, the schools look more like they are being dismantled than rebuilt. How can this be? If Americans over a broad political spectrum regard education as vital, why has nothing been done?

I have spent thirty years as a scholar examining the nature of democracy, and even more as a citizen optimistically celebrating its possibilities, but today I am increasingly persuaded that the reason for the country's inaction is that Americans do not really care about education—the country has grown comfortable with the game of "let's pretend we care."

As America's educational system crumbles, the pundits, instead of looking for solutions, search busily for scapegoats. Some assail the teachers—those "Profscam" pedagogues trained in the licentious Sixties who, as aging hippies, are supposedly still subverting the schools—for producing a dire illiteracy. Others turn on the kids themselves, so that at the same moment as we are transferring our responsibilities to the shoulders of the next generation, we are blaming them for our own generation's most conspicuous failures. Allan Bloom was typical of the many recent critics who have condemned the young as vapid, lazy, selfish, complacent, self-seeking, materialistic, small-minded, apathetic, greedy, and, of course, illiterate. E. D. Hirsch in his *Cultural Literacy* and Diane Ravitch and Chester E. Finn Jr. in their *What Do Our Seventeen-Year-Olds Know?* have lambasted the schools, the teachers, and the children for betraying the adult generation from which they were to inherit, the critics seemed confident, a precious cultural legacy.

How this captious literature reeks of hypocrisy! How sanctimonious all the hand-wringing over still another "education crisis" seems. Are we ourselves really so literate? Are our kids stupid or smart for ignoring what we preach and copying what we practice? The young, with their keen noses for hypocrisy, are in fact adept readers—but not of books. They are society-smart rather than school-smart, and what they read so acutely are the social signals emanating from the world in which they will have to make a living. Their teachers in that world, the nation's true pedagogues, are television, advertising, movies, politics, and the celebrity domains they define. We prattle about deficient schools and the gullible youngsters they turn out, so vulnerable to the siren song of drugs, but think nothing of letting the advertisers into the classroom to fashion what an *Advertising Age* essay calls "brand and product loyalties through classroom-centered, peer-powered lifestyle patterning."

Our kids spend 900 hours a year in school (the ones who go to school) and from 1,200 to 1,800 hours a year in front of the television set. From which are they likely to learn more? Critics such as Hirsch and Ravitch want to find out what our seventeen-year-olds know, but it's really pretty simple: they know exactly what our forty-seven-year-olds know and teach them by example—on television, in the boardroom, around Washington, on Madison Avenue, in Hollywood. The very first lesson smart kids learn is that it is much more important to heed what society teaches implicitly by its deeds and reward structures than what school teaches explicitly in its lesson plans and civic sermons. Here is a test for adults that may help reveal what the kids see when they look at our world.

WE THINK NOTHING OF LETTING ADVERTISERS INTO THE CLASSROOM TO FASHION WHAT AN *ADVERTISING AGE* ESSAY CALLS "BRAND AND PRODUCT LOYALTIES THROUGH CLASSROOM-CENTERED, PEER-POWERED LIFESTYLE PATTERNING"

REAL-WORLD CULTURAL LITERACY

1. According to television, having fun in America means

    a) going blond
    b) drinking Pepsi
    c) playing Nintendo
    d) wearing Air Jordans
    e) reading Mark Twain

2. A good way to prepare for a high-income career and to acquire status in our society is to

    a) win a slam-dunk contest
    b) take over a company and sell off its assets
    c) start a successful rock band
    d) earn a professional degree
    e) become a kindergarten teacher

3. Book publishers are financially rewarded today for publishing

    a) mega-cookbooks
    b) mega–cat books
    c) megabooks by Michael Crichton
    d) megabooks by John Grisham
    e) mini-books by Voltaire

4. A major California bank that advertised "no previous credit history required" in inviting Berkeley students to apply for Visa cards nonetheless turned down one group of applicants because

    a) their parents had poor credit histories
    b) they had never held jobs
    c) they had outstanding student loans
    d) they were "humanities majors"

5. Colleges and universities are financially rewarded today for

    a) supporting bowl-quality football teams
    b) forging research relationships with large corporations
    c) sustaining professional programs in law and business
    d) stroking wealthy alumni
    e) fostering outstanding philosophy departments

6. Familiarity with *Henry IV, Part II* is likely to be of vital importance in

    a) planning a corporate takeover
    b) evaluating budget cuts in the Department of Education
    c) initiating a medical-malpractice lawsuit
    d) writing an impressive job résumé
    e) taking a test on what our seventeen-year-olds know

SCHOOLS CAN AND
SHOULD LEAD, BUT WHEN
THEY CONFRONT A SOCIETY
THAT IN EVERY INSTANCE TELLS
A STORY EXACTLY OPPOSITE
TO THE ONE THEY ARE TEACHING,
THEIR JOB BECOMES IMPOSSIBLE

7. To help the young learn that "history is a living thing," Scholastic, Inc., a publisher of school magazines and paperbacks, recently distributed to 40,000 junior and senior high-school classrooms

   a) a complimentary video of the award-winning series *The Civil War*
   b) free copies of Plato's *Dialogues*
   c) an abridgment of Alexis de Tocqueville's *Democracy in America*
   d) a wall-size Periodic Table of the Elements
   e) gratis copies of Billy Joel's hit single "We Didn't Start the Fire" (which recounts history via a vaguely chronological list of warbled celebrity names)

My sample of forty-seven-year-olds scored very well on the test. Not surprisingly, so did their seventeen-year-old children. (For each question, either the last entry is correct or all responses are correct *except* the last one.) The results of the test reveal again the deep hypocrisy that runs through our lamentations about education. The illiteracy of the young turns out to be our own reflected back to us with embarrassing force. We honor ambition, we reward greed, we celebrate materialism, we worship acquisitiveness, we cherish success, and we commercialize the classroom—and then we bark at the young about the gentle arts of the spirit. We recommend history to the kids but rarely consult it ourselves. We make a fuss about ethics but are satisfied to see it taught as an "add-on," as in "ethics in medicine" or "ethics in business"—as if Sunday morning in church could compensate for uninterrupted sinning from Monday to Saturday.

The children are onto this game. They know that if we really valued schooling, we'd pay teachers what we pay stockbrokers; if we valued books, we'd spend a little something on the libraries so that adults could read, too; if we valued citizenship, we'd give national service and civic education more than pilot status; if we valued children, we wouldn't let them be abused, manipulated, impoverished, and killed in their beds by gang-war cross fire and stray bullets. Schools can and should lead, but when they confront a society that in every instance tells a story exactly opposite to the one they are supposed to be teaching, their job becomes impossible. When the society undoes each workday what the school tries to do each school day, schooling can't make much of a difference.

Inner-city children are not the only ones who are learning the wrong lessons. TV sends the same messages to everyone, and the success of Donald Trump, Pete Rose, Henry Kravis, or George Steinbrenner makes them potent role models, whatever their values. Teen dropouts are not blind; teen drug sellers are not deaf; teen college students who avoid the humanities in favor of pre-business or pre-law are not stupid. Being apt pupils of reality, they learn their lessons well. If they see a man with a rubber arm and an empty head who can throw a ball at 95 miles per hour pulling down millions of dollars a year while a dedicated primary-school teacher is getting crumbs, they will avoid careers in teaching even if they can't make the major leagues. If they observe their government spending up to $35,000 a year to keep a young black behind bars but a fraction of that to keep him in school, they will write off school (and probably write off blacks as well).

Our children's illiteracy is merely our own, which they assume with commendable prowess. They know what we have taught them all too well: there is nothing in Homer or Virginia Woolf, in Shakespeare or Toni Morrison, that will advantage them in climbing to the top of the American heap. Academic credentials may still count, but schooling in and of itself is for losers. Bookworms. Nerds. Inner-city rappers and fraternity-house wise guys are in full agreement about that. The point is to start pulling down the big bucks. Some kids just go into business earlier than others. Dropping out is the national pastime, if by dropping out we mean giving up the precious things of the mind and the spirit in which America shows so little interest and for which it offers so little payback. While the professors argue about whether to teach the ancient history of a putatively white Athens or the ancient history of a putatively black Egypt, the kids are watching televised political campaigns driven by mindless image-mongering and inflammatory polemics that ignore history altogether. Why, then, are we so surprised when our students dismiss the debate over the origins of civilization, whether Eurocentric or Afrocentric, and concentrate on cash-and-carry careers? Isn't the choice a tribute not to their ignorance but to their adaptive intelligence? Although we can hardly be proud of ourselves for what we are teaching them, we should at least be proud of them for how well they've learned our lessons.

Not all Americans have stopped caring about the schools, however. In the final irony of the educational endgame, cynical entrepreneurs like Chris Whittle are insinuating television into the classroom itself, bribing impoverished school boards by offering free TV sets on which they can show advertising for children—sold to sponsors at premium rates. Whittle, the mergers and acquisitions mogul of education, is trying to get rich off the poverty of public schools and the fears of parents. Can he really believe advertising in the schools enhances education? Or is he helping to corrupt public schools in ways that will make parents even more anxious to use vouchers for private schools—which might one day be run by Whittle's latest entrepreneurial venture, the Edison Project.

According to Lifetime Learning Systems, an educational-software company, "kids spend 40 percent of each day . . . where traditional advertising can't reach them." Not to worry, says Lifetime Learning in an *Advertising Age* promo: "Now, you can enter the classroom through custom-made learning materials created with your specific marketing objectives in mind. Communicate with young spenders directly and, through them, their teachers and families as well." If we redefine young learners as "young spenders," are the young really to be blamed for acting like mindless consumers? Can they become young spenders and still become young critical thinkers, let alone informed citizens? If we are willing to give TV cartoons the government's imprimatur as "educational television" (as we did a few years ago, until the FCC changed its mind), can we blame kids for educating themselves on television trash?

Everyone can agree that we should educate our children to be something more than young spenders molded by "lifestyle patterning." But what should the goals of the classroom be? In recent years it has been fashionable to define the educational crisis in terms of global competition and minimal competence, as if schools were no more than vocational institutions. Although it has talked sensibly about education, the Clinton Administration has leaned toward this approach, under the tutelage of Secretary of Labor Robert Reich.

The classroom, however, should not be merely a trade school. The fundamental task of education in a democracy is what Tocqueville once called the apprenticeship of liberty: learning to be free. I wonder whether Americans still believe liberty has to be learned and that its skills are worth learning. Or have they been deluded by two centuries of rhetoric into thinking that freedom is "natural" and can be taken for granted?

The claim that all men are born free, upon which America was founded, is at best a promising fiction. In real life, as every parent knows, children are born fragile, born needy, born ignorant, born unformed, born weak, born foolish, born dependent—born in chains. We acquire our freedom over time, if at all. Embedded in families, clans, communities, and nations, we must learn to be free. We may be natural consumers and born narcissists, but citizens have to be made. Liberal-arts education actually means education in the arts of liberty; the "servile arts" were the trades learned by unfree men in the Middle Ages, the vocational education of their day. Perhaps this is why Thomas Jefferson preferred to memorialize his founding of the University of Virginia on his tombstone rather than his two terms as president; it is certainly why he viewed his Bill for the More General Diffusion of Knowledge in Virginia as a centerpiece of his career (although it failed passage as legislation—times were perhaps not so different). John Adams, too, boasted regularly about Mas-

SECURITY GUARDS AND
METAL DETECTORS ARE POOR
SURROGATES FOR CIVILITY, AND
THEY MAKE OUR SCHOOLS LOOK
INCREASINGLY LIKE PRISONS
(THOUGH THEY MAY BE LESS SAFE
THAN PRISONS)

sachusetts's high literacy rates and publicly funded education.

Jefferson and Adams both understood that the Bill of Rights offered little protection in a nation without informed citizens. Once educated, however, a people was safe from even the subtlest tyrannies. Jefferson's democratic proclivities rested on his conviction that education could turn a people into a safe refuge—indeed "the only safe depository" for the ultimate powers of society. "Cherish therefore the spirit of our people," he wrote to Edward Carrington in 1787, "and keep alive their attention. Do not be severe upon their errors, but reclaim them by enlightening them. If once they become inattentive to public affairs, you and I and Congress and Assemblies, judges and governors, shall all become wolves."

The logic of democracy begins with public education, proceeds to informed citizenship, and comes to fruition in the securing of rights and liberties. We have been nominally democratic for so long that we presume it is our natural condition rather than the product of persistent effort and tenacious responsibility. We have decoupled rights from civic responsibilities and severed citizenship from education on the false assumption that citizens just happen. We have forgotten that the "public" in public schools means not just paid for by the public but procreative of the very idea of a public. Public schools are how a public—a citizenry—is forged and how young, selfish individuals turn into conscientious, community-minded citizens.

Among the several literacies that have attracted the anxious attention of commentators, civic literacy has been the least visible. Yet this is the fundamental literacy by which we live in a civil society. It encompasses the competence to participate in democratic communities, the ability to think critically and act with deliberation in a pluralistic world, and the empathy to identify sufficiently with others to live with them despite conflicts of interest and differences in character. At the most elementary level, what our children suffer from most, whether they're hurling racial epithets from fraternity porches or shooting one another down in schoolyards, is the absence of civility. Security guards and metal detectors are poor surrogates for civility, and they make our schools look increasingly like prisons (though they may be less safe than prisons). Jefferson thought schools would produce free men: we prove him right by putting dropouts in jail.

Civility is a work of the imagination, for it is through the imagination that we render others sufficiently like ourselves for them to become subjects of tolerance and respect, if not always affection. Democracy is anything but a "natural" form of association. It is an extraordinary and rare contrivance of cultivated imagination. Give the uneducated the right to participate in making collective decisions, and what results is not democracy but, at best, mob rule: the government of private prejudice once known as the tyranny of opinion. For Jefferson, the difference between the democratic temperance he admired in agrarian America and the rule of the rabble he condemned when viewing the social unrest of Europe's teeming cities was quite simply education. Madison had hoped to "filter" out popular passion through the device of representation. Jefferson saw in education a filter that could be installed within each individual, giving to each the capacity to rule prudently. Education creates a ruling aristocracy constrained by temperance and wisdom; when that education is public and universal, it is an aristocracy to which all can belong. At its best, the American dream of a free and equal society governed by judicious citizens has been this dream of an aristocracy of everyone.

To dream this dream of freedom is easy, but to secure it is difficult as well as expensive. Notwithstanding their lamentations, Americans do not appear ready to pay the price. There is no magic bullet for education. But I no longer can accept that the problem lies in the lack of consensus about remedies—in a dearth of solutions. There is no shortage of debate over how to repair our educational infrastructure. National standards or more local control? Vouchers or better public schools? More parental involvement or more teacher autonomy? A greater federal presence (only 5 or 6 percent of the nation's education budget is federally funded) or fairer local school taxes? More multicultural diversity or more emphasis on what Americans share in common? These are honest disputes. But I am convinced that the problem is simpler and more fundamental. Twenty years ago, writer and activist Frances Moore Lappé captured the essence of the world food crisis when she argued that starvation was caused not by a scarcity of food but by a global scarcity in democracy. The education crisis has the same genealogy. It stems from a dearth of democracy: an absence of democratic will and a consequent refusal to take our children, our schools, and our future seriously.

Most educators, even while they quarrel among themselves, will agree that a genuine commitment to any one of a number of different solutions could help enormously. Most agree that although money can't by itself solve problems, without money few problems can be solved. Money also can't win wars or put men in space, but it is the crucial facilitator. It is also how America has traditionally announced, We are serious about this!

If we were serious, we would raise teachers' salaries to levels that would attract the best young professionals in our society: starting lawyers get from $70,000 to $80,000—why don't starting kindergarten teachers get the same? Is their role in vouchsafing our future less significant? And although there is evidence suggesting that an increase in general educational expenditures doesn't translate automatically into better schools, there is also evidence that an increase aimed specifically at instructional services does. Can we really take in earnest the chattering devotion to excellence of a country so wedded in practice to mediocrity, a nation so ready to relegate teachers—conservators of our common future—to the professional backwaters?

If we were serious, we would upgrade physical facilities so that every school met the minimum standards of our better suburban institutions. Good buildings do not equal good education, but can any education at all take place in leaky, broken-down habitats of the kind described by Jonathan Kozol in his *Savage Inequalities*? If money is not a critical factor, why are our most successful suburban school districts funded at nearly twice the level of our inner-city schools? Being even at the starting line cannot guarantee that the runners will win or even finish the race, but not being even pretty much assures failure. We would rectify the balance not by penalizing wealthier communities but by bringing poorer communities up to standard, perhaps by finding other sources of funding for our schools besides property taxes.

If we were serious, we'd extend the school year by a month or two so that learning could take place throughout the year. We'd reduce class size (which means more teachers) and nurture more cooperative learning so that kids could become actively responsible for their own education and that of their classmates. Perhaps most important, we'd raise standards and make teachers and students responsible for them. There are two ways to breed success: to lower standards so that everybody "passes" in a way that loses all meaning in the real world; and to raise standards and then meet them, so that school success translates into success beyond the classroom. From Confucian China to Imperial England, great nations have built their success in the world upon an education of excellence. The challenge in a democracy is to find a way to maintain excellence while extending educational opportunity to everyone.

Finally, if we were serious, parents, teachers, and students would be the real players while administrators, politicians, and experts would be secondary, at best advisers whose chief skill ought to be knowing when and how to facilitate the work of teachers and then get out of the way. If the Democrats can clean up federal government bureaucracy (the Gore plan), perhaps we can do the same for educational bureaucracy. In New York up to half of the city's teachers occupy jobs outside the classroom. No other enterprise is run that way: Half the soldiers at company headquarters? Half the cops at stationhouse desks? Half the working force in the assistant manager's office? Once the teachers are back in the classroom, they will need to be given more autonomy, more professional responsibility for the success or failure of their

JEFFERSON SAW IN EDUCATION A FILTER THAT COULD BE INSTALLED WITHIN EACH INDIVIDUAL, GIVING TO EACH THE CAPACITY TO RULE PRUDENTLY; UNIVERSAL AND PUBLIC EDUCATION CREATES AN ARISTOCRACY TO WHICH ALL CAN BELONG

EVEN AS OUR LOWER SCHOOLS
ARE AMONG THE WORST IN THE
WESTERN WORLD, OUR GRADUATE
INSTITUTIONS ARE AMONG THE
BEST, PARTLY BECAUSE CORPORATE
AMERICA BACKS UP STATE AND
FEDERAL PRIORITIES IN THIS
CRUCIAL DOMAIN

students. And parents will have to be drawn in not just because they have rights or because they are politically potent but because they have responsibilities and their children are unlikely to learn without parental engagement. How to define the parental role in the classroom would become serious business for educators.

Some Americans will say this is unrealistic. Times are tough, money's short, and the public is fed up with almost all of its public institutions: the schools are just one more frustrating disappointment. With all the goodwill in the world, it is still hard to know how schools can cure the ills that stem from the failure of so many other institutions. Saying we want education to come first won't put it first.

America, however, has historically been able to accomplish what it sets its mind to. When we wish it and will it, what we wish and will has happened. Our successes are willed; our failures seem to happen when will is absent. There are, of course, those who benefit from the bankruptcy of public education and the failure of democracy. But their blame is no greater than our own: in a world where doing nothing has such dire consequences, complacency has become a greater sin than malevolence.

In wartime, whenever we have known why we were fighting and believed in the cause, we have prevailed. Because we believe in profits, we are consummate salespersons and efficacious entrepreneurs. Because we love sports, ours are the dream teams. Why can't a Chicago junior high school be as good as the Chicago Bulls? Because we cherish individuality and mobility, we have created a magnificent (if costly) car culture and the world's largest automotive consumer market. Even as our lower schools are among the worst in the Western world, our graduate institutions are among the very best—because professional training in medicine, law, and technology is vital to our ambitions and because corporate America backs up state and federal priorities in this crucial domain. Look at the things we do well and observe how very well we do them: those are the things that as a nation we have willed.

Then observe what we do badly and ask yourself, Is it because the challenge is too great? Or is it because, finally, we aren't really serious? Would we will an end to the carnage and do whatever it took—more cops, state militias, federal marshals, the Marines?—if the dying children were white and middle class? Or is it a disdain for the young—white, brown, and black—that inures us to the pain? Why are we so sensitive to the retirees whose future (however foreshortened) we are quick to guarantee—don't worry, no reduced cost-of-living allowances, no taxes on social security except for the well-off—and so callous to the young? Have you noticed how health care is on every politician's agenda and education on no one's?

To me, the conclusion is inescapable: we are not serious. We have given up on the public schools because we have given up on the kids; and we have given up on the kids because we have given up on the future—perhaps because it looks too multicolored or too dim or too hard. "Liberty," said Jean-Jacques Rousseau, "is a food easy to eat but hard to digest." America is suffering from a bad case of indigestion. Finally, in giving up on the future, we have given up on democracy. Certainly there will be no liberty, no equality, no social justice without democracy, and there will be no democracy without citizens and the schools that forge civic identity and democratic responsibility. If I am wrong (I'd like to be), my error will be easy to discern, for before the year is out we will put education first on the nation's agenda. We will put it ahead of the deficit, for if the future is finished before it starts, the deficit doesn't matter. Ahead of defense, for without democracy, what liberties will be left to defend? Ahead of all the other public issues and public goods, for without public education there can be no public and hence no truly public issues or public goods to advance. When the polemics are spent and we are through hyperventilating about the crisis in education, there is only one question worth asking: are we serious? If we are, we can begin by honoring that old folk homily and put our money where for much too long our common American mouth has been. Our kids, for once, might even be grateful.

School Reform

What's Missing

*A master educator surveys America's urgent search for
better schools and proposes some answers. Among them: serious attention
to children's school-away-from-school, the TV tube, and adults who teach
by example—not hypocrisy.*

Theodore R. Sizer

*Theodore R. Sizer is a longtime educator whose books include
"Places for Learning, Places for Joy: Speculations on American
School Reform" and "Horace's Compromise: The Dilemma of
the American High School." Formerly dean of the Harvard
Graduate School of Education and headmaster of Phillips
Academy, Andover, Massachusetts, he teaches at Brown University and is chairman of the Coalition of Essential Schools
there.*

Political concern about the quality and shape of
American elementary and secondary education has
reached remarkable proportions—unprecedented
in the last 70 years.

Thirty-five years ago school reform was spurred by
exaggerated fears of Soviet scientific prowess. More recently, American concern has centered on economic competition from Japan and Germany. Today's pervasive
feeling of urgency grows out of deeper, intertwined
insecurities. As in the past, Americans are concerned
with the unfavorable comparison of US pupils' performance against that of their counterparts in other nations, in
particular in the form of global competition and test
scores. But today's worries eat at our internal integrity as
a nation, too: We fear that too many kids today don't
know how to cope, that too many drop out, that too many
enter second-generation poverty. Too many are unable to
fulfill the obligations of participating in a democratic
society, which threatens the very fabric of who we are
and what we stand for.

Proposals for school reform now come from every
quarter. And what was unthinkable only a couple of
decades ago—the creation at public expense of privately

managed systems of schools, even some of a for-profit
nature—is now seriously pursued.

CRUCIAL OMISSIONS

For the first time ever, the schools have been a central part
of a presidential campaign. We have witnessed debate:
What would each administration do to improve—and to
improve radically—the quality of education provided by
the public schools? This national debate has burst forth
even as the schools continue to be a constitutional responsibility of the states and a practical duty of the cities,
counties, and towns.

Education reform is now, political leaders tell us, a
national issue. First let's focus on some important areas
which will orient us on the long road to better schools.
Later we'll explore two equally crucial areas, crucial areas
strangely and unfortunately missing from the education
debate.

For all the palaver over education, one is struck not by
the immediacy or novelty of the debate but, in the context
of the last thirty years, by the seemingly persistent dissatisfaction with the institution of public education in the
United States. One can trace the roots of the dismay back
to the 1960s. The trigger there was not so much the
quality of the schools but, rather, the access to them by
poor and minority children. However, even as efforts
were made from two quarters—the Congress with legislation such as the Elementary and Secondary Education
Act of 1965 and the courts enforcing civil rights laws—
evidence began piling up that the schools were ineffective
not only in providing a ladder out of poverty but also in
providing an effective education for all children.

The criticism spread during the 1970s, fueled by a spate
of published critiques and the work of national commis-

From *World Monitor,* Vol. 5, No. 11, November 1992, pp. 20-27. © 1992 by Theodore R. Sizer. Reprinted by permission of the
author.

sions such as that chaired by former Secretary of Labor Willard Wirtz which undertook to explain the apparent drop in the nation's Scholastic Aptitude Test (SAT) scores. It had a remarkable fillip in 1983 with the publication of the report of a federal task force that found "our nation at risk."

If a foreign power imposed our mediocre educational performance on us, we might well view it as an act of war.

"If an unfriendly foreign power had attempted to impose on America the mediocre educational performance that exists today," the report asserted, *"we might well have viewed it as an act of war. . . ."*

The focus of the public argument turned away from issues of equity and toward the needs of the economy for a labor force that could compete globally.

More reports and unprecedented state action followed. President Bush and the 50 governors—led, ironically, by Bill Clinton of Arkansas—capped this surge of concern with their meeting on education in 1989 at Charlottesville, Virginia, and their issuance of a set of "national education goals" to be reached by the year 2000.

It used to be that the public schools were an icon, apple pie. Now it appears that they are the reverse, a blot on the American escutcheon. Their *reform* is the apple pie.

FLAWED REMEDIES

The remedies pursued by the early 1990s, while sometimes in contradiction, cluster in three rough categories.

I. The most familiar can be called the *oblique* strategy. Government here does not insist directly on fundamental reform of an individual school but, rather, promotes it at long range by means of a combination of three devices: (1) increased regulation, such as the requirement that students must "take" certain "courses"; (2) increased mass testing, both to tell how a school and a child are "doing" and to identify and thus humiliate the incompetent into reform; and (3) improved teacher salaries, more rigorous teacher education, and stricter teacher licensing, on the assumption that improved schools will come only with an "improved" teacher force. Key phrases for this strategy are "toughening up" and "holding schools accountable."

II. The second strategy is *direct*, the rethinking and redesign of individual schools. Government has promoted this approach less vigorously than has corporate America, especially those companies which for their own good reasons have themselves rethought and consequently "restructured" their ways and means of operation. The assumption here is that the means of education, however comfortably familiar and traditional, are pro-

foundly flawed and that reform requires fresh, sensibly designed sorts of institutions.

III. The third strategy is *systemic*, and assumes both that the oblique approach never gets boldly to the heart of the matter and that the direct approach will not work because it depends on the existing bureaucracy—with its predictable aversion to change—to reform itself. The device to do the job is generically labeled "choice": It posits that only a marketplace where parents *select* schools for their children will provide the force necessary to overcome inertia and the hammerlock that the professional interests appear to have on public education. The scare word is "vouchers," chits worth the costs of education which parents could "cash" at any school, whether public, private, parochial or for-profit. The system envisioned is not all that different from that now extant in American higher education. The GI Bill and Pell student-aid grants are, in their ways, "vouchers," and they follow the student not the school.

In practice to date, the oblique strategy has gotten the greatest play both because it is cheap (requiring other people to do things merely costs the paper to print the regulations), and it avoids the nasty political catfights which are inevitable when detailed institutional reform is attempted. The oblique strategy has had the further effect of undermining direct institutional reform, as the regulations and the syllabi implied by the required tests reinforce demonstrably ineffective but nonetheless vigorously defended traditional ways of schooling (for example, completely disconnecting the "subjects" from one another, mathematics from science, history from geography, and so forth; and favoring sweeping and thus largely useless "coverage" of material rather than thorough understanding).

Because the direct approach is expensive—people in schools, like people in business, need time to redesign their work and substantial retraining—it has gained little favor except at the well-publicized and controversial edges.

DOLLAR DEFICIENCY

Serious systemic change still provokes violent argument, and even political name-calling. Clearly American society has not yet gotten used to the possibilities of different sorts of systems, different sorts of policy incentives, different mechanisms for the learning up (as they said in the 19th century) of young citizens. However, if recent history about other sorts of educational change is any indication, Americans will get used to such possibilities, and soon. For example, the ambitious redesign of schools was considered both radical and fanciful in 1985; it is mainstream today.

The citizen watches all this and wonders how serious the politicians really are. Most governmental initiatives (and palliatives, such as the S&L bailout) involve money, investment in the desired change. Apart from bringing up teachers' salaries (which still lag behind America's first-world economic competitors) and supporting specific programs, such as those affecting handicapped students, the investment in reform *per se* has to date been trivial.

Some leaders argue that there is enough money already in the system and that the task is to reallocate those dollars. Persuasive though this sounds, the stubborn fact is that America invests proportionally less in its elementary and secondary schools than do its economic competitors (although when higher education is factored in, the United States appears a leader). And in many states and communities the traditional sources of school aid—the property tax and the sales tax—are drying up, and with them the core funding for the schools.

'THIS IS WHAT YOU WANT!'

In many regions, schools serving the poor are under a sort of financial siege not seen in America for decades. *How odd this is,* the citizen thinks, at the time the political leaders are calling for reform of education, a reform necessary for economic and civic renewal.

There is, then, remarkable silence about money for reform. Are there other silences, perhaps equally or more important? Indeed there are, at least two.

In 1950 less than 5% of US homes had television. Today almost every American home has at least one television set. The impact of this is not only that so many more homes have television but that, over the years, the average amount of time a television set is on in the household has increased dramatically—to the point where that set is on and being more or less watched more than seven hours a day.

Television has become the biggest school system, the principal shaper of culture.

The television revolution has occurred and, what's more, it has spawned progeny. For instance, 56.4% of households today have cable (nearly three times as many as in 1980), and though cable may provide a wider range of programming than that offered by the Big Three networks, it is in essence another opportunity to turn on the set.

Typical youngsters will be in a room with a TV set on for more hours a day than they spend per day in class in school—in fact, more hours a day than they spend doing anything else except sleeping. They may or may not attend to that set, just as each student may or may not attend to what goes on in the school classroom (when carefully observed, the students appear to attend to the

subject in a class about 40% of the class time). However, the likelihood of substantial influence—"education"—from television is exceedingly high.

Television has become the biggest school system, the principal shaper of culture. Across America (and the world) there is a new cultural homogeneity created by television, a sense of what is more or less important, what is news, what is to be admired, who the heroes are. While formal research is thin on this conclusion, one has merely to visit schools and listen to the students, to what they think is "in," to whom they admire, to what they want to buy at the cookie-cutter malls found from Seattle to Atlanta, to what they think the good and decent life is and might be.

Willy nilly, television is powerfully influencing the young on what it is to be an American. And because of the way that television is financed, that influence is unrelievedly consumerist. *This is what you want! This person whom you should admire wants this!* These are hardly messages that are to deepen a young person's analytical or critical powers or to expose him or her to the unknown or to press for values that are unconnected from those which appear to the marketeers to "entertain" and thus draw the maximum number of desired watchers. That is, TV's messages are "educative" in that they influence; but they are not "educative" in the sense that the school reform movement deems essential.

Programs are "sponsored" by businesses in order to extend their business. That is, television is an agent of commerce, an electronic billboard. Given the huge costs of the medium, business can justify "sponsorship" to its stockholders only if that investment creates or increases a market. It would be unreasonable to argue otherwise, save at the margins—a public service program here and a modest subsidy of public television there. The way the television "system" works means that it must be consumerist in its intent; because the bottom line is audience size (the Nielsen ratings—how many are watching—determine the advertising rates), high-quality programming is in this climate nothing short of altruistic.

However, must this be so? If the school "system" can be changed, why might not also the wireless and cable television apparatus, the telecommunications "system" be changed? Must it be almost entirely commercial, or is there a significant way both to protect the advertising function of the medium and to use it as itself a sort of "school"? Can it be turned to profound educative purposes, to do on a large scale what the Children's Television Workshop has attempted to do on a small scale with "Sesame Street" and associated programs? Though merely reserving cable "channels" for local not-for-profit use was not enough to change viewing fare (any more than merely "ordering" through regulation that schools should change), even that foothold was destroyed: In 1985 the United States Court of Appeals determined that cable systems no longer were required (as they once were) to carry *any* local broadcast stations.

THE NEXT LEAP FORWARD

Simply, can the "system" be altered so that the communications environment—*which we all own*, as free for each of us as the air we breathe—is to some significant and secure degree commandeered for central and public educational purposes? The right to broadcast is limited to those with licenses, and licenses are awarded by the Federal Communications Commission with the supposed understanding that a broadcaster is obligated to use those public airwaves in a way that "serves the public interest."

Clearly, the interests served now are less public than private, and more profit- than service-oriented.

Even more radical, can we change the very nature of what it is to watch TV? Can the incentives for a student's use of that medium be made powerful so that "watching a television program" is an active, engaging experience more than merely an "extra credit," supplementary (and ultimately passive) sort of thing? Can the existing schooling system be changed to accommodate this electronic "school" as something unique and powerful in its own right and not merely an adjunct to the familiar pedagogy of the traditional classroom?

Most of us follow people even more than ideas: We do what those whom we admire do.

Americans are but a decade from yet another technological leap forward, their connection by means of a nationwide fiber-optic network linking ever larger numbers of individuals, schools, homes, universities, and businesses to a massive national data base—in effect, giving the individual access to a vast library. And there is more: It may be possible for the individual to interact with that "library" in creative ways; that is, to be far more than just a passive recipient of what is "there to see." The computer, the telephone, and the television set will blend together—creating a yet more powerful "school" than even the ubiquitous TV set is today.

What will be the economics of this new system? What public interest can it serve, and how will that public interest be stalwartly safeguarded? How will its existence change the purposes and shape of the schools, and what measures must be taken even now to energize the schools to accept and then to make those changes?

Can mass education be both improved and made more efficient with a "configuration" (as the late historian Lawrence A. Cremin put it in 1965) of educating resources rather than leaving the public's interest for "education" only to what goes on within the walls of a school building?

The simple facts today are that we already confront in television an educating system *outside of school buildings* which powerfully influences virtually all kids, and that this electronic educating system is sure to increase its power exponentially over the next two decades.

The citizen asks, *where do these realities appear in the debate over contemporary educational reform?* Why is the discussion today only over the familiar—courses given for a certain number of hours a year in schools staffed by professionals? Why is the nation's most powerful cultural medium left virtually to a commercial interest, and rarely to a deeper public interest? The silence is as puzzling and troubling as it is deafening.

I WILL SHOW YOU HONEST KIDS

There is another "silence," one which arises from the simple fact that we all, young and old, learn much from example. Most of us follow people even more than ideas: We do what those whom we admire do. Personages from Jesus to Albert Schweitzer to Mother Teresa to Martin Luther King Jr. have symbolized that truism; and, as the Nazis showed the world, there are other kinds of models to follow.

Kids copy kids, but even more they copy adults. The adolescents among them are exquisitely attuned to evidence of hypocrisy; they deeply resent dicta from their elders that signal "do what I say not as I do." The citizen asks, *if emulation is so powerful, what place does it have in school reform?* If we want our young to think and behave in certain principled, thoughtful ways, how do we model these for them, providing by our example models of the values we espouse?

Show me an English teacher who is a published, practicing poet, and I'll show you students who take creative writing seriously.

Show me math and science and art and social studies teachers who are known regularly to speak a foreign language, and I will show you a school where the foreign language requirement is sincerely honored.

Show me a community with a first-class, accessible, and widely used public library, and I'll show you young citizens who care about reading.

Show me parents and politicians who do not lie, or deliberately skid along the edges of untruth, and I will show you honest kids.

Show me public media that do not demean women or minorities, and I will show you schools where discrimination and sarcastic stereotyping are readily addressed.

It is difficult to persuade young people to read carefully and hard, to respect serious academic demands, to tell the truth and not to cheat, to understand the differences among people and to make the best of them—in a word, to take even the practical, civic life of the mind seriously—if the culture outside of the school does otherwise. One cannot reform the school if the older folk in the community by their actions signal contempt for the desired school's values.

1. HOW OTHERS SEE US AND HOW WE SEE OURSELVES

OUR CHILDREN'S BEST TEACHERS

The citizen asks, *then school reform starts with us?* Indeed it does. The leader who argues for traditional academic values but who practices them little is not only a hypocrite but also a corrupt teacher. So are older folks who "mandate" community service activity for kids—to teach them about the world, to make them empathetic and generous—but do nothing of this sort themselves. ("Too busy. . . ." on the golf course.) And older folks who do not vote, or vote on what is clear to be ill-informed prejudice. And older folks who ignore the collective needs of society, arguing that "what is mine is mine."

And a particularly delicious irony is found with the state lottery systems, often justified as a device to support education: They depend wholly on a population that does not understand the first thing about mathematical probability.

"Getting the people behind the public schools" is not just the politics of annual budgets and bond issues. It is about living the values which school stands for, whatever one's age. One hears little about that in the school reform debate, and there's the pity. We adults—all of us—are our children's best teachers. Silence about our responsibilities as models is a costly oversight. Adult lives that mock the schools' proper values are living hypocrisy and breed cynicism in the young.

The evidence is all around us that many of our young people are not well served by our schools. We all can do better. Those of us who would undertake the necessary reforms must attend carefully not only to the agenda that our political leaders have put before us, but also to *the silences*—the silences that mask aspects of our culture which must be accounted for if true reform is to take hold and flourish.

What's Behind the
DECLINE OF
PUBLIC SCHOOLS?

The growth of teacher unions, loss of local control, the push for desegregation, and the decline of blue-collar jobs— all have contributed to the problem.

Sam Peltzman

Dr. Peltzman is Sears Roebuck Professor of Economics, University of Chicago (Ill.) Business School.

IMAGINE TAKING a trip back through time to a classroom of a generation ago. Many things are different. Perhaps the most obvious is there are a large amount of students, about 40% more than a typical classroom of today. One can look around in vain for a teaching assistant or a lot of equipment. Instead of modern audio/visual gear, there may be a scratchy old record player in the corner, probably shared with a few other classes. There are far less books and art materials, and they are doled out more sparingly. There is an altogether forbidding austerity about it, compared to today's more intimate and friendly place. Austerity is the appropriate word. This classroom is getting by with about one-third the real dollar expenditures of those of the 1990s.

There is another fact that comes as a considerable embarrassment to the voyagers from this generation—this classroom seems to be turning out better-educated students. At least in terms of basic knowledge, of literacy and numeracy, the average high-school graduate apparently is no match for his or her counterpart of a generation ago. While it is possible to quibble with the details, the broad facts are beyond any serious dispute. Performance of students has declined noticeably.

The most widely cited statistic is the drop in SAT scores. While there is some dispute about whether these exaggerate or understate a little bit, they do convey the essential point: In today's crop of college freshmen, only one-third are doing better than the average freshman of a generation ago. In an important respect, this is old news. At least it can be said that, over the last 10 or 15 years, things have not gotten worse; in some respects, they have gotten better. Yet, on the whole, as a broad generalization, schools today are performing at roughly the level they were in 1980. The intriguing question is: What happened in the half-generation prior to 1980 to bring American schools to where essentially they are today?

During that period (approximately 1965-80), real expenditures per student doubled as teacher ratios declined by one-fourth. Meanwhile, student achievement deteriorated badly by every available measure. For an ordinary business to double its inputs, yet somehow manage to produce less is unthinkable, but that's what happened to American education in this roughly 15-year period leading up to 1980.

Why did this occur? Attempts of social scientists to uncover the source of this deterioration have been largely unsuccessful. The difficulty is that the decline was so sudden, sharp, and pervasive, it affected every region and socioeconomic group. Virtually nothing that distinguishes the 1960s and the 1970s from other decades can be ruled out as a cause. On the other hand, the suddenness rules out the operation or important contribution of any long-run trend that was well under way by 1960.

Rather than seeking a single answer to the question of what went wrong, let us examine one aspect of the problem that often is neglected—the political context within which American schools operate. American elementary and secondary education overwhelmingly is a public enterprise. The public sector accounts for about nine out of every 10 students and an even larger share of the expenditures. Taken as a whole, it is

As a result of overcrowding and insufficient classrooms, large areas such as cafeterias and gymnasiums have had to be pressed into service utilizing jerry-built dividers, producing an environment that hardly is compatible with teaching and learning.

probably the nation's largest public enterprise.

American schools are funded publicly and administered by public employees, so they inevitably are going to be subject to the pulling and tugging of political forces. The way these political forces have evolved has contributed to some degree to the way schools have declined.

Politics and public education

Under the decentralized organization of American public schools, public education almost entirely is a state and local concern. There are 50 different state departments of education making policy, thousands of local school boards with some degree of autonomy, and, whatever the political influences that are operating on education, they inevitably are local.

Accordingly, there is substantial local variety in the way school systems seem to perform, at least as measured by what their students achieve. Consider state-by-state data on trends for high-school students going on to college. Typically, they are taking a college entrance exam, either the SAT or the ACT, which between them test roughly 2,000,000 students a year. During the 15-year pre-1980 period, SAT scores were dropping by five points a year. While no state completely avoided this trend, declines half as large were not uncommon. Obviously, some school systems are doing a better

job in avoiding whatever these forces are than others.

In examining states that are relatively less successful and asking what type of political environment seems to characterize them, the rise of teacher unionization comes up as one answer, beginning just about the time that student performance began to decline nationally. Before 1960, there was essentially no teacher unionization. Then, in the 1960s, there was very rapid growth. By the end of that decade, more than half the teachers in the country were unionized; today, about three-quarters belong to one or the other of the major national teachers' unions. This rapid early growth, with over half the teachers becoming unionized in less than 10 years, was accompanied by pressure on state legislatures to grant unions new rights. These days, it is almost an annual rite of fall to have teachers' strikes. Generally, most public employees didn't have the right to strike in 1960. There was a lot of political pressure on state legislatures to give these workers—including teachers—that option.

The result of these efforts was very uneven. The initial success of teacher unions in New York City and New York State spread to a few urban centers and the states that contained them, then beyond those places. Even today, there are a few states where teacher unionization essentially is nonexistent. What happened to student achievement in those places where the push for teacher organization was most suc-

cessful most quickly and those states where the legislatures were the most receptive to union pressures for things like the right to strike? The broad answer is that it tended to deteriorate more than average in those areas where the early success of these union efforts was most pronounced. This is not to imply that teacher unions are indifferent or hostile to student achievement; in fact, the opposite is more nearly true. Albert Shanker, head of the American Federation of Teachers, has emerged as a very powerful voice for improving the academic performance of students in recent years. However, unions also have other concerns —for job security, promotion, pay differential rules, etc.—so inevitably there are going to be tradeoffs. For instance, union-style job security and a flexible ability to replace underperforming teachers can not always co-exist.

Another powerful trend operating on the political environment of schools when their performance deteriorated was that political control became considerably more centralized, a tendency that began after World War II with a movement to consolidate local school districts. At the end of the war, there were 100,000 school districts in the U.S. By 1970, when the consolidation movement was at an end, that number had fallen to 20,000, approximately what there are today. About 15 years after this movement began, around 1960, a shift toward financial centralization began. Until then, local school boards raised most of their own funds. About 60% of money for the public schools was raised at that level, typically by real estate taxes that went to local school boards; the bulk of the rest was provided by state governments. By 1980, the state government had become the senior financial partner, and local school boards generated about 40% of their own funds—again, roughly where they are today.

This financial centralization is not associated with improved school performance—quite the contrary. Those states that moved earliest and most extensively to replace local with state financing tended to have—other things being the same—sharper deterioration in school performance. These facts are consistent with the theory that school performance is inhibited by the layering of bureaucratic controls over them that are remote from and less responsive to parents.

A third important change in the political environment of education was the push for desegregation. At the time these pressures arose, there was a fear that the disruption caused by the need to deal with this issue would compromise school performance. The pressures led to two distinct responses. Southern schools desegregated massively, while northern systems remain as segregated today as they were in the 1960s. Neither response, however, is associated with a marked decline in school performance. In fact, the southern systems which desegregated most completely tend to have done better than the average system in the country in terms of both black and white student achievement.

Business influences performance

A more subtle change in the political environment of schools has not received much attention, but has had a profound impact on school performance. Business groups are at the forefront in pressing for education reform for obviously good reasons. They bear a direct and substantial cost from the decline in the performance of public schools in terms of decreased productivity that accompanies a less well-educated workforce and, in many cases, the need to provide remedial education in-house. It is perhaps a sad commentary on the state of the schools that a lot of basic literacy and numeracy education today goes on inside businesses, rather than the schools.

Their demand for educated labor has grown over time as the role of traditional blue-collar jobs has declined. This massive push toward employing more knowledgeable workers occurred precisely when public education performance was declining. During the two decades from 1960 to 1980, the share of the experienced labor force with college degrees more than doubled, from under 10% to over 20%. College-educated labor accounted for more than half of the net growth in jobs in these two decades.

This rate of growth in credentialization, if not education, of the labor force is unprecedented.

It might be expected that this massive increase in demand for educated labor would have mobilized businesses to resist the forces of deterioration in public schools. After all, their demand for education is growing substantially and, as the forces of decline begin to assert themselves, employers should be out front to put pressure on the political process to reverse it. Obviously, either the business community didn't do that or it didn't succeed. Why did business pressure fail to stem the slide of public education?

First, business interests have to be translated into political pressure. In the case of education, that means at the state and local levels. Second, not all business interests are going to be equally important at these levels—or indeed at any level. For instance, a politician in Wisconsin is going to be more receptive to the interests of the dairy industry than to those of college professors, as are those from Michigan to the needs of auto makers or politicians from New Jersey to pharmaceutical companies. When it comes to an issue as broad as public education, those industries which have some political clout already have weak incentives to get involved heavily.

To see why, take as an example the electronics companies in Silicon Valley. If that industry uses its local political clout to improve California schools, most of the benefits are going to accrue to other employers in the state. Perhaps, therefore, it would be more advantageous for Silicon Valley to spend the limited political capital this industry has on something of more direct benefit, say convincing local politicians to go to Washington to lobby for protection against foreign competition. The point is, influential industries have a fairly weak incentive to push for broad improvement in the public schools. Now consider how much weaker these incentives become when Silicon Valley begins hiring mainly college graduates and Ph.D.s.

A generation ago, when Silicon Valley, or its appropriate predecessor, the defense industry, was bending metal with a largely blue-collar force, a lot of these workers were products of the local schools. A failure of that system could not be overcome easily by recruiting replacements from afar. The relative immobility of these less-educated workers at least gave some incentive for an industry like defense to exert pressure for better local schools. When it comes to college graduates and beyond, however, these are employees who are vastly more mobile than the less-educated labor that merely graduates from high school.

In the case of something like Silicon Valley, proportionately fewer of their employees today are the products of California public schools than the blue-collar workers of a generation ago. In that par-

ticular case, many of them are the products of the local public school systems in India, Korea, and Taiwan. The direct interests of an industry in local schools weakens as its employment base shifts to more mobile college-educated workers. In those states where the locally prominent industries shifted most extensively to college-educated labor in the decades from 1960 to 1980, the performance of the state school system slipped noticeably more than the national average.

While this fact can not be linked to any direct evidence of weakened political pressure for better schools, it does raise a red flag about the plausible role of business interest in public education. The politics of public education remains at state and local levels. In a world where employees and their employers increasingly are mobile without long-term ties to one locality, making the business interest in public education effective is going to be more difficult than it used to be.

Is American public education likely to turn around decisively and substantially improve as it hasn't done for the last 30 years? One easily can come up with a pessimistic answer considering the forces that have produced the drop in performance. The rise of teacher unions, decline of local financial responsibility, and weakening of a direct immediate business interest in the way local schools perform seem largely irreversible. Nevertheless, there is a larger message that can give grounds for optimism: The performance of public schools is susceptible to pressures for change that emanate from its political environment. That is, the public schools are not irremediably unresponsive institutions, beyond all hope of salvation. The question is: Where will the big pressure for change come from?

One possible answer is the business community, provided it can overcome the obstacles to collective action outlined above. That's a big "if." The plausible business interest in the quality of the public schools cuts across geographical and industry boundaries. Therefore, it is going to require a broad-based coalition of business interests with very powerful arms in each state. It is doubtful whether a change of that type can be brought off.

A more immediate source of pressure is likely to come from the burgeoning demand for what is called "choice" today—the buzzword of the political debate about the public schools. If the kind of choice that leads to an effective response, and perhaps the only kind is one in which students' parents can deny resources to the public schools, becomes a widespread possibility, public school performance could turn up decisively. In terms of the levers of public policy, some countervailing competitive pressure on the public schools probably offers the most immediate method of reversing the dismal history of the past generation.

International Report Card Shows U.S. Schools Work

William Celis 3d

Contrary to the grim portrait often painted of American education, a new report finds that compared with other industrialized nations, the United States does a reasonably good job of educating its citizens and preparing them for work.

The report, issued yesterday by the Organization for Economic Cooperation and Development, based in Paris, indicated that American students lag only slightly behind their counterparts around the world in math and science and that a higher than average percentage of American students get college educations.

The United States spends more per student on higher education each year than any other nation—about $13,000 compared with the average of $6,000 to $7,000 for the 24 countries surveyed. Thirty-six percent of Americans between the ages of 25 and 64 have college degrees—among the highest percentage in the world. In addition, the percentage of women enrolled in colleges or universities is higher in the United States than in other countries.

More Private Support

At a time when all industrialized nations are grappling with how to train a workforce for the future, the report calls for stronger ties between employers and educational systems. It notes in particular "the need for sound initial education" for "better integration between academic and vocational studies" and for "an adult training system adapted to the needs of employers, workers and nonworkers."

Although American colleges and universities are improving their efforts to prepare students for the workplace, much of the real training is being done by two-year community colleges, whose long tradition of vocational education is being strengthened through Federal, state and local grants.

The report offers a statistical portrait of American education that is far more favorable than several studies undertaken in recent years by American educators. Much of their research has indicated that American students lag their counterparts elsewhere in core academic subjects and that scores on standardized college entrance exams have been sliding in recent years.

Scores Are Stabilizing

But in recent years, the free fall in entrance exams has stopped, and scores in math and science have also stabilized. The study released today finds, for example, that American students score above average in reading comprehension and about average in science.

The study also showed that, despite criticism of early childhood education in the United States, 90.2 percent of all 5-year-olds attend public or private early childhood programs, a percentage that places the country among the top five nations surveyed out of 24.

Describing the report as "full of pluses and minuses," Education Secretary Richard W. Riley said yesterday that the study "illustrates why the American habit of being comfortable with just being average comes up short in the new global economic environment." Mr. Riley said the report "confirms why there is an urgent need to press ahead in our continuing efforts to give every American child a world-class education."

The United States has a slightly higher number of science graduates as a proportion of the labor force—653 per 100,000—than other nations. While lagging behind Britain and Japan, it is about the same as Germany.

While only 15.3 percent of all college degrees awarded in 1991 in the United States were in the sciences—math, computer science, engineering and natural science—more people attended college, feeding the workforce.

In Germany, 32 percent of all degrees are in the sciences, but the percentage of people attending college is less than half that of the United States. In Japan, 25.7 percent of degrees are in the sciences, but the percentage of people attending college is only two-thirds the rate for the United States.

On the whole, American colleges and universities continue to outstrip competing systems, not only in the total number of graduates but in dollars spent for education. The United States spends $13,639 on each college and university student, by far eclipsing the $10,415 spent by Australia. The vast majority of other countries spend between $6,000 to $7,000 per student, the study indicated.

Not surprisingly, the study indicated, the better a worker's education, the better his or her financial rewards. This is especially true in free-market systems.

Other nations had similar highs and lows. France and Finland, for example, had the highest literacy rates. Belgium had the lowest student-teacher ratio. Portugal, which has recently expanded public education, ranks lowest in math achievement, behind the United States and Spain.

Competing Pressures

The report is a systematic comparison of education in the industrialized world by what is essentially an international research center specializing in the economies of its member nations. The first such study by the 33-year-old organization, which includes the European Community and the G-7 nations, was done last year. This year's study is more encompassing, taking into account differing structures in educational systems.

While the report calls for increased attention to linking educational systems with employment, United States educators have a history of resisting what they perceive as the vocationalizing of education.

"There's pressure pushing the university to emphasize occupational education, and there's counterpressure to offer all kids a liberal arts education," said 'Michael W. Kirst, a professor of education at Stanford University and an expert on the politics of education. "The way American colleges and universities have dealt with this is specialized institutions."

Some institutions, particularly comprehensive state university systems, have established professional schools in engineering, nursing, medicine and other professions. "The question is whether you want to standardize higher education in America," said Mr. Kirst. "Our response in America has been pluralism."

The report and its authors also helped explain some of the shortcomings of American public schools, in which high school students spend about 25 hours a week in actual course work, compared with 38 hours for Finnish students.

Difference in Focus

"In the United States, schools are given a wider mandate than almost all of your competitive countries," said Albert Tuijnman, an economist who is one of the three authors of the study. "The health, social services and sports functions are considered important, but there is a distinct difference in the focus of an American school."

Mr. Tuijnman also suggested that inefficiencies in spending, on everything from books to buildings, and little involvement by teachers in decisions involving schools contributed to the mixed academic performance by American students.

The United States spent $5,177 per student in primary grades for the 1990–91 academic year, the highest of any nation, and $6,472 per student in secondary grades, the third highest, Mr. Tuijnman said.

In reading, American 14-year-olds outperformed students in 12 other nations. (Not all comparisons covered all 24 member nations because of incompatible data.)

In math, American students scored at the bottom of the scale, about the same as Spanish and Portuguese students.

In science, American students scored about the same as their counterparts in Canada, England, France, Scotland and Spain.

The United States' scores were derived from 16 public school systems, a representative sampling that included suburban and rural systems as well as schools in New York City, Washington, Chicago, Atlanta and Dallas.

While the United States spends considerable sums for public education, the authors of the report said many of the additional educational dollars go not into the classroom but to personnel other than teachers.

Teachers make up 2.6 percent of the American workforce. Custodians, bus drivers, cafeteria workers and maintenance workers represent 2.9 percent of the workforce and typically are paid from a school system's budget. Such services in other nations are supported by private enterprise, a movement only now beginning to take root in the United States as evidence grows that private companies can provide services like transportation and cleaning for less money than school systems spend.

The center is part of the Organization for Economic Cooperation and Development, a group of the world's industrialized nations that was formed in 1960 to study common issues. The organization measures unemployment rates, tracks trade volume, and studies how economic decisions made by individual nations affect the world economy.

The 26th Annual Phi Delta Kappa/ Gallup Poll

Of the Public's Attitudes Toward the Public Schools

Stanley M. Elam, Lowell C. Rose, and Alec M. Gallup

STANLEY M. ELAM is contributing editor of the Phi Delta Kappan. *He was* Kappan *editor from 1956 through 1980 and has been coordinating Phi Delta Kappa's polling program since his retirement. LOWELL C. ROSE is executive director of Phi Delta Kappa. ALEC M. GALLUP is co-chairman, with George Gallup, Jr., of the Gallup Organization, Princeton, N.J.*

TWO PROBLEMS — the growth of fighting/violence/ gangs and poor discipline — are by far the most serious problems facing U.S. public schools today, according to the 26th annual Phi Delta Kappa/ Gallup Poll of the Public's Attitudes Toward the Public Schools. Each of these problems was mentioned by 18% of the 1,326 adults surveyed. Lack of adequate financial support and drug abuse were also frequently mentioned.

People cited a web of causes for violence in and around schools, including the abuse of drugs and alcohol by students, the growth of gangs, the easy availability of weapons, and the breakdown of the American family. Remedies for most of these problems may be beyond the direct control of the schools, but people would like to see stronger penalties for student possession of weapons and more training for school personnel in how to deal with student violence. Other measures people consider potentially effective include more job training for students in the public schools, drug and alcohol abuse programs, courses in values and ethics, and education in ways to reduce racial and ethnic tensions. Courses in how to be a good parent and in conflict resolution were judged less likely to be effective.

Other highlights of the 26th Phi Delta Kappa/Gallup education poll:

• People gave the school attended by their eldest child good grades — 70% gave it an A or a B, and 92% gave it a passing grade. But they continue to give the nation's schools considerably lower grades: only 22% award the nation's schools an A or a B, while 49% give them a C.

• The vast majority of respondents looked favorably on such Clinton Administration initiatives as financial help with college expenses in return for public service; efforts to improve school-to-work transition programs; full funding of Head Start and concentration of the program in schools with the highest proportions of poor children; and the establishment of academic achievement goals for children, with financial help from the federal government so that states and districts can meet these standards.

• Americans reaffirmed their historic opposition to government assistance (in the form of vouchers) for those who choose nonpublic schools for their children's education. The 1991 Phi Delta Kappa/Gallup education poll showed majority support for the voucher idea for the first time since 1983.

• The trend in opinion favoring character education in the public schools continues. Moreover, Americans also approve nondevotional instruction in the world's religions.

• Americans have decidedly mixed reactions to the recent flurry of interest in contracting with private corporations to operate public schools.

• Americans give mixed signals on Channel One, the plan whereby Whittle Communications provides free television equipment and 10 minutes of news programming to the schools in return for the right to include as much as 2½ minutes of advertising in the program. Those without knowledge of such a program in their community oppose it, while those with knowledge of such a program in their local schools support it.

• By a 3-1 majority, Americans believe that public schools should give equal emphasis to a common cultural tradition and to the cultural traditions of growing minorities in the U.S.

From *Phi Delta Kappan*, Vol. 76, No. 1, September 1994, pp. 41-56. © 1994 by Phi Delta Kappa, Inc. Reprinted by permission.

• People generally believe that the existing U.S. system of tax funding for public schools is unfair to the average taxpayer.

• A majority of respondents like the idea of charter schools that would be free to try out promising reform measures.

• More people are currently involved in local school activities and reform efforts than at any time in the past decade.

• People continue to believe that the traditional A to F or numeric grades are useful in reporting student progress, but they give even higher grades to two newer forms of reporting: written descriptions of students' progress and checklists indicating what students can and cannot do.

The report and tables that follow provide details about these and other findings of the 26th annual Phi Delta Kappa/Gallup poll.

Biggest Problems Facing Local Public Schools

For the first time ever, the category "fighting, violence, and gangs" shares the number-one position with "lack of discipline" as the biggest problem confronting local public schools. Why has this happened in 1994, only a year after inadequate financing and drug abuse were most frequently mentioned?

Is the current uproar about violence in the schools merely a media phenomenon? To some extent, yes. For all the hoopla in the national press, there is no crime wave in America — except among blacks. Although one-third of Americans rate crime as the nation's most important problem, crime statistics have been declining steadily since 1981, according to the Bureau of Justice. But not in the black community. Between 1968 and 1994 murder rates for whites actually decreased. By contrast, the rate among blacks increased by 65%. A black person is now seven times as likely as a white person to be murdered, four times as likely to be raped, three times as likely to be robbed, and twice as likely to be assaulted or to have his or her car stolen. The total number of murders in the U.S. — about 22,000 last year — has remained constant since 1980, but murder now disproportionately affects the black community.

Contrary to popular perceptions, cities with populations of one million or more experienced the greatest decline in serious crimes last year (5%), while suburban law enforcement agencies reported 3% fewer serious crimes and police in rural areas reported a 2% drop, according to a preliminary crime report issued by the Federal Bureau of Investigation in March.

A Louis Harris survey of U.S. public school teachers, students, and police department officials, conducted for the Metropolitan Life Insurance Company in the fall of 1993, showed 77% of the teachers feeling "very safe" in their schools, 22% feeling "somewhat safe," 1% feeling "not very safe," and less than 1% feeling "not at all safe."* A somewhat smaller majority of teachers (60%) in schools with all or many minority students felt very safe. Students felt less safe than teachers: 50% very safe, 40% somewhat safe, 4% not very safe, 3% not at all safe, and 3% not sure.

Among teachers and students overall, only small pluralities felt that violence has increased in the past year. However, among some schools dominated by minority and low-income students, the perception that violence had increased was considerably stronger. Law enforcement officers, especially those in urban areas, thought violence in schools had increased.

*A summary of the Metropolitan Life survey results can be obtained by writing MetLife, P.O. Box 807, New York, NY 10159-0807. Ask for *MetLife Survey of the American Teacher: Violence in America's Schools*.

A majority of teachers and law enforcement officers believe that the major factors contributing to violence in the public schools include lack of supervision at home, lack of family involvement in the schools, and exposure to violence in the mass media. Students see a wider variety of sources, many related to peer relations.

The accompanying tables present 1994 Phi Delta Kappa/Gallup poll findings on the biggest problems facing the schools and compare the frequency with which certain problems have been mentioned in these polls over the past decade.

The question:

What do you think are the biggest problems with which the public schools of this community must deal?

Problems	National Totals %	No Children In School %	Public School Parents %	Nonpublic School Parents %
Fighting/violence/gangs	18	19	16	17
Lack of discipline	18	18	17	22
Lack of proper financial support	13	12	16	9
Drug abuse	11	11	13	7
Standards/quality of education	8	8	5	11
Overcrowded schools	7	5	11	10
Lack of family structure/ problems of home life*	5	5	3	4
Crime/vandalism	4	5	4	3
Pupils' lack of interest/ truancy/poor attitudes	3	3	3	5
Parents' lack of support/ interest	3	4	2	3
Difficulty in getting good teachers	3	4	2	2
Poor curriculum/low curriculum standards	3	2	3	2
Lack of respect	3	2	3	1
Integration/segregation, racial discrimination	3	3	2	2
There are no problems	1	1	2	2
Miscellaneous**	9	9	8	13
Don't know	11	12	9	11

*New category.

**A total of 33 different kinds of problems were mentioned by 2% or fewer respondents.

(Figures add to more than 100% because of multiple answers.)

The table below shows how public perceptions of the biggest problems facing local public schools have fluctuated over the past decade, a period when four different problems have ranked number one at least once.

Percentages Mentioning Each Major Problem

	1994 %	1993 %	1992 %	1991 %	1990 %	1989 %	1988 %	1987 %	1986 %	1985 %
Fighting/violence/ gangs	18*	13	9	3	2**	1**	1**	1**	2**	1**
Lack of discipline	18*	15	17	20	19	19	19	22	24	25*
Lack of proper financial support	13	21*	22*	18	13	13	12	14	11	9
Drug abuse	11	16	22*	22*	38*	34*	32*	30*	28*	18

*Indicates first rank (or tie)

**Category was "fighting."

There was considerable uniformity among demographic groups as to the nature of local public school problems. However, these differences stood out: fighting/violence/gangs was mentioned more often by residents of urban areas (27%), by nonwhites (31%), by 18- to 29-year-olds (28%), and by people living in the West (23%) and South (21%).

Cause	Very Important %	Quite Important %	Not Very Important %	Not at All Important %	Don't Know %
Cutbacks in many school support programs	45	27	18	6	4
Increased poverty among parents	44	29	20	6	1
Increased cultural, racial, and ethnic diversity among the public school student population	43	26	22	7	2

*Less than one-half of 1%.

Causes of and Cures for Violence

Note that if one combines "lack of discipline" with "fighting/violence/gangs," the figure for total "net" mentions reaches 35% in 1994, whereas it was 27% in 1993. Something appears to have happened, and it was most likely a media creation. There is no gainsaying, however, that Americans live in a violent culture — four times more violent, some experts say, than that of Western Europe.

By coincidence, poll planners decided to ask 1994 respondents two questions: the first to judge the importance of several putative causes of violent behavior among schoolchildren and the second to make judgments about the effectiveness of certain measures the schools might take to combat or ameliorate violence.

To determine what the public believes to be the main causes for increased violence in the nation's public schools, respondents were asked to rate the importance of each of 13 possible causes of school violence. At least 70% of respondents rate the increased use of drugs and alcohol, the growth of youth gangs, the easy availability of weapons, and a general breakdown in the American family as very important causes of violence in the nation's schools.

The first question:

As you probably know, there has been an increase in violence in the nation's public schools over the last decade. How important do you consider each of the following as a cause for this increased violence — very important, quite important, not very important, or not at all important?

Cause	Very Important %	Quite Important %	Not Very Important %	Not at All Important %	Don't Know %
Increased use of drugs and alcohol among school-age youth	78	17	3	2	*
Growth of youth gangs	72	19	4	3	2
Easy availability of weapons (guns, knives)	72	15	6	6	1
A breakdown in the American family (e.g., an increase in one-parent and dysfunctional families)	70	20	7	2	1
Schools do not have the authority to discipline that they once had	65	22	9	3	1
Increased portrayal of violence in the media (especially in movies and on TV)	60	20	14	5	1
Inability of school staff to resolve conflicts between students	59	26	11	3	1
Shortages in school personnel	52	26	15	5	2
Trying to deal with troubled or emotionally disturbed students in the regular classroom instead of in special classes or schools	51	27	16	4	2
A school curriculum that is out of touch with the needs of today's students	48	28	17	4	3

Obviously, such a list of causes ignores the relationships between various causes and makes no attempt to distinguish between root causes and immediate causes of violence among young people. But the strength of the responses indicates that the public sees youth violence as part of the larger problem of social breakdown in America, a breakdown that is the subject of countless seminars, sermons, and sociological studies.

The role of the schools in combating or ameliorating this breakdown is being sorted out by policy makers in thousands of settings. However, considering just the causes of school violence deemed most important by the public, we must go to the seventh on the list before we find one that attributes responsibility to the school. The schools have little control over the first six.

Analysis of the findings by population group reveals that public school parents are about as likely as are other groups to rate these causes of school violence very important. However, blacks are substantially more likely than whites to judge the following causes very important: easy availability of weapons (88% to 69%); shortages in school personnel (76% to 49%); increased cultural, racial, and ethnic diversity among student populations (63% to 39%); cutbacks in school support programs (67% to 42%), and increased poverty among parents (65% to 41%). There is little difference between blacks and whites with regard to the importance of drug and alcohol use and the growth of youth gangs.

The second question:

How effective do you think each of the following measures would be in reducing violence in the public schools — very effective, somewhat effective, not very effective, or not at all effective?

Measure	Very Effective %	Somewhat Effective %	Not Very Effective %	Not at All Effective %	Don't Know %
Stronger penalties for possession of weapons by students	86	8	3	2	1
Training school staffs in how to deal with student violence	72	20	5	2	1
More vocational or job-training courses in public schools	67	25	7	1	*
Drug and alcohol abuse programs for students	66	23	7	3	1
Values and ethics education for students	60	27	9	3	1
Education designed to reduce racial and ethnic tensions	57	27	10	4	2
Courses offered by the public schools in how to be a good parent	51	28	15	5	1
Conflict education for students	45	35	11	3	6

*Less than one-half of 1%.

People tended to be hopeful about all the measures proposed. Not a single one was judged likely to be "not very effective" or "not at all effective" by a majority of respondents. In fact, majorities rated all but one of the remedies likely to be "very effective."

There were virtually no differences in the responses of public school parents and those with no children in schools. It is interesting to note that better-educated respondents were somewhat more skeptical of the likely success of every measure proposed than were the less-educated respondents. In addition, by an average margin of about 20 percentage points, more blacks than whites felt that the following measures would be very effective ways to curb school violence: courses in how to be good parents (70% to 48%), more vocational or job-training courses (85% to 64%), conflict education to reduce racial and ethnic tensions (65% to 42%), and drug and alcohol abuse programs (82% to 64%).

The People Grade Their Schools

Ever since 1974 respondents to the Phi Delta Kappa/Gallup education poll have been asked to rate their local public schools' performance on a scale of A to F. Over the years related questions have been added, including one that secures judgments about the performance of public schools nationally. The most revealing question, however, was one first asked of public school parents in 1982: What grade would you give the school your oldest child attends? Parents' responses made it clear that the more one knows about a school, the more likely one is to think well of its performance. (Certainly, parents have more direct information than nonparents.)

In 1994 more than four Americans in 10 (44%) give the public schools in their community an A or a B, about the same proportion as reported in every Phi Delta Kappa/Gallup survey since these ratings were introduced two decades ago. Three-quarters of the public (74%) award their local public schools at least a grade of C. Only 7% say their local schools deserve a grade of F. These relatively high grades are awarded despite the fact that the grading is strongly based on the views of the large majority of the public (70%) with no children in school or with children enrolled in nonpublic schools.

The first question:

Students are often given the grades A, B, C, D, and FAIL to denote the quality of their work. Suppose the *public* schools themselves, in this community, were graded in the same way. What grade would you give the public schools here — A, B, C, D, or FAIL?

	National Totals %	No Children In School %	Public School Parents %	Nonpublic School Parents %
A & B	44	39	57	28
A	9	8	12	4
B	35	31	45	24
C	30	30	30	39
D	14	16	9	16
FAIL	7	8	3	13
Don't know	5	7	1	4

5. Phi Delta Kappa/Gallup Poll

Ratings Given the Local Public Schools

	1994 %	1993 %	1992 %	1991 %	1990 %	1989 %	1988 %	1987 %	1986 %	1985 %	1984 %
A & B	44	47	40	42	41	43	40	43	41	43	42
A	9	10	9	10	8	8	9	12	11	9	10
B	35	37	31	32	33	35	31	31	30	34	32
C	30	31	33	33	34	33	34	30	28	30	35
D	14	11	12	10	12	11	10	9	11	10	11
FAIL	7	4	5	5	5	4	4	4	5	4	4
Don't know	5	7	10	10	8	9	12	14	15	13	8

The second question:

How about the public schools in the nation as a whole? What grade would you give the public schools nationally — A, B, C, D, or FAIL?

	National Totals %	No Children In School %	Public School Parents %	Nonpublic School Parents %
A & B	22	23	19	18
A	2	2	2	4
B	20	21	17	14
C	49	50	48	45
D	17	14	22	23
FAIL	6	8	4	6
Don't know	6	5	7	8

Ratings Given the Nation's Public Schools

	1994 %	1993 %	1992 %	1991 %	1990 %	1989 %	1988 %	1987 %	1986 %	1985 %	1984 %
A & B	22	19	18	21	21	22	23	26	28	27	25
A	2	2	2	2	2	2	3	4	3	3	2
B	20	17	16	19	19	20	20	22	25	24	23
C	49	48	48	47	49	47	48	44	41	43	49
D	17	17	18	13	16	15	11	11	10	12	11
FAIL	6	4	4	5	4	4	3	2	5	3	4
Don't know	6	12	12	14	10	12	13	17	16	15	11

When respondents likely to be most familiar with the schools — i.e., public school parents — are asked to grade the school their oldest child attends, seven in 10 (70%) would award that school a grade of A or B. This has been true for the last decade. More than nine in 10 public school parents (92%) give the school their oldest child attends at least a passing grade of C. Public school parents' tendency to rate their children's schools high extends to their perceptions of local schools. For example, 57% of public school parents give the local public schools a grade of A or B, and 87% give the local public schools at least a C.

The third question:

Using the A, B, C, D, FAIL scale again, what grade would you give the school your oldest child attends?

Ratings Given School Oldest Child Attends

	1994 %	1993 %	1992 %	1991 %	1990 %	1989 %	1988 %	1987 %	1986 %
A & B	70	72	64	73	72	71	70	69	65
A	28	27	22	29	27	25	22	28	28
B	42	45	42	44	45	46	48	41	37
C	22	18	24	21	19	19	22	20	26
D	6	5	6	2	5	5	3	5	4
FAIL	1	2	4	4	2	1	2	2	2
Don't know	1	3	2	*	2	4	3	4	3

*Less than one-half of 1%.

1. HOW OTHERS SEE US AND HOW WE SEE OURSELVES

There were few demographic differences in parental ratings. However, parents of children in elementary school were more likely to give high grades than parents of children in high school. This is consistent with poll reports in other years.

This year the poll planners added another question to the series on grading the public schools. People were asked to grade the public schools "in their neighborhood." The ratings of neighborhood schools were higher than those for the nation's schools and for schools in the community. While 44% of respondents gave schools in the local community a grade of A or B, 50% of respondents gave schools in their neighborhood similarly high grades. These results should not be too surprising, because a "community" may have a great many schools about which respondents know little more than they do about the nation's schools, whereas respondents are most likely to be familiar with the schools attended by children from the more limited area of their own neighborhood.

The question:

How about the public schools attended by children from your neighborhood? What grade would you give them — A, B, C, D, or FAIL?

	National Totals %	No Children In School %	Public School Parents %	Nonpublic School Parents %
A & B	50	46	60	39
A	12	10	16	11
B	38	36	44	28
C	30	30	29	35
D	9	10	7	12
FAIL	6	7	3	8
Don't know	5	7	1	6

The most significant demographic differences in responses to this question were found in the category of community size. More than 50% of people living in suburban and rural communities give schools attended by neighborhood children a grade of A or B, while only 43% of those living in urban areas give similarly high grades.

Have Schools Improved or Deteriorated?

In three of the last seven Phi Delta Kappa/Gallup education polls, people have been asked whether they think that their local public schools have improved, deteriorated, or stayed about the same over the previous five years. This year, as was the case when the question was last asked in 1990, more people perceived deterioration (37%) than saw improvement (26%); in 1988, more people saw improvement than deterioration.

The question:

Just your own impression, would you say that the public schools in your community have improved from, say, five years ago, gotten worse, or stayed about the same?

	National Totals %	No Children In School %	Public School Parents %	Nonpublic School Parents %
Improved	26	23	32	20
Gotten worse	37	39	30	43
Stayed about the same	33	33	34	33
Don't know	4	5	4	4

	National Totals		
	1994 %	1990 %	1988 %
Improved	26	22	29
Gotten worse	37	30	19
Stayed about the same	33	36	37
Don't know	4	12	15

Poll interviewers followed the question about improvement/deterioration of *local* public schools with the same question about the *nation's* schools. The findings were far more negative. For every individual who believed that the nation's public schools have improved (16%), there were three (51%) who thought they have deteriorated.

The question:

What about public schools in the nation as a whole? Would you say they have improved from five years ago, gotten worse, or stayed about the same?

	National Totals %	No Children In School %	Public School Parents %	Nonpublic School Parents %
Improved	16	15	18	18
Gotten worse	51	51	51	55
Stayed about the same	26	28	24	20
Don't know	7	6	7	7

But when *parents* were asked the same question about public schools their children attended, the findings were nearly reversed. For every parent who believed that the school attended by his or her oldest child had gotten worse in the past five years (15%), there were more than two (36%) who thought it had improved.

The question:

Would you say the public school your oldest child attends has improved from five years ago, gotten worse, or stayed about the same?

	Local Schools %	Nation's Schools %	School Attended By Oldest Child %
Improved	26	16	36
Gotten worse	37	51	15
Stayed about the same	33	26	41
Don't know	4	7	8

What can one make of these responses? It seems likely that the general public has come to believe public education's critics regarding the state of the *nation's* schools, which have been blamed for everything from ignorance of geography to economic recession. Parents with children in school know better; a comfortable majority of them believe that the schools their children attend are improving.

Clinton's Education Initiatives

When President Clinton signed his education reform strategy into law in March 1994, he called the Goals 2000: Educate America Act a "new and different approach for the federal government." He said that the measure would establish "world class" national education standards and rely on school districts at the grassroots to help students achieve them.

The centerpiece of Goals 2000 is a new program, authorized at $400 million a year (appropriations to come later) that would provide grants to states and districts that adopt reform plans consistent with the legislation. The plans must call for setting high standards for curriculum content and student performance, as well as opportunity-to-learn standards or strategies for insuring adequate school services.

Enactment of Goals 2000 was the culmination of a process begun in 1989 when the National Governors' Association and President Bush agreed at an education summit to set six national goals for education. Clinton, then governor of Arkansas, was a key player in drafting the goals. The current version of this ambitious strategy includes two additional goals, dealing with teacher training and parent participation.

Three major initiatives of the Clinton Administration were already in place: increases in Head Start funding, with more of it targeted directly to children living in poverty; a modest program that will allow a limited number of students to earn money for college by performing public service; and a school-to-work bill authorizing $300 million a year to help high schools create work-based learning programs for students who do not go to college.

Respondents to the current poll were asked to indicate approval or disapproval of four of the Clinton Administration initiatives. All four proved highly popular.

The question:

Here are some education programs currently being advanced by the federal government. As I read off each program, would you tell me whether you favor or oppose it?

	National Totals		
	Favor %	Oppose %	Don't Know %
Assistance with high school students' college expenses in return for performing some kind of public service	81	17	2
Greater emphasis on, including additional money for, work-study vocational programs for high school students who do not plan to go to college	79	20	1
A large increase in funds for early childhood education in those public schools with the highest percentage of children living in poverty	74	22	4

More effort to reach agreement on academic achievement goals for children at various stages of school, without specifying how the schools should reach these goals	63	32	5

	Those Who Favor These Initiatives			
	National Totals %	No Children In School %	Public School Parents %	Nonpublic School Parents %
Assistance with high school students' college expenses in return for performing some kind of public service	81	80	83	83
Greater emphasis on, including additional money for, work-study vocational programs for high school students who do not plan to go to college	79	78	82	74
A large increase in funds for early childhood education in those public schools with the highest percentage of children living in poverty	74	74	75	66
More effort to reach agreement on academic achievement goals for children at various stages of school, without specifying how the schools should reach these goals	63	62	66	56

Strong majority support for these initiatives was registered in all demographic groups. Young adults (aged 18-29) and blacks were particularly enthusiastic about improved funding for early childhood education. The percentages in favor were 90% and 84%, respectively. There was even considerable bipartisan support for all four of the measures.

National Curriculum and National Assessment

The question about federal initiatives was followed by another focusing on the idea of a national curriculum and national assessment of achievement. Once again, as in earlier polls, people made clear their approval of a basic curriculum of subject matter for all schools (read "national curriculum") and of standardized national examinations that students must pass for grade promotion and high school graduation.

Although most respondents probably do not understand the full implications of such a significant change in U.S. tradition, every poll in this series that has explored the idea shows strong support for it. In 1989, for example, poll respondents favored national standards and goals for schools by a 70% to 19% margin. In the same poll, 69% said that they favored the use of a standardized national curriculum in the local public schools, while only 21% opposed the idea. The same questions asked in 1991 yielded similar results.

The current poll examined these issues using questions that were worded somewhat differently, but the results only confirm the earlier findings. For example, instead of being asked whether they favored or opposed a national curriculum and standardized national exams for grade promotion and high school graduation, respondents were asked how important they considered each factor to be as a way to improve the nation's public schools.

More than eight in ten (83%) responded that a standardized national curriculum was either very important or quite important; similarly, about seven in ten (73%) thought standardized national exams were either very or quite important.

The question:

How important do you think each of the following is as a way to improve the nation's public schools: very important, quite important, not too important, or not at all important?

	Very Important %	Quite Important %	Not Too Important %	Not at All Important %	Don't Know %
Establishing a basic curriculum of subject matter or program of courses for all schools	49	34	12	4	1

	Very Important %	Quite Important %	Not Too Important %	Not at All Important %	Don't Know %
Establishing standardized national examinations, based on a national curriculum, that students must pass for grade promotion and for high school graduation	46	27	18	7	2

	Those Who Said 'Very Important'			
	National Totals %	No Children In School %	Public School Parents %	Nonpublic School Parents %
Establishing a basic curriculum of subject matter or program of courses for all schools	49	47	54	58
Establishing standardized national examinations, based on a national curriculum, that students must pass for grade promotion and for high school graduation	46	46	45	44

School Choice and Vouchers

Since 1970, these polls have traced trends in opinion about government financial aid to parochial schools, about the use of government-issued vouchers that would help parents finance a private or church-related school for their children, and about public school choice proposals. People have consistently opposed any form of government aid to nonpublic schools and have favored public school choice by sizable margins. But no consensus has developed on the voucher question.

Here in table form is the history of responses to a question worded as follows: "In some nations the government allots a certain amount of money for each child for his education. The parents can send the child to any public, parochial, or private school they choose. This is called the 'voucher system.' Would you like to see such an idea adopted in this country?"

	National Totals							
	1991 %	1987 %	1986 %	1985 %	1983 %	1981 %	1971 %	1970 %
Favor	50	44	46	45	51	43	38	43
Oppose	39	41	41	40	38	41	44	46
Don't know	11	15	13	15	11	16	18	11

Over the past two or three years, Oregon, Colorado, and California have held referendums on various forms of vouchers. Although all three referendums were defeated by sizable majorities, voucher proponents vow to keep trying. Californians may vote on the proposition again as soon as next year.

In the current poll the issue was presented again, without mentioning the word *vouchers* but making clear that government money would pay "all or part" of a child's tuition if the parents chose to send the child to a nonpublic school.

Presented with this somewhat different question, the public opposes the voucher idea by a 54% to 45% majority. The response to this year's question suggests that opinion for and against the voucher idea has begun to crystallize. For example, when the long-term trend question was asked most recently (in 1991), 11% of the public had no opinion. In response to the new question, however, only 1% of respondents expressed no opinion.

In only two demographic groups did majorities favor the voucher idea as stated. Not surprisingly, nonpublic school parents (representing 9% of Americans) supported vouchers by more than a 2-1 margin (69% to 29%). In addition, Catholics (24% of Americans) approved the idea by a 55% to 44% majority.

The question:

A proposal has been made which would allow parents to send their school-age children to any public, private, or church-related school they choose. For those parents choosing nonpublic schools, the government would pay all or part of the tuition. Would you favor or oppose this proposal in your state?

	National Totals %	No Children In School %	Public School Parents %	Nonpublic School Parents %
Favor	45	42	48	69
Oppose	54	57	51	29
Don't know	1	1	1	2

Support for Character Education

"The fundamental tragedy of American education is not that we are turning out ignoramuses but that we are turning out savages," says Frederick Close, director of education for the Ethics Resource Center in Washington, D.C. Close would institute moral education or character education in the schools in an effort to counteract what he calls "a continuously rising crime wave among the younger generation." He echoes the sentiments found in a growing body of literature that includes the best-selling *Book of Virtues*, by William Bennett, who used his office as secretary of education in the late Eighties to campaign for "moral literacy" in the public schools. (*The Book of Virtues* is subtitled *A Treasury of Great Moral Stories* and is intended for home and school use.) Like many of his fundamentalist backers, Bennett believes that we must recover paradigms that we once shared as a nation "before the triviality of television absorbed most of children's attention and before a prevailing cynicism made virtue seem laughable.''

Kevin Ryan, a professor of education at Boston University, points out that public schools have bent over backwards in their efforts not to offend anyone about anything. To make themselves inoffensive and studiously neutral, they have all but cleansed the curriculum of religious and ethical content. He speaks of schools as ''morally dangerous places for children.''*

It was Thomas Jefferson who first used the phrase ''the wall of separation between church and state'' in 1802, and it describes one of the most settled doctrines in American constitutional law. In his majority opinion in *Everson* (1947), Justice Hugo Black repeated Jefferson's phrase in a case that blocked out some of the last vestiges of religion in the public schools. Has the doctrine designed to protect the individual from tyranny diminished the role of virtues and values in civic life? Many people are beginning to think so.

In last year's poll Americans said that they believe their local communities could agree on a set of basic values, such as honesty and patriotism, that could be taught in the public schools. This year poll planners framed three questions related to issues of character education and the teaching of moral values in the schools.

The first question, repeated from the 1987 Phi Delta Kappa/Gallup education poll, asked respondents whether ethics should be taught in the public schools or left to parents and religious institutions. As in 1987, when 43% favored ethics and character education courses and 36% opposed them, in 1994 a small plurality of the public supported such courses (49% in favor, 39% opposed). Support was a good deal stronger among public school parents, however (57% in favor, 34% opposed).

The first question:

It has been proposed that the public schools include courses on ''character education'' to help students develop personal values and ethical behavior. Do you think that courses on values and ethical behavior should be taught in the public schools, or do you think that this should be left to the students' parents and/or the churches?

Should Be Taught	National Totals %		No Children In School %		Public School Parents %		Nonpublic School Parents %	
	'94	'87	'94	'87	'94	'87	'94	'87
Yes, schools	49	43	44	42	57	45	54	54
No, parents and/or churches	39	36	42	36	34	38	38	31
Both (volunteered)	12	13	14	13	8	13	8	11
Don't know	*	8	*	9	1	4	*	4

*Less than one-half of 1%.

To find out what personal traits or virtues the public believes should be taught as part of character education courses, survey respondents were asked to indicate whether each of nine virtues should or should not be included in such courses. The vote in favor of teaching these virtues was practically unanimous, with the single exception of ''thrift'' — and even this old-fashioned virtue was judged worthy of inclusion by 74% of respondents.

The second question:

*Quoted by John Merrow in '' 'Don't Offend': Our High-Level Policy of Cowardice,'' *Education Week*, 16 February 1994, p. 56.

Now, here is a list of personal traits or virtues that might be taught in the public schools in your community. As I read off each item, would you tell me whether you think it should be taught or should not be taught in the local public schools?

Should Be Taught	National Totals %	No Children In School %	Public School Parents %	Nonpublic School Parents %
Respect for others	94	94	93	91
Industry or hard work	93	93	93	95
Persistence or the ability to follow through	93	92	94	94
Fairness in dealing with others	92	93	92	90
Compassion for others	91	91	91	89
Civility, politeness	91	91	90	91
Self-esteem	90	90	92	80
High expectations for oneself	87	87	88	82
Thrift	74	73	74	71

In the 1993 poll, a different list of character traits (some better described as attitudes) was offered, with the following results: honesty, 97%; democracy, 93%; acceptance of people of different races and ethnic backgrounds, 93%; patriotism or love of country, 91%; caring for friends and family members, 91%; moral courage, 91%; the golden rule, 90%; acceptance of people who hold different religious beliefs, 87%; acceptance of people who hold unpopular or controversial political or social views, 73%; sexual abstinence outside of marriage, 66%; acceptance of the right of a woman to choose abortion, 56%; acceptance of people with different sexual orientations (i.e., homosexuals or bisexuals), 51%.

The third question:

The public schools in America are constitutionally prohibited from teaching any particular religion. Would you favor or oppose nondevotional instruction about various world religions in the public schools in your community?

	National Totals %	No Children In School %	Public School Parents %	Nonpublic School Parents %
Favor	66	65	67	61
Oppose	33	33	32	39
Don't know	1	2	1	*

*Less than one-half of 1%.

There were few significant demographic differences in the responses to this question. However, respondents living in the South (71%) and Midwest (69%) were slightly more likely to favor nondevotional religious instruction than those in the East (59%) or those in the West (62%).

Jury Still Out on Privatization

In a development reminiscent of the ill-fated experiments with performance contracting in the early 1970s, public school boards in several U.S. cities have recently contracted with private companies to manage some of their schools. For example, nine Baltimore schools are now being run by Education Alternatives, Inc., of Minneapolis. The same company was hoping to operate as many as 15 schools in Washington, D.C., but that plan has been put on hold for further study. The Baltimore and Washington superintendents have said that they sought contracts with private firms because they were frustrated by bureaucracies so complex and cumbersome that they could not get leaking roofs repaired or teachers transferred from under- to overenrolled schools in a timely way.

The Edison Project, established in 1991 by Whittle Communications, Inc., and now based in New York City, expects to begin operating the first of several hundred public schools in the fall of 1995, investing its own capital. Meanwhile, former Yale University President Benno Schmidt, Jr., who heads the Edison Project, hopes to contract with the board of education in Chicago to operate a number of that city's public schools. Schmidt has hinted that Edison schools will have a student/teacher ratio of about 17 to 1, that students will be organized in "houses" of about 100 each with a team of teachers to stay with them for three years, and that schools will be open from 7 a.m. to 6 p.m., including an optional 1½ hours at the beginning and end of the day for families who need child-care services.

To determine public acceptance of the concept of privatization of some facets of the public school system, respondents were asked whether they favored or opposed the idea of private, profit-making companies operating the schools. Opinion is almost evenly divided on the privatization idea.

The question:

Do you favor or oppose an idea now being tested in a few cities in which private, profit-making corporations contract to operate schools within certain jurisdictions?

	National Totals %	No Children In School %	Public School Parents %	Nonpublic School Parents %
Favor	45	46	43	50
Oppose	47	46	49	41
Don't know	8	8	8	9

There were few significant demographic differences in the responses. However, younger respondents and Republicans show considerably more support for this form of privatization than do older respondents and Democrats. Among those under 50 years of age, 50% support the idea, while only 39% of those older than 50 do. Fifty-one percent of Republicans favor the idea, while 38% of Democrats do.

More 'Basics' but Broader Curriculum

In several previous Phi Delta Kappa/Gallup education polls, a majority of respondents favored more emphasis on curriculum "basics," which people generally conceive to be "reading, writing, and arithmetic," often with science and history/ U.S. government included. Generally, people do not think that the public schools pay enough attention to these subjects. Nevertheless, the 1990 poll (whose results for the "basics" are reported in the accompanying table) showed that people also want more emphasis on computer training (79%), vocational education (65%), health education (62%), business (60%), and even physical education (32%).

To determine the public's preferences concerning curriculum content, respondents to this year's poll were asked whether they would favor more, less, or about the same emphasis in eight subject areas. Music, art, and foreign language have posted remarkable gains since 1990. Nonwhites are more likely than whites to say they desire more emphasis on most of the subjects listed. The differences are largest in the case of music and art.

The first question:

As I read off each high school subject, would you tell me if you think that subject should be given more emphasis, less emphasis, or the same emphasis it now receives in high school, regardless of whether or not you think it should be required?

	More Emphasis %	Less Emphasis %	Same Emphasis %	Don't Know %
Mathematics	82	1	17	*
English	79	2	19	*
Science	75	3	22	*
History/U.S. government	62	6	31	1
Geography	61	7	31	1
Foreign language	52	16	32	*
Music	31	22	46	1
Art	29	24	46	1

*Less than one-half of 1%.

	1990 Results			
	More Emphasis %	Less Emphasis %	Same Emphasis %	Don't Know %
Mathematics	80	3	14	3
English	79	3	15	3
Science	68	11	18	3
History/U.S. government	65	9	23	3
Geography	53	18	25	4
Foreign language	37	34	25	4
Music	13	39	43	5
Art	12	42	40	6

Are Students Capable of Learning More Math and Science?

Do some students avoid math and science simply because they don't want to invest the effort to master these subjects? Or does mastery elude them despite their efforts? To ascertain whether Americans believe that public school students can learn more about these subjects, survey respondents were asked two questions.

The questions:

Do you believe that most public school students have the capacity to learn more math than they generally do today?

Do you believe that most public school students have the capacity to learn more science than they generally do today?

Yes, Have Capacity	National Totals %	No Children In School %	Public School Parents %	Nonpublic School Parents %
Math	89	88	90	94
Science	88	88	88	92

The answers reveal that virtually the entire U.S. public believes that most students are capable of learning more math and more science than they generally do.

Support for and Opposition to Channel One

Channel One, the 12½-minute news and information program (with commercials) produced by Whittle Communications, Inc., for the past four years, is the subject of considerable debate in educational circles. But it has gained only modest media attention.

To determine how the public feels about the Whittle experiment, survey respondents were first read a description of the Whittle program and asked whether they were aware of any such arrangement in their own communities. Those who thought the Whittle experiment was in effect in their local public schools were then asked whether they were in favor of or opposed to it.

Those respondents who thought the experiment was not in operation in their communities or who did not know whether or not it existed there were asked whether they would be in favor of or opposed to having such an arrangement in their local schools.

The survey findings reveal that the relatively few (11% of respondents) who are aware of the use of the Whittle program in their local schools *favor* it by more than a 2-1 margin. (Channel One is now employed in more than 12,000 schools, most of these with high concentrations of poor students.) By contrast, those who are unaware of such a program in their communities oppose the introduction of the experiment into their schools by a substantial 57% to 38% margin.

The first question:

A company has been loaning TV sets and satellite dishes to public schools that agree to show their students daily 10-minute news and feature broadcasts from this company. Each broadcast includes two to 2½ minutes of commercial advertising directed to the students. The company makes money by selling this television time to advertisers. Do you happen to know whether any of the public schools in your community have entered into an arrangement of this kind, or not?

	National Totals %	No Children In School %	Public School Parents %	Nonpublic School Parents %
Yes, have arrangement	11	11	13	10
No, do not have	48	46	51	55
Don't know	41	43	36	35

The second question (asked of those who indicated awareness of the arrangement):

Are you in favor of this arrangement in the local public schools or opposed to it?

	National Totals %
Yes, favor	66
No, opposed	30
Don't know	4

The third question (asked of those "not aware" of any local arrangement):

Would you be in favor of your local public schools' entering into this kind of arrangement, or opposed to it?

	National Totals %	No Children In School %	Public School Parents %	Nonpublic School Parents %
Yes, favor	38	39	36	34
No, opposed	57	56	58	54
Don't know	5	5	6	12

Those *unaware* of the Whittle experiment registered opposition by substantial majorities in most demographic groups. However, there were two notable exceptions: young adults (ages 18-29) favored the Whittle experiment (60% to 37%), whereas those 30 and older opposed it (63% to 31%); and nonwhites were evenly divided between support and opposition (48% to 49%), whereas whites were opposed to the program (36% in favor, 58% opposed).

Unmotivated High School Students

Educators often speculate about reasons for the lack of academic motivation that afflicts many high school students. There appears to be no consensus among them about causes.

To obtain some idea of the public's perceptions on this topic, respondents were presented with a question offering three possible explanations. Respondents were asked how important they considered each explanation. The public considered *all of them* important; between seven and eight in 10 respondents felt that each of the three explanations was either very important or somewhat important.

The question:

Many high school students are not motivated to do well academically. To indicate why you think this is the case, would you rate each of the following reasons as very important, somewhat important, not very important, or not at all important?

	Very Important %	Somewhat Important %	Not Very Important %	Not at All Important %	Don't Know %
The negative attitudes of fellow students about high academic performance	63	25	7	3	2
The fact that employers of high school graduates seldom seem to care about high school records	49	29	15	5	2
The fact that many colleges will admit any student with a high school diploma, regardless of his or her high school record	49	28	15	6	2

Rated Very Important	National Totals %	No Children In School %	Public School Parents %	Nonpublic School Parents %
The negative attitudes of fellow students about high academic performance	63	64	61	59
The fact that employers of high school graduates seldom seem to care about high school records	49	50	49	44
The fact that many colleges will admit any student with a high school diploma, regardless of his or her high school record	49	52	45	47

Monoculturalism or Multiculturalism?

The long-running debate over multiculturalism in the schools has heated up in recent years, as some groups protest a tendency to abandon the melting-pot metaphor in favor of "tossed salad" and as the number and size of racial and ethnic minority groups increase. In Lake County, Florida, for example, fundamentalists holding a 3-2 edge on the school board voted in May 1994 to teach students that American culture and institutions are "superior to other foreign or historic cultures."

Answers to the following two questions in the current poll suggest that there is a commodious middle ground on the issue of multiculturalism, and, as the first table shows, three out of four Americans choose to occupy it.

The first question:

In your opinion, which should the public schools in your community promote — one common, predominant cultural tradition only, or both a common cultural tradition and the diverse cultural traditions of the different population groups in America?

	National Totals %	No Children In School %	Public School Parents %	Nonpublic School Parents %
Promote one common tradition only	18	18	19	19
Promote both one common tradition and diverse traditions of different populations	75	74	76	72
Don't know	7	8	5	9

The second question (asked of the 75% who said that schools should promote both one common tradition and diverse traditions of different peoples):

Which one do you think should receive more emphasis — one common cultural tradition, diverse cultural traditions, or should both receive the same emphasis?

	National Totals %	No Children In School %	Public School Parents %	Nonpublic School Parents %
More emphasis on one common cultural tradition	10	10	9	11
More emphasis on diverse cultural traditions	11	11	11	9
Equal emphasis on both	53	53	56	51
Don't know	8	8	5	10

(Figures add to 100% when those who believe that the schools should promote one common culture *only* — see responses to the first question in this series — are included.)

As the first table [in this section] shows, about one citizen in five (18%) would agree that the public schools should promote only a single common cultural tradition. (Those most in favor of monoculturalism are Republicans [23%] and those 65 years of age and older [24%].) The great majority of Americans think that the public schools should advocate a diversity of traditions — although with varying emphases. One American in 10 believes that, while diverse traditions should be taught, the common cultural tradition should be emphasized; a similar number (11%) believe that, while both the common culture and diverse cultures should be taught, diversity should be given more emphasis. Roughly half (53%) of those polled believe that a common cultural tradition and diverse traditions should be given equal attention.

Tax System for Schools

Many questions in past Phi Delta Kappa/Gallup polls have shown that people are unhappy with the forms of taxation used to support U.S. public schools, and they are particularly disturbed by the inequalities in funding that result from features of the tax system in most states. Tax revolts occur with some regularity. Among the most recent was last year's upheaval in Michigan, which led to the virtual abandonment of the local property tax, backbone of school finance in most states for generations, in favor of a massive state sales tax increase and new mechanisms to equalize funding among districts.

A question in the current poll shows that the U.S. public, by a 54% to 43% majority, regards tax policies that fund education in the U.S. as unfair to taxpayers.

The question:

In your opinion, is the existing system of funding public education in this country fair or unfair to the average taxpayer?

	National Totals %	No Children In School %	Public School Parents %	Nonpublic School Parents %
Fair	43	48	36	30
Unfair	54	50	61	65
Don't know	3	2	3	5

Bare Majority for Charter Schools

A charter school is a tax-funded school given broad freedom from state regulations in exchange for such favorable "outcomes" as improved test scores, attendance rates, dropout rates, and the like. Most charter contracts provide for the loss of the charter, typically granted by a public school board, if results aren't evident within a specified period.

In Minnesota, whose pioneering legislation was passed in 1991, charter schools include one with a year-round program for 35 students between the ages of 13 and 21, a private Montessori school, and a school for deaf students. In California, where 1992 legislation authorized 100 charter schools, one will have an English-as-a-second-language curriculum, and two will be resource centers for home schooling.

Despite growing support for charter schools among state governing bodies, some people fear that the movement is a step on the road to vouchers for private schools, which many believe would create a two-tiered education system that would shut out the poor, since private schools would raise tuition beyond the value of the vouchers.

The current poll shows that a 54% to 39% majority of the public favors charter schools.

The question:

A number of states have passed, or are considering, legislation that frees some public schools from certain state regulations and permits them to function independently. Some people say that these charter schools would be a good thing because, with fewer regulations, they would be able to try out new ideas for improving education. Others say charter schools would be a bad thing because regulations are necessary to guard against inferior or poor educational practices. Which position do you agree with more — that charter schools are a good thing for education or that they are a bad thing for education?

	National Totals %	No Children In School %	Public School Parents %	Nonpublic School Parents %
Charter schools are a good thing for education	54	53	55	60
Charter schools are a bad thing for education	39	39	39	32
Don't know	7	8	6	8

Majorities in virtually every demographic group support the idea of charter schools. Age is a key determinant, however. Those between the ages of 18 and 29 favor the idea (66% to 31%), as do those between the ages of 30 and 49 (57% to 37%). But those over age 50 oppose charter schools (47% to 42%).

Citizen Contact with the Schools

Recent emphasis on the importance of parental knowledge about and involvement in the life of the public schools may be paying off. Over the last decade the frequency of many forms of public contact with the schools has doubled or nearly so. Areas showing the greatest gains are attendance at school board meetings, attendance at meetings dealing with school problems, and attendance at plays, concerts, and athletic events. Even adults with no children in school now claim to participate in the life of the schools to a considerable degree.

The question:

Since last September, which of the following, if any, have you yourself done?

	National Totals %	No Children In School %	Public School Parents %	Nonpublic School Parents %
Attended a school play or concert in any local public school	54	43	79	51
Attended a local public school athletic event	53	46	70	59
Met with any teachers or administrators in the local public schools about your own child	31	6*	87	48
Attended any meeting dealing with the local public school situation	28	18	51	34
Attended a PTA meeting	21	7	49	50
Attended a meeting to discuss any of the school reforms being proposed	20	13	35	34
Attended a school board meeting	16	10	27	38
Been a member of any public-school-related committee	15	8	31	18

*Parents of a child approaching school age might consult school personnel about enrolling him or her.

	National Totals			Public School Parents		
	1994 %	1991 %	1983 %	1994 %	1991 %	1983 %
Attended a school play or concert in any local public school	54	30	24	79	56	42
Attended a local public school athletic event	53	30	25	70	49	42
Met with any teachers or administrators in the local public schools about your own child	31	27	21	87	77	62
Attended any meeting dealing with the local public school situation	28	16*	10	51	36*	18
Attended a PTA meeting	21	14	14	49	38	36
Attended a school board meeting	16	7	8	27	13	16

*In 1991 this category was worded: "Attended any meeting dealing with the local public schools."

New Formats for Reporting Student Progress

The always-simmering dissatisfaction with time-honored forms of reporting student progress has resulted in much experimentation in recent years. To the discomfiture of college admissions officials, a growing number of high schools have even abandoned calculating rank in class, which depends on letter grades that can be converted to numbers.

To determine which format for reporting students' progress was considered preferable, parents of public school children were asked how useful they found each of the following systems: A to F or numeric grades to denote excellent to failing achievement, A to F or numeric grades to describe the student's efforts, a written description of the student's progress, or a checklist that indicates what the student knows and is able to do. Parents felt that the two newer formats were preferable to the more traditional A to F systems. For example, about seven in 10 called both the written description and the checklist "very useful." Two more traditional A to F grading systems, by contrast, were judged very useful by smaller percentages.

The question (asked of parents of public school children):

Here is a list of different types of reports that the public schools use to inform parents of their children's progress in school. As I read off a description of each type, would you tell me if you consider it very useful, quite useful, not very useful, or not useful at all for informing you about the progress of your child?

	Very Useful %	Quite Useful %	Not Very Useful %	Not Useful At All %	Don't Know %
A written description of the student's progress in a number of areas	74	20	5	*	1
A checklist which indicates what the student knows and is able to do in each subject	70	22	6	1	1
A to F or numeric grades in each subject to denote excellent to failing achievement	58	32	8	1	1
A to F or numeric grades to describe the student's *effort* in each subject	56	32	9	1	2

*Less than one-half of 1%.

Interesting Cross Comparisons

Some of the most interesting information in the Phi Delta Kappa/Gallup education poll comes from cross comparisons that can be made among the various subgroups in the sample. (Care should be taken, of course, to observe the confidence intervals described in the table of sampling tolerances that appears elsewhere in this report.) A sampling of some interesting cross comparisons follows.

• Of those surveyed, 18% mention fighting/violence/gangs as the biggest problem facing the public schools; however, this figure rises to 31% among nonwhites.

• Of those living in the West, 35% give the public schools in their communities an A or a B. This compares to 52% in the Midwest and 48% in the East.

• Of nonpublic school parents, 69% favor allowing parents to send their school-age children to any public, private, or church-related school (with the government paying all or part of the tuition for those who choose nonpublic schools). This percentage falls to 48% among public school parents and to 42% among those with no children in school.

• Men and women differ over the teaching of "character education" in the schools, with 54% of women — but only 43% of men — in favor.

• Of young respondents — in the 18-29 group — 52% favor private, profit-making corporations contracting to operate schools within a certain jurisdiction. However, only 33% of those 65 and older are in favor.

Cross comparisons of this kind can be produced from the data contained in the 415-page document that is the basis for this report. Persons who wish to order this document should write to Phi Delta Kappa, P.O. Box 789, Bloomington, IN 47402. Ph. 800/766-1156. The price is $95, postage included.

Sampling Tolerances

In interpreting survey results, it should be borne in mind that all sample surveys are subject to sampling error, i.e., the extent to which the results may differ from what would be obtained if the whole population surveyed had been interviewed. The size of such sampling error depends largely on the number of interviews.

The following tables may be used in estimating the sampling error of any percentage in this report. The computed allowances have taken into account the effect of the sample design upon sampling error. They may be interpreted as indicating the range (plus or minus the figure shown) within which the results of repeated samplings in the same time period could be expected to vary 95% of the time, assuming the same sampling procedure, the same interviewers, and the same questionnaire.

The first table shows how much allowance should be made for the sampling error of a percentage:

Recommended Allowance for Sampling Error of a Percentage

In Percentage Points (at 95 in 100 confidence level)*

Sample Size	1,500	1,000	750	600	400	200	100
Percentages near 10	2	2	3	3	4	5	8
Percentages near 20	3	3	4	4	5	7	10
Percentages near 30	3	4	4	5	6	8	12
Percentages near 40	3	4	5	5	6	9	12
Percentages near 50	3	4	5	5	6	9	13
Percentages near 60	3	4	5	5	6	9	12
Percentages near 70	3	4	4	5	6	8	12
Percentages near 80	3	3	4	4	5	7	10
Percentages near 90	2	2	3	3	4	5	8

*The chances are 95 in 100 that the sampling error is not larger than the figures shown.

The table would be used in the following manner: Let us say that a reported percentage is 33 for a group that includes 1,000 respondents. We go to the row for "percentages near 30" in the table and across to the column headed "1,000."

The number at this point is 4, which means that the 33% obtained in the sample is subject to a sampling error of plus or minus four points. In other words, it is very probable (95 chances out of 100) that the true figure would be somewhere between 29% and 37%, with the most likely figure the 33% obtained.

In comparing survey results in two samples, such as, for example, men and women, the question arises as to how large a difference between them must be before one can be reasonably sure that it reflects a real difference. In the tables below, the number of points that must be allowed for in such comparisons is indicated.

Two tables are provided. One is for percentages near 20 or 80; the other, for percentages near 50. For percentages in between, the error to be allowed for lies between those shown in the two tables.

Recommended Allowance for Sampling Error of the Difference

In Percentage Points (at 95 in 100 confidence level)*

TABLE A — Percentages near 20 or percentages near 80

Size of Sample	1,500	1,000	750	600	400	200
1,500	4					
1,000	4	5				
750	5	5	5			
600	5	5	6	6		
400	6	6	6	7	7	
200	8	8	8	8	9	10

TABLE B — Percentages near 50

Size of Sample	1,500	1,000	750	600	400	200
1,500	5					
1,000	5	6				
750	6	6	7			
600	6	7	7	7		
400	7	8	8	8	9	
200	10	10	10	10	11	13

*The chances are 95 in 100 that the sampling error is not larger than the figures shown.

Here is an example of how the tables would be used: Let us say that 50% of men respond a certain way and 40% of women respond that way also, for a difference of 10 percentage points between them. Can we say with any assurance that the 10-point difference reflects a real difference between men and women on the question? Let us consider a sample that contains approximately 750 men and 750 women.

Since the percentages are near 50, we consult Table B, and, since the two samples are about 750 persons each, we look for the number in the column headed "750," which is also in the row designated "750." We find the number 7 here. This means that the allowance for error should be seven points and that, in concluding that the percentage among men is somewhere between three and 17 points higher than the percentage among women, we should be wrong only about 5% of the time. In other words, we can conclude with considerable confidence that a difference exists in the direction observed and that it amounts to at least three percentage points.

If, in another case, men's responses amount to 22%, say, and women's to 24%, we consult Table A, because these percentages are near 20. We look in the column headed "750" and see that the number is 5. Obviously, then, the two-point difference is inconclusive.

Acknowledgments

The authors of this report gratefully acknowledge the assistance of the following advisory panel in originating and prioritizing questions for the 26th Phi Delta Kappa/Gallup survey. The panel should not be held responsible, however, for the final form in which the questions were asked or for the way in which answers were interpreted.

Douglas Bedient, president of Phi Delta Kappa and professor of curriculum and instruction, Southern Illinois University; David L. Clark, Kenan Professor of Education, University of North Carolina, Chapel Hill; Chester E. Finn, Jr., founding partner and senior scholar, the Edison Project; Pascal D. Forgione, Jr., state superintendent of public instruction, Delaware; Betty Hale, vice president and director, Leadership Programs, Institute for Educational Leadership; Katie Haycock, director, Education Roundtable, American Association for Higher Education; Vinetta Jones, national director, Equity 2000 Program; James A. Kelly, president, National Board for Professional Teaching Standards; Sally B. Kilgore, senior fellow and director of educational policy studies, Hudson Institute; Joanne Kogan, communications manager, National Board for Professional Teaching Standards; Anne Lynch, past president, National Congress of Parents and Teachers; Gene Maeroff, senior research associate, Carnegie Foundation for the Advancement of Teaching; John Merrow, executive officer, Learning Matters; Richard A. Miller, executive director, American Association of School Administrators; John Murphy, superintendent, Charlotte-Mecklenburg (N.C.) Schools; Joe Nathan, director, Center for School Change, University of Minnesota; Peter J. Negroni, superintendent, Springfield (Mass.) Schools; Ted Sanders, superintendent of public instruction, Ohio; Gilbert T. Sewall, director, American Textbook Council, and editor, *Social Studies Review*; Thomas A. Shannon, executive director, National School Boards Association; and Brenda Wellburn, executive director, National Association of State Boards of Education.

Research Procedure

The Sample. The sample used in this survey embraced a total of 1,326 adults (18 years of age and older). A description of the sample and methodology can be found elsewhere in this report.

Time of Interviewing. The fieldwork for this study was carried out during the period of 10 May to 8 June 1994.

The Report. In the tables used in this report, "Nonpublic School Parents" includes parents of students who attend parochial schools and parents of students who attend private and independent schools.

Due allowance must be made for statistical variation, especially in the case of findings for groups consisting of relatively few respondents, e.g., nonpublic school parents.

The findings of this report apply only to the U.S. as a whole and not to individual communities. Local surveys, using the same questions, can be conducted to determine how local areas compare with the national norm.

Design of the Sample

For the 1994 survey the Gallup Organization used its standard national telephone sample, i.e., an unclustered, directory-assisted, random-digit telephone sample, based on a proportionate stratified sampling design.

The random-digit aspect of the sample was used to avoid "listing" bias. Numerous studies have shown that households with unlisted telephone numbers are different in important ways from listed households. "Unlistedness" is due to household mobility or to customer requests to prevent publication of the telephone number.

To avoid this source of bias, a random-digit procedure designed to provide representation of both listed and unlisted (including not-yet-listed) numbers was used.

Telephone numbers for the continental United States were stratified into four regions of the country and, within each region, further stratified into three size-of-community strata.

Only working banks of telephone numbers were selected. Eliminating nonworking banks from the sample increased the likelihood that any sampled telephone number would be associated with a residence.

The sample of telephone numbers produced by the described method is representative of all telephone households within the continental United States.

Within each contacted household, an interview was sought with the youngest man 18 years of age or older who was at home. If no man was home, an interview was sought with the oldest woman at home. This method of respondent selection within households produced an age distribution by sex that closely approximates the age distribution by sex of the total population.

Up to three calls were made to each selected telephone number to complete an interview. The time of day and the day of the week for callbacks were varied so as to maximize the chances of finding a respondent at home. All interviews were conducted on weekends or weekday evenings in order to contact potential respondents among the working population.

The final sample was weighted so that the distribution of the sample matched current estimates derived from the U.S. Census Bureau's Current Population Survey (CPS) for the adult population living in telephone households in the continental U.S.

As has been the case in recent years in the Phi Delta Kappa/Gallup poll series, parents of public school children were oversampled in the 1994 poll. This procedure produced a large enough sample to ensure that findings reported for "public school parents" are statistically significant.

Composition of the Sample

Adults	%	Farm	2
No children in school	66	Undesignated	23
Public school parents	30*	**Income**	**%**
Nonpublic school parents	6*	$40,000 and over	34
		$30,000-$39,999	15
*Total exceeds 34% because		$20,000-$29,999	16
some parents have children at-		$10,000-$19,999	17
tending more than one kind of		Under $10,000	9
school.		Undesignated	9
		Region	**%**
Sex	**%**	East	24
Men	47	Midwest	25
Women	53	South	31
Race	**%**	West	20
White	83	**Community Size**	**%**
Nonwhite	14	Urban	33
Undesignated	3	Suburban	35
Age	**%**	Rural	23
18-29 years	23	Undesignated	9
30-49 years	44	**Education**	**%**
50 and over	33	Total College	52
Occupation	**%**	College graduate	22
(Chief Wage Earner)		College incomplete	30
Business and professional	34	Total high school	47
Clerical and sales	10	High school graduate	33
Manual labor	29	High school incomplete	14
Nonlabor force	2	Undesignated	1

Conducting Your Own Poll

The Phi Delta Kappa Center for Dissemination of Innovative Programs makes available PACE (Polling Attitudes of the Community on Education) materials to enable nonspecialists to conduct scientific polls of attitude and opinion on education. The PACE manual provides detailed information on constructing questionnaires, sampling, interviewing, and analyzing data. It also includes updated census figures and new material on conducting a telephone survey. The price is $55.

For information about using PACE materials, write or phone Neville Robertson at Phi Delta Kappa, P.O. Box 789, Bloomington, IN 47402-0789. Ph. 800/766-1156.

How to Order the Poll

The minimum order for reprints of the published version of the Phi Delta Kappa/Gallup education poll is 25 copies for $10. Additional copies are 25 cents each. This price includes postage for delivery (at the library rate). Where possible, enclose a check or money order. Address your order to Phi Delta Kappa, P.O. Box 789, Bloomington, IN 47402. Ph. 800/766-1156.

If faster delivery is desired, do not include a remittance with your order. You will be billed at the above rates plus any additional cost involved in the method of delivery.

Rethinking and Changing the Educative Effort

American educators could have a much better sense of their own past as a profession, and the public could have a better sense of understanding the history of public education. In the United States, a fundamental cycle of similar ideas and practices reappears in school curricula every so many years. The decades of the 1970s and 1980s witnessed the rise of "behavioral objectives" and "management by objectives," and the 1990s have brought us "outcome-based education" and "benchmarking" in educational discourse within the public school system's leadership. These are related behavioral concepts focusing on measurable ways to pinpoint and evaluate the results of educational efforts. Why do we seem to reinvent the "wheel" of educational thought and practice every so many decades? This is an important question worth addressing. Many of our ideas about change and reform in educational practice have been wrongheaded. There is in the mid-1990s a stronger focus on more qualitative, as opposed to empirical, means of assessing the outcomes of our educative efforts; yet state departments of education still insist on external, objective assessments and verifications of students' mastery of predetermined academic skills. How does this affect the development of creative, imaginative teaching in schools? We are not sure; but all of us in the education system are concerned, and many of us believe that there really are some new and generative ideas to help students learn basic intellectual skills and content.

The essays in this and later units of this volume explore some of these ideas. There are a variety of myths about what did or did not happen in some "golden age" of our educational past. Our current realities in the field of education reflect very differing conceptions of how schooling ought to change. It is difficult to generalize reliably regarding school quality across several decades because of several factors; high schools, for instance, were more selective in 1900, when only 7 percent of American youth graduated from them, whereas today we encourage as many youth as are able to graduate from high school. The social purposes of schooling have been broadened; now we want all youth to complete some form of higher education.

The school situation today is further complicated by two other issues: the "choice" issue and the efforts to "privatize" some sectors of our public school systems. Some private corporations have formed for the sole purpose of offering educational services to these systems. Such developments have generated intense feelings and debate. Whether parents should have the right to choose to send their children to private schools with public tax monies is at the center of the choice issue. Whether or not public tax monies should "follow the child" outside of the public school systems is one issue under debate. Whether or not private corporations should provide instructional services to public school systems is the question in the privatization issue. The articles in this unit reflect the debate over these issues.

We have to consider the social and ideological differences among those representing opposing school reform agendas for change. The differences over how and in what directions change is to occur in our educational systems rest on which educational values are to prevail. These values form the bases for differing conceptions of the purposes of schooling. Thus the differing agendas for change in American education have to be positioned within the context of the different ideological value systems that underpin each alternative agenda for change.

There are several currently contending (and frequently conceptually conflicting) strategies for restructuring life in schools as well as the options open to parents in choosing the schools that they want their children to attend. On the one hand, we have to find ways to empower students and teachers to improve the quality of academic life in classrooms. On the other hand, there appear to be powerful forces contending over whether control of educational services should be even more centralized or more decentralized (site-based). Those who favor greater parental and teacher control of schools support greater decentralized site management and community control conceptions of school governance. Yet the ratio of teachers to nonteaching personnel (administrators, counselors, school psychologists, and others) continues to decline as public school system bureaucracies become more and more "top heavy."

In this unit, we consider the efforts to reconceive, redefine, and reconstruct existing patterns of curriculum and instruction at the elementary and secondary levels of schooling and compare them with the efforts to reconceive existing conflicting patterns of teacher education. There is a broad spectrum of dialogue developing in North America, the British Commonwealth, Russia, Central Eurasia, and other areas of the world regarding the redirecting of the learning opportunities for all its citizens.

Prospective teachers here are being encouraged to question their own individual educational experiences as part of the process of their becoming what all communities view as rural institutions. We must acknowledge that our values affect our ideas about curriculum content and the purpose of educating others. This is perceived as vitally important in the developing dialogue over liberating all students' capacities to function as independent inquirers. The dramatic economic and demographic changes in our society necessitate a fundamental reconceptualization of how schools ought to respond to the many social contexts in which they are located. This effort to reassess and reconceive the education of others is a vital part of broader reform efforts in society as well as a dynamic dialectic in its own right. How can schools, for instance, better reflect the varied communities of interest that they serve? What must they do to become better perceived as just and equitable places in which all young people can seek to achieve learning and self-fulfillment?

This is not the first period in which our citizens have searched their minds and souls to redirect, construct, and, if necessary, deconstruct their understandings regarding formal educational systems. The debate over what ought to be the conceptual and structural underpinnings of national educational opportunity structures has continued since the first mass educational system was formed in the nineteenth century.

When we think of continuity and change, we think of the conceptual balance between cherished traditions and innovations that will facilitate learning without compromising cherished core values and standards. When we think of change in education, we are reminded of such great educational experiments of earlier times as John Dewey's Laboratory School at the University of Chicago, Maria Montessori's Casi di Bambini (children's houses), and A. S. Neill's controversial Summerhill School in England, as well as many other innovative experiments in learning theories. Our own time has seen similarly dramatic experimentation.

What constitutes desirable change is directly related to one's own core values regarding the purposes and content of educational experiences. When considering a proposed change in an educational system or a particular classroom, we need to ask some pointed questions: What is the purpose of the proposed change? What are the human and social benefits and costs of the proposed change (in teachers' work, in students' learning tasks, and so on)? What defensible alternatives are possible? What are our best ideas? How does the proposed change affect traditional practice? The past 30 or more years of research on teaching and learning have shown us that we must improve the quality of learning while also broadening educational opportunity structures for our young people.

Each of the essays in this unit relates directly to the conceptual tension involved in reconceiving how educational development should proceed in response to all these dramatic social and economic changes in society.

Looking Ahead: Challenge Questions

What are some issues in the debate regarding educational reform?

Why is choice such a controversial issue in American education today?

Why do you think that public monies should or should not be used in private school settings?

What are the issues related to privatization efforts? Should private corporate enterprises contract to deliver instructional services in public school systems? Why, or why not?

What social, political, and economic pressures are placed on our public school systems?

Why are comparisons made of the school performance of students from different nations, and what can be learned from these comparisons? What are some limitations of such comparisons?

—F. S.

On to the Past
Wrong-Headed School Reform

The assumption that comparative testing is the best means for changing schools rests, Mr. Moffett maintains, on the equally unfounded assumption that public education will improve if schools operate by free-market competition, as businesses are alleged to do.

James Moffett

James Moffett is an author and consultant in education living in Mariposa, Calif. This article is adapted, with the permission of the publisher, from his book The Universal Schoolhouse: Spiritual Awakening Through Education, *published by Jossey-Bass. For ordering information, write to Jossey-Bass Publishers, 350 Sansome St., San Francisco, CA 94104; ph. 415/433-1767 or fax 415/433-0499. ©1994, Jossey-Bass, Inc.*

THE GOVERNMENTAL initiative to reform schooling has been based on two of the very assumptions most responsible for the problems that reform aims to solve. One is that assessment is the instrument of change because schools teach to tests. The second is that business knows best because public education is really just another business. Since the notion of reforming schools through national assessment has already received considerable criticism, I will focus here on the tendency to treat schooling like a business.

PRIVATIZING PUBLIC EDUCATION

It is impossible to understand the movement toward a national curriculum, which does not fit American ideals, or the railroading of national assessment, which is a wildly irrational way of dealing with the problems of schooling, unless you realize how closely these initiatives are tied to business, state legislatures, and other non-educational managers. For example, the New Standards Project that works so closely with the governors' National Education Goals Panel is co-directed by Marc Tucker, author of *America's Choice— High Skills or Low Wages?* and head of the National Center on Education and the Economy. Business should indeed be served by a good system of public education, but the higher-order thinking abilities and creative problem solving that it correctly believes graduates must now bring to the work force are precisely what have suffered most from testing, standardizing, and centralizing—that is, from an education system driven by government and industry.

The assumption that comparative testing is the best means for changing schools rests on the equally unfounded assumption that public education will improve if schools operate by free-market competition, as businesses are alleged to do. Corporations that were forced to reform themselves to meet foreign competition now come on like born-again revivalists: "We did it, so we can show you how to do it." Chrysler's president, Lee Iacocca, became a folk hero for saving his company, when in fact it was taxpayers' money that saved Chrysler through a bailout or subsidy that, had it been paid to a single mother living with her children in poverty, would have been called welfare. Had Chrysler's cost-benefit management by objectives not arrogantly exploited the Big Three's monopoly through such practices as deliberate obsolescence, Chrysler would have been able to cope with real competition when it finally came — from abroad. Ford would *already* have made "quality" job one. And General Motors would already have adopted the production methods of its Saturn division throughout the corporation. Thus endangered by serious foreign competition, American corporations have indeed had to make some practical changes — but not in the direction of a moral conversion.

During recent decades, leading companies in every field — pharmaceuticals, chemicals, defense contractors, automobiles, brokerage, savings and loans, insurance — have been convicted or indicted for breaking laws. Indeed, industry analysts are saying that even the oldest and most revered names can no longer be trusted. Criminal behavior aside, what about just plain morality? How much honest public concern can we expect from corporations that fire older employees to avoid paying retirement benefits, keep secret their own unfavorable findings about their products, and mount massively expensive campaigns — paid for by the consumer through increased prices of goods

— to lobby against environmental protection?

Douglas Noble, author of *The Classroom Arsenal: Military Research Information Technology and Public Education*, compiled brief profiles of members of the board of the New American Schools Development Corporation (NASDC) as a way of asking, "Are these really the people we want to be shaping our children's schools?"

Norman R. Augustine, CEO of Martin-Marietta, formerly served in six positions at the Department of Defense, including undersecretary of the Army. According to *Business Month*, he has "played a key role in the shaping of the modern U.S. arsenal," and remains a "consummate insider" in U.S. defense policy. . . .

James K. Baker is vice chairman of NASDC, CEO of . . . Arvin Industries, and a founding member of Commit, Inc., a business group involved in Indiana school reform. According to *Education Week*, Indiana teacher organizations are currently engaged in "all out war" with Commit, whose adversarial agenda "confirms the worst fears public educators hold about their new and powerful partner. . . ."

Frank Shrontz, vice chair of NASDC and CEO of Boeing, . . . a major defense contractor, served in the 1970s as both assistant secretary of defense and assistant secretary of the Air Force. In the past year, Shrontz has been battling Washington State teachers to prevent "fair tax" legislation that would increase Boeing's taxes by $500 million, with much of the money targeted for the state's beleaguered schools. . . .

Kay Whitmore [is] CEO of Eastman Kodak, . . . which has been reeling . . . from [among other things] huge fines for patent infringements and environmental pollution. . . .

Louis Gerstner, Jr., vice chair of NASDC and CEO of tobacco-food conglomerate RJR Nabisco, is known for his marketing genius. [Today Gerstner is CEO of IBM.] As former president of American Express, he . . . exploited an elitist image with the slogan "membership has its privileges." Gerstner was hired as CEO of RJR Nabisco by the firm whose leveraged buyout of RJR was called by *Time* magazine "the

worst display of greed since the . . . robber barons." The buyout has also been immortalized in such books as *Barbarians at the Gate* and *True Greed*. Since taking charge, Gerstner's top priority has been to stem the erosion of cigarette sales, which account for over 60% of the firm's operating income. Under his leadership, the company has recently been hit with several scandals: its targeted marketing toward poor black youth and young, white, working-class females; its aggressive cigarette exports to Third World populations; and . . . its exploitation of young people through its "Old Joe Camel" advertising campaign. Meanwhile, the RJR Nabisco Foundation has channeled $30 million into its own Next Century Schools program, a prototype of NASDC that funds model ventures stressing extended schooling, productivity, and strict accountability.[1]

America 2000, the Bush Administration's school reform strategy (now adopted by President Clinton and renamed Goals 2000), proposed that, under the direction of such people, the New American Schools Development Corporation should fund and guide the research and development of experimental projects to reinvent schooling.

Behind this federal sponsoring of partnership between public schools and for-profit companies lies tremendous anger in the business world that corporations' efforts to survive in global competition are being thwarted by poorly educated employees. Efficiency experts have convinced business leaders, as they did earlier regarding company alcoholism, that fixing employees is more cost-effective than replacing employees — in this case with ones who can communicate, collaborate, and cogitate. Companies are furious about having to pay both school taxes and the costs of running their own "in-house" schools to do what they believe public education should be doing.

They have a just complaint here. The best way to respond to it, however, is to reform schooling in the most effective way, considering *all* educational goals. Business does not know what is best for schooling, and it is suffering no more

from poor education than is the rest of the society, including many individuals. As a stakeholder and as a possible learning resource, business should indeed participate in school reform, but it has too narrow a perspective and too limited a motive to guide it. The results would surely be skewed and not even in business' own interest. Both the corporate model and its money are dangerous.

THE GOVERNMENT'S conviction that business can show the schools how to set their house in order derives not only from a concern about the employability of the populace but also from the old false analogy that running schools is like manufacturing and marketing commodities. When Lee Iacocca addressed the Association for Supervision and Curriculum Development (ASCD) at its annual convention in May 1991, he said, "Your product needs a lot of work, and in the end, it's your job." His tough talk on the problem of the increasing numbers of children in poverty was that "your customers don't want to hear about your raw materials problem — they care about results."

So children are raw materials. After complaining that Chrysler spends $60,000,000 for school taxes and still has to teach basic skills to many workers, Iacocca likened graduating a student who can't read to selling a car without an engine. "It's massive consumer fraud." (How good it must have felt to be able to level against another "industry" a charge that has so often been leveled against his own.) Iacocca pursued the theme of consumerism: "Right now, American education has a lot of dissatisfied customers."[2]

Comparing children to metal, rubber, and plastic is hard to forgive. Comparing human growth to factory production implies the putting together of inert parts into subassemblies that eventually go into that final assemblage, the product. This applies an inorganic, particle approach to an organic, holistic process. But what irrational thinking anyway to compare students to products when these "products" are also the "consumers," both as students and later as parents and taxpayers. Fur-

Business should indeed participate in school reform, but it has too narrow a perspective to guide it.

thermore, these consumers are taxpaying voters who also *run* schools. Chrysler's customers don't run the company. What possible sense can this analogy between school and business make when the raw materials, the products, and the consumers of schooling are all one and the same?

But it is part of the current CEO thinking to lump all large enterprises together from a purely managerial viewpoint and thus to ignore the actual nature of each enterprise. Managing is managing, it is thought, regardless of whether the organization is a foundation, a government agency, a for-profit company, or a public institution. A manufacturing executive can tell an education system what it ought to do because he looks on schooling as just another outfit to run. But what the outfit *does* is critical.

A politically conservative educational initiative — Republican or Democratic — classifies education as just another consumer good in order to push privatization, which is the real goal of its brand of "school reform." In his ASCD speech, Iacocca also said, "People are not just going to settle for an inferior product — they want to shop around." There it is, the "free-market" concept of education whereby parental choice is extended by vouchers to private schools. Thus conservatives can graft privatization onto school restructuring. After all, wasn't free enterprise the way for *perestroika* to cure the ills of the Soviet Union?

In May 1991, the same month that Iacocca addressed the ASCD, *Harper's Magazine* ran an article describing Britain's national curriculum and national assessment, quickly installed at the beginning of the 1990s by Margaret Thatcher's education secretary, Kenneth Baker, whom she later made chairman of the Conservative Party and then home secretary. "Thatcher and Baker chose to see education as an enterprise that could be made more efficient by making schools subject to market forces."[3] Brits are unembarrassed by privatization of their education system, which has always combined both public and private schools, but their teachers are now complaining that they can't teach for testing.

In America the advocacy of vouchers incorporating private schools into public education remains controversial. So the privatization of schooling proceeds unannounced as such but clearly marked by proposals to 1) encourage business to fund school projects, 2) extend parental choice to private schools, and 3) throw all schools into free-market competition.

A full-page ad in the same issue of *Harper's Magazine* that contained the article on Britain's national curriculum bares the strategy of parlaying school restructuring into privatization:

> A well-established practice from the business world could do wonders: management by exception. . . . Deregulate and decentralize. Encourage teachers to design and implement teacher cooperatives or collaboratives. Give principals the authority they need to run schools without red tape. Permit parents to choose the public school their children attend. In short, permit schools — some of them at least — to be market-sensitive.[4]

The company that paid for the ad was a prime defense contractor, Rockwell International. The main author of the ad was Denis Doyle, who is co-author of *Winning the Brain Race: A Bold Plan to Make Our Schools More Competitive* and a senior fellow at the Hudson Institute, a conservative think tank.

National assessment and national curriculum contradict by nature this call for deregulation and decentralization, which are being used here to justify competition among schools considered as businesses. The decentralization of education need have no connection whatsoever with

> *The nationalizing of education through testing is a move to cut spending for social services.*

"free markets," since education could perfectly well decentralize and remain totally public. What enables the authors of the ad to modulate from the now-popular idea of decentralized schools to their ultimate goal of "market-sensitive" schools is precisely the deceptive confusion between the public and private sectors. For *business*, decentralization of government

does mean deregulation, which can indeed create a free market. That is simply not the case for education.

But it is not just the false analogy between the two sectors that misleads. It's also the boast that business holds the patent on "management by exception," which presumably means creative thinking that waives bureaucratic rules. Since when does American business practice this in an exemplary way? And for whose benefit if it does?

Of course it is true that, since government regulates business far less than education, business is freer to develop and exercise creativity. That freedom defines in fact much of the difference between the public and private sectors. This should give business a reason to help liberate schools from regulation, which the ad purports to do, not prolong it, as national assessment and a national curriculum would certainly do in providing the score comparisons on which free-market schooling would be based. The ad argues for freeing teachers and principals from *school district* centralization but not from control by *state and federal government*, with which large corporations are more naturally allied. School districts respond more to local businesses, which are more apt to include total community welfare in their aspirations for schools than is Rockwell International.

In both Britain and the U.S. the nationalizing of education through testing is a move to cut spending for social services, one of the biggest of which is schooling. The ostensible motive is accountability — to get more out of schools while putting no more into them. Conservative constituents want to get their kids out of public schools and send them to private schools without paying for both, or at least to get their kids out of the worst public schools and into the better ones.

Teachers of English to Speakers of Other Languages (TESOL), which tends much more than other educational subject organizations to see things from the viewpoint of minorities or poor people, spotted this favoritism immediately:

> What about children of parents who don't have transportation options? Who can't pay the difference between their voucher and the private school tuition? Who can't read the brochures comparing the schools they may choose from? Who are so busy with two or three jobs that they can't visit the schools to make a choice?[5]

Too many local factors determine success and failure, most of which schools have no control over.

This article in *TESOL Matters* cites 1991 Teacher of the Year Jeffrey White's objection to school choice: that it presupposes good and bad schools and therefore favored and unfavored children. The article continues:

> Providing seed money for innovative schools is an exciting concept, yet the New American Schools are limited in advance by the requirement of consensus on World Class Standards and the focus on scoring well on the "National Achievement Tests." Bush's recommendations for leadership in this process muffle the voices of educators, parents, and students while amplifying the voices of business officials and politicians.[6]

The Pennsylvania legislature rejected a plan that would have provided each child a $900 voucher to attend a public school in another district or a private school, because the amount would discriminate against the poor, $900 being too little to pay tuition at most private schools. The 1991 Massachusetts "choice" plan "flatly encourages students to leave poor districts for rich ones" since "the 'home' districts are charged a 'tuition' roughly equivalent to the per-pupil expenditure in the receiving district." As Robert Lowe has written, "This market ethos ignored any responsibility for other children's education, any obligation for community control of education, any commitment to schools as sites of democratic discourse."[7]

The whole point of comparing schools, which otherwise seems irrational as a way to improve them, makes perfect sense when viewed from the standpoint of a constituency of business executives and conservative individuals. Comparing schools will expose ineffectuality, spurring the bad ones to shape up and permitting parents to identify the good ones. But it is obviously not mere dereliction that causes school failure. In any case, comparative testing cannot possibly be a fair way to sort schools for efficiency because too many local factors determine success and failure, most of which — such as population to be served, local history, and ma-terial resources — schools have no control over.

This "market-sensitive" approach will simply increase the differential between "good" and "bad" schools. It will not improve overall quality, because nothing intrinsic to better learning will necessarily have occurred. Most private schools to which some ghetto students have been admitted on vouchers run essentially the same curriculum as do the public schools from which the students have been rescued. But they have smaller classes, little bureaucracy, and a more serene atmosphere — all attributes that reform should bring to public education. Were these private schools to be incorporated into the public system or enlarged enough to make room for other lucky refugees, they too would come to resemble regular schools — unless the whole system were reformed. A few havens for the favored prove nothing.

In other words, we can't afford to have *any* bad schools. There is nothing efficient or cost-effective about polarizing education in this way. *All* schools must improve. Losers may be acceptable and necessary in business but not in education. Applying free-market thinking to education is sacrificing some children to others. Inefficiency becomes an excuse for inequality. And how far are you going to carry free enterprise in education? Will the schools that fail file for bankruptcy? What do you do with them? And with the children still stuck in them? Imposing the rules of the private sector on the public sector destroys the point of the public sector, which is to act collectively for the benefit of all.

The idea that business knows best and that education should imitate the secret of its "success" — free-market competition — underlies the movement toward national assessment, which is supposed to act as a consumer's guide. This approach to reform is faulty from one end to the other — both the assumptions and the strategies built on them. If rationalization were not standing in for rationality and if it were not backed by government and business, this line of thinking would not even have to be refuted. It is simply not true that educators have no idea of how to improve learning unless their dereliction is exposed and they are forced to cast about for something better.

THE RIGHT MEANS ARE RIGHT HERE

The real truth about school failure is that educators aren't doing what they know to do. The right things to do in literacy, for example, have been known for decades and could give us a nation of readers any time we could succeed in *implementing* them. We have to ask why the changes that educators themselves propose for literacy never happen. And the reasons are systemic.

For example, the classic overemphasis on the receptive activities of listening and reading suits bureaucratization and politicization better. Authentic speaking and writing are much harder to control and centralize, precisely because, as *pro-*

> *The real truth about school failure is that educators aren't doing what they know to do.*

ductive activities, they shift decision making to the learner and call for an individualized curriculum. And yet learning to read through writing is one of the most promising roads to literacy. In the 1920s and 1930s some educators championed other badly needed practices, such as individualized or free reading, which would likewise have greatly improved literacy learning but also never became more than marginal methods, especially in secondary schools. Individualized reading also challenges centralized control, as does individualized learning generally. And yet individualization may more nearly meet the needs of reform than any other single practice.

One of the most often repeated slogans of today's reform effort in math and science asserts that "less is more" — meaning that instead of mistakenly trying to incorporate all the new knowledge in these fields, schools should more thoroughly cover fewer topics, selected for their representation of the field. In 1913 Alfred North Whitehead wrote, "Mathematics, if it is to be used in general education, must be subjected to a rigorous process of selection and adaptation. . . . It must . . . deal directly and simply with a few general ideas of far-reaching importance."[8] On the broader question of curricular integration, which educators likewise advocate repeatedly, Whitehead wrote in 1916, "The solution which I am urging is to eradicate the fatal disconnection of subjects which kills the vitality of our modern curriculum. There is only one subject-matter for education, and that is Life in all its manifestations. . . . Unless quadratic equations fit into a connected curriculum, of course there is no reason to teach anything about them."[9]

It is simply not true that change in education awaits new ideas or higher goals or more information. What we know to do far exceeds what we are free to do. Neither more research, nor assessment data, nor bright ideas, nor money will improve public education if we can't act on what we already know. The blockages are the key. Unless you analyze and remove the obstacles, education reform is impossible. And this takes realistic prob-

lem solving, which conceits of national assessment merely defer.

The assumption that educators are nonplused and that schools have to be fixed by outsiders not only generates a tremendously negative feeling in schoolpeople — who know just how much they already suffer from being political footballs in a top-down approach — but it stymies still further the implementation of changes schoolpeople already know should be made. Most teachers I work with are doing many things they don't believe in and are not doing much of what they do believe in.

The mandate to "reinvent schooling" does not mean we have to scrap everything and start from scratch. If a way is cleared, most of the desired reform can consist simply of throwing out unjustified practices that now fill the curriculum and pulling together into a unified learning field the many excellent practices that generations of educators have long advocated and that some schools have managed to implement in bits and pieces. Imagine the exasperation of those educators who *have* begun successful changes only to have the government announce with a flourish of trumpets that it is going to reassert even more strongly the standardized testing and other centralization that such experimental enclaves have fought to waive in order to succeed.

Maybe formalization and centralization served a worthy purpose before teaching became a serious profession, in the Prussia of Frederick the Great or in the Massachusetts of Horace Mann. But considering the sophisticated operations of today's professional organizations for educators, they are no longer necessary. In-

deed, it is downright destructive for government at any level to continue to standardize learning and to specify the subjects and methods of public education.

The best ways of learning are not recondite exotica. They are taking place all around us, all the time — if not often in public schools, then in some private schools. But if not in any schools at all, then everywhere else — at home, in the workplace, on the playground. People are learners, and they are learning all the time. We already know what works. More practical evidence exists for effective learning practices than special research could ever amass. So the prospect for reform is much more positive than it looks: act on what we know about learning, and don't let politics and economics obscure the obvious practical knowledge staring us in the face from the whole environment.

1. Douglas D. Noble, "Who Are These Guys? Corporate Involvement in the 'New American Schools,' " *Rethinking Schools*, March/April 1992, p. 20.
2. These quotations are from "Sound Bites," *ASCD Update*, Association for Supervision and Curriculum Development, May 1991, p. 5.
3. Tim Brookes, "A Lesson to Us All," *Harper's Magazine*, May 1991, p. 27.
4. *Harper's Magazine*, May 1991, no page number.
5. Mary Lou McClosky and D. Scott Enright, "America 2000 — Two TESOL Members Respond," *TESOL Matters*, August/ September 1991, p. 1.
6. Ibid., p. 8.
7. Robert Lowe, "The Illusion of 'Choice,' " *Rethinking Schools*, March/April 1992, p. 22.
8. Alfred North Whitehead, "The Mathematical Curriculum," presidential address to the London branch of the Mathematical Association, in *The Aims of Education* (1929; reprint, New York: New American Library/Dutton, 1949), p. 85.
9. Ibid., pp. 18-19.

European Schools Offer Contrasts and Similarities

Nations vary in beginning ages, years of compulsory schooling, and numbers going on to higher education

Arlette Delhaxhe

Arlette Delhaxhe is chief of the Department of Studies and Analyses, United European Eurydice.

As the demand for more training grows and the required levels of qualification keep going up and up, Europe's schools have had to take in a growing number of pupils for a greater number of years.

Today, compulsory schooling generally spans nine or 10 years, and as many as 12 in Belgium and Germany. Southern Europe is slowly bringing itself up to date: Although Turkey and Italy still have only five and eight years of compulsory school attendance, respectively, Portugal and Spain are catching up with their northern neighbors: Portugal requires nine years of schooling, and Spain, which currently requires eight years, will have 10 years of compulsory schooling beginning in 1996.

With the creation of all sorts of educational centers and the recognized importance of the education of young children,

Eurydice information network was created in 1976 to support cooperation in education within the European Community. It was acknowledged in 1990 to be a major means of information about national and Community education structures, systems, and developments. According to their education structures, each member-state has delegated at least one unit to participate in the network, and the EC Commission has established the Eurydice European Unit to coordinate the network. Eurydice is funded in cooperation among the units.

it is no longer the law that determines at what age a child starts school. Children start very young even though it is still optional (except in Northern Ireland and Luxembourg): usually age 3 or 4, and sometimes as young as age 2 or 3, as in France and Belgium. Northern countries, on the other hand, where the role of the family in the small child's life is greater, put off school until much later (age 5 in Denmark and Norway, for example).

Even if they agree with the principle of early education, not all southern European countries have the capacity to cater to the young child. In the countryside, for example, preschool education is often a luxury few can afford.

All the same, it is true to say that the majority of children start school at least a year before they are obliged to by law. The striking exceptions: Only 50 percent of Greek children, 40 percent of Portuguese, and a mere 5 percent of Turks preempt their summons to school.

Countries that require their young people to stay in school the longest also turn out the most university students: On average 30 to 40 percent of their 18-to-24-year-olds go to university. Yet some of these countries are so selective that university attendance rates fall to the level of countries such as Turkey: fewer than 15 percent for England and the Swiss canton of Zurich. In the United States, by contrast, more than half the 18-to-24-year-olds are in higher education.

Systems may differ, but European elementary-school classrooms look much the same. Coeducation, an average class size of 20 to 22 pupils (except in Turkey, where it can reach 45), and one teacher

for all subjects per age-group (except in Scandinavia): All Europe's primary schools are built on more or less the same pattern.

The choice of the basic subjects to be taught varies little: reading and writing, mathematics, an introduction to the sciences, sports, and art. One difference is in the importance given to foreign languages. At first, only the Anglo-Saxon countries went for it, but it is growing steadily throughout the European Community.

As for the new technology, it has not found its way into all European schools. France and Belgium allow only a minimum of educational television programs, and Greece has just banned them completely. Northern and central European countries have included the ABC's of computers in their general educational aims (especially at secondary level) and have equipped most schools. Southern Europe, along with France and Belgium, uses the computer simply as a teaching aid.

Timetables are where the real differences show. Greece, Norway, Germany, and Italy all favor a half day, usually the morning from 8 a.m. to 1 p.m. Other countries—France, Belgium, Turkey, or Switzerland—prefer a full day with a break for lunch.

Schoolchildren in southern Europe get the longest summer holidays, between 10 and 12 weeks. The others have eight weeks or even as few as five or six, as in Switzerland, England, Germany, and Denmark.

Having to repeat a year is the bugbear of German, Swiss, and Turkish schoolchildren, while their Scandinavian and

2. RETHINKING AND CHANGING THE EDUCATIVE EFFORT

British counterparts automatically move up from one class to the next. For pupils in France, Spain, and Portugal, the threat of repeating looms only when they are about to move from one cycle of studies to the next. Some countries, such as Belgium and Spain, have decided to limit the number of times a student can repeat a year.

Northern Europe makes no distinction between elementary and secondary school: School just flows from Day 1 until the end of compulsory schooling at 16. At the other extreme, the Benelux countries, the German-speaking countries, Switzerland, and Ireland oblige their pupils to make a choice between general, technical, or even professional education as they are entering the sec-ondary cycle or after only one transitional year.

Other countries lie between the two poles: Everyone follows the same junior cycle of secondary school, with few optional extras. Such is France's *collège unique,* the Italian *scuola media,* the Greek *Gymnasio,* and the last stage of basic teaching in Spain and Portugal. This puts off the moment of decision until the pupils reach 15 or so.

The experience European pupils have as they work their way up in school varies considerably from country to country. The same is less true for their teachers. The profession is going through a crisis, barely mitigated by the social recognition teachers enjoy in Austria, Switzerland, or Hungary.

Except in Luxembourg and Switzerland, where teachers earn more than similarly qualified workers in the private sector, teachers' pay is never an inducement. As a general rule, university teachers are better paid than primary-school teachers even if, as in Scandinavia, the difference is small.

In spite of it all, teachers practice their profession on a full-time basis, rarely seeking to add to their earnings through other work. The exception is Greece, where lessons given outside school represent the larger part of teachers' earnings. Over the years, the teaching profession has become feminized, especially at the elementary level. In most European countries, two-thirds of all teachers are women.

ANGELA ULM – STAFF

How Much Schooling: An International Comparison

This information about the amount of time students around the world spend in school is based on a World Media questionnaire sent to the participating newspapers.

	How many hours in an average school day?		How many days are there in a school year?		How many years of compulsory education?		At what age must students make decisions affecting their education and vocational prospects?
	PRIMARY	SECONDARY	PRIMARY	SECONDARY	YEARS	AGES	
ARGENTINA	n/a	n/a	180	150	7	7-14	17-18
AUSTRIA	4-5	6-7	237	237	9	6-15	15
BELGIUM	4.5	5	182	182	12	6-18	12
BRAZIL	3.5	4	180	180	n/a	n/a	16-17
BRITAIN	6	7	190	190	11	5-16	14
DENMARK	5-7	7	200	200	9	7-16	15-17
FRANCE	6	6	180	180	10	6-16	15-16
GERMANY	5	7	200*	200*	12	6-18	10
GREECE	4-5	7	175†	175†	9	6-15	14
HUNGARY	5	6-8	170	170	10	6-16	14 or18
MEXICO	4.5-5	4-6	188	188	9	n/a	15-16
NORWAY	5	6	190	190	9	7-16	16
PORTUGAL	5-6	6-7	172	172	9	6-15	14-15
SENEGAL	5	7	168	168	5	6-11	17
SPAIN	5	6	175	170	8	6-14	14
SWITZERLAND	5-6	6-7	195	195	9	6-16*	15-16
TURKEY	5	6-8	180	180	5	9-14	15
UNITED STATES	7	7	180	180	10	6-16	16

Source: World Media Project, 1993   *Except in areas with six-day school week   † Half-days   ★ Canton Zurich

Selling the schools

Is private enterprise the future of public education in America?

The Osceola County school board in Florida is scheduled to approve the construction of a $36 million public school next week. William Rawn, the noted U.S. architect, has been hired to design the campus, just outside Orlando, and the Celebration School and Teaching Academy, as it's called, is scheduled to open in 1996, with 1,400 students in pre-kindergarten through 12th grade. New public schools are built all the time, of course, but in a host of ways, from its design to its teaching techniques and use of technology, Celebration breaks sharply from American public schooling tradition. Who is behind the school's innovations? The Walt Disney Co.

For-profit companies have long been involved in servicing the nation's public schools, running the cafeterias and operating the bus systems, for instance. But now, amid mounting frustration with the slow pace of promised school reforms and the increasing privatization of other public institutions, the heretical idea of commercial enterprises *educating* public school students is fast gathering momentum. Dozens of school systems from Portsmouth, Va., to San Jose, Calif., have begun discussing the running of their schools with private companies. President Clinton stunned the public education establishment earlier this year when he threw the weight of his office behind the movement, urging school systems in his State of the Union address to "experiment with ideas like chartering their schools to be run by private corporations." Last week, the first lady tacitly endorsed the radical notion when she toured one of the nation's first privately managed schools in Baltimore.

Runaway rhetoric? But the rhetoric of public school privatization may be running ahead of practicality. Privatization is touted as a way of bringing the efficiency of the marketplace to education and as a more palatable alternative to controversial private school vouchers. If widely introduced, the idea would bring about a sea change in American schooling. Yet the spread of the nascent movement is far from a given. To date, school management has attracted a small number of businesses with questionable or untested educational programs.

Nor is it clear that private firms will be able to make money running public schools. One of the early lessons of the privatization movement in education is that it's all but impossible to attract the capital needed to build a national network of new private schools because the returns on such investments don't warrant the risk of investment. At the same time, the firms already in the business are coming under intensifying attacks by the nation's powerful teachers' unions, further clouding the question of whether school privatization will spread.

Nonetheless, there has been a flurry of recent privatization activity:

■ The Hartford, Conn., school board voted last week to entertain a proposal by a private firm, Education Alternatives Inc. of Minneapolis, to manage all of the city's 32 schools. The firm's fee would be as much as $50 million over five years.

■ President Clinton this month signed a bill that permits states to spend federal education money to explore the running of public schools by private firms.

■ Baltimore, meanwhile, is in the second year of a five-year contract with EAI to run nine city schools for $133 million. The city has hired Sylvan Learning Systems, a private tutoring firm, to supply federally funded instruction to disadvantaged students. Sylvan recently went public and is aggressively pursuing contracts in other school systems.

■ Whittle Schools L.P., a new company created by media entrepreneur Chris Whittle, last month won the right to run three new publicly funded schools in Massachusetts, beginning in 1995.

■ The Maryland State Board of Education in November gave itself the authority to turn poorly performing schools over to for-profit companies.

No fantasy land. Next week's vote in Osceola will cap two years of planning by the Disney Development Co. The Walt Disney Co. division quietly launched the Celebration School project in 1992, as part of a planned community of 20,000 it is building near Walt Disney World. The company hired Deborah Claesgens, an expert in public-private partnerships, who forged a partnership with the Osceola schools and nearby Stetson University and brought in prominent reformers like Harvard psychologist Howard Gardner to consult.

Designers in Disney's Consumer Products Division are creating new multimedia curriculum materials to be used in the school (and marketed nationally in about two years). Celebration will also have an outdoor ecology lab on its 34-acre campus, fiber optics linking the school to the neighboring community and reconfigured buildings that create "neighborhoods" where groups of students and teachers spend the bulk of the school day together. A teacher-training center is planned as well. The school will be run by a three-member board of trustees that reports to the Osceola school board. Disney, Osceola and Stetson will each appoint one trustee.

But shocking as it might be to have the cartoon king designing a public school, Disney doesn't plan to get into the school-management business. Indeed, there are presently only two fledgling private firms in business to run public schools: EAI and Whittle Schools L.P., known popularly as the Edison Project.

Only EAI is already running schools. The firm has been widely praised for its early success in cleaning up and making safer the dilapidated inner-city schools it inherited in Baltimore. In a school system with a $350 million repair backlog, where it takes months to replace a broken window, EAI responds to requests for repairs within 48 hours. And both students and teachers are responding to the improvements—by showing up for school more often.

But it's not clear that EAI's results with teaching and learning will match its record in physical plant maintenance. The company does not offer school systems a new curriculum but rather a series of teaching strategies that it calls the Tesseract Way. Curriculum experts say it's essentially a collection of reforms that already have been introduced in public education—hands-on science and math, group learning and team teaching, literature-oriented reading instruction, mainstreaming special education students, individualized educational plans and well-supplied classrooms.

It's an ambitious agenda, and EAI has by many accounts made progress in the nearly two years it has been in Baltimore. Classrooms have more teaching materials, and special ed rolls have been reduced. Teachers are being trained in new teaching techniques, and minimally qualified classroom aides have been replaced by mostly college-educated "interns."

On the other side of the ledger, there has been too much turnover among the interns, critics charge, and many "mainstreamed" special ed students lack the classroom help they need. But the most compelling criticism of EAI is that it concentrates too much attention on students' basic-skills test scores at the expense of high standards — and that it does so for business purposes. EAI has put the bulk of its classroom resources into raising students' scores on basic-skills tests, installing 1,100 computers and requiring that each student spend 30 minutes a day on them doing drills in math and reading. EAI's computer drilling system is widely employed in remedial education; the drills match the skills measured by tests like Maryland's basic-skills exam, and EAI monitors its teachers to ensure they are keeping students at their computers.

At a time when basic-skills testing is under sharp attack as a detriment to true learning, EAI is making the tests the primary measure of its ability to run schools. "The whole thing is based on improving the test scores of students we serve," says EAI founder and Chairman John Golle. Golle admits that "there's a lot wrong with standardized testing." But he insists "that's the way schools are measured." To its critics, EAI is touting scores on simplistic tests to improve its image — at the expense of its students. Unfortunately for EAI, reading or math test scores at its eight Baltimore elementary schools declined last year, albeit before EAI had Tesseract fully in place.

Loftier vision. The Edison Project proposes to educate students to a far higher standard than EAI. In the three years since media entrepreneur Chris Whittle launched the company, its staff has fashioned a plan that would have students speaking two languages by the end of the fifth grade and passing six advanced placement exams before graduating.

Edison is aiming to open its first 10 to 15 elementary schools, enrolling 10,000 students, in fall 1995. But its lofty classroom goals hinge on a longer school day, a longer year and a host of other reforms, and it's far from clear that Edison will be able to win the concessions it needs. Indeed, if the response to the privatization movement by the nation's teachers' unions is any measure, it won't be easy.

Viewing privatization as a threat to jobs and to the influence of teachers' unions in schools, the American Federation of Teachers and the National Education Association and their local affiliates have attacked EAI relentlessly in recent months. The AFT affiliate in Baltimore has taken EAI to court and has lodged complaints with the Department of Education; lobbying by the NEA's local killed talks with EAI in San Diego. If anything, Edison is likely to encounter tougher union opposition as its negotiations with school systems intensify. It's no accident that Edison won its first three public school contracts through a Massachusetts law that permits Edison to bypass local school boards and unions.

Edison also needs over $50 million in financing by year's end to stay in business and open its first schools in 1995, company officials say. Adding to that challenge are the financial woes of Whittle Communications L.P., the Knoxville-based media company. Though Edison is an independent company, several of Whittle Communications' general partners are funding Edison, and Whittle is expected to post losses of $30 million this year. What's more, the red ink resulted in a major leadership shake-up last month that was widely interpreted in Knoxville as stripping Chris Whittle of day-to-day control of the company that bears his name.

In search of profits. Ultimately, the future of the nascent privatization movement depends upon whether Edison and EAI are able to turn a profit. EAI has cut costs in Baltimore by improving the management of its schools' physical plants, by moving many students out of special education classes and by replacing unionized teachers' aides with the interns, who are lower paid and don't receive benefits, a move that has enraged local labor leaders.

The financial frailty of EAI is reflected in the wild fluctuations of its stock price. Issued in 1991 at $4 a share, the stock hit a high of nearly $49 last fall in anticipation of new contracts but fell below $10 recently when the contracts (in Milwaukee and the District of Columbia) didn't materialize. In another sign of the company's weakness, institutional short sellers—investors who make money when a stock's price falls—control 1.4 million of EAI's 6.5 million shares.

The Edison Project's financial future is just as insecure. The company's computer models project that 70 percent of the nation's school systems could be run at a profit. But it's a long way from a computer model to money in the bank.

Myths & Facts

About Private School Choice

Numerous studies and test results have shown us that the academic performance of American students is very poor. Most citizens, be they elected officials or teachers, parents or retirees, agree that this crisis in education affects us all because it threatens our capacity to sustain our democracy and to meet the challenges of a global economy. The question is how to overcome that crisis.

For the past few years—with increasing intensity—Americans have been told that private school choice is the solution to our problems in education. Private school choice (also commonly known as vouchers) means allowing parents to use public dollars to send their children to private and religious schools. Proponents say private school choice will break up the public school "monopoly" and force schools to improve as they compete to attract customers. The result, they say, will be good schools and high student achievement.

This is an attractive argument, but one based more on myth than on fact. The American Federation of Teachers believes that educators have a special responsibility to help the public distinguish between myth and fact and that informed debate is essential to the democratic process. In publishing Myths and Facts about Private School Choice, we hope to advance citizens' understanding of this important and controversial public policy issue.

Some may ask, "Why should we take the AFT's word about private school choice? Doesn't the AFT have a vested interest in public education?" Sure we do, and so do all Americans. And we are not asking anyone to take our word—or anyone else's, for that matter—on private school choice. We have documented all our facts, as well as the claims made by private school choice supporters. Check out the evidence and ask further questions—of both sides in this debate.

The AFT is proud of its role in and support of public education, but that has not blinded us to the reality that the American education system must do a much better job. Teachers were the first to blow the whistle on declining academic standards and poor student performance, and when the studies came out that confirmed what teachers already knew, the AFT did not whitewash the findings. Just as we are uncovering here the myths about private school choice, we publicized the sad facts about American student achievement.

If private school choice is not the answer, what is? We believe the keys to turning around both our public and private schools are: clear and challenging academic standards; student assessments based on these standards; and accountability for students and schools based on performance. We also advocate rigorous standards for teachers; firm and fair discipline in schools, and the removal of chronically disruptive and violent youngsters to alternative schools; and restoring parents' involvement in helping their children succeed in school.

These are commonsense solutions favored by most Americans. These solutions are within our reach. We hope you will work with us to achieve them and at the same time strengthen and preserve the vital role of public education in our democracy.

From *American Educator*, Vol. 17, No. 3, Fall 1993, pp. 26A-26H. Reprinted by permission of *American Educator*, the quarterly journal of the American Federation of Teachers. © 1993.

MYTH: Private school choice lets parents pick the best school for a child by giving them a voucher to use at a public or private school.

FACT: Parents may choose a private school, but that doesn't mean the school will choose their child. Public schools have to take all children. Private schools don't.

Private schools pick children on the basis of grades, recommendations, scores on entrance exams, and personal interviews. For example, 71 percent of Catholic high schools require an entrance exam, as do 43 percent of other religious schools and 66 percent of independent private schools.[1]

Unless a child is well-behaved, belongs to the "right" social class or religion, or has the right mix of intellectual, creative, and athletic abilities, he or she may not get into a private school. And since private schools are private, the public—the taxpayers who would foot the bill for vouchers—have no say in private schools' admission and other policies.

The term "private school choice" is therefore misleading, because money isn't the only barrier to choosing a private school, especially one with a good reputation. Ask any wealthy family if money alone can get a child into a private school of choice. The answer is No.

Disadvantaged children would have even less choice of private schools. For example, very few private schools serve children with disabilities.[2] In Milwaukee, where poor families can get vouchers for private schools, 40 percent of the children who sought to participate could not find a school that would take them.[3]

MYTH: Private school choice would increase accountability in education by breaking up the public school monopoly and making schools more responsive to parents.

FACT: Private school choice would *reduce* accountability in education. The reason is simple: Private schools are exempt from almost all public regulations.

Most private schools don't have to account to the public for their admission, discipline, or expulsion policies; curriculum; teacher qualifications; the source of their funds or how they spend those funds; the needs of children with disabilities; or their students' test results. Private schools are controlled by their owners, and they need not involve anyone, including parents, in school governance.

This lack of accountability does not mean private schools are irresponsible. Private schools are free from regulation because what they teach and how they teach are not supposed to be the public's business and *can't* be the public's business—unless private schools are willing to give up their autonomy and religious schools are willing to have the wall between church and state broken down.

Advocates of private school choice say that parents will hold the schools accountable. But vouchers create incentives for schools to attract customers and not necessarily to improve achievement, so there's no assurance that what schools would sell—or what parents would buy—would be a better education. Where would busy parents get the information they need to choose among schools? Should we just assume that all private schools would be honest? Moreover, is parental satisfaction an adequate standard of accountability when all taxpayers—not just parents with school-age children—bear the cost of education?

Public schools should be more accountable for their performance. But at least they show how they spend taxpayers' money; follow regulations about discipline, safety, equal opportunity, curriculum, and teacher credentials; and publish information about student performance, good or bad. And they are governed by the people's elected representatives.

If we want stricter accountability in education, that's what we should demand—rather than giving public dollars to schools that don't have to answer to the public.

MYTH: Private school choice would promote healthy competition between public and private schools and make all schools better.

FACT: Competition *is* healthy—when everyone has to play by the same rules. But the playing field for public and private schools is far from level.

As noted earlier, public schools must serve all children; private schools don't have to. Public schools must obey state and local regulations concerning discipline; health and safety; civil rights; special education; curriculum; student testing; teacher qualifications—the list goes on. Private schools are exempt from most of these rules.

In the name of fair competition, are proponents of choice ready to subject private and religious schools to the rules now governing public schools? Not a chance. Are they proposing to ask Congress, state legislatures, school boards, and the courts to roll back the laws and regulations governing public schools and allow them to behave like private schools? No. Can a competition be fair if competitors play by different rules? And can its results prove anything of value? No on both counts.

At any rate, it would be a riverboat gamble to entrust education to the chance of the market. Markets develop products to satisfy people's tastes or needs, according to their ability to pay. But satisfying consumers is not the goal of education: Learning is. Education is a vital *public* good that cannot be guaranteed through markets (that's why we developed public schools in the first place).

Supporters of private school choice glamorize the market and ignore its failures and abuses. If markets only penalize poor performance and encourage quality goods, why are junk food and violent movies so common? Why have so many private trade schools pocketed millions of dollars in federal aid for higher education without giving students the training they were promised?[4] Why are taxpayers shelling out $200 billion to rescue banks that failed when their owners speculated recklessly with other people's money?

In a market system, some parents might choose topnotch schools, but others might choose cult schools or football factories. When a referendum on private school choice was called in California, a group of avowed witches announced plans to open a "pagan" school that would combine reading, writing, and arithmetic with magic. Indeed, vouchers would create a lot of chances for hocus-pocus.

MYTH: Private schools are as nonselective, open, and diverse as public schools.

FACT: Private schools serve a hand-picked and more advantaged group of students than public schools do because of the purposes, admission policies, and tuition costs of private schools.

Religious schools dominate the private sector in education: 81 percent of private elementary and secondary schools are religious schools, and 84 percent of private school students attend religious schools.[5]

Also, most private schools educate students from families having greater resources than those of public school students. Private school students are much more likely to have college-educated parents than public school students (see Chart 1). Likewise, private school students are much more likely to be well-off than public school students (see Chart 2). Private schools are also less racially diverse: The share of white students attending private school (11 percent) is double that of Hispanic and black students (5 percent and 6 percent, respectively).[6]

What about the claims that Catholic schools are a special case—that they are as open and diverse as public schools? The facts show otherwise. For example, only 2 percent of Catholic schools fall into the lowest quartile of student socioeconomic status (SES), compared with 28 percent of public schools. Even in urban areas, only 18 percent of Catholic schools fall into the lowest SES quartile, compared with 42 percent of public schools.[7]

CHART 1

PARENTAL EDUCATION LEVELS OF ELEMENTARY AND SECONDARY STUDENTS IN PUBLIC, PAROCHIAL, AND OTHER PRIVATE SCHOOLS

Public schools: < 4 years high school 25, 4 years high school 38, 1-3 years of college 18, 4+ years of college 19

Church-related schools: < 4 years high school 10, 4 years high school 35, 1-3 years of college 25, 4+ years of college 30

Nonsectarian schools: < 4 years high school 8, 4 years high school 21, 1-3 years of college 14, 4+ years of college 57

Legend:
- < 4 years high school
- 4 years high school
- 1-3 years of college
- 4+ years of college

Source: Private Schools in the United States: A Statistical Profile, With Comparisons to Public Schools, Figure 3-6, p. 47, U.S. Department of Education, National Center for Education Statistics, February 1991.

CHART 2

FAMILY INCOME OF ELEMENTARY AND SECONDARY STUDENTS IN PUBLIC, PAROCHIAL, AND OTHER PRIVATE SCHOOLS

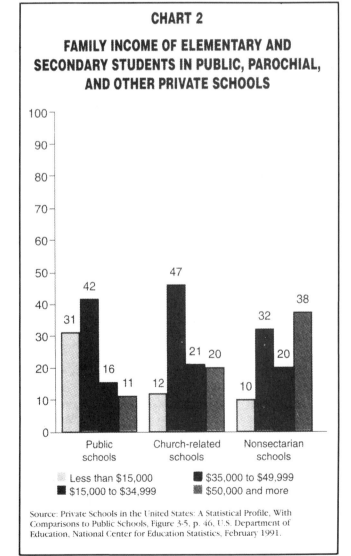

Public schools: Less than $15,000 31, $15,000 to $34,999 42, $35,000 to $49,999 16, $50,000 and more 11

Church-related schools: Less than $15,000 12, $15,000 to $34,999 47, $35,000 to $49,999 21, $50,000 and more 20

Nonsectarian schools: Less than $15,000 10, $15,000 to $34,999 32, $35,000 to $49,999 20, $50,000 and more 38

Legend:
- Less than $15,000
- $15,000 to $34,999
- $35,000 to $49,999
- $50,000 and more

Source: Private Schools in the United States: A Statistical Profile, With Comparisons to Public Schools, Figure 3-5, p. 46, U.S. Department of Education, National Center for Education Statistics, February 1991.

2. RETHINKING AND CHANGING THE EDUCATIVE EFFORT

Catholic schools do perform an important service by educating some poor children, many of whom are not Catholic. But even in such cases, Catholic schools handpick these students and can always expel their mistakes. Public schools must accept all comers.

None of these differences between public and private schools should be surprising, because private schools cater to particular needs and wants—"market niches." This undercuts the claim that private school choice will benefit a wide range of children, not because private schools are irresponsible, but because the nature of private schools—and private businesses—is to carve out market niches. Public and private schools serve very different groups of children—and would continue doing so under a voucher plan.

MYTH: The evidence shows that private schools outperform public schools.

FACT: The evidence shows no such thing. Because private schools are able to handpick students, many of whom have highly educated parents and high family incomes, you'd expect private schools to substantially outperform public schools. The surprise is they don't. Private schools do only slightly better, and their edge disappears when one compares public and private school students from similar backgrounds.

TABLE 1

AVERAGE PROFICIENCY AND PERCENTAGE OF STUDENTS AT OR ABOVE FOUR ANCHOR LEVELS ON THE NAEP MATHEMATICS SCALE BY TYPE OF SCHOOL

	Percent of Students	Average Proficiency	Percentage of Students at or Above			
			Level 200	Level 250	Level 300	Level 350
GRADE 4						
Public Schools	88 (1.2)	214 (0.9)	70 (1.3)	10 (0.8)	0 (0.0)	0 (0.0)
Catholic Schools	8 (1.1)	224 (2.0)	83 (2.6)	16 (2.2)	0 (0.0)	0 (0.0)
Other Private Schools	4 (0.8)	231 (2.8)	89 (3.8)	22 (3.4)	0 (0.0)	0 (0.0)
GRADE 8						
Public Schools	89 (1.3)	264 (1.2)	97 (0.5)	66 (1.3)	13 (1.3)	0 (0.1)
Catholic Schools	7 (1.1)	278 (2.6)	100 (0.2)	84 (2.6)	22 (3.4)	0 (0.2)
Other Private Schools	4 (0.7)	274 (2.4)	100 (0.5)	80 (3.8)	18 (2.9)	0 (0.0)
GRADE 12						
Public Schools	90 (1.3)	295 (1.1)	100 (0.1)	90 (0.7)	45 (1.4)	5 (0.6)
Catholic Schools	6 (1.1)	302 (3.0)	100 (0.0)	96 (1.2)	54 (4.5)	4 (1.0)
Other Private Schools	4 (0.8)	301 (3.1)	100 (0.0)	97 (1.1)	51 (4.8)	4 (1.8)

The standard errors of the estimated percentages and proficiencies appear in parentheses. It can be said with 95 percent certainty that for each population of interest, the value for the whole population is within plus or minus two standard errors of the estimate for the sample. When the proportion of students is 0 percent, the standard error is inestimable. Although percentages less than 0.5 percent are rounded to 0 percent, a few eighth-grade public school students (0.2 percent) and Catholic school students (0.1 percent) reached Level 350.

DESCRIPTION OF NAEP LEVELS:

Level 200: Simple additive reasoning and problem solving with whole numbers; content typically covered by 3rd grade.

Level 250: Simple multiplicative reasoning and two-step problem solving; content typically covered by 5th grade.

Level 300: Reasoning and problem solving involving fractions, decimals, percents, elementary geometry, and simple algebra; content introduced by 7th grade.

Level 350: Reasoning and problem solving involving geometry, algebra, and beginning statistics and probability; content generally covered in high school math courses in preparation for the study of advanced math.

Source: The State of Mathematics Achievement: NAEP's 1990 Assessment of the Nation and the Trial Assessment of the States, U.S. Department of Education, National Center for Education Statistics, June 1991, Table 2.6 and Executive Summary, pp. 6-7.

Let's examine the evidence from three sources: (1) the National Assessment of Educational Progress, (2) the High School and Beyond study, and (3) Milwaukee's experiment with vouchers for low-income families.

The National Assessment of Educational Progress (NAEP)

The NAEP is a national survey that has tracked student achievement in major subjects since 1969. The 1990 NAEP math assessment was the first to report results separately for public and private school students.

Overall, private school students had only a slim advantage on the NAEP math test (see Table 1). In grades 4 and 8, private school students averaged 10 to 17 more points on NAEP's 500-point scale. This margin dropped to between 6 and 7 points by grade 12. Even more surprising is the fact that, compared with private school seniors, a slightly higher percentage of public school seniors attained the top level of achievement on the 1990 math exam.[8]

Research has shown again and again that parent education and family income have powerful effects on educational achievement. So, given the much higher levels of parent education and family income enjoyed by private school students, one would expect them to achieve much more. But they don't.

If one compares the 1990 NAEP math scores of private and public school students with the same level of parent education or the same math coursework, *the achievement gap vanishes completely* (see Charts 3, 4, and 5).[9] The 1990 NAEP exam in science and the 1992 math results show the same pattern.[10]

Chester Finn, Jr., an Assistant Secretary of Education under President Reagan and a fervent backer of private school choice, found similar results in an analysis of unpublished NAEP test results for history and literature.

Finn concluded that, "With differences that large in parent education, it is conceivable that there is no (private) school effect showing up here at all."[11]

None of this is anything for public schools to crow about. Neither public nor private school students are performing well. For example, only about half of high school seniors—in either school sector—can solve problems involving decimals, fractions, percents, basic geometry, and simple algebra. These topics typically are taught in junior high math.

But the fact that private schools, despite their considerable advantages, do not perform much better than public schools indicates that private school choice is not a panacea. Even if all public school students entered private schools tomorrow, we'd still have an educational crisis on our hands.

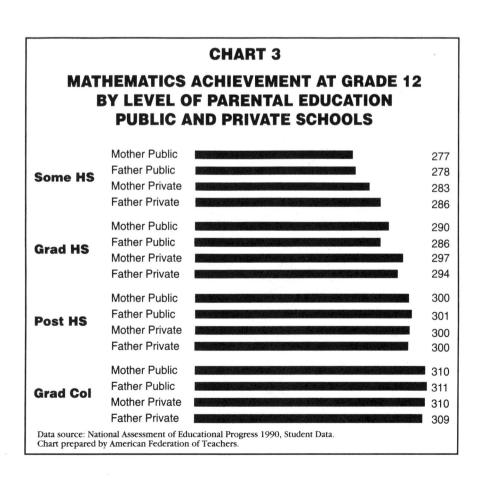

CHART 3

**MATHEMATICS ACHIEVEMENT AT GRADE 12
BY LEVEL OF PARENTAL EDUCATION
PUBLIC AND PRIVATE SCHOOLS**

Some HS		
Mother Public		277
Father Public		278
Mother Private		283
Father Private		286

Grad HS		
Mother Public		290
Father Public		286
Mother Private		297
Father Private		294

Post HS		
Mother Public		300
Father Public		301
Mother Private		300
Father Private		300

Grad Col		
Mother Public		310
Father Public		311
Mother Private		310
Father Private		309

Data source: National Assessment of Educational Progress 1990, Student Data.
Chart prepared by American Federation of Teachers.

High School and Beyond (HS&B)

HS&B is a federal survey of student achievement in 1,000 public and private high schools. The research findings based on HS&B mirror the NAEP results: The private school advantage is very small and almost disappears when similar students are compared.

A 1982 analysis of HS&B data by James Coleman reported that Catholic high school students scored one grade level higher on achievement tests than their public school counterparts.[12] This finding fueled the popular impression that private schools are better than public schools. Unfortunately, Coleman failed to control for student ability or learning prior to high school. Once those errors were corrected, the private school edge in achievement was tiny.

Leading researchers who have studied the HS&B data echo that point. For example: Professor John Witte, University of Wisconsin at Madison: "The size of the differences in achievement between sectors is simply so small that we can draw almost no conclusions from them."[13]

Professor Christopher Jencks, Northwestern University: "The annual increment attributable to Catholic schooling . . . averages .03 or .04 standard deviations per year. By conventional standards, this is a tiny effect."[14]

But what about the latest book using HS&B, *Politics, Markets, and America's Schools,* by John Chubb and Terry Moe? Doesn't the book prove that private schools outdo public schools because of market control?

It's true that Chubb and Moe received a lot of media attention for their conclusion that private schools perform better than public schools. However, when experts looked at the book, they found it was highly flawed, based more on ideology than on evidence. In fact, Chubb and Moe never directly compared the performance of public and private schools. Instead, they simply assumed that the qualities of effective schools are associated with free markets and private schools. Can we afford to make decisions about the future of public schools on the basis of faith instead of evidence?

The flaws in Chubb and Moe's research are well-documented, but too numerous to describe here. However, two leading education scholars, Valerie Lee of the University of Michigan and Anthony Bryk of the University of Chicago, summed it up when they wrote: *"Politics, Markets, and America's Schools* comes up short as a piece of disciplined policy research" and goes "substantially beyond what the empirical evidence can support."[15]

Milwaukee's voucher experiment

Milwaukee's voucher experiment reinforces the conclusion that private schools don't outperform public schools and that private school choice won't improve student achievement. Moreover, this program vividly shows the risks of giving tax dollars to schools not accountable to the public.

The Milwaukee program offers vouchers for up to 950 low-income, public school students to use at non-religious private schools. Yet the private schools have

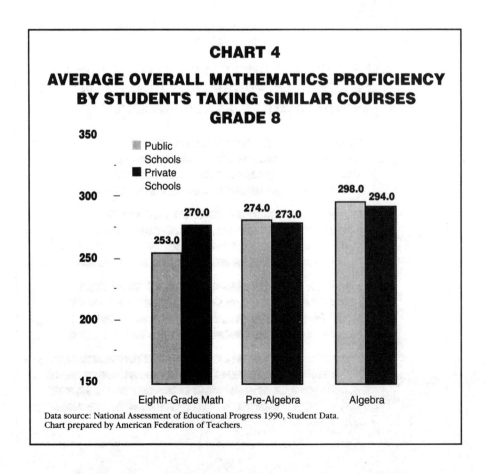

CHART 4

AVERAGE OVERALL MATHEMATICS PROFICIENCY BY STUDENTS TAKING SIMILAR COURSES GRADE 8

Public Schools
Private Schools

Eighth-Grade Math: 253.0 / 270.0
Pre-Algebra: 274.0 / 273.0
Algebra: 298.0 / 294.0

Data source: National Assessment of Educational Progress 1990, Student Data.
Chart prepared by American Federation of Teachers.

been unable or unwilling to serve even such a small number of children. In the most recent year, only 613 students participated, while almost 400 could not find a school that would take them. Only 11 of 21 eligible private schools were willing to take voucher students.

Parents whose children participated in the voucher program report satisfaction with their choice. Yet the annual student attrition from Milwaukee's voucher schools has been 35 percent; and, teaching methods in Milwaukee do not differ much in the public and private schools. In addition, the voucher schools are characterized by low teacher salaries and high teacher turnover.

Accountability is almost completely absent in the Milwaukee program. During the first year, one of the voucher schools withdrew from the program when it reintroduced religious instruction, sending 63 students back to the public schools. Several weeks later, the school went bankrupt amid claims of theft and financial mismanagement. Parents also complained about food, transportation, a lack of books and materials, and discipline problems. The school lacked formal bylaws or a governing board with open meetings and did not submit to an external financial audit. Because private schools are exempt from almost all regulations, there are no safeguards to prevent similar abuses. Advocates of private school choice say that parents will hold the schools accountable, but how many parents have the time or expertise to check a school's budget, review its curriculum, or even make sure that the bus driver has a license?

Of course, the bottom line is whether the choice program increases learning. In the second year, voucher students lost ground in reading and held steady in math, while public school students stayed constant in both reading and math scores. Although it is still too early for firm conclusions about Milwaukee's voucher experiment, the voucher schools are, if anything, doing worse than the public schools.[16]

The evidence is overwhelming: Private schools do not educate the same kinds of students as public schools, and private schools do not outperform public schools.

MYTH: American colleges and universities, which are forced to compete, are the best in the world. If our elementary and secondary schools had to compete, they would also reach the same level of excellence.

FACT: American colleges and universities vary widely: Some are outstanding, some are mediocre, and some are abysmal. The competition for customers does nothing to promote academic excellence. Indeed, some colleges will take any warm body, regardless of whether the student learned anything in high school, just to keep enrollments up.

A recent ranking of admission standards at American colleges reflects this sorry state of affairs. Only 39 colleges qualified as "most difficult"—most of their students are in the top 10 percent of their high school class and have SAT scores above 1250. By contrast, 188

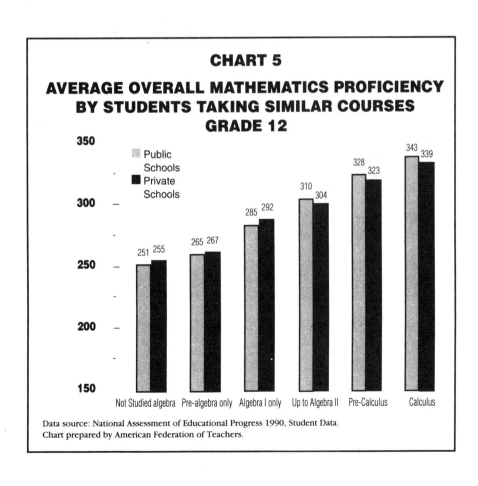

CHART 5

AVERAGE OVERALL MATHEMATICS PROFICIENCY BY STUDENTS TAKING SIMILAR COURSES GRADE 12

Public Schools / Private Schools

Course	Public	Private
Not Studied algebra	251	255
Pre-algebra only	265	267
Algebra I only	285	292
Up to Algebra II	310	304
Pre-Calculus	328	323
Calculus	343	339

Data source: National Assessment of Educational Progress 1990, Student Data.
Chart prepared by American Federation of Teachers.

colleges—almost five times as many—were "non-competitive," accepting almost all applicants regardless of high school record and SAT scores.[17]

Why are college admission standards so low? The answer is easy: Colleges are competing for customers to keep the flow of tuition and federal aid dollars coming in. A former college professor recently told the *Wall Street Journal,* "When the institution needs to recruit and retain students to survive . . . intellectual standards are at risk of being compromised."[18]

With such powerful pressure for colleges to attract customers, it comes as no surprise that many students don't do well or learn much in college. The dropout rate is enormous: Only half of full-time entrants to four-year colleges have earned a college degree six years later.[19] That's much worse than high school dropout rates. Studies have also shown that many college graduates can't make sense of bus schedules, contrast two opposing editorial views, or calculate the tip for a restaurant bill.[20]

Other nations' universities show that high standards, not competition, are vital to education. To attend college in Australia, Great Britain, France, Germany, and Japan, students must pass demanding national or provincial exams based on high school curriculum. The United States lacks such standards. Many or most American college students could not get into European universities.

Competition does force schools to seek out customers, but that doesn't necessarily mean the schools are selling anything of value.

MYTH: Giving parents the right to choose a private school would not cost taxpayers anything. In fact, it would save money.

FACT: Private school choice would be very expensive, even before a single child changed from public to private schools. Why? Taxpayers would provide vouchers for children *already* attending private school. The total cost would exceed $30 billion annually if each of the nation's 5.4 million children in private school got a voucher worth the average expenditure ($5,900) for each public school student.[21] In effect, people would be subject to double taxation for public and private schools.

This would represent a large transfer of income from the public to the mostly high-income families with children in private schools. Even if half of these families refused the voucher, the cost still would exceed the $12 billion in federal spending on elementary and secondary education in 1992.[22]

It's true that most voucher plans offer less than the average cost of educating a student. For example, California's voucher proposal (subject to a voter referendum in November 1993) offers $2,600 per student; Milwaukee's voucher program offered $2,745 per student in 1992-93. But smaller vouchers mean that more families—particularly poor families—won't be able to pay for good private schools (top private schools cost as much as $6,000 to $12,000 per year).

Advocates of private school choice say their plan would pare down the public school bureaucracy. But they neglect to tell us that choice would require a huge new bureaucracy—and hence, more money—to give parents information about the array of schools and to transport children to schools outside their neighborhoods.

With federal, state, and local budgets already severely strained, can taxpayers afford to subsidize high-income families who already can afford to send their children to private school?

MYTH: Public education in the United States is beyond repair. Years of reform efforts have achieved nothing, so we have no alternative but to try private school choice.

FACT: Public schools must do a much better job. But the doomsayers mislead us when they claim public schools are getting worse and worse. The fact is that public schools have been doing a better job recently, even as child poverty and family breakup increased. Instead of rolling the dice with private school choice, we need to continue to improve the public schools.

Education reform during the 1970s and 1980s was mostly an effort to shore up basic skills. Remedial programs expanded; student testing (mostly low-level) increased; and graduation requirements were toughened. What happened? Test scores in science, math, and reading for students in grades 4, 8, and 12 have risen slowly but steadily. The gains were sizable in basic skills, but absent in more advanced skills.[23]

Is this good enough? No. We need to insist on higher standards. The main reason American children don't learn much—in public *or* private schools—is that our educational standards are so low. Most college-bound students know they can find a school that will accept them, no matter how poor their grades are or how little they know. Job-bound students know that employers don't check high school transcripts. The solution is an education system driven by clear and challenging curriculum standards, student assessments tied to those standards, and direct accountability for student and school performance—the same formula used by other industrialized democracies whose students outperform our own.

By contrast, private school choice offers no benefits and entails enormous risks. We've seen that private schools are not doing better than public schools. What are the risks? Private school choice would reduce accountability and risk further separating us by class, race, ethnicity, and religion. Markets are inherently unstable. Businesses constantly open and close, merge and restructure. What would happen if a child's school closed in the middle of the school year? Would the child wait until next year if other schools are filled to capacity? Would public schools be used as dumping grounds? What if public school buildings were sold, closed, or privatized? Many neighborhood schools would disappear. Private school choice might seem like a harmless experiment, but—like Humpty Dumpty—if public schools fall, they will be hard to put back together again.

Should we sacrifice public schools for a perilous and untested market fantasy? We think the answer is No.

REFERENCES

1. U.S. Department of Education, National Center for Education Statistics, *Private Schools and Private School Teachers: Final Report of the 1985-86 Private School Study* (Washington, D.C.: U.S. Government Printing Office, 1987), p. 22.
2. According to the U.S. Department of Education, 7 percent of public school students participate in programs for the handicapped, compared with 2 percent of private school students. See U.S. Department of Education, National Center for Education Statistics, *Digest of Education Statistics, 1992* (Washington, D.C.: U.S. Government Printing Office, 1992), p. 69.
3. John Witte, Andrea Bailey, and Christopher Thorn, "Second-Year Report: Milwaukee Parental Choice Program" (paper published at the Department of Political Science and the Robert M. LaFollette Institute of Public Affairs, University of Wisconsin at Madison, December 1992), p. iv.
4. For examples of fraud and mismanagement among recipients of federal higher education aid, see U.S. Department of Education, Office of the Inspector General, *Semiannual Report to Congress,* No. 26 (Washington, D.C.: Office of the Inspector General, 1993)), pp. vii-viii.
5. See National Center for Education Statistics, *Digest of Education Statistics, 1992,* p. 69.
6. U.S. Department of Commerce, Bureau of the Census, *School Enrollment—Social and Economic Characteristics of Students: October 1991,* Current Population Reports, Series P-20, No. 469 (Washington, D.C.: U.S. Government Printing Office, 1993), p. x.
7. John Witte, "Understanding High School Achievement: After a Decade of Research, Do We Have Any Confident Policy Recommendations?" (paper presented at the 1990 annual meeting of the American Political Science Association), Table 10.
8. U.S. Department of Education, National Center for Education Statistics, *The State of Mathematics Achievement: NAEP's 1990 Assessment of the Nation and the Trial Assessment of the States* (Washington, D.C.: U.S. Department of Education, 1991), p. 90.
9. See Albert Shanker and Bella Rosenberg, "Do Private Schools Outperform Public Schools?" in *The Task Before Us: A QuEST Reader* (Washington, D.C.: American Federation of Teachers, 1993), pp. 40–43.
10. See U.S. Department of Education, National Center for Education Statistics, *The 1990 Science Report Card: NAEP's Assessment of Fourth, Eighth, and Twelfth Graders* (Washington, D.C.: U.S. Department of Education, 1991), p. 15, and U.S. Department of Education, National Center for Education Statistics, *NAEP 1992 Mathematics Report Card for the Nation and the States* (Washington, D.C.: U.S. Department of Education, 1993), p. 149.
11. Kristen Goldberg, "Gravest Threat to Private Schools Is Better Public Ones, Finn Warns," in *Education Week,* March 9, 1988, p. 1.
12. See James Coleman, Thomas Hoffer, and Sally Kilgore, *High School Achievement* (New York: Basic Books, 1982).
13. Witte, "Understanding High School Achievement: After a Decade of Research, Do We Have Any Confident Policy Recommendations?" p. 27.
14. As quoted in Witte, "Understanding High School Achievement: After a Decade of Research, Do We Have Any Confident Policy Recommendations?" p. 27.
15. Valerie Lee and Anthony Bryk, "Science or Policy Argument: A Review of the Quantitative Evidence in Chubb and Moe's *Politics, Markets, and America's Schools* (paper prepared for conference sponsored by the Economic Policy Institute, Washington, D.C., October 1, 1992), p. 17. See also Nicholas Lemann, "A False Panacea," in *The Atlantic,* January 1991, pp. 101-105; Abigail Thernstrom, "Is Choice a Necessity?" in *The Public Interest,* Fall 1990, pp. 124-132; Amy Stuart Wells, "Choice in Education: Examining the Evidence on Equity," in *Teacher's College Record,,* Fall 1991, pp. 137-155; and Witte, "Understanding High School Achievement: After a Decade of Research, Do We Have Any Confident Policy Recommendations?" pp. 18-22.
16. The information about the Milwaukee voucher program presented here is based on Witte, Bailey, and Thorn, as well as John Witte, "First-Year Report: Milwaukee Parental Choice Program" (paper published at the Department of Political Science and the Robert M. LaFollette Institute of Public Affairs, University of Wisconsin at Madison, November 1991).
17. Peterson's Guides, *Peterson's Four-Year Colleges, 1993* (Princeton, N.J.: Peterson's Guides, 1993), pp. 57-62.
18. Albert Shanker, "Competing for Customers," Where We Stand, in the *New York Times,* June 27, 1993.
19. U.S. Department of Education, *Digest of Education Statistics, 1992,* p. 304.
20. See U.S. Department of Education, *Digest of Education Statistics, 1992,* p. 399, and Irwin Kirsch, Ann Jungeblut, Lynn Jenkins, and Andrew Kolstad, *Adult Literacy in America: A First Look at the Results of the National Adult Literacy Survey* (Washington, D.C.: U.S. Department of Education, 1993), pp. 25-27.
21. The number of private school students is from U.S. Department of Education, National Center for Education Statistics, *Public and Private Elementary and Secondary Education Statistics: School Year 1992-93* (Washington, D.C.: U.S. Department of Education, 1993), p. 7. The figure for average education expenditures is from U.S. Department of Education, *Digest of Education Statistics,* p. 159.
22. Executive Office of the President, Office of Management and Budget, *Budget of the United States Government, Fiscal Year 1994* (Washington, D.C.: U.S. Government Printing Office, 1993), p. A-25.
23. See Ina Mullis, John Dossey, Mary Foertsch, Lee Jones and Claudia Gentile, *Trends in Academic Progress* (Washington, D.C.: U.S. Department of Education, 1991), pp. 1–21.

The Precarious Politics Of Privatizing Schools

CHARLES MAHTESIAN

At first glance, it's hard to imagine what Franklin Smith could have done differently to avert the political train wreck that occurred on his watch. After proposing the privatized management of schools in late 1993, the District of Columbia school superintendent followed up with the requisite political feather-smoothing and barnstormed across the city to explain the idea to community groups.

But the D.C. Board of Education never had a chance to vote on the proposal. Four months after introducing it, Smith decided to shelve the idea. While he figured at least five of the board's 11 members were with him—and three were still undecided—the fractious debate that had ensued convinced him that the time was not right for a vote. A decision to proceed, the superintendent said, would have caused "chaos and confusion."

Smith was right: It would have. Even if privatization had been approved, its slim margin of victory would have underscored the deep divisions within the community. But in retreat, Smith ended up in worse shape than when he began his crusade.

On the one hand, privatization advocates in the business community were so upset that they threatened to scale back their involvement with city schools—and they were Smith's friends. On the other, opponents of private management—namely, teachers' union leaders—continued to bloody Smith with a barrage of criticism. A group of parents and community activists initiated an effort to oust him from office. And at one noisy school board meeting, a brawl broke out over the subject of privatization.

Upon closer examination, perhaps Smith could have handled the whole affair better. To begin with, the initial announcement caught many in the city's educational establishment off guard. The teachers' union was angered and the prospect of outsiders taking control of

Many places have been looking at private companies to run their schools. But public officials are finding the idea hard to sell.

inner city schools made far too many parents uneasy. The election-year timing was also questionable. Five school board members and embattled Mayor Sharon Pratt Kelly are up for reelection in 1994, and the last thing they wanted on voters' minds was the privatization vote.

The irony, of course, is that for all the fury surrounding D.C.'s attempt at privatization, the issue of whether private management of public schools would actually work was never really addressed.

Indeed, with the practical application of school privatization still in its infancy, it is nearly impossible to assess its impact on student achievement and performance. But as the Washington donnybrook demonstrated, one thing is certain: The philosophical debate has run headlong into political reality.

Dozens of school systems across the country are openly or privately discussing the private-management option. Hartford, Connecticut, is seriously considering turning over its entire 32-school, 26,000-student school system to private management, as is the 4,000-student school system in suburban Pinckney, Michigan.

They are looking to the two giants in the field—Educational Alternatives Inc. and the Edison Project. There are other, smaller firms, but most of them are local in nature and lack the financial resources of EAI and Edison.

So far, Minneapolis-based Educational Alternatives is the only for-profit firm with any public school management experience. Besides running nine Baltimore public schools, EAI operates South Pointe Elementary School in Miami Beach—the first in the nation to contract with a private company. In addition to providing school management and consulting services, EAI has developed its own custom-designed curriculum, known as Tesseract.

The Edison Project, based in New York City, is a spinoff from Whittle

Communications, which produces the advertising-supported Channel One classroom news show. Edison also offers a specialized curriculum, and advocates longer school days and extended school years. At the moment, Edison does not operate any schools but has contracted to run three charter schools in Massachusetts beginning in 1995. So far, the Bay State's charter school law is the only one that directly permits applications from private companies.

Both EAI and Edison ask only for the amount of money currently spent per pupil, and in return promise improved student performance, increased capital investment and high-tech equipment. Edison even plans to offer a home computer to every student. The firms expect to realize a profit by streamlining school bureaucracies, contracting out various services and establishing economies of scale.

Sound too good to be true? Well, if you listen to the teachers' unions, it is. In virtually every large city where the concept has been or is currently being considered, teachers have aggressively attacked the idea. And in San Diego and Nashville, as well as D.C., the unions' opposition was enough to kill or indefinitely postpone privatization efforts.

"They have clearly taken out against the privatization idea. It's something they want to nip in the bud," says Chester Finn, a former U.S. assistant secretary of education and founding partner of the Edison Project. "It's probably Public Enemy Number 2 in their world view. Vouchers is Number 1."

If the experiences in San Diego and Nashville are any indication, it seems that teachers consider the two enemies about equally loathsome. In San Diego, for example, privatization proponent Kay Davis of the Chamber of Commerce's Business Roundtable actually became Public Enemy Number 1.

Earlier this year, disgruntled teachers distributed a flier detailing Davis' role as a voting board member of the State Teachers Retirement System, which happens to include 8,000 shares of EAI stock in its portfolio. The letter, which Davis describes as a "hit piece," also noted that another member of the Business Roundtable—of which Davis serves as executive director—sits on EAI's board of directors. While the school board managed to pass a resolution supporting privatization as an option, the effort stalled without a final vote.

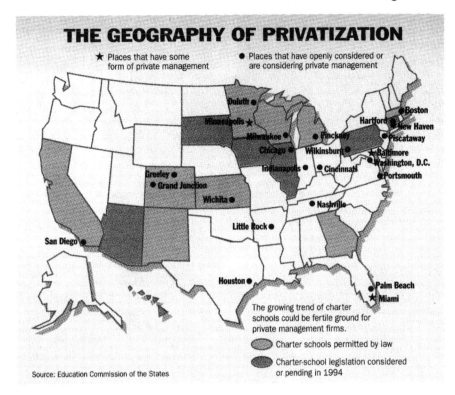

THE GEOGRAPHY OF PRIVATIZATION

★ Places that have some form of private management

● Places that have openly considered or are considering private management

The growing trend of charter schools could be fertile ground for private management firms.

⬭ Charter schools permitted by law

⬤ Charter-school legislation considered or pending in 1994

Source: Education Commission of the States

Nashville teachers were also agitated when privatization reared its head—and perhaps with even better reason: They sensed their jobs were on the line. Under the terms of its single-school proposal, a locally based firm known as Alternative Public Schools wanted the autonomy to hire and fire its own teachers. That's a big step beyond where EAI and the Edison Project are willing to go. In most cases, they both take on existing contracts and use unionized teachers.

"If you want maximum improvement in a school, it is essential that the management entity control the personnel," argues Bill DeLoache of APS. That may be true. But if you want maximum political mileage, DeLoache learned, it is essential that you not alienate the union.

So despite having the support of the mayor, the Metro Council, the chamber of commerce, prominent minority leaders and Nashville's two major daily newspapers, the privatization proposal was mothballed by a school board that had no intention of crossing one of its key constituencies—the teachers.

Still, teacher opposition is not nearly as divisive as the racial dynamic of privatization. Even if cities manage to persuade their teachers to get on board, the accompanying racial baggage is often enough to derail it.

To date, no major city has escaped a racially charged process. Part of the reason is that, in virtually all cases, the prospective management firms are headed by white entrepreneurs who are attempting to run urban schools with large minority enrollments.

"Is this targeted toward the inner city, basically poor, minority-populated schools? The answer is yes. It's a large market and there is a lot of need," says John McLaughlin, editor of *The Education Investor* and an assistant professor of education at St. Cloud State University in Minnesota. "But it shouldn't be a racial issue. The issues are not really race-based, they are children-based."

In the District of Columbia, though, privatization advocates could never quite get beyond one parent's well-publicized comment. "With 89.9 percent of the school student body African-American," she asked, "why would we bring in rich, white folks who don't have credentials of educating anybody to run our schools?"

Minorities pressed essentially the same argument in Minneapolis, where the school board recently hired Peter Hutchinson of the Public Strategies Group as school superintendent. Some minority groups sought to block his appointment because they wanted an executive of color. A white male, hailing from a private consulting firm and lacking the usual education credentials, was not exactly what they had in mind when they called for the selection of a "non-traditional" candidate.

It did not seem to matter that the school district had solicited Hutchinson's application. Or that he was a city resident with extensive local business ties, two children in Minneapolis public schools and credited with cleaning up the district's finances under a previous consulting contract with his firm. The Minneapolis Urban League still called the selection process a "sham."

But underscoring the racial component is an economic one. In many cities, newly empowered minorities are reluctant to relinquish the administrative control—and accompanying jobs—that took them so long to attain. Privatization looks to be a painful tradeoff, especially when it could mean giving up control of jobs that have been a stepping stone to the middle class for many minorities.

"You know what kind of jobs would go first," says Carolyn Smith, president of the Portsmouth, Virginia, Education Association, and a leader in the local fight against privatization. "Cafeteria workers and custodians—the basic support systems for the buildings."

Indeed, since private firms such as EAI and the Edison Project intend to make their profits from cost savings in instructional delivery and overall program management, a significant number of non-teaching positions are certain to be affected. In Baltimore, for example, EAI contracts with Johnson Controls for facility management services and with KPMG Peat Marwick for accounting services. EAI also uses lower-paid interns in place of unionized paraprofessionals as teachers' assistants.

So, given such determined opposition, how did Baltimore win approval for school privatization? First, it is important to remember that the deal Baltimore signed with EAI in 1992 covers just one middle school and eight elementary schools. Only 4,800 of the city's 113,000 public school students are affected. And the Baltimore school board remains ultimately accountable for the experiment. The five-year contract with EAI can be terminated by the school board at any time, for any reason, upon 90 days notice.

Still, no other city has managed to replicate even this feat. Baltimore's relatively smooth path was largely due to

circumstances that were unique to the place and time.

Of particular significance is the design of Baltimore's political structure, which allowed Mayor Kurt Schmoke and Superintendent Walter Amprey to work together and bypass potential opposition. From the outset, they were looking to make fundamental changes in the way the city educates its children. And privatization is about as fundamentally different as it gets. Both officials backed the idea wholeheartedly.

Schmoke's support was no small matter in a city where the mayor has an unusually firm grip on the school system. Since the Baltimore school board is appointed by the mayor—a structure unlike that in most other cities—there were no loose cannons to deal with. The board was not subject to the same political pressures faced by the Nashville, San Diego and Washington, D.C., school boards.

Compare Schmoke's role to that of D.C. Mayor Kelly, who, with a tough election coming up, sat on her hands. Not that it mattered much anyway: Kelly has no direct control over the District's elected school board.

The respective school superintendents were another key difference between Baltimore and the District of Columbia. Amprey, a Baltimore native and graduate of the local public schools, drew from a deep reservoir of goodwill and respect accumulated over a long career. His stature provided a degree of political

> **Given the ideological baggage of privatization, some officials have learned to avoid using the P word.**

cover while blunting criticism about "outsiders" running the schools, a charge that Franklin Smith—a non-native—was unable to silence in Washington.

The prospect of out-of-towners making a buck off of children's education is

an especially effective scare tactic since opponents invariably make the case that entrepreneurs do not have a community's best interests at heart. "Public education grows out of—and is connected to—the community organically," argues Alex Molnar, a professor of education at the University of Wisconsin-Milwaukee. "That cannot be reproduced by looking at students as customers." And the fact that the educational firms exist as for-profit ventures only heightens suspicions about their motives.

It also helped that the Baltimore union was unusually docile at the outset. Without any other experiences to draw from, they were ill-prepared to put up a fight. "Because we were the first in the country, we didn't have anyone to look at," says Linda Prudente, spokesperson for the Baltimore Teachers Union. "There wasn't any opportunity for open discussion or debate. It was almost a closed-door deal."

Though the union did not initially oppose privatization, its membership soured on the idea before the ink on the contract dried. Prior to the first day of classes at EAI schools, teachers boycotted training sessions over issues of job displacement and working conditions. Many complained that they learned most of the details of the arrangement only by reading about them in the newspapers. "They set the tone immediately that it was 'our way or the highway,'" says Prudente. "The relationship has progressively deteriorated from that point."

The union filed suit against the district to challenge the city's contract with EAI and sought to block pending agreements with other city schools. Then the American Federation of Teachers weighed in with a scathing report claiming that EAI makes its profits by cutting classroom services and increasing class size, and concluded it by requesting a U.S. Department of Education investigation.

The truth about EAI's performance to date likely lies somewhere between the unions' harsh rhetoric and the company's own glowing assessment, which notes an improvement in test scores. In any case, conclusions about the success of the Baltimore experiment after only a year and a half are, for the most part, premature.

Given the volatile nature of privatization efforts, local officials in Baltimore and a few other cities have learned to refrain altogether from even uttering the P word.

It may seem like splitting hairs, but privatization carries enough ideological baggage that, at least politically speaking, the most prudent course of action seems to be to find a less offensive term.

"This is not privatization," insisted Baltimore's Walter Amprey at a press conference announcing the agreement. "We are not handing our schools over to the private sector." Rather, he called it a "cooperative venture." In Portsmouth, Virginia, the pending proposal is referred to as "contract management."

"They've tried like the devil to avoid using the word privatization in Portsmouth," says McLaughlin of *The Education Investor*. "And that's a good idea because they are not privatizing the schools. They are contracting out a segment of public education. It is only one aspect."

Advocates are also quick to point out that it's not like public schools are a profit-free zone to begin with. Making money from the public schools is not a revolutionary concept. School districts regularly contract out for goods and support services such as textbooks, classroom materials, transportation and food preparation.

Privatizing curriculum and management services, though, is a bit different than signing a deal to provide students with pizzas or pencils. Any way you look at it, contracting out the three Rs to firms with little, if any, experience in educating kids is a voyage into uncharted waters. Add to that the open hostility of several important constituencies, and the result for public officials is that the fight to privatize low-performing schools may prove to be almost as difficult as turning them around.

Striving for Excellence: The Drive for Quality

We each wish the best quality of life that we can attain, and we each desire the opportunity for an education that will optimize our chances to achieve our objectives. The rhetoric on excellence and quality in schooling has been heated, and numerous opposing conceptions of how schools can achieve these goals have been presented for public consideration in recent years. The debate over how to achieve such qualitative improvement has led to some hopes realized of improved academic achievement goals on the part of students as well as to major changes in how teacher education programs are structured. But we also are beginning to see some fascinating alternatives open to us if we have the will to make them happen.

In the decade of the 1980s, those reforms instituted to encourage the qualitative growth in the conduct of schooling tended to be what education historian David Tyack referred to in *The One Best System* (Harvard University Press, 1974) as "structural" reforms. Structural reforms consisted of demands for standardized testing of students and teaching, reorganization of teacher education programs, legalized actions to provide alternative routes into

the teaching profession, efforts to recruit more people into teaching, and laws to enable greater parental choice as to where their children may attend school. These structural reforms cannot, however, as Tyack noted as early as 1974, in and of themselves produce higher levels of student achievement. We need to explore a broader range of the essential purposes of schooling, which will require our redefining what it means to be a literate person. We need also to reconsider what we mean by the "quality" of education and to reassess the effects on our children being schooled.

When we speak of quality and excellence as aims of education, we must remember that these terms encompass aesthetic and affective, as well as cognitive, processes. Young people cannot achieve that full range of intellectual capacity to solve problems on their own simply by being obedient and by memorizing data. How students encounter their teachers in classrooms and how teachers interact with their students are concerns that encompass aesthetic as well as cognitive dimensions. We see reflected in the current literature on this topic critical reactions to standardized testing as well as vigorous defenses of it. There is a real need in the 1990s to enforce intellectual (cognitive) standards and yet also to make schools more creative places in which to learn, places where students will yearn to explore, to imagine, and to hope.

Compared to the United States, European nations appear to achieve more qualitative assessments of students' skills in mathematics and the sciences, in written essay examinations in the humanities and social sciences, and in the routine oral examinations given by committees of teachers to students as they exit secondary schools. This approach contrasts the "top-down" solutions that have been the traditional way to resolve educational problems in the United States and Canada. Perhaps this is not avoidable, due to the obvious necessity of governmental financing of our public, tax-supported school systems. This top-down pattern of national-state (provincial) policy development for schooling needs to be tempered by even more of the "bottom-up," grassroots efforts to improve the quality of schools that are now under way in many communities in North America. New and imaginative inquiry-and-assessment strategies need to be developed by teachers working in their classrooms, and they must nurture the support of professional colleagues and parents.

Excellence is the goal: the means to achieve it is what is in dispute. There is a new dimension to the debate over assessment of academic achievement of elementary and secondary school students. In addition, the struggle continues of conflicting academic (as well as political) interests in the quest to improve the quality of preparation of our future teachers, and we need to sort these issues out as well.

No conscientious educator would oppose the idea of excellence in education. The problem in gaining consensus over how to attain it is that excellence of both teacher and student performance is always defined against some preset standards. Which standards of assessment should prevail? The current debate over excellence in teacher education clearly demonstrates how conflicting academic values can lead to conflicting programmatic recommendations for educational reform.

The 1980s provided educators with many insightful individual and commissioned evaluations of ways to improve the educational system at all levels. Some of the reports addressed higher education concerns (particularly relating to general studies requirements and teacher education), but most of them focused on the academic performance problems of elementary and secondary school students. From literally dozens of such reports, some common themes developed. Some have been challenged by professional teaching organizations as being too heavily laden with hidden business and political agendas. The rhetoric on school reform extends to the educators in teacher education, who are not in agreement either.

What forms of teacher education and inservice reeducation are needed? Who pays for these programmatic options? Where and how will funds be raised or redirected from other priorities to pay for this? Will the "streaming and tracking" model of secondary school student placement that exists in Europe be adopted? How can we best assess academic performance? Can we commit to a more heterogeneous grouping of students and to mainstreaming handicapped students in our schools? Many individual, private, and governmental reform efforts did *not* address these questions.

Other industrialized nations champion the need for alternative secondary schools to prepare their young people for varied life goals and civic work. The American dream of the common school translated into what has become the comprehensive high school of the twentieth century. But does it provide all the people with alternative diploma options? If not, what is the next step? What must be changed? For one, concepts related to our educational goals must be clarified and political motivation must be separated from the realities of student performance. We must clarify our goals. We must get a clearer picture of "what knowledge is of most worth."

Looking Ahead: Challenge Questions

Identify some of the different points of view on achieving excellence in education. What value conflicts can be easily defined?

Do teachers see educational reform in the same light as governmental, philanthropic, and corporate-based school reform groups? On what matters would they agree—and disagree?

What can we learn from other nations regarding excellence in education?

What are the minimum academic standards that all high school graduates should meet?

How can the National Board for Professional Teaching Standards improve the quality of the teaching force in the United States?

What are some assumptions about achieving excellence in student achievement that you would challenge?

What can educators do to improve the quality of student learning?

—F. S.

Redirecting Reform

Challenges to Popular Assumptions About Teachers and Students

No one can reform our schools for us, Mr. Clark and Ms. Astuto aver. Systemic reformers will have to be resisted systematically, for they are distracting us from the job at hand.

David L. Clark and Terry A. Astuto

David L. Clark (Indiana University Chapter) is Kenan Professor of Education in the Program in Educational Leadership at the University of North Carolina, Chapel Hill. Terry A. Astuto (University of Virginia Chapter) is a professor of educational administration and director of the Program in Educational Administration and Supervision at New York University. *This article was adapted and excerpted from* Challenges to Dominant Assumptions Controlling Educational Reform, *by Terry A. Astuto, David L. Clark, Anne-Marie Read, Kathleen McGree, and de-Koven Pelton Fernandez. Development of the original monograph was supported by the Regional Laboratory for Educational Improvement of the Northeast and Islands.* Roots of Reform: Challenging the Assumptions That Control Change in Education, *a monograph based on this document, was published by Phi Delta Kappa [March 1994].*

The Education Reform Movement of the 1980s and 1990s has produced disappointing results. Policy makers who have la-bored over federal, state, and local reform initiatives blame these results on the reluctance or incompetence of practitioners. Educators who work at the school and classroom levels blame policy makers for their lack of understanding of the real life of schools. Many of the parties involved blame the victims, or, more accurately, they would blame the victims if they had not been told that it is inappropriate to do so. (By "victims" we mean both students who are unprepared to cope with conventional school regulations, procedures, and requirements and their parents.) Everyone wants to blame the delivery systems that fragment the social, medical, psychological, nutritional, and educational resources and services provided for children.

Whoever or whatever is to blame for the failure of reform, many of the reform initiatives that are currently most popular could be dismissed as ridiculous on their face if they were not devised and supported by powerful and apparently credible advocates and if the consequences of their failure were not so devastating for a generation of American youth. Education reform in the U.S. must not fail. City school systems cannot be dismissed as unworkable. Youngsters from low-income households cannot be consigned to poverty-ridden schools and bleak futures. Despair over the state of American schools is unthinkable.

The root cause of the failure of reform is the limited imagination that has informed the reform proposals. For example, the establishment of state-level testing (with sanctions for districts that do not meet the minimum standards) is essentially a paper transaction that threatens a handful of underproducing districts. Not surprisingly, these are almost always districts with high concentrations of children living in poverty. For such districts, a proposal to convert their schools into youth service centers that would be open 24 hours a day, 365 days a year, serving three healthy meals to students and providing social, psychological, and medical services would be an authentic proposal for reform. Instead, school districts are counseled to adopt outcome-based programs that are in alignment with the

From *Phi Delta Kappan*, Vol. 75, No. 7, March 1994, pp. 513-520. © 1994 by Phi Delta Kappa, Inc. Reprinted by permission.

standardized tests being used to assess the effectiveness of schools.

Why do we focus on implementing site-based management systems for high schools while we retain the daily schedule of six to eight 50-minute class periods, which ensures that most high school teachers will never get to know about the lives of the 150 to 200 students whom they see each day? Does anyone believe that such an organizational structure provides the time for English teachers to tutor their students in writing? Or that it provides responsible adult role models for youngsters who have few such models in their homes or communities? Or that it provides an opportunity for individualized instruction and counseling? Do we really believe that schools are so different from other organizations that testing to weed out "rejects" is an effective system for improving the quality of the school's core processes?

What sort of reform is this, anyway? Why are we overlooking commonsense options that are supported by the experience of research and practice? We believe that the current reform movement is rooted in a set of nested assumptions that constrain the range of changes proposed for — or implemented in — our schools. For the past two years we have been attempting to identify the assumptions of policy makers, educational researchers, administrators, and teachers that govern the reform proposals they consider feasible. Our hunch was that many of these assumptions should be challenged; we believed that the axiomatic standing they had been granted in the reform movement was unwarranted.

Thus we examined the literatures of research, policy, and practice in search of information about: 1) the political context of education, 2) the social context of education, 3) the organizational structure of schools, 4) the organizational and educational processes in schools, and 5) the people who live and work in educational organizations. In this article we focus on the people associated with schools — especially the teachers and students.

In our search we were looking for the central assumptions held by policy makers, practitioners, and scholars about the best ways to run schools and to educate children. We recorded conventional, neoorthodox, and nonorthodox theoretical positions; data-based research findings; and reports of ordinary and exceptional practice. Whenever we discovered dominant, conventional views, we searched

for counterpoints to challenge the assumptions. If the counterpoints were justified by research evidence, successful practice, or persuasive logic, we noted them.

In the pages that follow we present a brief set of assumptions that are currently controlling education reforms directed toward teachers and students. We have reexamined each controlling assumption in relation to a counter-assumption for which equally convincing evidence could be found. We do not claim axiomatic standing for either assumptions or counterassumptions, although our polemic will support the counter-assumptions. Our intention in the study and in this article is to broaden rather than narrow the dialogue surrounding education reform. And while our imaginations may be insufficient to summon up the most effective vision of education reform, the evidence we discovered and will present here convinced us that merely doing more of the same will not be adequate for the 1990s. Indeed, the dominant policy direction today often works against the authentic reform of American schools.

> ## THE EVIDENCE WE DISCOVERED AND WILL PRESENT HERE CONVINCED US THAT MERELY DOING MORE OF THE SAME WILL NOT BE ADEQUATE.

ASSUMPTIONS ABOUT INDIVIDUALS IN SCHOOLS

Are people the reason for the failure or the success of organizations? This issue is reflected in contemporary education reform strategies. For example, recent reforms in teacher education include extended field experiences, increased requirements for initial certification, support systems for new teachers, required participation in professional development

activities for recertification, and the formation of the National Board for Professional Teaching Standards. These reforms reveal the underlying beliefs that teaching is a professional activity and that professionals responsible for the growth and development of children need advanced levels of expertise.

Yet, even as these reforms were being put in place around the nation, many states were reducing the professional requirements for initial certification of teachers. Some even created alternative routes to certification that reflect the belief that schools would be better if talented people who did not originally choose teaching as a career could be recruited to the teaching profession. These recruits are not required to commit themselves to advanced training or to demonstrate the same level of professional expertise as those who selected teaching as a career. Their preparation is largely through an apprenticeship model of "on-the-job" training and stresses mentorships and practice-oriented instruction.

The public and policy makers (and perhaps educators themselves) are puzzled about how to think about teachers and teaching. Are teachers experts or skilled technicians? Are they objects of public trust or targets for suspicion? Are they the main reason for school failures or the best hope for school improvement? And what about students? What explains their varying levels of engagement in and curiosity about learning?

Assumptions about the people in the school community — teachers, support staff, administrators, students, and their families — shape practice, sometimes subtly, sometimes overtly. Understanding both the widely accepted conventional assumptions and the challenging alternative beliefs about these people is critical to designing meaningful education reforms. These assumptions cluster in three major areas of concern and confusion: 1) motivation, 2) ability, and 3) level and type of contribution to organizational outcomes.

MOTIVATION

People direct their energy toward achieving individual and organizational purposes. Why? What explains the variations in levels of engagement in work? Motivation is a complicated and multidimensional concept that becomes still more confusing when applied to the workplace. Experience, popular theoretical frameworks, and research about organizations all combine to create our beliefs about motivation. And, of course, different perspectives yield different insights. One of the deepest differences in the basic assumptions with regard to motivation is evident in the fact that many people believe that individuals are motivated to achieve institutional objectives by institutional incentives, while others believe that individuals are self-motivated to achieve institutional objectives unless blocked by the organizational environment.

External and internal motivation. The assumption that people are externally motivated stems from traditional views about people in the workplace. Traditional organizational perspectives recognize the existence of the informal organization that includes the purposes, needs, and aspirations of workers. Yet management is urged to subordinate these purposes, needs, and aspirations to predetermined organizational objectives. The formal organization matters; the informal organization is but unavoidable noise in the system.

A generation ago Douglas McGregor observed that much managerial practice reflects the belief that workers, left to their own initiative, are not interested in high-quality performance. Designated as Theory X, this managerial perspective asserts that people inherently dislike work and will avoid it whenever possible, that people must be directed and coerced to put forth enough effort to achieve organizational objectives, and that people prefer to be directed and to avoid responsibility.[1]

While these bald assertions of Theory X might seem too extreme to be relevant to discussions of contemporary education reforms, most of the recent efforts to reform and restructure schools have been guided by these very assumptions. For example, state monitoring and accountability systems reflect a concern that local educators will not work hard enough to support student learning unless coerced to do so. The promotion of national achievement tests shows a lack of trust that state and local educators will focus instruction wisely unless the preferred instructional outcomes are specified. National statements of goals, state identification of the components of a common core of knowledge, and local administrative efforts to articulate a clear vision of the purposes of the school all stem from the belief that teachers and principals need to have their professional lives externally controlled.

These reforms reflect similar beliefs about students: that testing will lead students to work harder, that an agreed-upon curricular core will focus students' attention on important knowledge, and that students need to have their days structured by adults. Relationships between teachers and students and between prin-

> ACCORDING TO THEORY Y, PEOPLE WILL EXERCISE SELF-DIRECTION IN THE SERVICE OF OBJECTIVES TO WHICH THEY ARE COMMITTED.

cipals and students — especially those relationships routinized by school rules — also reflect the belief that improvement in student performance requires the use of "carrots" and "sticks."

The assumption that motivation requires incentives and control mechanisms conflicts with motivation theory and with the principles of human growth and development. For example, Abraham Maslow's theory of motivation contends that people progress through a hierarchy of human needs — from needs for basic physical requirements, to safety, to affiliation, to esteem, to self-actualization.[2] The idea that human beings strive for personal fulfillment is quite different from the belief that human beings are unmotivated and uninterested in their own growth and achievement.

Even more to the point, Frederick Herzberg's research argues that such external incentives as salary, safety, and relationships with administrators can be sources of dissatisfaction in the workplace if basic expectations are not met. Once these basic needs have been met, these incentives are not sources of motivation. True motivators are linked to personal growth and achievement. They include individual responsibility for the work to be done,

recognition of individual contributions to the organization, and the challenges of the work itself.[3]

Herzberg's theory and his research findings with regard to motivation are consistent with McGregor's Theory Y. Briefly, Theory Y states that both physical and mental effort in work are as natural as play or rest; that people will exercise self-direction and self-control in the service of objectives to which they are committed; that commitment to objectives is a function of the rewards associated with their achievement (and that satisfaction of ego and self-actualization needs are the most significant rewards); that people not only accept but seek responsibility; and that imagination, ingenuity, and creativity are widely distributed in the population.[4]

The assumption that people are self-motivated is supported by motivation theory and research and is also consistent with the reports of teachers that the intrinsic rewards of teaching — reaching a child, seeing growth and development, fostering learning — are most significant to them. Self-motivation is also characteristic of young people. Research into students' thought processes has focused on reinforcement, the need for achievement, locus of control, and attribution (i.e., students' understandings of themselves as learners).[5] This literature demonstrates the importance of the student's assuming responsibility for learning and building a sense of efficacy as a learner. As children mature, their capacity for self-direction also increases, yet they find themselves in even more controlled learning environments at the secondary school level.

When we consider the role of motivation in the workplace, we encounter a peculiar characteristic: responsibility for motivating others mirrors the hierarchy of power. Teachers motivate students; principals motivate teachers; superintendents motivate principals. Apparently, the higher an individual is in the administrative hierarchy, the more credit he or she is given for being self-motivated and self-directed and the more responsibility he or she is given for motivating others. This connection between motivation, control, and power highlights another interesting observation made by McGregor. The extent to which individuals in subordinate roles avoid responsibility or lack ambition would appear to be a consequence of past opportunity and experience, not an inherent characteristic.[6]

This raises another important question: What type of work environment best sustains an individual's sense of motivation? Two competing assumptions help frame this discussion: competition stimulates individuals to higher levels of individual achievement, or cooperation provides the nurturance, support, and colleagueship that stimulate individual achievement.

Competition and cooperation. Competition is highly valued in American society. But does it sustain the self-motivation of individuals in the workplace? The argument in support of competition is based on the belief that an individual can push beyond current levels of skill and achieve at the highest possible levels when pressed to do so in the heat of competition. As early as the era of scientific management, Frederick Taylor argued that competitive work environments within an organization stimulate productivity.[7] In factories, this idea was operationalized as piecework; in professional work, it takes the form of comparative measures of individual performance in relation to organizational outcomes.

Establishing competitive environments in schools is at the heart of many personnel policies. The fascination with merit

> THE CONCEPT OF COMMUNITY RECOGNIZES THE VALUE OF SHARED EFFORTS IN AN ENVIRONMENT THAT IS SAFE FOR EXPERIMENTATION.

pay and recognition programs for teachers stems from the belief that a direct connection between individual work and individual reward will lead teachers to increase their efforts to promote student achievement. Testing programs that monitor student achievement and make possible comparisons between classrooms, schools, or districts establish conditions for identifying winners — and losers.

Does all this competition actually create conditions that are appropriate for in-

dividual achievement? The counter-argument is that self-motivation is sustained when individuals maintain a sense of their own efficacy and work in a context in which people help one another develop skills, take risks, and challenge standard operating procedures. Competitive environments isolate people; cooperative environments bring people together and protect diversity of experience, preference, and interest.

School improvement, like individual learning, is an interactive, mutually reinforcing activity that requires the collaborative efforts of all participants in collegial, supportive work environments. Cooperation is enhanced by personal actions and organizational support. That is, to build cooperative environments, individuals need to exhibit cooperative behaviors and to voice the benefits of cooperation. At the same time, organizational support needs to signal the benefits of cooperation for collective purposes.

Cooperative work environments characterize high-producing organizations because they foster the sharing of ideas, allow idiosyncrasy to be a strength rather than a weakness, support innovation and change, and broaden the range of perspectives on work problems. The question for restructuring and reforming schools is, What organizational forms are compatible with the demands of cooperative working environments? Bureaucratic structures isolate individuals and organize work around principles of efficiency, authority, and procedural specificity; they both establish and support the condition of competitiveness for which they were originally designed. The concept of community, on the other hand, recognizes the value of shared efforts in an environment that is safe for experimentation and that respects individual differences. Structures built on principles of community establish and support the condition of cooperation.

Organizational structures that are consistent with the principles of community are particularly relevant for schools. The work of schools involves three major communities: the professional community, various learning communities, and the stakeholder community. Structures supportive of the professional community provide time for dialogue and access to ideas both within the individual school community and throughout the broader professional arena, including practitioners in other schools, colleagues in higher education, and educational researchers.

Structures supportive of learning communities provide opportunities for interaction and caring between teachers and students and among students, as well as collaboration in learning activities. Structures supportive of the stakeholder community reach out to provide room for collaboration and strategies to enhance communication among parents, community residents, local businesses, and agencies that provide child and family support.

Theory and research about motivation and personality have demonstrated time and again that people are inherently and naturally drawn to learning, work, and responsibility. Decades ago, Chester Barnard, Chris Argyris, and Douglas McGregor described with force and eloquence the wide range of talents and positive predilections that people bring to their work.[8] Yet dominant beliefs about people in the workplace continue to assume that people are organizational problems and fail to acknowledge that the real problems may stem from the bureaucratic form of the organization.

ABILITY

The talents and intellectual abilities of people are only partially used at work in traditional organizations. Policy makers and reformers have introduced a number of initiatives to create conditions to increase the performance levels of teachers and students. These reforms reflect different assumptions about individual ability: outstanding educators demonstrate high levels of technical skill, or outstanding educators demonstrate high levels of professional expertise.

Technicians and professionals. Everyone agrees that the work of teachers is the critical element in effective schooling. However, everyone does not agree on whether the work of teachers involves only the mastery of relatively specific technical skills or the development of a professional repertoire of instructional options, in-depth understanding of the content of instruction, sensitivity to the wide range of student needs, and a comprehensive understanding of the principles of child and adolescent growth and development. These competing beliefs are played out in the choice of reforms for preservice teacher education, for inservice training programs, and for the improvement of school and classroom practices.

The reforms in teacher education mirror the limitations of vision found in school reform. Most teacher preparation programs continue to be undergraduate degree programs with little space or time for intense professional preparation. And these preservice training programs are spread across 1,300 colleges and universities, many of which commit few resources and little energy to teacher education.

Continuing education is an essential characteristic for all professional fields. Yet some states have narrowed the range of growth opportunities for teachers by expanding the coursework in the basic disciplines that is required for recertification and by reducing or eliminating coursework required in professional education — an arbitrary and unnecessary choice between bodies of necessary skill and knowledge. As their main program of faculty development, most school districts rely on "inservice days" devoted to the sharing of introductory information about district-directed initiatives. While effective organizations in the private sector expand their investment in staff development, school districts have reduced expenditures for staff development at exactly the time when the challenges of teaching are becoming more complex.

At the level of classroom practice, significant variation occurs in the amount of time teachers spend on different subjects,

> FOR TOO MANY STUDENTS, SCHOOLS ARE NOT EXCITING, LIVELY PLACES THAT ENGENDER ENTHUSI- ASM FOR AND ENGAGE- MENT IN LEARNING.

in the instructional focus on basic skills or on higher-order skills, in the amount of teacher direction, in the quality of instructional material, and in the level of responsiveness to individual student needs. Evidence exists of great variability in the quality of instruction for poor children, for children of color, for children with special needs, and for girls as opposed to boys.

Yet most of the popular initiatives intended to improve the practice of teaching are based on the belief that outstanding teaching is a technical skill. Technical experts are people trained in the skills and technical details of an endeavor. The technical dimensions of teaching involve the delivery of curricular content, the implementation of instructional methods, the assessment of student learning, and the application of methods of classroom control. Such reforms as outcome-based education focus on these dimensions, and, as a consequence, professional discretion is narrowed in an effort to ensure precision in the implementation of curricular and instructional decisions.

Rather than establish conditions that maximize the abilities of teachers, tightly linked instructional packages stunt performance, growth, imagination, and community. They are examples of the fact that, although people are naturally self-motivated, organizational factors often serve to depress individual ingenuity and achievement. Argyris made this point very clearly. Based on a synthesis of the literature about human growth and development, Argyris arrived at the chilling conclusion that organizational work environments demand less mature behavior from adults. Controlling, hierarchical, bureaucratic environments are more congruent with such less mature behaviors as passivity, dependence, subordinate position, and lack of self-control and awareness.[9]

As they play out in schools, bureaucratic structures exert a debilitating effect on students. Not only do these structures socialize students to view work as dull and constraining, but they also rein in the natural curiosity of children and youth. For too many students, schools are not exciting, lively places that engender enthusiasm for and engagement in learning and academic pursuits.

An alternative assumption about the work and abilities of educators stems from the belief that outstanding teaching requires professional expertise. Professionals draw from a broad range of relevant disciplines to make decisions about their practice. Teams of professionals often work together to determine the wisest course of instructional action. Some efforts to restructure schools — those that provide teachers with opportunities to make professional decisions about their work and about activities to support student learning — require a definition of teaching ability that incorporates an understanding of the dimensions of professional expertise.

Viewing teachers as members of a professional community focuses attention on norms of collegiality and on the ethics of professional practice. This shift has implications for the work of principals. Sources of control are built into the processes of professional work and collaboration, not into the hierarchy of authority. Principals' actions that focus on stability, goal setting, regularity, accountability, intervention, control, and efficiency are either redundant, destructive of cooperation and a sense of community, or both. Alternative actions that support the professional community, the learning community, and the stakeholder community require more complex, professional expertise on the part of principals. Facilitating the working communities of a school requires actions that foster activity, the development of a professional community that incorporates diversity and difference, and the creation of a sense of individual efficacy and empowerment among students and staff members.[10]

Under these conditions, principals work interactively with the professional community to design, critique, and improve structures and norms of professional practice. They support the learning community by working with staff members and students to implement a wide range of learning activities. They support the stakeholder community by working outside the school, creating connections with families, social agencies, and political structures. In short, a principal supports the school's communities and serves as the school's representative in the society at large.

Different assumptions about the work of teachers and administrators imply different assumptions about the environmental conditions necessary for school improvement: competitive work environments that use teacher evaluation and inservice training to improve teaching ability as opposed to collaborative work environments that provide opportunities for individual and collective learning designed by primary work groups to improve teaching ability.

Competitive and collaborative work environments. Most procedures for evaluating teachers are designed to provide principals with the opportunity to clarify school goals and purposes, assess the curricular and instructional decisions of teachers, observe classroom performance, and provide feedback on the quality of the teacher's performance. Discussions of teacher evaluation systems assert that their primary purpose is improvement, and their structure is consistent with the belief that quality performance requires administrative supervision and feedback. These strategies are much more in tune with a view of teachers' work as technical skill rather than as professional expertise. (Interestingly, such strategies are also compatible with perspectives that assume that motivation is external rather than internal.)

On the other hand, collaborative work environments are sensitive to the complexities of professional decision making. The wide range of student needs taxes the expertise of any individual. Opportunities for collaboration bring the knowledge and abilities of a number of professionals to bear on decisions about learning activities for individual students. Meaningful collaboration replaces the control that is characteristic of management-driven organizations with the empowerment of professional staff members. Collaboration reduces isolation, and, as a result, professional decisions become more public and more accessible for the scrutiny of colleagues who may offer useful advice.

This discussion of the supervision and evaluation of teachers can serve as a reminder that "administrators are people too." They vary in their levels of motivation. Nothing about the administrative role guarantees high intrinsic motivation to achieve; yet one has every reason to assume a Theory Y view of administra-

> ## GRADUATE TRAINING FOR EDUCATIONAL LEADERS IS ONE OF THE FEW AREAS IN EDUCATION THAT HAS REMAINED IMPERVIOUS TO REFORM.

tive behavior. The school-level administrator is just as likely to suffer from the negative effects of an achievement-based competitive testing environment as are the teachers — probably more so if the district administration believes that the buck stops in the principal's office.

Are these administrators managers or leaders? Professionals or technicians? What claim to expertise can they make if they are to be instructional leaders? They began as teachers. How have they now accumulated the expertise to establish school goals, assess curricular decisions, and evaluate teacher performance? Surely such changes have not come about as a consequence of their graduate study. Graduate training for educational leaders is one of the few areas in education that has remained impervious to reform over the past 20 years. Yet it is one of the areas most in need of reform.

Educational administrators should lay claim to professional status along with their teachers. Their work is endlessly complex. Its complexity is caused by the intensive demands made on administrators for interaction with staff members, students, parents, and their own superiors. Administrators should reflect on their own position in order to understand the roles of others in the organization. Administrators who can see their own working lives mirrored in those of the people in the schools in which they work will be able to increase their own contribution and that of others to the schools' goals. Their own sense of self-motivation will enable them to foster self-motivation in students and teachers. Their own commitment to continued professional development and their recognition that they will never know enough to fulfill their professional responsibilities will enable them to encourage the professional development of teachers and the learning of students. Such administrators will sustain the same environment of cooperation, support, and nurturance for teachers and students that they wish the central office to provide for them. And they will emphasize collaborative work and feedback because a setting characterized by control and evaluation will never tap the abilities of professionals.

CONTRIBUTION

People who participate in organized work are concerned about the quality of the outcome of their labors. In the case of education, policy makers and the general public expect schools to deliver according to their expectations; for example, they expect increased levels of student achievement and decreased dropout rates. Parents want schools to care about their children and to provide them with individualized opportunities to learn, grow, and develop. Children and young people want schools that are responsive to their needs and that engage them with opportunities for social interaction; they want schoolpeople to care about them and to show them respect. Principals and teachers want to create learning environments that are safe and secure and to foster the students' academic achievement and growth. They also want schools to be places that are good for adults and that provide professional support and opportunities for professional development.

How then do principals, teachers, support staff members, students, and community members contribute to the individual and collective achievement of all these outcomes? In their book *In Search of Excellence*, Thomas Peters and Robert Waterman popularized the catch phrase "productivity through people."[11] Subsequently, the popular literature on organizational effectiveness picked up this orientation. Corporate executives, managers, politicians, and union leaders all voice their agreement that people are the key to the success of an organization. However, what that means in practice depends on which underlying assumptions an individual holds about the contributions people make to the work of an organization. A discussion follows of two opposing assumptions: people are the means of production within an organization, or people are the initiators of action and the shapers of a working environment that fosters individual and collective achievement.

People as means of production or as initiators of action? Many years ago Chester Barnard identified an important dilemma about the place of the individual in the organization:

> Sometimes in everyday work an individual is something absolutely unique, with a special history in every respect. This is usually the sense in which we regard ourselves, and so also our nearest relations, then our friends and associates. . . . The farther we push away from ourselves, the less the word "individual" means what it means when applied to you and me.[12]

Barnard hit on a peculiar but well-documented human trait: people are quite generous in self-evaluation. Individuals tend to overrate their own performance and underestimate that of others. Experience and observation of individuals in the workplace verify that the farther we move from ourselves, the less confident we are in the ability, commitment, energy, and good will of people.

The assumptions that underlie organizational forms and structures reinforce assumptions about the contribution of people in the workplace. Traditional organizational structures that are consistent with the principles of bureaucracy do not take a chance on people. An uptight, orderly work environment is promoted through the hierarchy of authority; through job specifications; through rules, regulations, and standard operating procedures; and through an impersonal orientation toward an organization's people.

Instead of dealing with the dilemmas and troubles natural to collective work, traditional structures solve the problem by taking the people completely out of the picture. The hierarchy of authority reflects the belief that people lack ability and initiative. Consequently, domination is accepted as a necessary feature of work, and people are viewed as instruments of organizational productivity. This depersonalization not only results in treating people as cogs in the organizational machinery, but also convinces people over time that they are unable to influence the direction of their own work. When an organization conveys the message that it does not depend on people in any significant way, the sensible human response for workers is to disengage from the organization. When personal and professional interactions occur within power relationships, distrust is a reasonable reaction. When the structures and processes of work are standardized, no room exists for difference.

The principles and beliefs that flow from the bureaucratic mindset operate in most schools. Work is organized so that teachers are replaceable parts; long- and short-term substitutes can be handled smoothly. Under these conditions, the specification of responsibilities for teachers is limited solely to face-to-face instruction and supervision of students. A similar restriction applies to administrators' relationships with teachers. In such situations, teachers create their own worlds within the classroom and leave school-wide purposes and directions to others.

Viewing the contributions of individuals to an organization as merely the "means of production" depersonalizes and de-skills the work environment. At the same time, the unique talents of individuals are stifled. Viewing people as the means to organizational ends protects the organization from variations among workers,

> # THE LANGUAGE OF EDUCATION REFORM IS STILL DOMINATED BY THE HARSHNESS OF BUREAUCRACY, CONTROL, COMPETITION, AND INTERVENTION.

quiets dissenting voices, and flattens affective responses to organizational purposes and directions. The cost of this insurance is high, however. The organization loses the creativity and ingenuity of its people, and individuals lose their sense of efficacy and their opportunities for connection with others who share a common purpose.

The counter-assumption recognizes that people in organizations socially construct the meaning of their work, including conditions for success. Talented, self-directed, professionally committed individuals do not view their contributions as the mere implementation of work routines. They view their contributions in terms of participation in the design, enactment, and outcome of their efforts and those of their colleagues. However, the principles of bureaucracy are so persistent and pervasive that most people have limited experience working within structures that are built on principles of community, democracy, or social justice. Thus current efforts to increase participation through shared decision making or representative governance councils frequently are implemented within the boundaries of a bureaucratic framework.

A COMMONSENSE PROPOSAL

The language of education reform is still dominated by the harshness of bu-

reaucracy, control, competition, and intervention. It is a discouraging language of distrust and inspection. The current education reform movement is stuck in a worsening negative cycle, unable to deliver on its promises and destructive to the human spirit.

However, alternatives are possible. To begin, we could shuck off the assumptions that have led us to adopt the current reform agenda. That is not an impossible task. Examined one by one, their efficacy is certainly questionable.

We also need to place certain priorities at the top of our agenda. And we are not talking about radical priorities. We are talking about priorities that emphasize saving our children and youth through a reform movement that is sensitive to people. Will such a movement have tradeoffs? Of course. Every policy decision involves tradeoffs. But in this case the tradeoffs seem modest when stacked up against the neglect and deadening of human potential confronted by teachers and students in the current reform movement. Will a school reform movement that is child-centered and that brooks no talk of failure in caring for our children cost money? Of course it will. But it is no more than parents are willing to invest in their own children. Will a teacher-centered reform movement place different responsibilities in the hands of professional educators? Yes. But it will assign to teachers exactly the kind of responsibility, discretion, and colleagueship that make for a vital and responsive professional life.

Challenging the dominant assumptions about professional educators and students is necessary to generate a new sense of purpose. The metaphor for tomorrow's schools should be the successful home, guided by mature and caring adults. Such a school would:

• support success hopefully and tirelessly;

• adjust to the phases of childhood and young adulthood with trust, confidence, and support;

• believe in the efficacy of individuals during periods of failure as well as success;

• provide the basic conditions for nurturance, protection, and growth — including social, medical, nutritional, and psychological assistance;

• foster collegiality, cooperation, and collaboration as teachers and students learn and play together;

• introduce the wonder of a diverse and ever-changing world to learners;

• make time every day for the personal, interactive relationships needed to support learning; and

• assess success and failure — building on the former and learning from the latter.

No one can reform our schools for us. If there is to be authentic reform in American education, it must be a grass-roots movement. Systemic reformers will have to be resisted systematically, for they are distracting us from the job at hand. The only system we have is the local community school, and external agencies should be worrying about how they can help and support these school units — not about how they can dominate them. The current repressive and retro-

gressive policies will have to be rejected and replaced by teacher- and student-centered reforms. We are honestly sorry that those who would save our children and our schools by fiat cannot do so. But that is the simple truth. We will have to do it in individual communities, through hard work and the investment and effort of individuals who work on the front line. Isn't that always the way?

1. Douglas McGregor, *The Human Side of Enterprise* (New York: McGraw-Hill, 1960), pp. 33-34.
2. Abraham H. Maslow, "A Theory of Human Motivation," in Jay M. Shafritz and Albert C. Hyde, eds., *Classics of Public Administration* (Pacific Grove, Calif.: Brooks/Cole Publishing, 1987), pp. 135-51.
3. Frederick Herzberg, *The Managerial Choice: To Be Efficient and to Be Human* (Homewood, Ill.: Dow Jones-Irwin, 1976).
4. McGregor, pp. 47-48.
5. Merlin C. Wittrock, "Students' Thought Processes," in idem, ed., *Handbook of Research on Teaching*, 3rd ed. (New York: Macmillan), pp. 297-314.
6. McGregor, p. 48.
7. Frederick W. Taylor, "The Principles of Scientific Management," in Jay M. Shafritz and J. Steven Ott, eds., *Classics of Organization Theory* (Chicago: Dorsey Press, 1987), pp. 66-81.
8. See, for example, Chester A. Barnard, *The Functions of the Executive* (Cambridge, Mass.: Harvard University Printing Office, 1938); Chris Argyris, *Personality and Organization: The Conflict Between System and the Individual* (New York: Harper and Brothers, 1957); and McGregor, op. cit.
9. Argyris, op. cit.
10. David L. Clark and Terry A. Astuto, "Paradoxical Choice Options in Organizations," in Daniel E. Griffiths, Robert T. Stout, and Patrick B. Forsyth, eds., *Leaders for America's Schools* (Berkeley, Calif.: McCutchan, 1988), pp. 112-30.
11. Thomas J. Peters and Robert H. Waterman, Jr., *In Search of Excellence: Lessons from America's Best-Run Corporations* (New York: Harper & Row, 1982).
12. Barnard, p. 12.

HIGH STANDARDS FOR ALL?

The Struggle for Equality in the American High School Curriculum, 1890-1990

All children, like all men, rise easily to the common level. There the mass stop; strong minds only ascend higher. But raise the standard, and, by a spontaneous movement, the mass will rise again and reach it.
—from *Horace Mann's First Annual Report (1837)*

JEFFREY MIREL AND DAVID ANGUS

Jeffrey Mirel is associate professor of leadership and educational policy studies and a fellow at the Social Science Research Institute, Northern Illinois University, DeKalb. He is the author of The Rise and Fall of an Urban School System: Detroit, 1907-1981 *(Ann Arbor: University of Michigan Press, 1993). David Angus is professor of education and chair of the program in Educational Foundations at the University of Michigan, Ann Arbor. Material for this article was taken from a book they are writing entitled* Conflict and Curriculum in the American High School, 1890-1990 *(Teachers College Press, in progress).*

FOR MOST of this century the people who shaped the curriculum of the American high school were philosophically in line with many of the critics of national goals and standards today. They wholeheartedly believed that blanketly imposing high academic standards on all high school students would create greater educational *in*equality, arguing that such standards would reinforce and accentuate educational disparities between socio-economic and racial groups. Close investigation of actual trends in high school student course-taking since the 1920s, however, does not validate that belief. To the contrary, our analysis of data shows that it was curricular differentiation that had a profoundly negative effect on the education of large numbers of American young people, particularly working class and black students. We focus on these trends in 20th-century American high schools in order to provide some insights into the current debate about national goals and standards. Our study leads us to believe that national goals and standards, wisely developed and applied, can greatly benefit American education. Such measures could constitute major steps toward equalizing educational quality and ensuring that all American students, particularly poor and minority students, have access to the same challenging programs and courses that students in the nation's best schools now receive.

This essay is based on findings from a study of high school course-taking that we conducted for the U.S. Department of Education.[1] In that study we analyzed a series of national surveys of high school course-taking conducted by the U.S. Office of Education (USOE) from 1928, 1934, 1949, 1961, and 1973. These surveys grew out of a group of USOE studies beginning in the 1890s. While some of the earlier studies focused on specific courses such as Latin and Greek or on a limited range of subjects, by 1922 the studies were national in scope and comprehensive enough to provide a national perspective on curriculum change over time. For example, we found that between 1922 and 1973 the number of distinct courses reported to the USOE rose from about 175

From *American Educator*, Vol. 18, No. 2, Summer 1994, pp. 4-9, 40-42. Reprinted by permission of *American Educator*, the quarterly journal of the American Federation of Teachers. © 1994.

titles to more than 2,100. It is impossible to sort out the extent to which this increase represented new courses or merely variations or elaborations on older themes, but its magnitude makes it difficult to avoid the impression of curricular expansion running amok.

These surveys provide historians of the American high school with a series of increasingly detailed and trustworthy snapshots of high school course enrollments spanning the years from 1890 to 1973. In addition, researchers under contract to the National Center for Education Statistics have gathered similar data in 1982, 1987, and 1990, usually from student transcripts, which we linked to the earlier studies. All combined, the USOE surveys and the recent transcript studies provide a sweeping picture of high school curriculum development in the 20th century. Unfortunately, these data have rarely been utilized by scholars in describing the modern history of secondary education generally or the high school curriculum specifically.[2]

As rich as these data are, there are some limits to what they can show. Our study of course-taking and transcripts investigated only the courses that students took, not the content of courses nor the effectiveness of teaching and learning in these courses. Yet despite these limitations, our study highlights several important developments and trends in American secondary education.

■ Since the 1890s, educators and scholars have engaged in impassioned debate over whether all students should follow essentially an academic program or a differentiated program that included vocational and general tracks; both sides in the debate believed their approach would increase equal educational opportunity.

■ During the Great Depression, that debate was largely settled in favor of the advocates of curricular differentiation; as a consequence, between the 1930s and the 1970s the proportion of academic course-taking by American students fell steadily.

■ The "excellence" reforms of the late 1970s and early 1980s appear to have reversed the decline in academic course-taking; by 1990, more students and a greater percentage of students were taking academic courses than at any time since the late 1920s.

■ In the past decade, minority students have increased their amount of academic course-taking at a faster rate than white students. At the same time, the high school dropout rate has fallen, particularly among black students. These positive trends, however, have not been accompanied by increasing college enrollments by blacks.

We will discuss each of these findings in turn.

The Great Debate About the High School Curriculum

From their inception in the first half of the 19th century, high schools in the United States have been flashpoints of controversy about who would use them and what courses students would take. In 1893, these controversies coalesced around a report issued by the Committee of Ten, a group composed largely of college presidents who had been asked by the National Education Association to investigate the condition of high school education and recommend improvements. Chaired by Charles W. Eliot, president of Harvard, the committee argued that all high school students should receive an academic education. The Committee concluded that curricular standards must be high and, most importantly, they must be the same for all students regardless of whether these students drop out of school after only a few years, graduate from high school but do not seek further education, or go on to college.

As the Committee put it, "every subject which is taught at all in a secondary school should be taught in the same way and to the same extent to every pupil so long as he pursues it, no matter what the probable destination of the pupil may be, or at what point his education is to cease.... Not that all the pupils should pursue every subject for the same number of years; but so long as they do pursue it, they should all be treated alike."[3] Equal educational opportunity, in this report, primarily refers to the *means* of education, the courses that students take, as they move toward graduation. Schools fulfill the promise of equal educational opportunity by insisting that all students take essentially the same rigorous academic courses. Anticipating the accusation that this academic program of study would appeal mainly to the small number of high school students planning to go to college, the Committee argued simply that academic education was the best preparation for life regardless of students' future plans. Needless to say, such a program of study was also the best preparation for college.

Over the next quarter of a century, educators and scholars debated the appropriateness of the Committee of Ten's recommendations for the rapidly growing high school population. Between 1890 and 1930, the number of 14- to 17-year-olds attending high school soared from 359,949, under 7 percent of the age group, to 4,804,255, over 51 percent of the age group.[4] Educators widely believed that many of these new students pouring into high schools were less academically talented than previous generations of pupils. Based on this belief, critics of the Committee of Ten argued that the new students had neither the ability, interest, nor need for the rigorous academic program proposed by the Committee.

Leading this attack was the eminent psychologist G. Stanley Hall. As early as 1904, Hall denounced the idea that all students should follow the same academic program. Distorting the Committee's argument by reversing its terms, Hall chastised the Committee for assuming that the best preparation for college was also the best preparation for life. Moreover, he argued that such an academic program would inevitably be diluted in order to accommodate the flood of new students who were entering the high school. He deemed the new students a "great army of incapables ... who should be in schools for the dullards or subnormal children." For this diverse and increasingly large group of students, Hall proposed a wide-ranging program of instruction that would not be dominated by academic courses.[5]

Hall's critique of the Committee of Ten contained a number of assumptions that became central to the debate about standards and equality in the American high school. First, he assumed that a uniform, academic program stifled adolescents' needs to spontaneously explore the world around them. Second, he maintained that holding all pupils to high academic standards favored the small number of students planning to go to college. From this perspective the Committee's report became an elitist document representing the biases of the college presidents who helped draft it. Third, Hall presumed that the majority of young people entering high schools in this era were inferior students. Supported by this belief, Hall and other critics of the Committee of Ten contended that it had totally ignored the different needs and aspirations of these students.

Eventually, opponents of the Committee added a fourth assumption: that a rigorous, uniform academic program significantly contributed to high rates of student dropouts. In this line of reasoning, students were essentially forced out of school by difficult academic classes that were irrelevant to their lives, boring, and damaging to their self-esteem. Advocating curricular differentiation as the solution to these problems, critics of the Committee maintained that a uniform academic course of study actually violated the principle of equal educational opportunity because it increased the dropout rate and stratified society more rigidly along the lines of high school graduates and dropouts.

In 1918, another National Education Association report, *Cardinal Principles of Secondary Education*, captured these critics' sentiments precisely. Thoroughly rejecting the uniform, academic approach of the Committee of Ten, *Cardinal Principles* instead proposed a multifaceted high school offering students choices among distinct courses of study. The report declared, "The work of the senior high school should be organized into differentiated curriculums [sic].... The basis of differentiation should be, in the broad sense of the term, vocational, thus justifying the names commonly given,

> *The period from the 1920s to the 1970s was marked by an unbroken decline in the percentage of courses that high school students took in such core academic areas as English, foreign language, math, science, and social studies.*

such as agricultural, business, clerical, industrial, fine-arts, and household-arts curriculums. Provisions should be made also for those having distinctively academic needs and interests."[6]

Supporters of these multifaceted or, as the report labeled them, "comprehensive," high schools defined equal educational opportunity as equal access to different programs for different students. In this definition, equality was assured by permitting young people to choose from an array of courses suited to their individual needs, abilities, and interests. Although the reality of curricular tracking, which was well established in the

nation's leading urban school districts by the 1930s, often belied this egalitarian rhetoric, educators hailed differentiated high school programs as the key to democratizing the high school. Specifically, they argued that relevant and practical curricular options would encourage larger and larger numbers of students to stay in school and ultimately graduate. This view of equal educational opportunity referred primarily to the diploma that students received upon graduation, not to the actual education they had received. All graduates would receive the same ultimate credential despite having taken very different courses and having met very different standards along the way.[7]

For over a century, supporters of the Committee of Ten and *Cardinal Principles* have been debating these different definitions of equality of educational opportunity and the value of their respective curricular manifestations. It has become routine for historians to figuratively describe 20th century educational reform as a series of pendulum swings between these two distinct philosophical and curricular programs. Educational historians, for example, portray the 1950s as a period in which the curriculum swung away from the relevance-based Life-Adjustment Movement (a movement that drew heavily from the philosophy of *Cardinal Principles*) toward the more academic (and thus Committee of Ten-style) demands of the post-Sputnik era. During the 1960s, the pendulum then returned to a curriculum aimed at greater relevance, often implemented in "open classrooms." Finally in the 1970s, the pendulum swung once again toward academics in the back-to-basics movement.

Our study finds little evidence that these pendulum-like swings of curricular reform actually typify historical trends in secondary education. The rhetoric of curricular reform does not coincide with the reality of student course-taking. Rhetorically, 20th-century school reform *has* swung between the curricular options noted above with the ideas and language of "relevance" alternating with those of "academic rigor." Our data, however, demonstrate that until the late-1970s *these rhetorical swings did not correspond with student course-taking in high schools.* Rather, what occurred from the 1920s to the 1970s was the steady triumph of the philosophy embodied in *Cardinal Principles*. This triumph was marked by an unbroken decline in the percentage of courses that high school students took in such core academic areas as English, foreign language, math, science, and social studies. Instead, students took increasing percentages of less demanding, non-academic courses including physical education, health, and vocational education.

The crucial period of change was the Great Depression and the immediate post-World War II years. Prior to this time, high schools across the nation appeared to have followed a middle path in regard to the Committee of Ten-*Cardinal Principles* debate. Most schools strongly stressed an academic program but, by 1930, offered an increasing number and variety of vocational and elective courses to meet the more "practical" needs of youth. The situation, however, changed drastically in the 1930s when the national economic collapse sent a huge wave of new students into high schools. By 1940, 7,123,009

Beginning in the 1930s, working-class and black children were disproportionately assigned to non-academic tracks and courses and to academic classes that had lower standards and less rigorous content.

students between the ages of 14 to 17 were in high school, over 73 percent of the age group.[8]

This unprecedented flood of new pupils reinforced two key assumptions about high school students noted earlier. First, educational leaders believed that most of these students were even less academically talented (and therefore less worthy of a strong academic program) than previous generations of students. As a 1934 National Education Association report stated, "a very considerable portion of the new enrollment is comprised of pupils of a different sort—boys and girls who are almost mature physically, who are normal mentally, in the sense that they are capable of holding their own with the ordinary adult, but who are unwilling to deal successfully with continued study under the type of program which the secondary school is accustomed to provide [i.e., the traditional academic program]."[9]

Second, educational leaders assumed and feared that a regimen of tough academic courses would force many of these students to drop out, a particularly awful prospect in the 1930s given the desperate shortage of jobs. As a result, educators channeled increasing numbers of these students into undemanding, non-academic courses. In addition, we found in an earlier study, that in keeping with their definition of equal educational opportunity (holding students in school long enough to obtain a diploma), educational leaders diluted content and lowered standards in the remaining academic courses that these students were required to take. While these curricular decisions sought to promote equal educational opportunity, in reality they had a grossly *un*equal impact on working-class and black children who were beginning to attend high school in greater numbers during this time. Beginning in the 1930s, these students were disproportionately assigned to non-academic tracks and courses and to academic classes that had lower standards and less rigorous content.[10]

These Depression-era developments received an additional boost in the post-World War II years with the creation of the Life Adjustment Movement, a federally sponsored curricular reform effort that both justified and encouraged these anti-academic trends in American high schools.[11] These trends had a profound impact on the course-taking patterns of students for much of this century. In 1928, over 67 percent of the courses taken by American students were academic. Six years later, the amount of academic course-taking had dropped to slightly more than 62 percent. Over the next two decades the percentage of academic courses taken by U.S. high school students continued to fall from just over 59 per-

cent in 1949 to 57 percent in 1961 and then returned to 59 percent in 1973.

The growth of the non-academic share of the curriculum can be gauged by one startling fact: In 1910, the share of high school work devoted to *each* of the five basic academic subjects—English, foreign language, mathematics, science, and history—enrolled more students than all of the non-academic courses combined. Moreover, these data do not reveal the more subtle changes within academic subjects in which English courses were reorganized to relate "literature and life," and history and government courses were transformed into the social studies.[12]

Furthermore, and contrary to recent historical interpretation, the relative decline in academic enrollments was not matched by increases in vocational enrollments, except briefly during World War II. Rather, as noted above, a large proportion of the curricular shift is accounted for by such "personal development" courses as driver's training, health, and physical education. Behind this development was the generally negative assessment of both the academic *and* vocational abilities of the new waves of students who entered the high school in the 1930s and after the war. What many historians fail to recognize, but our data show quite clearly, is that these students were often tracked away not only from academic courses but from vocational ones as well.

The decline in the percentage of academic course-taking and the rise in less demanding "personal service" courses by American high school students should have given many Americans serious cause for concern. Certainly some critics, most notably Arthur Bestor in 1953, decried the expanding "educational wastelands."[13] But many, if not most, Americans—even those deeply concerned about the future of the academic subjects—simply ignored the problem. Why? The simplest explanation lies in the rising number of high school students. Between 1949-50 and 1969-70, the number of students in grades nine through twelve more than doubled from 6,397,000 to 14,322,000.[14] Growing high school enrollments masked the steady decline in the *percentage* of academic course-taking because the absolute number of students in various academic courses was increasing steadily. Between 1928 and 1973, for example, while the share of the total courses devoted to foreign language fell from 9.5 percent to 3.9 percent, the enrollment in such classes rose from 1,377,000 to 3,659,000. Such trends tended to mute criticism by Bestor and others because high school leaders routinely pointed out that more students were taking academic courses than ever before and because the high schools were supplying enough students to fill college classrooms. However, what these defenders of the status quo failed to mention was that at the same time more students than ever before were also enrolling in less rigorous, non-academic courses.

Occasionally, social commentators voiced concern that high school graduates did not seem as well prepared for jobs or higher education as students in the past, which was probably the case. One newspaper exposé in Detroit at this time, for example, found that students in the college preparatory track in 1958 took fewer academic courses than did students in the general track in

1933. In other words, in the late 1950s students in both the college preparatory and non-college tracks received a less rigorous education than did the non-college bound students of the 1930s. Such criticism, however, had little effect on school policy or practice.[15]

Over the next two decades a number of policy changes in schools across the country helped sustain this transformation of the high school curriculum. The first involved a subtle but important shift in the way some academic courses were delivered to students. In 1960, 93 percent of students enrolled in English courses took these courses in a two-semester sequence. Twelve years later, this proportion dropped to only 63 percent. We found the same trend in social studies. These changes indicate that by the early 1970s schools were increasingly offering English and social studies courses in a one-semester rather than two-semester format. Students still had to take two courses to get a year's credit, but the courses that they took to get that credit did not necessarily have to relate to one another. The one-semester format fit quite nicely into educational programs that placed a high priority on catering to students' needs, interests, and scheduling demands. However, it reduced the opportunity for students to explore complex topics in a continuous and in-depth manner over the course of an entire year.

In addition, our analysis reveals an expansion in the range of activities that school leaders deem worthy of academic credit, specifically granting Carnegie credits to activities that formerly had been labeled extracurricular. The most notable examples of this trend include giving course credit for working on the school newspaper and yearbook. Undoubtedly students gain important skills and knowledge in these activities. Nonetheless, granting them credit further diminished the role that academic courses play in high school education. Finally, we find evidence of students receiving credit for such courses as Consumer Math and Refresher Math, largely non-academic courses that many school systems use to fulfill graduation requirements in mathematics.

In all, our study finds clear evidence of a decline in academic course-taking beginning in the 1930s. As in economics where bad money drives out good, so in education for much of this century easier and weaker curricula appear to have driven out strong. Until the 1970s, however, few people were disturbed enough about these trends to take action.

The Positive Impact of the "Excellence" Reforms

In the late-1970s, the decline in academic course-taking began to reverse, and high school students increased the percentage of these courses for the first time in almost half a century. Throughout the 1980s, that trend gained momentum, and by 1990 a full-fledged shift toward greater academic course-taking was under way. Between 1973 and 1990, the percentage of academic course-taking jumped from 59 percent to over two-thirds. This substantial increase in the percentage of academic courses taken by American students in the past 20 years is as great as the decline that took place between 1928 and 1961.

The causes of this shift are varied, but they unquestionably include the following: a changing economic situation in which a high school diploma carried less value than previously; demands of parents for higher quality education for their children; alarm about the steady decline in SAT scores; the publication of such manifestos as *A Nation at Risk;* enactment of more stringent high school graduation requirements by state legislatures; and the setting of higher standards for student performance by school districts. By late 1986, for example, 45 states and the District of Columbia had raised their graduation requirements, 42 states increased math requirements, and 34 states bolstered science requirements.[16]

Two additional factors are also worth noting. First, school leaders could no longer rely on demographic trends to mask the decline in the percentage of academic course-taking by American students. Between 1976 and 1991, the number of students in grades nine through twelve fell steadily from 15,656,000 to 12,655,000.[17] Had earlier policies continued unchanged, both the absolute number of students in academic courses and the percentage of these courses taken by students would have been falling by the late 1970s. Second, many colleges and universities (at times prompted by state boards of higher education) increased entrance requirements for incoming freshmen, thereby adding considerable support to complementary efforts on the high school level regarding graduation requirements.

As positive as these trends in academic course-taking are, some very important questions still need to be asked. Specifically, are the courses that we identified as academic truly academic in content or have we simply cataloged changes in course titles while content has either remained unchanged or has been diluted? As noted earlier, our data could not answer these questions. However, a new study conducted by the Wisconsin Center for Educational Research (WCER) does provide some answers at least in regard to math and science courses. Led by WCER Director Andrew Porter, researchers intensively studied course content and teaching strategies in 18 schools in six states. These states—Arizona, California, Florida, Missouri, Pennsylvania, and South Carolina—all had introduced "relatively major increases in their standards for high school mathematics and science." Porter summarized the results of the study noting, "Some education scholars wondered if course content would get watered down as more average and below average students enrolled in more advanced courses. However, our data indicate that, in the schools in the states that we studied, the content of the math and science was as rigorous after standards were increased."[18] These are very exciting findings that support our belief that the trend toward greater academic course-taking is more than a cosmetic change. However, additional studies need to be conducted to see if the same patterns regarding the quality of teaching and material hold true in other content areas.

As promising as these trends are, much remains to be done. As late as 1990, when the percentage of academic course-taking had improved to over 66 percent, the ratio of academic to non-academic courses still had not returned to 1928 levels. In other words, the progress that has been made should be viewed as a first step but not an end in itself.

The Impact of "Excellence" Reforms on the Dropout Problem and Minority Students

Any demand for more rigorous curricula and higher academic standards inevitably must confront the question, won't such curricula and standards increase the dropout rate in general and have a negative impact on the educational opportunities of poor and minority students in particular? As noted earlier, for more than half a century, educational policy makers have made decisions based on the presumption that tougher course requirements automatically increase the dropout rate, especially among poor and minority students. Moreover, these policy makers assumed that the only way to keep the dropout rate from soaring was to make the high school curriculum less challenging and more entertaining. Consequently, these educational leaders routinely condemned efforts to raise academic standards because of their fear that such measures would contribute to greater educational inequality.

Is that specter of higher dropout rates validated by findings on the effects of academically oriented reforms? The short answer is no. Between 1973 and 1990, when higher standards and tougher graduation requirements were widely enacted and the percentage of academic course-taking jumped by almost 10 percent, the national dropout rate declined from 14 percent to 12 percent. These numbers are even more impressive for minority students. Between 1982 and 1990, African Americans and Hispanics increased their academic course-taking to a greater extent than whites and Asian Americans. In 1982, only 28 percent of African Americans and a quarter of Hispanic students took a regimen of four years of English, three years of social studies, and two years of math and science. By 1990, the percentages had nearly tripled to 72 percent and 70 percent respectively. The share of minority students taking three years of math and science has risen even more dramatically, from 10 percent to 41 percent of black students and from 6 percent to a third of Hispanic students. During the same period, the dropout rate for black students *fell* from 18 percent to 13 percent while the dropout rate for Hispanic students remained unchanged at about 32 percent.[19] These data should put to rest the ritualized invocation of the threat of increased dropouts every time someone suggests that U.S. schools demand more from their students.

Not only are more minority students taking an increasing percentage of tougher academic courses, but they are performing better on national standardized exams, as well. During the late 1970s and 1980s, SAT scores for both blacks and Hispanics rose significantly *especially among students who took the most advanced academic courses.* Between 1976 and 1993, black students' scores on the verbal section of the SAT rose 21 points and in math increased 34 points. During the same period, Mexican-American students' scores rose 21 points on the verbal section and 18 points in math, while Puerto Rican students' scores rose three points and eight points respectively. In addition, since 1988, the number of minority students taking Advanced Placement Tests has grown at "record rates" according to the College Board. The number of black students taking the tests grew from under 10,000 in 1988 to more than 15,000 in 1993, and the number of Latino students soared from just over 10,000 to just under 30,000 in the same period.[20]

In short, demanding more academic course work from students appears to have contributed to improved student outcomes especially among minorities, and it *has*

> *Critics who argue that national standards and national assessment will damage the educational prospects for poor and minority students simply are ignoring the historical record.*

not led to increases in the dropout rate among these groups. Unfortunately, the increases in academic course-taking by minority students have not resulted in subsequent increases in college enrollments, especially on the part of black students. In fact, that group's enrollment in colleges has fallen since the mid-1970s. Between 1976 and 1988, the proportion of black 18- to 24-year-olds going to college fell from 22.6 percent to 21.1 percent of the age group. At the same time, the percentage of whites rose from 27.1 to 31.3.[21]

No finding from our research is more troubling than this one. If large numbers of black students are taking the courses that meet college entrance requirements but are still not entering college, something is seriously wrong. We suspect that economic factors rather than educational preparation have been primarily responsible for the decline in black college enrollment in the 1980s. Specifically, it appears that a 1975 change in federal student aid policy that replaced large numbers of grants (that did not have to be repaid) with loans (that did have to be repaid) had a negative impact on black college attendance. Black students generally come from poorer families than whites and consequently may be less willing and less able to accept the burden of long term debt.[22]

Conclusion

How do these findings relate to the questions about goals and standards that we considered at the beginning of this essay? Our study of high school course-taking points to four important conclusions.

First, it is clear that equal educational opportunity was not achieved by lowering academic standards through curricular differentiation, tracking, shortening courses from two semesters to one, and giving academic credit to previously extracurricular activities. Indeed, the students most harmed by these policies were the children of working-class and minority families. Critics who argue that national standards and national assessment will damage the educational prospects for poor and minority students simply are ignoring the historical record. In the past, poor and minority students have been the most frequent casualties of such standard-lowering policies as allowing less rigorous courses to meet academic requirements for graduation or diluting content in academic courses while keeping course titles the same. The second-class education that resulted from these policies undoubtedly contributed to social, racial, and gender inequality. We believe that clearly articulated national content and performance standards and well-designed national methods of assessment can make such policies more difficult to implement and thus make an important contribution to equality of educational opportunity.

Second, the recent process of raising academic standards in high schools by strengthening graduation requirements and reducing the number of electives that students may take has moved us closer to the goal of equal educational opportunity for larger numbers of students than ever before in our history. No group has responded more positively to these changes than African-American students who have increased their proportion of academic course-taking more dramatically than whites. Equally striking is the fact that during the very time that high school standards were being raised, the dropout rate fell, particularly among black students.

Third, such factors as resources do play an important role in ensuring educational equality, but the struggle for greater equity in resources should not be allowed to sidetrack the push for national goals and standards. The decline in black college attendance, which appears to be due to changes in federal financial aid policy, provides evidence of the importance of adequate resources for achieving equal educational opportunity. However, we take issue with critics of Goals 2000 who argue that unless and until resources are equalized among school districts the setting of national goals and standards will increase educational inequality. That stance tacitly acquiesces to the low educational standards currently in place in many impoverished communities across the country. Moreover, if goals and standards are put on hold while activists, politicians, policy makers, and judges battle over equalization, the practical consequence will be to consign yet another generation of students in impoverished districts to a second-rate, second-class education. That stance seems to us sadly reminiscent of the arguments for curricular differentiation early in this century. While the reasons have changed, the theme remains the same, namely that children from poor and minority backgrounds cannot be expected to rise to the challenge of high academic standards. We reject that assumption.

Finally, we see the setting of national goals and standards as the beginning not the end of the struggle. What remains to be done will be extremely difficult because it demands a massive effort to create developmentally appropriate, challenging course materials and methods for students of differing ability on every grade level. The idea that all students should meet high standards (and essentially follow the same curriculum) does not deny that there are educationally relevant differences among individuals in interests and abilities. Nor does it rule out approaches that would recognize different levels of mastery or that would offer a solid core of academically rigorous courses within a career-related focus. But implicit in the idea of high standards for all is the belief that differences in students' interests and abilities should challenge educators to explore a host of alternative instructional methods and approaches that will enable students to meet demanding performance standards rather than adopt what has been the traditional policy of curricular differentiation.

Much of the modern failure of American K-12 education lies in our avoiding the formidable task of discovering how to teach difficult subjects in ways that are both accessible to young people and yet still true to the complexity and richness of the material. Over 30 years ago, Jerome Bruner declared that "any subject can be taught effectively in some intellectually honest form to any child at any stage of development."[23] Goals 2000 challenges us to make that happen.

REFERENCES

[1] David Angus and Jeffrey Mirel, "Rhetoric and Reality: American High School Course Taking, 1928-1990" in Diane Ravitch and Maris Vinovskis, eds. *Learning from the Past: What History Teaches Us About School Reform* (Baltimore: Johns Hopkins University Press, forthcoming in 1995).

[2] There are two notable exceptions both of whom strongly influenced our interpretation of the history of high school curriculum. They are John F. Latimer, *What's Happened to Our High Schools?* (Washington, D.C.: Public Affairs Press, 1958) and David Cohen whose outstanding essay on the history of the high school can be found in Arthur Powell, Eleanor Farrar, and David K. Cohen, *The Shopping Mall High School: Winners and Losers in the Educational Marketplace* (Boston: Houghton Mifflin, 1985), pp. 233-308.

[3] National Education Association, "The Report of the Committee of Ten on Secondary-School Studies" (Washington, D.C.: The Association, 1893) in Sol Cohen, ed., *Education in the United States: A Documentary History, Vol. 3* (New York: Random House, 1974), 1935.

[4] U.S. Office of Education, *The Biennial Survey of Education in the United States, 1955-56* (Washington, D.C.: The Office, 1956). p. 30.

[5] On Hall's critique see Herbert M. Kliebard, *The Struggle for the American Curriculum, 1893-1958* (New York: Routledge and Kegan Paul, 1986), pp. 14-15.

[6] National Education Association, *The Cardinal Principles of Secondary Education* (Washington, D.C.: U.S. Government Printing Office, 1918), p. 22.

[7] Indeed, *Cardinal Principles* explicitly declared that secondary "education should be so reorganized that every normal boy and girl will be encouraged to remain in school to the age of 18, on full time if possible, otherwise on part time." Ibid., p. 30.

[8] U.S. Office of Education, *The Biennial Survey of Education in the United States, 1955-56*, p. 30.

[9] Quoted in Jeffrey Mirel, *The Rise and Fall of an Urban School System: Detroit, 1907-1981* (Ann Arbor: University of Michigan Press, 1993), p. 132.

[10] David Angus and Jeffrey Mirel, "Equality, Curriculum and the Decline of the Academic Ideal: Detroit, 1928-68," *History of Education Quarterly* 33 (Summer 1993), pp. 179-209.

See also, Patricia Cayo Sexton, *Education and Income: Inequalities of Opportunity in Our Public Schools* (New York: Viking, 1961).

11 On these trends see, Diane Ravitch, *The Troubled Crusade: American Education, 1945-1980* (New York: Basic Books, 1983), pp. 43-80.

12 On these changes see Latimer, *What's Happened to Our High Schools?* p. 118.

13 Arthur Bestor, *Educational Wastelands: The Retreat from Learning in Our Public Schools* (Urbana: University of Illinois Press, 1953/1985).

14 National Center for Education Statistics, *Digest of Education Statistics, 1988* (Washington, D.C.: U.S. Government Printing Office, 1988), pp. 10, 98, 141, 142.

15 Mirel, *The Rise and Fall of an Urban School System,* pp. 235-39, 254-56.

16 James B. Stedman and K. Forbis Jordan, *Education Reform Reports: Content and Impact,* Report No. 86-56 EPW (Washington, D.C.: Congressional Research Service, 1986), pp. 12-41.

17 National Center for Education Statistics, *Digest of Education Statistics, 1993* (Washington, D.C.: U.S. Government Printing Office, 1993), p. 12.

18 "Standard Setting in High School Mathematics and Science Has Positive Effect," *WCER Highlights* 5 (Winter 1993), p. 4.

19 National Center for Education Statistics, *Dropout Rates in the United States: 1991* (Washington, D.C.: U.S. Government Printing Office, 1992), p. 83.

20 Karen De Witt, "College Board Scores Are Up For Second Consecutive Year," *The New York Times,* 19 August 1993, Section I: 1,8; Meg Sommerfeld, "Number of Minorities Taking A.P. Exams Continues To Go Up," *Education Week,* 10 November 1993, p. 10.

21 National Research Council, Committee on the Status of Black Americans, *A Common Destiny: Blacks and American Society, Summary and Conclusions* (Washington, D.C.: National Academy Press, 1989), 19; Thomas Byrne Edsall with Mary D. Edsall, *Chain Reaction: The Impact of Race, Rights, and Taxes on American Politics* (New York: W.W. Norton, 1992), p. 245.

22 Edsall and Edsall, *Chain Reaction,* p. 247. See also, National Research Council, Committee on the Status of Black Americans, *A Common Destiny,* p. 19.

23 Jerome Bruner, *The Process of Education* (Cambridge, Mass.: Harvard University Press, 1960), p. 33.

Blueprint For Renewal

A unique experiment in grass-roots governance reinvents the school board

JEAN M. ZLOTKIN

Jean M. Zlotkin is a member of the school board of the Aromas/San Juan Unified School District in San Juan Bautista, Calif., and served as its first board president. She previously served seven years on the board of the San Juan Union Elementary District in San Juan Bautista. A practicing attorney and credentialed school teacher, she is the parent of two sons, ages 15 and 8.

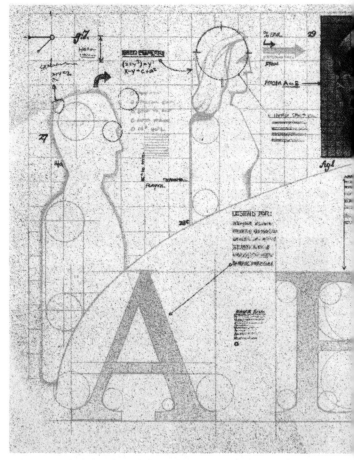

This is the story of parents who learned they can be front-runners as well as followers. It's the story of how a group of volunteers formed a new school district in California and of how the newly formed school board learned to leave management to the superintendent it had hired. It's an old story, too, retelling the tale of democracy at work—of ordinary people joining hands; believing in consensus, each other, and the purpose that brought them together; and succeeding in changing the governance of schools in their communities. That the end product of our grass-roots effort is—at least so far—a traditional board/superintendent governance model says something about the resilience and suitability of that model. How we arrived at that end product is a story of enfranchisement—and a powerful reminder that board service is indeed a public trust.

The story begins in 1988 in the small town of Aromas, about 40 miles south of San Jose in the Monterey Bay area. Aromas parents—spending time together at their elementary school (the only school in town), at community functions, and at social gatherings—found themselves lamenting the sad state of their children's education.

They were distressed to see their children being educated in a large school district that, back in the 1950s, had swallowed up little Aromas School and proceeded thereafter largely to ignore the 400-student, K-8 school. The big district, Pajaro Unified (K-12; enrollment 14,000), had closed the Aromas School cafeteria, had let the facility deteriorate, had sent in short-stay administrators and many temporary teachers, and had seemed more interested in developing

magnet schools elsewhere than in improving Aromas School.

The parents were frustrated. They went to school board meetings to voice their concerns—to no avail. Several of them sought interdistrict transfers to enroll their children in a small neighboring school district located about 10 miles away in the San Juan Union Elementary District (where, in fact, I was a board member at the time). The district had only one K-8 school of about 550 children, named San Juan School.

Meanwhile, unbeknownst to the group that had transferred in from Aromas, parents in San Juan Union were voicing similar concerns about the quality of education and inability of parents to be heard. True, the San Juan School facility looked good, the staff was largely competent and well-liked, the class sizes (at least for California) weren't bad, and the school climate seemed safe and friendly. Still, somehow, children were coming home saying they didn't like school. And it wasn't just the bright kids—although they complained, too, of boredom, lack of challenge, and lack of meaning in their studies.

The San Juan parents weren't sure what was the matter—only that they, too, felt somewhat disenfranchised by administrators and teachers who listened politely but changed nothing significant. Community and school staff morale was sinking; kids didn't have a positive sense of school pride; something was amiss.

Joining forces

Then something happened that caused these isolated groups to come together. It was a fluke, really, that started

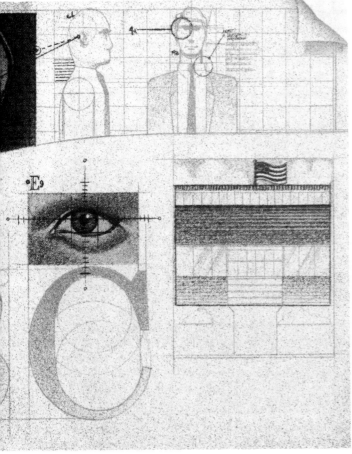

Illustration by Michael Hill.

an avalanche of activity. Although I was a school board member in the district, I also was one of the uneasy parents. And if I was concerned about our little elementary district, as the mother of two young sons in the district, I was even more concerned about the high school my sons would attend. The high school, in yet another district some 12 miles away, had a school enrollment of close to 2,000, 90 percent from another community. I feared parents would be even less effective there than in San Juan and didn't relish the commute or the prospect of a big "shopping mall" high school.

One day, I asked the superintendent of San Juan Union if it might not be possible to keep the ninth-graders in San Juan. Although he seemed to be largely satisfied with the quality of education at both the elementary and high school

levels, he mentioned his own concerns about San Juan students not having their own community high school.

He replied that I shouldn't think just about ninth-graders but about all the community's high school kids. "Why not," he said, "bring all of them back?"

"Can we?" I asked.

He answered that, as a district with only a few thousand residents and approximately 600 students, San Juan was too small to qualify for its own unified school district under California law. But, he went on, it would be possible to form a K-12 unified school district if we had at least 1,501 students. We would need to join with another elementary school district to come up with the numbers required for forming a unified district.

The matter was left at that for a while, but neither the superintendent nor I forgot the idea. Later, when a group of Aromas residents suggested changing the district boundaries to correspond with the county lines—a change that would officially pull the interdistrict transfer students from Aromas into San Juan Union—the subject soon changed to unifying the district altogether.

So began a process that brought together people with different concerns and different agendas but similar desires: better schools that would be more responsive to their communities. A grass-roots movement was born that ultimately had an impact on three existing school districts while creating one entirely new one. The focal point for the campaign became building a new community high school for two towns, but the driving force, for us as parents, was the underlying belief that we could improve all levels of education, including elementary grades.

The core group

Although many people took part in the campaign to form the new district and elect a new school board to govern it, a central group—made up of fewer than 10 people and at times of only two or three—sustained the endeavor. All volunteers and all parents, the members of this group formed the critical core of leaders that carried the movement forward.

The San Juan Union superintendent—with whom I'd initially discussed the idea—might have joined the cause, but that possibility died when the existing San Juan Union school board voted 4-1 against the idea. As the only dissenting member, I stuck with the movement to promote the change. But the San Juan Union board, which opposed the idea at the state-level hearings, forbade any administrator or teacher from assisting with, supporting, or spending district-paid hours with any of the organizers for unification. (Pajaro Unified was also in opposition and brought suit against us; we prevailed.)

The volunteer parents were a diverse group, including an experienced group organizer, an artist, a building contractor, a naturalist, a lawyer, and several teachers or former teachers not employed by any of the affected districts.

From this initial group, five people (of whom I was one) were tapped to run as candidates for the school board of the newly formed district, if the vote to form the district was favorable. We five agreed to run jointly, as a slate, and to share a platform and a vision of what we wanted to build. As with all the group's decisions, these were made by brainstorming and consensus, each participant considering the group's needs as well as individual strengths, weaknesses, and preferences.

Perhaps consensus came easily because no one was on the payroll and none of us knew for certain what we were supposed to do from one step to the next. Or maybe it was just that people with similar concerns work together more effectively than those with divergent interests. Whatever the case, the process of creating a new district never bogged down in power plays, ego trips, or arguments. The task was too big and faced too much opposition for that.

For the next two years, our parent group, using other help whenever it was available, persuaded the California Board of Education—over powerful, multidistrict, professional opposition—to allow the issue to go to the ballot. This triumph was followed by a hard-fought, highly publicized campaign that deeply divided both communities. It seemed clear to us that the opposition in each town was trying to save its power base and, in some cases, jobs within the existing district structures.

But when the vote was tallied in June 1990, approval for the reorganization carried the day, and all the leadership group's candidates, five in a field of 11, won election with close to 70 percent of the vote or higher. The Aromas/San Juan Unified School District was born.

Operating without professionals

In the heat of winning, though, we realized the central educational issues had slipped away. In the necessity of selling people on the district concept and the need for a high school, we had neglected the issue that had brought us together in the first place, a high-quality education for all our children.

Happily, during the summer of 1990, the librarian for Central Park East High School, an experimental 7-12 secondary school in New York City, happened to visit. He exposed us to some ideas we hadn't heard about before—the principles of Theodore Sizer's Coalition of Essential Schools. (The principles include personalized teaching and learning, the concept of the student as worker, and a focus on helping adolescents to learn to use their minds well.) From these core beliefs came our ideas for restructuring—and our focus for the new school board and district.

The first order of business was to define a set of goals and principles—a philosophical base that expressed what we were about and why we were letting this task affect the rest of our lives. Recognizing the importance of this foundation, we instituted the practice of discussing educational issues first at all board meetings, before dealing with nuts-and-bolts business items. The motto we adopted for the board letterhead seemed an appropriate reminder of what we were about: "Learning to Learn."

The board was seated in October 1990. But getting started wasn't quite as simple as that. The old San Juan Union Elementary District was to continue in existence until June 1991, so we parents in the new district were still on our own. The outgoing board of San Juan Union declined to provide staff or money for the new district. So, as newly elected board members, we parents found ourselves acting as both board members and administrators on a nearly full-time, daily basis, to launch our new district. It wasn't something we'd initially anticipated or desired, but there it was.

Still working as unpaid volunteers, we found an office, developed a budget, got a loan from the California Department of Education and the local county office of education, and began district operations—in a district that, at the time,

was staffed only by board members and one part-time paid secretary.

On July 1, 1991, the old San Juan Union Elementary District ceased to exist. Thereafter, our new board found itself dealing with a myriad of operational problems we had not adequately anticipated or planned for. We also found the political resistance to change in San Juan a force to be reckoned with at times. The newly hired principal for San Juan School, selected for his personal strengths and powerful belief in the board's stated goals, was challenged to his limits. And the principal assigned to Aromas School—who trans-

A unique situation

The story of the creation of the Aromas/San Juan Unified School District demonstrates that volunteer community members still can make a major difference in education on the local level, despite powerful opposition.

Even so, it's important to note that a combination of unique needs dictated our choice of remedy. It is not a course of action I or the others in my district would recommend—unless such exceptional circumstances existed that working within the current organizational structure and with the professional educators in the community could not achieve the objective at hand. The best thing for kids is usually joint leadership—a partnership of parents and professionals built on respect, trust, and open sharing of information.

A few points:

• **Healing the wounds.** Wounds take a long time to heal, and morale is a fragile thing. One of our primary objectives since beginning this district has been to implement an inclusionary policy for all—especially for those who doubted the wisdom of this direction and were bitter about the change. Most of the parents who opposed the idea left their children in our public schools, and many, happily, now are part of the core of people working hard to improve our district. Some even say they're glad we won. Of course, others still prefer grumbling.

Until our high school is built, the jury is out about the wisdom of the change at that level. (We project the high

ferred to Aromas, at his choice, from his former position as vice principal at San Juan School—also was under pressure to succeed with a teaching staff of 95 percent new hires.

As board members, we found ourselves frequently exhausted and sometimes overwhelmed by the work and energy required of us to make the district function. We had never intended to run the district ourselves. Our families, too, began to tire of the seemingly endless meetings and work sessions. And, at last, owing to both the magnitude of the undertaking and the resurfacing of uncertainties and fears that had been stifled in the surge of creating the new district, board members and other supporters were beginning to express anxieties and doubts about the endeavor.

Critical choices

Shortly into the 1991-92 academic year, the superintendent (who continued from San Juan Union Elementary District) announced his intent to retire in July 1992. He had voiced this possibility four years earlier—and now he was ready to take the step.

His retirement forced us to make some critical decisions. Our own weariness and the vast amount of learning we'd had to do over the past three years had taught us that a committee of volunteers—even elected, energetic, committed, passionate volunteers—was not the answer to governance over the long haul.

The board met to decide, one more time, what to do. We considered the traditional model of governance and admin-

istration—that is, a school board and superintendent. But we also discussed the idea of not having a superintendent at all—that is, having the school board act as the policy-making body and principals operate as site-based managers, with other administrative assistance for district-level responsibilities. We even looked at the possibility of contracting with an outside school-management firm—such as Education Alternatives Inc. based in Bloomington, Minn.—to run the district for us.

We looked again at our adopted goals and principles, found them still to be a good expression of our beliefs, and decided to seek a new superintendent who would work to implement those beliefs. We contracted with a professor from a nearby university known for his own commitment to our beliefs and to restructuring, and we asked him to act as the board's adviser for the search.

A community-based superintendent selection committee

came together—including many people who had opposed forming the new district, and also including an equal balance of members from both San Juan and Aromas. This committee sought and selected a new superintendent, who officially began work last July 1.

As yet, it's too early to draw conclusions about the success of our new district. And it's too early to be certain we made the right decision in choosing a traditional board/superintendent governance model. But it has been done. We parents have chosen to remain traditional policymakers rather than policy implementers and to trust staff to carry forward our vision, consistent with the strategic planning we're now undertaking.

But for me, one thing is different: Unlike my role on the old San Juan board, I am now a fully informed leader, no longer dependent on a superintendent to tell me what's going on or how to interpret it. We have learned how to do things ourselves and to understand them through our own eyes and ears.

Nonetheless, as a board, we chose to surrender our power and our leadership to a superintendent, knowing through our own experience what "administration" really means. Although it's not at all unusual for school boards to surrender power to superintendents, it is unusual for boards to understand, firsthand, what power they really hold and what they really can do to effect change in the public schools.

One thing is certain: Our new superintendent knows that this school board and these communities will accept nothing less than success. The challenge he must meet is the one our grass-roots movement set out to achieve in the first place: making sure all students find school a place where they are comfortable, safe, and progressing academically and where they feel engaged, excited, positive, eager, proud, and certain that what they learn will take them where they want to go and allow them to be whatever they dream of being.

The creation of the Aromas/San Juan Unified School District shows that parents—simple community people—can make a difference in what is possible for public schools. The birth of this district recognizes that leadership and good ideas can spring from anyone, regardless of position, title, length of service, age, or compensation.

But creation, while difficult, is easy compared to implementation. As we all know, consensus on ideas is one thing; agreeing on the details is quite another. To make this effort take hold, shared belief and shared vision must exist among staff members and students as well as the community at large. Partnerships between professionals and parents, adults and children, and teachers and administrators are required for success.

Our endeavor helped us and our district employees recognize that it doesn't necessarily take lots of money or power to be effective. Leaders arise when a need for them appears. Indeed, leadership and followership are just two sides of the same coin, each dependent on the other to have real value. Recognizing that truth—and the fact that we all must take turns in both roles—should help us better serve our children and our communities.

The next step for Aromas/San Juan will be to make good on our promise: achieving a lifelong learning environment that meets the needs and interests of all our citizens, children and adults alike.

school will not be built until 1996; in the meanwhile, our high school students are being farmed out to several districts around us.) Of course, those who lost power positions (such as former board members) or had economic reasons for opposing the change (such as employees of the affected districts) still think this was a bad move. But then, that's the nature of the democratic process.

- **What our experiences say for your school board.** If your district has parents like us, what should your board do? Honest communication with parents, openness, and responsiveness on the part of my old school board would have avoided much of the bitterness and animosity that resulted from the confrontational position we were forced to take. I don't question the right of those individuals to disagree with me on this matter, but I do think board members, as elected representatives, need to respond to issues and provide internal processes to air them and discuss pros and cons. Hostility begets hostility. What should your school board do? Keep in touch, and make external attack unnecessary.

- **P.S. I'm still a dissatisfied parent.** Change is a long, hard, slow process, and we still have a long way to go to meet the needs of our students, many of whom are not thriving today. Organizational change is only a step. Until our beliefs are incorporated into practice and made personal and real in our schools, meaningful education for all will remain a goal, not a reality. We're still finding our way and learning just how difficult the task before us is.—J.M.Z.

Stop Expecting The Worst Of Schools

For one thing, the scores aren't falling; for another, U.S. schools measure up better than you think on international comparisons

Gerald W. Bracey

Gerald W. Bracey is a research psychologist and education consultant who lives in Alexandria, Va.

Ever since that "paper *Sputnik*" *A Nation at Risk* appeared in April 1983, this nation has come to expect the worst about its schools. The prevailing atmosphere of gloom is so strong even well-meaning people write things that are not true. A few examples will show what I mean.

The March 10, 1993, edition of *Education Week* stated that "in the last decade the number and proportion of students scoring above 650 on either the SAT verbal or mathematics sections declined." Not so: The proportion of students who score above 650 on the verbal section is the same as it was 10 years ago—3 percent. But the proportion who score that high on the math section has risen from 7 percent to 10 percent. That might sound like a small increase. But remember that the Scholastic Aptitude Test was designed so that only 6.5 percent of students attained a score of 650 or better. In addition, the group that set the standards on the SAT was an all-white, mostly male elite living in the Northeast. The nationwide pool of students who take the test now is far more diverse than that, yet we still see a 50 percent increase in the percentage of high scorers.

A second example comes from the magazine you're reading right now. A headline in the November 1992 issue stated, "Good news: Our 9-year-olds read well. Bad news: Our 14-year-olds don't." In fact, U.S. 14-year-olds finished ninth among students of 31 nations, and their scores were close to the top. (More on this later.)

International comparisons such as this reading study are used to great effect by school critics, who claim that two facts emerge from these studies. First, they say, our students do not achieve well compared to students in other nations. And second, they say, our students' failure has lowered our international competitiveness. Neither of these "facts" turns out to be true.

U.S. schools are racking up numerous successes at home. To some, though, these home-grown test scores do not have the importance they once did. We are a global economy, they say, and we must measure our students on a global scale. It is the international comparisons that count, this argument runs, and in these comparisons we finish low, often last.

Four legitimate responses can be made to this allegation: (1) The methodological problems of the international studies are so numerous that the results are virtually meaningless; (2) international comparisons have other problems that have nothing to do with methodology; (3) we compare favorably on many international indicators of achievement other than test scores; and (4) we often finish better than has been reported. I will consider each response in turn.

Methodology is just one problem

Most of the design problems with international studies have to do with some aspect of selection, and selection biases can have powerful effects. For example, in the Second International Mathematics Study, the results of which were published in 1987, eighth-graders in Hungary finished first, while those in Hong Kong finished in the middle of the pack (as did U.S. eighth-graders). By 12th grade, however, Hong Kong's students were

No. 1, and Hungary's were only average. This reversal might occur because Hong Kong's high schools are superior, but it is more likely due to selection differences: By the 12th grade, only an elite 2 percent of Hong Kong's students were still taking math, compared to 50 percent of 12th-graders in Hungary.*

The holding power of schools also affects the way different countries select and present their curricula. Because of tracking or dropout rates, if a country values some aspect of learning for all its children, it might need to present that material by the eighth grade, or many students will never be exposed to it. In the United States, however, more students stay in school longer than is the case in most other countries. That means U.S. schools can teach geometry in the 10th grade, comfortable in the knowledge that virtually everyone will be around to take it if they want to (or if their parents tell them to). Many countries do not have this luxury. And so when U.S. students score low on tests with geometry questions, the explanation is not a failure of education but a matter of curriculum sequence.

Different kinds of selection problems afflict the studies conducted by Harold Stevenson and his colleagues at the University of Michigan—studies whose conclusions about the superiority of Japanese education have, unfortunately, entered the popular culture. Stevenson conducted studies in Beijing, Taipei, Minneapolis, Chicago, and Sendai, Japan. The first selection problem with these studies is that Stevenson studied only first and fifth graders. All of his writings through the 1992 publication of his book, *The Learning Gap,* depend solely on multiple-choice test scores in mathematics in grades one and five. Yet the cover of the book heralds Stevenson's findings as, "Why Our Schools Are Failing and What We Can Learn From Japanese and Chinese Education."

Who would dare draw conclusions in any other field about the functioning of an entire system by looking at only two early points in that system? How can anyone who looks at only one curriculum subject and two elementary grades make wholesale pronouncements about "American Schools"?

Stevenson's studies also use small groups—240 students per grade per country. (The large international studies, by comparison, usually involve more than 1,000 students and often as many as 10,000.) Moreover, the U.S. samples were not representative: The Chicago sample had many more poor families, many more minorities, and many more students who did not speak English at home than we find in the nation as a whole—characteristics associated with low test scores. (Stevenson did not provide a similar description of his Minneapolis sample.) This might be the reason Stevenson's findings do not accord with those of other larger, more sophisticated studies.

These larger studies find that most countries look very much alike. Typically, only the very top country and the very bottom are exceptional. This fact often gets lost because the news media do not report average scores on these studies but only the ranks of the countries. And when you use ranks, someone must finish last. This obscures the quality of the performance: In the Olympic 100-meter dash, someone finishes last, but probably no one calls him "Pokey."

*For a complete list of references for the material referred to in this article, see Gerald W. Bracey, "Why Can't They Be Like We Were?" *Phi Delta Kappan,* October 1991, 104–117, and Gerald W. Bracey, "The Second Bracey Report on the Condition of Public Education." *Phi Delta Kappan,* October 1992, 104–117.

When you look at actual scores, rather than ranks, the differences among countries are very small indeed. Among the top scores for each country—at the 95th percentile—the differences among countries are smaller still. In fact, our top performers actually finish ahead of the top performers in a number of countries whose average test scores are higher. It is simply not the case that only a small percentage of U.S. students performs as well as average students in other countries.

Stevenson's work also illustrates problems that simply cannot be solved through advances in research design. For example, the families in Stevenson's Chicago sample have almost three children per home. Because of China's rigid birth-control policy, most of the students in his Beijing sample were from families with only one child. Stories abound about how these children receive almost constant adult attention. We cannot know exactly how this lavishing of attention affects achievement, but other research has found that children who interact with adults a lot score higher on tests than those who spend more time with their peers.

In addition to being the only child in the family, 50 percent of the Beijing kids had at least one grandparent living with them. Only 10 percent of the Chicago sample did. How can we take this "granny factor" into account? The answer is, we cannot. Again, we cannot know its precise impact, but the Chinese students clearly are in a position to interact with more adults.

Accentuating individuality

Once we turn away from the narrow confines of multiple-choice tests to other indicators of quality, we find more reason for cheer. For example, we send 58 percent of our high school students on to college and produce more college graduates than any other nation. Only Canada comes close, with 48 percent. The Japanese send 37 percent of their students to college. Moreover, Asian students are flocking to American colleges, which they consider the best in the world. But if American K–12 education is so bad, how can our colleges be so good? How could our high school graduates cope? How could professors produce such a silk purse from such a sow's ear?

Others before me have pointed out that the Nobel prize is virtually an American monopoly, and although Nobel prizes are few, they making a telling point about the United States versus Japan in culture and education. In *The Enigma of Japanese Power,* Karel van Wolferen, a Dutch journalist who lived in Japan for 25 years, reports the curious tale of a Japanese scientist who did win a Nobel prize. He was living in the United States at the time and had lived in Europe earlier. In Japan, the conclusion was obvious: He could never have won if he had stayed home. There, the pressure for group think and conformity to group norms would have prevented him from taking the personal, individual risks necessary to win the Nobel.

Our emphasis on individual attainment extends to everyone, not just Nobel laureates: International studies show that Japanese students get more alike on tests as they get older, but U.S. students become more diverse. We celebrate individual differences; the Japanese deplore them. "The nail that stands up gets hammered down," goes an old Japanese saying. Japanese schools regulate everything from the permissible tread on a tennis shoe to the color of your underwear. Girls who have curly or less-than-jet-black hair have to produce papers to prove they did not perm or dye it. Boys who dare to part their hair are in trouble. An op-ed piece in the *Washington Post* this spring declared that the Japanese state does not trust parents to train their children properly. Ours, we should remember, is a nation founded by parents who did not trust the state.

Descending from the rarefied air in which Nobel laureates dwell, we find that American scientists, mathematicians, and engineers write between 30 percent and 40 percent of the world's professional articles in these disciplines. No one else even comes close: The United Kingdom, Japan, and the former Soviet Union are tied at 8 percent each. The figures have been stable since at least 1973.

Only Japan has more engineers than we do, 188 per 10,000 workers to our 184. Almost all of Japan's engineers are free to work on improving domestic products, of course, while one-third of ours work in defense industries. We have so many scientists, mathematicians, and engineers that some cannot find work. In a Mar. 10, 1992, article, the *New York Times* reported that 12 percent of U.S. graduate students receiving a doctorate in physics in 1991 received not a single job offer, while another 50 percent received only one.

Better than people think

Even on multiple-choice tests, U.S. students often do better than people think they do. I have already observed that looking at scores instead of ranks washes out most differences among nations, but in some studies we rank quite well also.

Remember that November 1992 *School Board* headline about good news and bad news? The story reported the results of an international comparison in reading, which tested 200,000 9 and 14-year-olds in 31 countries. American 9-year-olds finished second, and our 14-year-olds finished ninth. Among 31 countries, a 15th-place finish is "average," so how can a ninth-place finish be bad news? More important, our 14-year-olds had scores very close to the top. On a scale of 600, American kids scored 535; the second place French scored 549. A difference of 14 points out of 600 is a trivial difference. (First-place honors went to Finland, a small, homogeneous nation with a superb social service system; its students scored 560.)

We do better than many people think even in mathematics, where we have taken our worst lumps in the news media. The Second International Mathematics Study (SIMS) administered an algebra test to eighth-graders. Only about 20 percent of U.S. eighth-graders take algebra; most European and Asian students do. Comparing the scores of these 20 percent to those of Japanese eighth-graders, American kids score well ahead. This comparison, of course has a selection bias of its own: I compared 20 percent of American students in a specific grade, presumably the academically most able 20 percent, to almost 100 percent of Japanese students in the same grade. But when this select group of U.S. students is compared to the top 20 percent of Japanese students, the U.S. kids still finish ahead by a tiny amount.

This finding reassures us that American students learn well what they are taught, but it doesn't take American education off the hook entirely. It shifts the question: Should 100 percent of American students take algebra in the eighth grade? Every math educator I've asked virtually shouts, "No!" Many aspects of mathematics are more important than algebra: One analysis of 1,400 jobs found that 78 percent of them required no algebra at all; only 8 percent required more than a little.

Education and global competition

Ultimately, though, how well U.S. schools perform in international comparisons isn't the issue. The real crux of the matter is the role of public education in determining our economic competitiveness. No doubt if we had no schools at all—or if we had truly awful schools—our work force would suffer greatly in comparison to those of other nations. However, the late education historian Lawrence Cremin, in his 1989 book, *Popular Education and Its Discontents,* provided the proper perspective on how important the schools can be:

"American economic competitiveness with Japan and other nations is to a considerable degree a function of monetary, trade, and industrial policy, and of decisions made by the President and Congress, the Federal Reserve Board, and the federal departments of the Treasury, and Commerce and Labor," Cremin wrote. "Therefore, to contend that problems of international competitiveness can be solved by educational reform, especially educational reform defined solely as school reform, is not merely Utopian and millenialist, it is at best foolish and at worst a crass effort to direct attention away from those truly responsible for doing something about competitiveness and to lay the burden on the schools. It is a device that has been used repeatedly in the history of American education."

One Japanese official called American workers lazy and illiterate and advised Americans not to buy a car made on Friday when everyone was thinking about the weekend or on Monday when everyone had a hangover, but another Japanese official said the American worker was the most productive in the world. The second official was not just being diplomatic. He was right.

Several studies verify his assertion. In one, the productivity of the American worker was set at an arbitrary 100, and other productivity rates were calculated appropriately. German workers finished with a score of 77, Japanese workers with 73. When the study factored out the number of hours Japanese workers worked, their productivity fell to 57, little more than half that of an American worker.

Perhaps the most telling story about American labor came out of Fremont, Calif., where General Motors closed a plant, saying that it had the worst labor force in the world. Toyota reopened the plant with more than 80 percent of those same lousy workers and shortly announced that it was competitive with anything in Japan.

As one after another mammoth American company— General Motors, IBM, Sears, American Express—experienced massive losses and layoffs, numerous articles have discussed what went wrong. But nowhere in the stories in the *New York Times,* the *Washington Post, Time, Newsweek,* or *U.S. News & World Report* was there a hint that low-quality labor had played even a small role in the company's troubles. Instead, these articles talked about CEOs and managers who, like the Swiss watchmakers who got wiped out when the world went digital, failed to see the world had changed. These corporate leaders persevered in making products no one wanted, using outmoded manufacturing techniques. (If we're going to bash education at all, we ought to start with the business schools for churning out such poor managers.)

This country does have a major labor problem, though— one that Europe has not solved. (The Asian countries are not really comparable because of the strong involvement of government in industry.) The problem is this: The jobs that are growing at the fastest rates—such as paralegals or radiology technicians—all require skilled workers, but these jobs account for only a tiny fraction of the labor force. The fastest growing jobs in terms of numbers are all unskilled—janitors, maids, waiters, sales clerks. The largest industry in this nation is tourism, which does not generate specialized positions.

In other words—and I know this will come as a shock—the U.S. labor force as it is currently configured does not need more and more highly skilled workers. Estimates of the number of college graduates taking jobs that require no college range from 18 percent to 26 percent, and the figure is rising. One approach to get out of this bind, an approach not without risk, is to reorganize work so that unskilled jobs become skilled jobs and decisions once made by supervisors are made on the front line. As economist Lawrence Mishel, an advocate of this approach says, industry has used schools as "an avenue of convenience" to hide its own failure to innovate. "An intelligent labor policy would create skilled jobs, not expect them to happen by themselves," says Mishel.

But this approach is risky, as shown by an example from *America's Choice: High Skills or Low Wages,* a report from the National Center on Education and the Economy: The old way of organizing work, according to this scenario, had six laborers on the front line and 18 in support positions. The new organization shows eight workers on the front line and six in support. What is not discussed is that the new organization results in a net loss of 10 workers. The Europeans have moved farther down this road than we have, and the price they have paid is much higher unemployment and social suffering. Fifty percent of people polled in England say they would leave their island if they could. And as Germany sinks into a recession, it seems to be sinking into a similar malaise, accompanied by much racial violence.

In this country, those businesses that have successfully reorganized work along these lines have usually had to install no-layoff policies. That is clearly the humane response. But how many companies can afford to do it? And what will be the net change in productivity if they do?

The shift to a service economy—under way more in Europe even than here—does not mean education has become less important, however. Just the reverse. People of all levels of education attainment are more likely to work in low-paying jobs now than 15 years ago, but the difference between wages for different levels of education has increased. A study of identical twins with different amounts of schooling estimated that each year of education beyond high school is worth an additional 16 percent in salary. Census figures are even more dramatic: In 1990, high school dropouts earned an average of $492 a month. Getting a diploma more than doubled that. Obtaining a bachelor's degree doubled the monthly income again, and a doctorate almost doubled the monthly intake once more: A Ph.D. makes in a month 65 percent of what a high school dropout earns in a year.

Lost in most of the discussion of international competitiveness is a good fix on the reality of what it all means. Typically, we respond with chagrin to some economic advance

in Japan or Germany. We see the global economy as a zero sum game: If they win, we lose. But this ignores the fact that after World War II, Japan and Germany had lost virtually everything and used our advances in technology to build themselves up. According to economist Robert Samuelson, the same thing applies now.

"What we're being asked to believe is that if another country (say, Japan) pioneers a new technology, we won't benefit," writes Samuelson. "This defies logic and history. After World War II, the United States led in most technologies. That hardly prevented Europe and Japan from rapidly raising their living standards. Just the opposite: the availability of proven U.S. technologies accelerated their economic growth."

The task ahead

Where does this all leave us? Clearly, U.S. schools are doing a much better job overall now than in the past. Clearly, we are doing better in international comparisons than we have been led to believe. And clearly, the link between schools and the work force is tenuous once we progress beyond a certain threshold level of schooling. (In my two articles for *Phi Delta Kappan,* "Why Can't They Be Like We Were?" and "The Second Bracey Report on the Condition of Education," I amassed mountains of evidence to prove these points.)

But that does not mean American public education has no shortcomings. Indeed, as is clear from such works as *Savage Inequalities,* by Jonathan Kozol, and "The Rural Underclass," a report from the Population Reference Bureau, large numbers of children do not receive anything approaching a minimal education. Writing in the March 7, 1993, *Washington Post,* high school English teacher Patrick Welsh (author of *Tales Out of School*) made this clear. "It may be hard for outsiders—or even school boards—to understand just how far behind many lower-income high school students are in even the most basic academic tasks," Welsh says. "The profundity of their difficulties—and thus their threat to classroom learning at large—is at the root of many parents' desire to preserve ability grouping."

Welsh presents examples of totally inadequate work by graduates and discusses kids who think that if they get more than a D on an assignment, they've wasted too much time on schoolwork. Yet, he says, "Worse than kids who just want a D for being medically alive are those who seem unable to behave in a group." And these students, unfortunately, are growing in number.

I have been called a messenger of complacency. Certainly I am not that. But the problems we have do not come from an inadequate system that cannot compete internationally. An education reform agenda that treats all schools as in need of radical restructuring will fail. Instead, we need a more focused reform approach that treats poor schools as patients in an intensive-care ward. We need to start with poor urban schools, but we must not forget poor rural schools. These schools have even more intractable problems, but, because they are dispersed across the countryside, they remain largely invisible. In the case of both urban and rural poverty, however, the threat lies within, not without. We must stop worrying about how we compare with other nations and attend to this threat on the home front.

Morality and Values in Education

It is amazing to consider the many ethical issues with which teachers must contend. Whether schools should have a major role in the moral development of students and what that role might be are fiercely debated issues. Some teachers describe their concern that students need to develop a stronger sense of character rooted in a more defensible system of values. Other teachers express concern that they cannot "do everything" and are hesitant to instruct on morality and values. Most believe that they must do something to help students become reasoning and ethical decision makers. Some organized groups do not want the public school system to do anything in this area, while a large number of persons in the general public believe that there are certain cherished social values that schools should teach. We can, I think, agree at least that teachers themselves ought to be good examples of rational, ethical decision makers to their students.

What teachers perceive to be worthwhile and defensible behavior informs our reflections on what we as educators should teach. We are conscious immediately of some of the values that inform our behavior, but we may not be aware of all that informs our preferences. Values that we hold without being conscious of them are referred to as tacit values—values derived indirectly after reasoned reflection on our thoughts about teaching and learning. Much of our knowledge about teaching is tacit knowledge, which we need to bring into conscious cognition by analyzing the concepts that "drive" our practice. We need to acknowledge how all our values inform, and influence, our thoughts about teaching.

Teachers need to help students develop within themselves a sense of critical social consciousness and a genuine concern for social justice. The debate on this issue continues in professional literature. Insight into the nature of moral decision making should be taught in the context of real current and past social problems and should lead students to develop their own skills in social analysis relating to the ethical dilemmas of human beings.

There is a need for teachers to develop principles of professional practice that will enable them to respond reasonably to the many ethical dilemmas that they now face. A knowledge base on how teachers derive their knowledge of professional ethics is developing; further study of how teachers' values shape their professional practice is very important. Educational systems at all levels are based on the desirability to teach certain fundamental beliefs and the disciplines of knowledge (however they may be organized in different cultures). School curricula are based on certain moral assumptions (secular or religious) as to the worth of knowledge—and the belief that certain forms of knowledge are more worthy than others. Schooling should not only transmit national and cultural heritages, including our intellectual heritage; it is also a fundamentally moral enterprise in which students need to learn how to develop tenable moral standards in the contexts of their own visions of the world.

We see, therefore, that when we speak of morality and education, there are process issues as to the most basic knowledge-seeking, epistemological foundations of learning. Hence, the controversy over teaching morality deals with more than just the tensions between secular and religious interests in society—although acknowledging such tensions is valuable. Moral education is also more than a debate over the merits of methods used to teach students to make morally sound, ethical choices in their lives—although this also is critically important and ought to be done. Thus we argue that the construction of educational processes and the decisions about the substantive content of school curricula are also moral issues as well as epistemological ones having to do with how we discover, verify, and transmit knowledge.

One of the most compelling responsibilities of both Canadian and U.S. schools is the responsibility of preparing young persons for their moral duties as free citizens of free nations. The Canadian and U.S. governments have always wanted their schools to teach the principles of civic morality based on their respective constitutional traditions. Indeed, when the public school movement began in the United States in the 1830s and 1840s, the concept of universal public schooling as a mechanism for instilling a sense of national identity and civic morality was supported. Indeed, in every nation, school curricula have certain value preferences imbedded in them.

Significant constitutional issues are at stake in the forms and directions that moral education should take in the schools. Both theistic and nontheistic conceptions of what constitutes moral behavior compete for the loyalties of teachers and students. Extremist forces representing the ideological left and right, both religious and secular, wish to see their moral agendas incorporated into school curricula.

Do teachers have a responsibility to respond to student requests for information on sexuality, sexual morality, sexually transmitted diseases, and so on? Or should they deny these requests? For whom do the schools exist? Is a teacher's primary responsibility to his or her client, the student, or to the student's parents? Do secondary school students have the right to study and to inquire into subjects not in officially sanctioned curricula? What are the moral issues surrounding censorship of student reading material? What ethical questions are raised by arbitrarily withholding information regarding alternative viewpoints on controversial topics?

Teachers cannot hide all of their moral preferences. They can, however, learn to conduct just and open discussions of moral topics without succumbing to the temptation to indoctrinate students with their own views.

Teaching students to respect all people, to revere the sanctity of life, to uphold the right of every citizen to dissent, to believe in the equality of all people before the law, to cherish the freedom to learn, and to respect the right of all people to their own convictions—these are principles of democracy and ideals worthy of being cherished. An understanding of the processes of ethical decision making is needed by the citizens of any free nation; thus, this process should be taught in a free nation's schools.

What part ought the schooling experience play in the formation of such things as character, informed compassion, conscience, honor, and respect for self and others? From Socrates onward (and, no doubt, before him), we have wrestled with these concerns. Aristotle noted in his *Politics* that there was no consensus as to what the purposes of education should be in Athens, that people disputed what Athenian youth ought to be taught by their teachers, and that youth did not always address their elders with respect. Apparently, we do not have a new problem on our hands. The issue of public morality and the question of how best to educate for individually and collectively responsible social behavior are matters of great significance in North America today.

The essays in this unit constitute a comprehensive overview of moral education with considerable historical and textual interpretation. Topics covered include public pressures on schools and the social responsibilities of schools. This unit can be used in courses dealing with the historical or philosophical foundations of education.

Looking Ahead: Challenge Questions

What is moral education? Why do so many people wish to see a form of moral education in schools?

Are there certain values about which most of us can agree? Should they be taught in schools? Why, or why not?

Should local communities have total control of the content of moral instruction in their schools, as they did in the nineteenth century? Defend your answer.

Should schools be involved in teaching people to reason about moral questions? Why, or why not? If not, *who* should do it? Why?

What is the difference between indoctrination and instruction?

Is there a national consensus concerning the form that moral education should take in schools? Is such a consensus likely if it does not now exist?

What attitudes and skills are most important to a responsible approach to moral decision making?

—F. S.

The Return of Character Education

Concern over the moral condition of American society is prompting a reevaluation of the schools' role in teaching values.

Thomas Lickona

Thomas Lickona is a developmental psychologist and Professor, Education Department, State University of New York at Cortland, Cortland, NY 13045. He is author of *Educating for Character: How Our Schools Can Teach Respect and Responsibility* (New York: Bantam Books, 1991.)

To educate a person in mind and not in morals is to educate a menace to society.
—*Theodore Roosevelt*

Increasing numbers of people across the ideological spectrum believe that our society is in deep moral trouble. The disheartening signs are everywhere: the breakdown of the family; the deterioration of civility in everyday life; rampant greed at a time when one in five children is poor; an omnipresent sexual culture that fills our television and movie screens with sleaze, beckoning the young toward sexual activity at ever earlier ages; the enormous betrayal of children through sexual abuse; and the 1992 report of the National Research Council that says the United States is now *the* most violent of all industrialized nations.

As we become more aware of this societal crisis, the feeling grows that schools cannot be ethical bystanders. As a result, character education is making a comeback in American schools.

Early Character Education

Character Education is as old as education itself. Down through history, education has had two great goals: to help people become smart and to help them become good.

Acting on that belief, schools in the earliest days of our republic tackled character education head on—through discipline, the teacher's example, and the daily school curriculum. The Bible was the public schools' sourcebook for both moral and religious instruction. When struggles eventually arose over whose Bible to use and which doctrines to teach, William McGuffey stepped onto the stage in 1836 to offer his McGuffey Readers, ultimately to sell more than 100 million copies.

McGuffey retained many favorite Biblical stories but added poems, exhortations, and heroic tales. While children practiced their reading or arithmetic, they also learned lessons about honesty, love of neighbor, kindness to animals, hard work, thriftiness, patriotism, and courage.

Why Character Education Declined

In the 20th century, the consensus supporting character education began to crumble under the blows of several powerful forces.

Darwinism introduced a new metaphor—evolution—that led people to see all things, including morality, as being in flux.

The philosophy of logical positivism, arriving at American universities from Europe, asserted a radical distinction between *facts* (which could be scientifically proven) and *values* (which positivism held were mere expressions of feeling, not objective truth). As a result of positivism, morality was relativized and privatized—made to seem a matter of personal "value judgment," not a subject for public debate and transmission through the schools.

In the 1960s, a worldwide rise in personalism celebrated the worth, autonomy, and subjectivity of the person, emphasizing individual rights and freedom over responsibility. Personalism rightly protested societal oppression and injustice, but it also delegitimized moral authority, eroded belief in objective moral norms, turned people inward toward self-fulfillment, weakened social commitments (for example, to marriage and parenting), and fueled the socially destabilizing sexual revolution.

Finally, the rapidly intensifying pluralism of American society (Whose values should we teach?) and the increasing secularization of the public arena (Won't moral education violate the separation of church and state?), became two more barriers to achieving the moral consensus indispensable for character education in the public schools. Public schools retreated from their once central role as moral and character educators.

The 1970s saw a return of values education, but in new forms: values clarification and Kohlberg's moral dilemma discussions. In different ways, both expressed the individualist spirit of the age. Values clarification said, don't impose values; help students choose

From *Educational Leadership*, Vol. 51. No. 3, November 1993, pp. 6-11. © 1993 by the Association for Supervision and Curriculum Development. All rights reserved. Reprinted by permission.

their values freely. Kohlberg said, develop students' powers of moral reasoning so they can judge which values are better than others.

Each approach made contributions, but each had problems. Values clarification, though rich in methodology, failed to distinguish between personal preferences (truly a matter of free choice) and moral values (a matter of obligation). Kohlberg focused on moral reasoning, which is necessary but not sufficient for good character, and underestimated the school's role as a moral socializer.

The New Character Education

In the 1990s we are seeing the beginnings of a new character education movement, one which restores "good character" to his historical place as the central desirable outcome of the schools' moral enterprise. No one knows yet how broad or deep this movement is; we have no studies to tell us what percentage of schools are making what kind of effort. But something significant is afoot.

In July 1992, the Josephson Institute of Ethics called together more than 30 educational leaders representing state school boards, teachers' unions, universities, ethics centers, youth organizations, and religious groups. This diverse assemblage drafted the Aspen Declaration on Character Education, setting forth eight principles of character education.[1]

The Character Education Partnership was launched in March 1993, as a national coalition committed to putting character development at the top of the nation's educational agenda. Members include representatives from business, labor, government, youth, parents, faith communities, and the media.

The last two years have seen the publication of a spate of books—such as *Moral, Character, and Civic Education in the Elementary School, Why Johnny Can't Tell Right From Wrong,* and *Reclaiming Our Schools: A Handbook on Teaching Character, Academics, and Discipline*—that make the case for character education and describe promising programs around the country. A new periodical,

the *Journal of Character Education,* is devoted entirely to covering the field.[2]

Why Character Education Now?

Why this groundswell of interest in character education? There are at least three causes:

1. *The decline of the family.* The family, traditionally a child's primary moral teacher, is for vast numbers of children today failing to perform that role, thus creating a moral vacuum. In her recent book *When the Bough Breaks: The Cost of Neglecting Our Children,* economist Sylvia Hewlett documents that American children, rich and poor, suffer a level of neglect unique among developed nations (1991). Overall, child well-being has declined despite a decrease in the number of children per family, an increase in the educational level of parents, and historically high levels of public spending in education.

In "Dan Quayle Was Right," (April 1993) Barbara Dafoe Whitehead synthesizes the social science research on the decline of the two biological-parent family in America:

> If current trends continue, less than half of children born today will live continuously with their own mother and father throughout childhood.... An increasing number of children will experience family break-up two or even three times during childhood.

Children of marriages that end in divorce and children of single mothers are more likely to be poor, have emotional and behavioral problems, fail to achieve academically, get pregnant, abuse drugs and alcohol, get in trouble with the law, and be sexually and physically abused. Children in stepfamilies are generally worse off (more likely to be sexually abused, for example) than children in single-parent homes.

No one has felt the impact of family disruption more than schools. Whitehead writes:

> Across the nation, principals report a dramatic rise in the aggressive, acting-out behavior characteristic of children, especially boys, who are living in

single-parent families. Moreover, teachers find that many children are so upset and preoccupied by the explosive drama of their own family lives that they are unable to concentrate on such mundane matters as multiplication tables.

Family disintegration, then, drives the character education movement in two ways: schools have to teach the values kids aren't learning at home; and schools, in order to conduct teaching and learning, must become caring moral communities that help children from unhappy homes focus on their work, control their anger, feel cared about, and become responsible students.

2. *Troubling trends in youth character.* A second impetus for renewed character education is the sense that young people in general, not just those from fractured families, have been adversely affected by poor parenting (in intact as well as broken families); the wrong kind of adult role models; the sex, violence, and materialism portrayed in the mass media; and the pressures of the peer group. Evidence that this hostile moral environment is taking a toll on youth character can be found in 10 troubling trends: rising youth violence; increasing dishonesty (lying, cheating, and stealing); growing disrespect for authority; peer cruelty; a resurgence of bigotry on school campuses, from preschool through higher education; a decline in the work ethic; sexual precocity; a growing self-centeredness and declining civic responsibility; an increase in self-destructive behavior; and ethical illiteracy.

The statistics supporting these trends are overwhelming.[3] For example, the U.S. homicide rate for 15- to 24-year-old males is 7 times higher than Canada's and 40 times higher than Japan's. The U.S. has one of the highest teenage pregnancy rates, the highest teen abortion rate, and the highest level of drug use among young people in the developed world. Youth suicide has tripled in the past 25 years, and a survey of more than 2,000 Rhode Island students, grades six through nine, found that two out of three boys and one of two girls thought it "acceptable for a man to force sex on a woman" if they had been dating for six months or more (Kikuchi 1988).

3. *A recovery of shared, objectively important ethical values.* Moral decline in society has gotten bad enough to jolt us out of the privatism and relativism dominant in recent decades. We are recovering the wisdom that we do share a basic morality, essential for our survival; that adults must promote this morality by teaching the young, directly and indirectly, such values as respect, responsibility, trustworthiness, fairness, caring, and civic virtue; and that these values are not merely subjective preferences but that they have objective worth and a claim on our collective conscience.

Such values affirm our human dignity, promote the good of the individual and the common good, and protect our human rights. They meet the classic ethical tests of reversibility (Would you want to be treated this way?) and universalizability (Would you want all persons to act this way in a similar situation?). They define our responsibilities in a democracy, and they are recognized by all civilized people and taught by all enlightened creeds. *Not* to teach children these core ethical values is a grave moral failure.

What Character Education Must Do

In the face of a deteriorating social fabric, what must character education do to develop good character in the young?

First, it must have an adequate theory of what good character is, one which gives schools a clear idea of their goals. Character must be broadly conceived to encompass the cognitive, affective, and behavioral aspects of morality. Good character consists of knowing the good, desiring the good, and doing the good. Schools must help children *understand* the core values, *adopt* or commit to them, and then *act upon* them in their own lives.

The cognitive side of character includes at least six specific moral qualities: awareness of the moral dimensions of the situation at hand, knowing moral values and what they require of us in concrete cases, perspective-taking, moral reasoning, thoughtful decision-making, and moral self-knowledge. All these powers of rational moral thought are required for full moral maturity and citizenship in a democratic society.

People can be very smart about matters of right and wrong, however, and still choose the wrong. Moral education that is merely intellectual misses the crucial emotional side of character, which serves as the bridge between judgment and action. The emotional side includes at least the following qualities: conscience (the felt obligation to do what one judges to be right), self-respect, empathy, loving the good, self-control, and humility (a willingness to both recognize and correct our moral failings).

At times, we know what we should do, feel strongly that we should do it, yet still fail to translate moral judgment and feeling into effective moral behavior. Moral action, the third part of character, draws upon three additional moral qualities: competence (skills such as listening, communicating, and cooperating), will (which mobilizes our judgment and energy), and moral habit (a reliable inner disposition to respond to situations in a morally good way).

Developing Character

Once we have a comprehensive concept of character, we need a comprehensive approach to developing it. This approach tells schools to look at themselves through a moral lens and consider how virtually everything that goes on there affects the values and character of students. Then, plan how to use all phases of classroom and school life as deliberate tools of character development.

If schools wish to maximize their moral clout, make a lasting difference in students' character, and engage and develop all three parts of character (knowing, feeling, and behavior), they need a comprehensive, holistic approach. Having a comprehensive approach includes asking, Do present school practices support, neglect, or contradict the school's professed values and character education aims?

In classroom practice, a comprehensive approach to character education calls upon the individual teacher to:

■ *Act as caregiver, model, and mentor,* treating students with love and respect, setting a good example, supporting positive social behavior, and correcting hurtful actions through one-on-one guidance and whole-class discussion;

■ *Create a moral community,* helping students know one another as persons, respect and care about one another, and feel valued membership in, and responsibility to, the group;

■ *Practice moral discipline,* using the creation and enforcement of rules as opportunities to foster moral reasoning, voluntary compliance with rules, and a respect for others;

■ *Create a democratic classroom environment,* involving students in decision making and the responsibility for making the classroom a good place to be and learn;

■ *Teach values through the curriculum,* using the ethically rich content of academic subjects (such as literature, history, and science), as well as outstanding programs (such as *Facing History and Ourselves*[4] and *The Heartwood Ethics Curriculum for Children*[5]), as vehicles for teaching values and examining moral questions;

■ *Use cooperative learning* to develop students' appreciation of others, perspective taking, and ability to work with others toward common goals;

■ *Develop the "conscience of craft"* by fostering students' appreciation of learning, capacity for hard work, commitment to excellence, and sense of work as affecting the lives of others;

■ *Encourage moral reflection* through reading, research, essay writing, journal keeping, discussion, and debate;

■ *Teach conflict resolution,* so that students acquire the essential moral skills of solving conflicts fairly and without force.

Besides making full use of the moral life of classrooms, a comprehensive approach calls upon the school *as a whole* to:

■ *Foster caring beyond the classroom,* using positive role models to inspire altruistic behavior and providing opportunities at every grade level to perform school and community service;

■ *Create a positive moral culture in the school,* developing a schoolwide ethos (through the leadership of the principal, discipline, a schoolwide sense of community, meaningful student government, a moral community among adults, and making time for moral concerns) that supports and amplifies the values taught in classrooms;

■ *Recruit parents and the community as partners in character education,* letting parents know that the school considers them their child's first and most important moral teacher, giving parents specific ways they can reinforce the values the school is trying to teach, and seeking the help of the community, churches, businesses, local government, and the media in promoting the core ethical values.

The Challenges Ahead

Whether character education will take hold in American schools remains to be seen. Among the factors that will determine the movement's long-range success are:

■ *Support for schools.* Can schools recruit the help they need from the other key formative institutions that shape the values of the young—including families, faith communities, and the media? Will public policy act

to strengthen and support families, and will parents make the stability of their families and the needs of their children their highest priority?

■ *The role of religion.* Both liberal and conservative groups are asking, How can students be sensitively engaged in considering the role of religion in the origins and moral development of our nation? How can students be encouraged to use their intellectual and moral resources, including their faith traditions, when confronting social issues (For example, what is my obligation to the poor?) and making personal moral decisions (For example, should I have sex before marriage?)?

■ *Moral leadership.* Many schools lack a positive, cohesive moral culture. Especially at the building level, it is absolutely essential to have moral leadership that sets, models, and consistently enforces high standards of respect and responsibility. Without a positive schoolwide ethos, teachers will feel demoralized in their individual efforts to teach good values.

■ *Teacher education.* Character education is far more complex than teaching math or reading; it requires personal growth as well as skills development. Yet teachers typically receive almost no preservice or inservice training in the moral aspects of their craft. Many teachers do not feel comfortable or competent in the values domain. How will teacher education colleges and school staff development programs meet this need?

"Character is destiny," wrote the ancient Greek philosopher Heraclitus. As we confront the causes of our deepest societal problems, whether in our intimate relationships or public institutions, questions of character loom large. As we close out a turbulent century and ready our schools for the next, educating for character

is a moral imperative if we care about the future of our society and our children.

---

[1]For a copy of the Aspen Declaration and the issue of *Ethics* magazine reporting on the conference, write the Josephson Institute of Ethics, 310 Washington Blvd., Suite 104, Marina del Rey, CA 90292.

[2]For information write Mark Kann, Editor, *The Journal of Character Education,* Jefferson Center for Character Education, 202 S. Lake Ave., Suite 240, Pasadena, CA 91101.

[3]For documentation of these youth trends, see T. Lickona, (1991), *Educating for Character:How Our Schools Can Teach Respect and Responsibility* (New York: Bantam Books).

[4]*Facing History and Ourselves* is an 8-week Holocaust curriculum for 8th graders. Write Facing History and Ourselves National Foundation, 25 Kennard Rd., Brookline, MA 02146.

[5]*The Heartwood Ethics Curriculum for Children* uses multicultural children's literature to teach universal values. Write The Heartwood Institute, 12300 Perry Highway, Wexford, PA 15090.

References

Benninga, J.S., ed. (1991). *Moral, Character, and Civic Education in the Elementary School.* New York: Teachers College Press.

Hewlett, S. (1991). *When the Bough Breaks: The Cost of Neglecting Our Children.* New York: Basic Books.

Kikuchi, J. (Fall 1988). "Rhode Island Develops Successful Intervention Program for Adolescents." *National Coalition Against Sexual Assault Newsletter.*

National Research Council. (1992). *Understanding and Preventing Violence.* Washington, D.C.: National Research Council.

Whitehead, B. D. (April 1993) "Dan Quayle Was Right." *The Atlantic* 271: 47-84.

Wynne, E. A., and K. Ryan. (1992). *Reclaiming Our Schools: A Handbook on Teaching Character, Academics, and Discipline.* New York: Merrill.

Ethnic Studies
and Ethics Studies:
A Study in Contrasts?

Dorothy Engan-Barker

Dorothy Engan-Barker is a faculty member in the Department of Educational Foundations, College of Education, Mankato State University, Mankato, Minnesota.

"I've never yet seen an ethnics studies class that doesn't divide instead of unify." This comment was made by a faculty member responding to a survey in which opinions were sought regarding the proposal that students should take at least one course in ethics as a condition for college graduation. There was, in the questionnaire, no direct reference to multicultural issues or ethnic studies, but the comment clearly reflects the growing disenchantment some feel in higher education with the proliferation of culture-specific courses.

The relationship of these courses to the ethics question is illustrated by the fact that culture-specific courses send the implicit—or perhaps—explicit message that ethnic and cultural behaviors and beliefs, including beliefs on what constitutes moral behavior, are so different they must be studied individually. At the same time, most agree that, central to studies in ethics, is the notion that human beings can arrive at some universally-accepted guidelines for moral human behavior, and that these can and do cut across ethnic and cultural boundaries.

In ethnic studies, a variety of people come together to pursue knowledge about "the other." In ethics courses, a variety of people come together with the goal of finding out about "the us." The statement made earlier about division and unity is a cryptic example of what many of us have been grappling with for a long time: the seeming conflict which results from attempts to identify a universal "ethical culture" which transcends but does not transgress beliefs of the many individual cultures.

When Rhetoric of Ethics Meets Practice. Nearly any educational institution these days will include, in its philosophy or mission statement, some mention of equality and the need to acknowledge and value all human beings. It may use such phrases as "building cultural literacy" or "fostering a sense of connectedness to the world community." Such efforts are generally encouraged and applauded by all. But to get beyond the rhetoric requires real-life action in the form of courses, curriculum, and programs. As these grow ever more numerous—taking up space, funds, and time in a period of intense competition for diminishing educational resources—the terms "fragmentation" and "divisive" are heard more and more frequently.

This is a dilemma for teachers at all levels who find themselves in schools, or even states, which have mandated the incorporation of both ethics education and multicultural education into their curricula and who take this charge seriously. The dilemma is made more complex by the fact that many, particularly those in monocultural communities, do not feel the immediacy of cultural conflicts nor understand the urgency of learning about other groups and incorporating this knowledge into the teaching repertoire. The task is further complicated by the growing opposition to "political correctness." In my own classes over the past couple of years, there are significantly greater numbers of students who express their opposition to "so much stress on differences." In homogeneous classrooms, how does one make real the need to hear and know "the other?"

Multicultural Education in Monocultural Settings. The majority of outlying schools in Minnesota have few students of color. The exceptions are those areas which include American Indian children or districts in which the children of Hispanic migrant farm workers are intermittently enrolled. However, while the state has a minority population of barely four per cent, about 40 per cent of the students in the major metropolitan areas are African-American, American Indian, Chicano-Hispanic, or Asian. In an effort to bring cultural balance to the curriculum, if not to actual school populations, in 1989, the State Department of Education decreed that all schools develop inclusive K-12 curricula that reflect, in all subject areas, multicultural, gender-fair, disability-sensitive perspectives. By June of 1990, of the state's 400-plus school districts, only a handful had submitted plans which were subsequently approved.

Those of us who are teacher educators must ask ourselves, "How can we expect classroom teachers to embrace and carry out state-prescribed multicultural curricula if little in their own preservice education has prepared them for this task?" Even more pressing is the question, "How good a job are we doing at helping preservice teachers come to **be** multicultural as opposed to merely "knowing about?" Teacher education programs, especially those where natural opportunities for intercultural experiences are rare, must attempt to create these experiences for students who will live in an increasingly globalized society. It is critical that those of us who work with preservice teachers emphasize and clarify not only the state's multicultural policy, but the seriousness with which it should be viewed. Again, with an overwhelmingly homogeneous population whose roots are in rural America, this task at times seems impossible.

In the introductory foundations course which I teach, students are exposed to a great deal of information on social issues which impact the institution called school. The text includes sections on Black Americans, Hispanic Americans, Native Americans, Asian Americans, the wealthy versus the poor, family configurations as a factor in student achievement, and so on. But we know that abstract knowledge of other cultures is not necessarily internalized so that it affects behaviors and atti-

From *Multicultural Education*, Vol. 2, No. 1, Fall 1994, pp. 24-26. Reprinted by permission of *Multicultural Education*, the magazine of the National Association for Multicultural Education. © 1994.

tudes. We also know that experience precedes conceptualization so that students, even at the college level, who have not experienced the internal discomfort or dissonance which can arise when opposing cultural norms meet, have great difficulty seeing themselves as other than tolerant and accepting in the classroom. Therefore, deliberate activities need to be developed to nurture and build the kind of understanding that is remembered and practiced. How to do this?

A Case Study: Expanding Cultural Comfort Zones. It was 8:05 a.m. and the faces that looked back at me appeared less than enthusiastic. The readings for the week covered chapters entitled, "Cultural Diversity in American Education" and "The Struggle for Equal Educational Opportunity."

I looked out over the 30 or so members of my "School and Society" class and thought, "What a fraud I am. An Iowa-farm-girl-turned-professor 'teaching' the next generation of rural or small-town students how to make their future classrooms 'multicultural.'" I abandoned my prepared presentation and, more as a function of my own curiosity than anything else, asked, "Think a moment and then identify just one piece of information from this week's readings which stands out more than anything else." At first no one said anything. Then their responses came, stilted and academically precise.

Teachers praise white students more than non-white students.

Disciplinary action is taken more often against black students than white students.

Over 50 per cent of American Indian students don't finish high school.

Mexican-American children, with limited English skills, fall farther and farther behind in school achievement.

In an attempt to engage the students at a less cerebral level, I asked for more personal responses. "You're all going to be teachers; how do you feel about this stuff you're reading? How do you think it will affect you as a professional?"

It was certainly an unfair question—how could they possibly know, given their own backgrounds and their minimal experience with culturally diverse classrooms—but one brave student volunteered, "Well, no matter what the book says about all the problems of those people, I think most of them are just normal folks—you know, just like us."

I swallowed my first response, which was to ask, "And all those who are not 'just like us' are abnormal?" Instead, I posed the following: "Imagine yourself in a college classroom where everyone else's background, customs, perhaps even language is different from yours. What is 'normal'?" It was at this point that students began to consider the "What ifs" and whose job it is to adapt, to adjust, to fit in. Eventually, all agreed that, mostly because of the power differential, it is the teacher's ethical responsibility to try to make each of her students feel comfortable in the classroom that becomes home for so many hours of the day. What is the first step in achieving this? For the teacher to not only know about but feel at least a little comfortable in the child's culture, the world that is 'normal' to her.

This then led to my final statement. "So you all agree that, even without a law, we are bound by professional ethics to become 'culturally literate' because we know this is positively linked to students' school success. How do teacher education students in an institution such as this (just look around, there's not a single non-white face in this room) really learn to become comfortable with those who are unlike ourselves? How do we get beyond the statistics I just heard and begin to focus on how we become comfortable with fellow humans who are not just like you and me?"

A number of suggestions were offered: "More speakers from different groups should come in...." "There could be videos on other cultures brought into the classroom...." "We could change texts..."

Interestingly, all the solutions relied on the instructor facilitating some sort of change in course content. When asked if they would support a course requirement that each student make a personal connection with someone from a group with which they were unfamiliar, an immediate collective reluctance was expressed. Furthermore, the overwhelming cause for their reluctance was placed squarely on "the other": "Those people usually don't even want to get involved with us."

It was after this statement that the student who uttered it smiled somewhat sheepishly and added, "But I guess I can't say that unless I really have tried it, can I?" After a somewhat uncomfortable silence, another voice tentatively offered, "Maybe we don't know how."

Thus began the idea for a program which, in its trial run, achieved more success than any of us had hoped for.

"Linking Learners": School and College Classroom Collaboratives. I'd been working on a research project with faculty from the Afrocentric Educational Academy, a pilot middle-school program connected to the Minneapolis Public Schools. Not long after the above experience, I approached Grace Rogers, a teacher at the Academy, over coffee, "How might you and your staff feel about your kids coming down to Mankato State for a day in order to 'teach' my students in their college classrooms? In return, my students could escort your kids around campus and answer questions they might have about college life."

She immediately embraced the idea. The assistant principal of her school and the dean of my college both gave enthusiastic support and the two of us started planning. While I looked for dollars to bring the kids to campus (ultimately the costs were shared by the College of Education and the university's Center for Cultural Diversity), Grace and her colleague, John Cearnal, started helping their kids prepare for their new roles as "college instructors."

On a Thursday in May, 31 6th-, 7th-, and 8th-graders from the Afrocentric Educational Academy in Minneapolis boarded a chartered bus which brought them to our campus two hours west of the city and in the heart of Minnesota farm lands. None had been on a college campus before. Here, they visited four College of Education classrooms where they presented skits on African history, gave mini-lessons drawn from their own curriculum, and answered questions from the preservice teachers who were their audience.

At noon, students from both groups—college campus and inner city—hooked up in pairs or small groups and spent time "hanging out" together while Academy faculty participated in a luncheon round-table discussion with Mankato State University faculty. The students, after eating sack lunches provided by the College, toured the student union, took a look at the new library, explored dormitory rooms, or shot baskets in the gym. Before embarking for home, representatives from the university's Cultural Diversity Center met with the students and gave more information about college life.

Between 140 and 150 university students were directly involved with this project, either by their attendance at the presentations or by spending one-on-one time with the Academy students. Many chose to participate in both activities. Both groups—middle school and college age—completed questionnaires, anonymously, after the visit.

What The Questionnaires Revealed. Academy students were asked to rate the overall experience on a scale from 1 (low) to 10 (high) by answering eight specific questions regarding the activity, *e.g.*, their own willingness to participate, their interest level, and how much they listened to and learned from the project. Many respondents gave the experience a 9 or a 10 overall ranking; the mean ranking was 7.

Responses to the question, "I felt excited when..." seemed evenly divided between teaching students older than me, "playing footfall," and "eating!"

In answer to the question, "If I had this experience again I would change...," most students responded, "Nothing."

Terms used most often by these students in summarizing their campus experience were, "fun" and "exciting."

Responses from the College of Education students indicated growth in two areas: (1) knowledge of and interest in African-American culture in general; and (2) new awareness of their own lack of intercultural experiences and knowledge.

Expanded knowledge of culture was demonstarted by such statements as:

I was impressed by these children and the system of Afrocentric education. Why not instill this sense of pride in other cultures as well? It's important for both sides to gain from this. We all have a purpose, and the information I gained from them was educational and enlightening and meant to be passed on.

I thoroughly enjoyed the presentation that the students gave. This sort of presentation is such a benefit to us as future educators....in class we have such a homogeneous learning environment. In all reality, as educators we are going to be blessed and challenged with such a diverse classroom. These students have shown us only one of the many cultures that may be included in a classroom.

...by witnessing a live performance regarding the beliefs and stories told by these young people, I will better retain the messages conveyed...I will never forget the skit on Harriet Tubman.

I really learned a lot from the students....In some ways, it was like I could feel what their ancestors dealt with, when they talked about slavery. I thought that this classroom activity was a great success for both the Minneapolis students and our classroom as well.

I hope for other students in the future, this program and others like it will grow and become available to many others. It's very important for people to learn about others and gain respect for people's many differences for there to be peace and harmony in society.

Other statements focused on specific interactions:

It was 12:00, and I had a meeting with some inner-city youths that were coming to a college for the first time. I

really didn't know what to expect because this was my first time face-to-face with African Americans.

Being a person from rural Minnesota without much exposure to the African-American culture and heritage, it was a good way to open up the door to multicultural understanding in a non-threatening way for me.

It was fun just to hang out with someone from a different background....

I am glad that I had the opportunity to show three girls around during noon...I saw how proud they were of their culture. I would definitely want to have this experience offered to other MSU students.

I found spending time with the students from the Academy was a great learning experience. It broke down some of my stereotypes I've learned growing up.

I had a lot of reactions to the black students' visit to MSU. At first I was kind of reluctant to the idea of it helping us or them.... [Now] I think that it was worthwhile to bring them down for the day. It opened a lot of people's eyes. It was good for both groups. We learned a little about another culture and they learned a little about college life. I strongly feel that this should be continued.

Meeting all of these kids at one time was overwhelming for me.... I think we were all a little nervous right away. Nobody knew what to say or do during lunch. [But] I think this was a great idea for [this class]. It gave us a chance to learn things about people we don't get much contact with.

I didn't have one African-American student in my high school so I though it helped me to know only their color and cultures are different, not the way they act and respond. They were typical adolescents.

Taking a campus tour with a 14-year-old black boy was a very educational experience. I learned many things about this young teenager in a short time.... As the day went on I realized that the boy really was becoming more comfortable around me.... I really think that this is a good experience for all people and not just future teachers. Maybe if we had more of these kinds of exercises people would see that racism is really stupid.

The Follow-Up. Based on these positive responses, we immediately took the plunge and applied for funds to cover a full-year program—fall, winter, and spring quarter visits. Contacts were made with two other schools as potential partners in the project, one which has a large proportion of East Asian as well as African-American stu-

dents, and the other, an American Indian magnet school.

The program, initially referred to as "the Academy kids' visit," is now called "Linking Learners Across Cultures." It has been expanded so that each quarter three visits will occur between College of Education students and students in the public school classrooms: two will bring MSU students to the inner city classrooms where a "buddy system" between college and public school students will be set up. When the kids come for their campus visit, they will recognize some already-familiar faces.

As the project evolves, we are realizing just how much potential there is for additional opportunities as an outgrowth of the project. Most of our education students take clinical experiences in rural area schools and we have explored with at least one school the possibility of bringing the city kids—most of whom will already know the student teachers—for a day into these classrooms.

As the program continues, some of the inner-city students will have had opportunity for up to three college visits before they begin their high school studies. We hope to begin a longitudinal research project, tracking participating students' progress as they move through junior and senior high school, with the goal of comparing their school retention rates and college attendance rates with those students of similar cultural, socioeconomic backgrounds but who have not had pre-college experiences.

Even under the best of conditions, no one can argue that two or three experiences a year with kids from culturally diverse schools will enlarge these preservice teachers' "cultural comfort zones" so that they could successfully step into a culturally diverse classroom and feel totally at ease. However, there is every indication that these very human one-to-one connections have succeeded in significantly reducing students' anxieties about "the other" so that they may, on a voluntary basis, seek out additional experiences.

Most of those involved in the project are just beginning their professional education coursework. As they begin to feel more comfortable in diverse settings, they may request these for student-teaching placements—now an infrequent occurrence. The majority of teaching jobs in the future will be in urban areas and it is imperative that those who accept these positions have the best possible preparation for meeting the needs of their students. And even if they go back to their home-towns to teach, they'll bring with them not only some "multicultural curriculum," but the experiences which will bring that curriculum to life.

Why Johnny Can't Tell Right from Wrong

The most important lesson our schools don't teach

Kathleen Kennedy Townsend

Kathleen Kennedy Townsend is director of the Maryland Student Service Alliance of the Maryland Department of Education.

"What would you like to be when you graduate?" asked a grade school teacher of her students in a Baltimore County classroom I visited recently. A young man raised his hand: "A pimp. You can make good money." The teacher then turned to a female student and asked, "Would you work for him?" "I guess so," the young woman replied lethargically.

In my five years in the Maryland Department of Education, I've heard hundreds of similar stories—rueful teachers' lounge chronicles of abject moral collapse by children barely old enough to make grilled cheese sandwiches by themselves. But these days you don't need to work in education to hear such mind-numbing tales. Turn on the TV news and there you have it: Our schools are hotbeds of violence, vandalism, and unethical behavior. Recently we've heard of a student-run LSD ring in one Virginia school and the bartering of stolen college entrance exams in one of New York City's most selective high schools. Sixty-one percent of high school students say they cheated on an exam during the past year. Nationwide, assaults on teachers are up 700 percent since 1978. Each month 282,000 students are attacked. And for the first time ever, the risk of violence to teenagers is greater in school than on the streets.

Obviously, we've got a problem here—a problem not just of violence, but of values. Plain and simple, many of our kids don't seem to have any, or at least any of a socially constructive kind. But what to do about 12-year-old aspiring pimps and cheaters? You might think the solution lies with that "family values" constituency, the Republicans. Yet a year of podium-thumping in favor of "values" by the Bush administration was not backed by a single concrete plan of action. In his four years as president, George Bush offered nothing more substantial than a PR stunt—his Thousand Points of Light Foundation. Still, at least the Republicans have been willing to *talk* about values. For all of Bill Clinton's 12-point plans, he has yet to come up with a specific agenda for restoring values.

To explain away that omission, Democrats argue that the ultimate responsibility for inspiring values lies not with the government, but with the family. A day in one of the nation's public schools might well convince the average citizen that those Democrats need a reality check. Face it: In some homes, parents simply aren't paragons of civic or ethical virtue. If we rely on the family alone to instill values, we will fail. As one 21-year-old ex-con said, "Kids grow up with a father or an uncle who is robbing stores. They figure, 'If my father can do it, so can I.'" In other homes, parents simply aren't around. In a series of recent workshops sponsored by the Maryland state government, high school students suggested a number of solutions they thought would help them better withstand the antisocial pressures that buffet them. While much of what they said was expected—more information about drugs, greater student participation in school and county decisions-one was a real eye-opener: They asked that their parents have dinner with them more often.

A survey of 176 schools that have adopted a values curriculum found that 77 percent reported a decrease in discipline problems, 68 percent boasted an increase in attendance, and 64 percent showed a decrease in vandalism.

Ultimately, the goal should be to help parents raise kind and law-abiding children. But how do we get there? Why not turn to the one institution that sees the problem more closely than any, and that touches children on a regular and sustained basis: the public school. Why not teach values in school?

Before you dismiss this suggestion as a William Bennettesque ploy to end calls for more school resources, additional jobs programs, or parental-leave legislation—all worthy goals—hear me out. Teaching values does *not* mean using the classroom to push a particular point of view on any political issue—say, abortion or the death penalty—that has worked its way to the core of the values debate. We're not even talking about school prayer or requiring the Pledge of Allegiance. It's much simpler than that: Teaching values means quietly helping kids to learn honesty, responsibility, respect for others, the importance of serving one's community and nation—ideals which have sufficiently universal appeal to serve as the founding and guiding principles of this country. In the schools, values education means lessons about friendship and anger, stealing and responsibility, simply being polite, respecting others, serving the needs of those who may be less fortunate—all lessons sadly absent from today's curriculum.

Teaching these sorts of values does more than yield heartwarming anecdotes of students helping old ladies across the street. It brings results—tangible improvement to the lives of children and their families. A survey of 176 schools that have adopted a values curriculum found that 77 percent reported a decrease in discipline problems, 68 percent boasted an increase in attendance, and 64 percent showed a decrease in vandalism. Three years after the Jackie Robinson Middle School in New Haven, Connecticut, initiated a values curriculum, the number of student pregnancies went from 16 to zero. After the Merwin Elementary School in Irwindale, California, instituted a character education program, damage due to vandalism was reduced from $25,000 to $500; disciplinary action decreased by 80 percent; and—could it be?—academic test scores went up.

Teaching values is clearly worth the trouble. So why is "values education" still one of education's neglected stepchildren? Why is it that schools that now teach values are rare—most often independent efforts by one or two inspired educators? Because, despite the family values chitchat, there's been no political or popular consensus that values should be as much a part of the curriculum as reading and writing. We need a more organized approach. If we are ready to instill a sense of values in America's youth, it will take a concerted effort by both political leaders and educators to make it happen.

SELECTIVE SERVICE

So where to begin? How about with a notion relegated to the back burner in the get-it-while-you-can eighties: community service. Serving others is held in such low regard among our youth that 60 percent of high school students said in a recent survey they simply would not be willing to "volunteer to serve their community for a year." That's a remarkable figure not only because so many aren't willing to serve, but because so many of those who responded negatively have never served to begin with. The students' distaste for service could largely be a distaste for the unknown. But when students are exposed to this unknown—through activities such as tutoring, visiting the elderly, rehabilitating homeless shelters, lobbying for new laws—their reaction is appreciably different.

Alethea Kalandros, as a ninth-grade student in Baltimore County, missed more than 70 days of school and was tempted to drop out. The next year she missed two days of school. What happened? She enrolled in a program that allows her to volunteer at the Maryland School for the Blind. "It gives me a reason to come to school," she says. Alethea is part of Maryland's pioneering effort in promoting community service. While the program is now voluntarily offered by only a couple of schools, Maryland, after years of heated debate, recently became the first state to require all high school students to perform community service in order to graduate. Starting next year, all students entering the ninth grade must complete 75 hours of service or classes which incorporate service into the lesson, such as stream testing in an environmental course or writing about visits to the elderly in an English class. As part of the program, students are required to "prepare and reflect." This means, for instance, complementing working in a soup kitchen with learning about the most common causes of homelessness.

Any of a wide variety of activities fulfill the requirement, from repairing a local playground to tutoring fellow students. The impact, however, goes beyond helping the needy. Community service, as the limited experience in schools has shown, teaches students values and citizenship. For instance, while fourth, fifth, and sixth graders at Jackson Elementary School in Salt Lake City, Utah, were studying ground water pollution, they discovered that barrels of toxic waste were buried just four blocks from their school. They waged a vigorous public relations and fundraising campaign to clean up the site, eventually winning the support of the city's mayor. When this effort was stymied—Utah state law does not allow for private donations to clean up such sites—they lobbied the legislature and changed the statute. And while service programs can help students make a difference outside the school, they also have an impact inside the classroom: They make learning more interesting by simply helping students to understand how to apply textbook lessons in the real world.

Despite successes in experimental programs, stubborn resistance to community service from educators is still the norm, even in Maryland where the Superintendents Association, the PTA, and the local boards of education all fought against the new service requirement. One of the most common knee-jerk reactions is cost. But ask educators in Atlanta, Georgia, who have been operating a regional service program for eight years, and they'll tell you it doesn't cost a dime. Of course, that doesn't mean all service programs can be run as efficiently, but it does show that costs can be kept low.

Beyond that, the arguments against service become more strained. The president of the Maryland Teachers Association, for example, called the proposal "enforced servitude" and claimed that it violated the Thirteenth Amendment. What's really bothering the educators? Probably the fact that they would be required to change their teaching methods. As Pat McCarthy, vice-president of the Thomas Jefferson Center, a non-profit foundation specializing in values education, says, "The biggest impediment to values education is teacher education." You can't teach community service out of a textbook; it takes time and thought, which, of course, takes effort. And that, for some educators, is a tough concept to accept.

While community service teaches values through hands-on experience, that's but one piece of the puzzle. If we want to instill values, why not take an even more straightforward approach: Teach them directly. It may sound radical, especially when we are talking about methods like memorizing passages from the Bible, "bribing" kids with discounts at the school store to behave decently, permitting students in class discussions to describe problems they face at home, and allowing teachers to make it clear that they might not approve of some parents' values. But while students are sometimes taught that what happens at home is not always a good thing, teaching values does not mean separating the parents from the lessons. Quite the contrary, a smart values program includes parents, too. Before a values program at Gauger's Junior High in Newmark, Delaware, was implemented, 100 people—parents, teachers, students and community representatives—attended a two-day conference in which they learned about the purpose and goals of the program and the ways they could help implement it. Parents provided input and teachers knew they had community support. And in the end, nobody had to worry that little Petey would bounce home from values class clutching the collected works of Lyndon LaRouche.

Is it really possible to teach values that we all agree upon? Of course. In fact, schools in an indirect way already present students with a set of values that is universally respected: What are our efforts to integrate our schools and prohibitions against stealing or drinking in school if not an education in values? It's not difficult to take this type of thinking one step further, creating a curriculum that teaches other values that are universally accepted but are almost never actually taught directly to our youth. In districts such as Sweet Home, New York, and in Howard and Baltimore counties, Maryland, superintendents formed representative groups of community leaders that included people as ideologically diverse as fundamentalist ministers and ACLU attorneys. They held public forums and listened to community opinion and after months of extensive discussion, the groups produced a list of values with which everyone was comfortable. Now, when people in these communities ask, "Whose values?" they can proudly say "Ours.

At places like Hebbville Elementary in a low-income section of Baltimore County, the results are impressive. There, teachers hold out the promise of tutoring the mentally retarded as a reward for children who have finished their assignments, done well on a test, shown improvement, or been helpful in class. The students actually vie for the privilege. Tiesha was picked to help out in a class of 15 seven- and eight-year-olds whose IQs are in the 30–45 range. "I like being a helper," she says. "I tried to teach my cousin that 100 percent and 100 percent equal 200 percent. When I saw her write two, I was so happy."

At the Waverly Elementary school in Baltimore City, values lessons are taught through discussions about peer pressure. The teacher chooses 15 students, divides them into four groups, and asks them to perform skits about peer pressure. One skit involves Daniel, whose three hip classmates mock him because he wears non-brand-name tennis shoes. Daniel persuades his parents to buy Nikes and when he returns to school, the gang accepts him. In reflecting upon the skit, Daniel says, "All the friends were making the decision rather than me making my own decision." Another student said, "Daniel could have decided to be different." It is significant that the students made up this fact pattern. In the kids-and-sneakers stories you usually hear, children are assaulting each other for Air Jordans. Here, they are girding themselves to accept an alternative.

That's well and good, but we're still missing one crucial element: accountability. For values education to succeed and prosper, schools need to show that it's paying off in tangible ways. That means, for instance, keeping track of indicators such as rates of crime and vandalism in schools or the number of students involved in community service where values are being taught.

CLASS WAR

Many may resent this call for values as a way for parents to shirk their own responsibility onto someone else, or may see it as another passing fad. As for parents, they may cling to concerns about which values their children should learn. But our collective trepidations pale next to the alternative: another generation of children growing up without a moral compass.

Changing will take courage, but we can take heart from one fifth-grade class I watched where the topic was "the right to be an individual." The purpose was to help the children decide when their own actions are inappropriate and to develop strategies for improving their classmates' behavior. The discussion began with a very simple story about a boy named Bobby who never washed himself and had no friends. Eventually he realized that he'd have to take a bath if he wanted his classmates to ask him to play. The immediate lesson was about cleanliness—about as innocuous a value as you can find. But the moral had pertinence even for frequent bathers: Sometimes change is not only good, but necessary. That's a lesson that should resonate, not just with fifth-graders, but with the next administration. Clearly, the old ways of inculcating values in our kids are no longer working. We grownups have got to change our thinking, too.

Ethical Communication in the Classroom

Michelle Dabel

Michelle Dabel teaches high-school English and coordinates curriculum in Fremont County Schools in Lander, Wyoming. She is completing her dissertation for a doctorate in Education and Rhetoric at New Mexico State University. Ms. Dabel has been a secondary and postsecondary teacher since 1975.

Most teachers would probably contend that they are good, effective communicators. After all, what is education if not the practice of effective communication? All that is positive or negative ultimately depends on communication and the use of language. But is there good ethical communication in the classroom—communication that exhibits equity of dialogue, mutual respect, and values the audience over the message?

The film about Nazi Germany ends. The fluorescent lights flicker back on. The teacher walks to the front of the room before the silence is broken. "If any of you think that the Nazis were right, then you are warped. Go ahead, open your texts to the questions, and get started."

The teacher finishes reading the fairy tale about the princess choosing a husband as her prince. The teacher closes the book and says, "Well, guys, I guess you just have to accept that women like rich men. Okay, it's break time. You have five minutes to go to the restroom. If you come back late, you won't get another break for the rest of the week."

The teacher begins a social studies activity. "I know that you have all heard something about the Clarence Thomas hearings. Do you know that the reason he was so controversial is that his would be a decisive, tie-breaking vote on the Supreme Court? Now, I know that you might have opinions on his stance on certain issues. We can't really discuss them, but think about them."

Interchanges of this type are fairly common every day in some American classrooms. Observation by educators and researchers indicates that teacher-talk, instruction giving, seatwork, and passive learning dominate the classroom (Apple 1985; Cazden 1988; Goodlad 1984; Shor 1986). In his monumental research of 1,000 American public schools, Goodlad (1984, 194) found strong similarities of how teachers teach. He generally describes classrooms as emotionally flat. Even when teachers start out with sound pedagogy and strong communication skills, the demands after a few years make them turn "to routines that make the least physical and emotional demands." Yet he found that successful schools "are more different, it seems, in the somewhat elusive qualities making up their ambience—the ways students and teachers relate to one another . . . ." Could this ambience be the levels of ethical communication? In some schools this type of communication does not seem to flourish. Why?

One-Way Communication

Instead of two-way communication, many teachers use one-way communication. This practice may arise because of a teacher's need to control, feelings of fear, or simply the belief that school is supposed to be that way. One main concern of teachers is control. As Elbow (1986) put it, "much teaching behavior really stems from an unwarranted fear of things falling apart." Elbow realized after studying and teaching for many years that a great deal of fear drove his teaching practices, a fear that "some unspecifiable chaos or confusion would ensue." He came to feel that this fear was unwarranted and found that in his own teaching, even when all did not go as planned, the students recovered—or found a new idea—and went on having learned something from the experience. How much extra control or power do teachers hoard that is driven by this underlying fear? Perhaps this fear changes classroom communication to the point of disempowering students. Perhaps it is this fear that creates unethical communication.

Cazden's (1988, 168) research on classroom discourse revealed teachers' perceptions of their own authority and social distance. Comparing distance on a continuum from close family members to fearful strangers, many teachers place themselves rather far from their students. "Many classroom observers have commented on the social distance that teachers either feel or wish to maintain between themselves and their students." She asks, "Even if teachers start most school years feeling like strangers to their students, why do these features of distance persist? Is it possible without expressions of humor and affection to achieve a shared sense of community?" This is also a call for good communication, effective

From *Kappa Delta Pi Record*, Spring 1993, pp. 80-84. © 1993 by Kappa Delta Pi, an International Honor Society in Education. Reprinted by permission.

classroom discourse—ethical communication.

This distancing sounds like the old cliché told to new teachers, "Don't smile until Christmas unless you want them walking all over you." Can there be a balance between control and unalienating communication? If a teacher chooses to be an ethical communicator, certainly he or she does not have to give up leadership control. Can students handle the dialogic, two-way give-and-take of ethical communication? Surely teachers can. If a teacher avoids two-way communication to maintain control, is the alienation of students a certain outcome? It often looks like the issue of control is juxtaposed with ethical communication.

Booth (1963) identifies the pedantic stance as one of three "unbalanced stances," the other two being the entertainer and the advertiser. He claims that the pedant ignores or undervalues the audience and focuses on the subject. The speaker's attitude toward the audience is a take-it-or-leave-it stance of neutrality and indifference. This unbalanced pedantic stance seems present in the illustration given above of a teacher's comments about the Nazis. He does not value the students' (audience's) opinion, focuses on the subject, and delivers a take-it-or-leave-it comment before moving on to material he has predetermined, perhaps to distract them from formulating any kind of response. Would not the teacher's stance—making a personal value judgment about student beliefs and trying to control their thinking—alienate them, no matter what their beliefs about Hitler were? What about the other teacher who believes that students cannot discuss politics? Is this a fear of losing control or a feeling of indifference to student opinions? Do the teachers reflect a caring attitude? Scorn?

These interactions have raised the idea of communication as dialogue rather than monologue. After all, true communication is not a one-way but a two-way transaction. Equity in communication cannot exist where there is no chance for one of the parties involved to respond. Unethical communication exists when there is little or no chance for an exchange of ideas (Johannesen 1990).

Buber (1958) examined two basic models of human relationships: I-Thou and I-It. He believed that the stance taken in a relationship directly affects communication. The I-Thou stance is characterized by openness, respect, and mutuality. The I-It stance, on the other hand, is characterized as perfunctory, unequal, and exploitative. In the I-It stance, people become "things," and the emphasis is on the communicator's message, not on the audience. Consequences are exaggerated, and choice is remote. The communicator's purpose is to coerce and command the listener. Is not this unethical communication? Is not this descriptive of a teacher's stance common in the classroom? Is it possible to resolve this dilemma?

Equal Communication

Habermas (1982) sets forth the "ideal speech situation," which he further discusses in terms of a discourse ethic. The four criteria call for *equal* opportunities to those involved to (1) initiate and continue communication, (2) express feelings, (3) forbid or permit communication, and (4) air all significant opinions. What does this mean in terms of the teacher who did not think that her students had significant opinions about the princess's choice? Students did not have an equal opportunity to initiate communication or express feelings. If the teacher was not willing to deal with student response to the fairy tale, why did she read it? What about student reaction to the comment about "how women are"? If the speaker (teacher) diminishes the worth or opinions of the audience

(students)—no matter what age, what number, or what subject matter—a skewed communication will result. What price control?

Looking again from the perspective of classroom discourse, how does this control manifest itself in schools? There may be communication rules for students—no talking, no whispering, no laughing, no turning to look at classmates, no passing notes, etc.—yet teachers can interrupt anybody anytime. On one level, students come to accept this as a well-established pattern in school, but on another level—especially as they develop opinions and independence—students become resentful and alienated and begin to resist authority. As Cazden (1988) points out, this lopsided communication also means that often the ones who need to communicate the most receive the least. Students who are shy, linguistically different, or otherwise insecure about communicating need reinforcement, practice, and a chance to "read" cues about language usage.

Spoken language creates social identity. In order to learn and grow, students need to use language in a school or social setting to begin to understand differences in how and when one says certain things. "While other institutions such as hospitals serve their clients in nonlinguistic ways, the basic purpose of school is achieved through communication" (Cazden 1988, 2). Classroom discourse affects the thought processes of students. What do students learn from unethical communication? Probably they do not learn humane and democratic values.

Elbow (1986, 69) states that teaching behaviors will be right "so long as they rest upon a symmetrical premise: an equal affirmation of the student's experience, his right to ground his behaviors in his experience . . . to embark on his own voyage of change. . . ." He feels that many poor teaching behaviors result from "some kind of pathology . . . the hunger to tell people things they did not ask you to tell them . . . unsolicited telling" that detracts from student growth and understanding. Elbow humorously states that we should "set up other arenas where teachers can work off this appetite."

Perhaps some classroom teachers may find this whole argument naive. Perhaps they would claim that teachers cannot practice ethical communication in the classroom. Some of the arguments or comments they may make follow. "The students are an unequal element of the communication seesaw. The students are not "heavy" enough to hold the weight. If the teacher permitted students to freely choose options, initiate dialogue, or air significant ideas, they would go wild and spiral completely out of control, running roughshod over the teacher. The class would never get anything done. Students must know their boundaries. They have little to offer because they are inexperienced, lacking knowledge and worthwhile opinions. Teachers have far too many students to let them all give voice to their opinions. They only reflect their parents' ideas and have not developed real opinions yet. Teachers are not therapists. They do not have time to help every student work out an opinion. The teacher's purpose is to dispense content knowledge and assess the students' progress. Teachers have a job to do! Let people engage in ethical communication elsewhere! It simply isn't practical or feasible in schools!"

Ethical Communication Strategies

So, where does this leave the argument? Teachers at this point have three choices: (1) The teacher can accept that he is not an ethical communicator because of any number of other priorities and sign off. (2) The teacher can say he or she already is an ethical communicator, practicing all of the criteria listed above. (3) Or the teacher can say that he or she would like to move toward becoming a

> What do students learn from unethical communication? Probably they do not learn humane and democratic values.

more ethical communicator by working out effective methods to manage the classroom and/or large numbers of students.

From my work at the secondary and postsecondary levels, I have observed and practiced strategies that assist in my becoming a more ethical communicator. For example, a teacher needs to be careful who is reinforced with feedback. Rather than take the first articulated answer, usually by an outspoken and successful student, the teacher can encourage others to build on an initial response or challenge the first student to carry the thought further, to think more deeply or in a different way. The teacher must ask himself why he judges particular discourse meaningful or even profound. On what criteria does a teacher use to base a decision? Just asking a question creates meaning. Carlsen (1991), examining questioning from a sociolinguistic perspective, states that "classroom questions are not simply teacher behaviors but mutual constructions of teachers and students." Teachers need to encourage students to formulate questions and answers for themselves. After all, asking a good question is often the first step in acquiring knowledge.

Another strategy, using analogy and metaphor to present ideas and concepts, can often help students see old thoughts in a new light. This is part of ethical communication because, rather than pushing ideas and biases on students, the teacher can structure an opportunity for them to examine attitudes freely. The teacher could use the analogy of a leaky roof, for example, to describe to teacher education students how the

goal of multicultural education is a challenge to the schools. If the roof is not leaking, everything is fine. If the roof is obviously dripping into the room, measures will be taken to fix it, but again everything will be fine. But if the roof is leaking into the structure of the building, hidden from sight, measures will not be taken to fix it, and eventually, the roof will fall in, harming the students and staff. Using such an analogy may externalize or objectify an idea in a way that will allow students to think more abstractly. The teacher can use a premise or begin questions with "What if . . .?" statements.

The teacher can try to be thoughtful, if not guarded, about expressing "expert" views. Teachers can monitor teacher talk, which can be very intimidating to a free exchange of ideas or may encourage students to manipulate opinions to garnish favor. Teachers can create and nurture an environment for student voices. They can strive to create a place of respect and safety where silent voices can be heard. Encouraging reluctant students, especially minority students, to participate and communicate reduces their feelings of marginality and gives other students a chance to hear about alternate social realities (Bigelow 1990). The students can examine their historical and biographical identity development. This should give them a clearer sense of why they think as they do.

When striving for ethical communication, basic attention to interpersonal skills is helpful. As Cazden (1988) points out, "classrooms are among the most crowded human environments." As a result, communication becomes abrupt, perfunctory, and routine. Common courtesy , which would be practiced elsewhere, is often dropped, especially when dealing with difficult students. The teacher should know students' names and establish eye contact whenever possible.

Ethical communication has to contain a sense that the speaker values the listener. An ethical communicator must exhibit involvement and a desire to understand the audience. Taking time to listen indicates to the student that he or she is worth the extra time. Saying "thank you" and "you are welcome" can be quite uplifting to a student. These are the common social graces that are often abandoned in the classroom. The students need to believe that the teacher is genuine and wishes them to reach their potential. How often can a teacher be heard to say "If you flunk, it is your own problem," or "If you don't turn in the assignment, it is just one less paper for me to grade"?

This is not to turn ethical communication into a superficial exercise in polite conversation. True, teachers have heavy workloads, which lead to frustration and fatigue. However, knowing that teachers have reasons for being abrupt or indifferent probably will not help students on a day-to-day basis nor will this fact make an unethical communication an ethical one. Also, ethical communication does not rule out confrontation and debate. Teachers can usually find a way to help students articulate and vent their

frustrations. Working in small groups or writing about the topic can release much tension. Talking to students individually to promote mutual understanding can help a teacher see students' concerns more clearly. If the group is not too large, individual conferences can work miracles.

Teachers who want to be recognized as professionals have a mandate to practice ethical communication, regardless of the circumstances. If our school settings work against such a mandate, then we must change the circumstances under which we labor. Ours and our students' futures teeter in the balance.

The film about Nazi Germany ends. The fluorescent lights flicker back on. The teacher remains near the switch as students begin to talk. "That was a disturbing film, wasn't it? Let's take some time to discuss your reactions. We might consider that there are students of Jewish or German heritage among us who have mixed feelings about what happened. Let's hear some of your opinions."

The class finishes an oral reading of a fairy tale about a princess choosing a husband. The teacher says, "Wow, things have really changed in the way people choose spouses. Let's take some time to discuss our ideas about this tale. First, clarify your thoughts in a five-minute writing. What does this story say about men and women? How do you feel about the princess's choice? What would you have done if you were one of the characters? Okay, start writing, and in five minutes we will take our break. When we come back, we will begin talking about it."

The teacher opens the class. "How many of you heard about or watched the Clarence Thomas hearings? This will be the basis for discussion today. Remember the format we established: taking turns, no shouting or name-calling, respecting others' opinions. We all need to learn how to develop our opinions with others in society. That is how democracy works. Okay now, who wants to start?"

References

Apple, M. W. 1985. *Education and power.* Boston: Ark Paperbacks.

Bigelow, W. 1990. Inside the classroom: Social vision and critical pedagogy. *Teachers College Record* 91:437–48.

Booth, W. C. 1963. The rhetorical stance. *College Composition and Communication* 14:139–45.

Buber, M. 1958. *I and thou.* New York: Scribners.

Carlsen, W. S. 1991. Questioning in classrooms: A sociolinguistic perspective. *Review of Educational Research* 61:157–78.

Cazden, C. B. 1988. *Classroom discourse.* Portsmouth, N.H.: Heinemann Educational Books.

Elbow, P. 1986. *Embracing contraries: Explorations in learning and teaching.* New York: Oxford.

Goodlad, J. I. 1984. *A place called school.* New York: McGraw-Hill.

Habermas, J. 1982. A reply to my critics. In *Habermas: Critical debates,* ed. J. B. Thompson and D. Held. Cambridge: MIT Press.

Johannesen, R. L. 1990. *Ethics in human communication.* 3rd ed. Prospect Heights, Ill.: Waveland.

Shor, I. 1986. Equality is excellence: Transforming teacher education and the learning process. *Harvard Educational Review* 56:406–26.

Managing Life in Classrooms

All teachers have concerns regarding the quality of "life" in classroom settings. All teachers and students want to feel safe and accepted when they are in school. There exists today a reliable, effective knowledge base on classroom management and the prevention of disorder in schools. This knowledge base has been developed from hundreds of studies of teacher-student interaction and student-student interaction that have been conducted in schools in North America and Europe. We speak of managing life in classrooms because we now know that there are many factors that go into building effective teacher-student and student-student relationships. The traditional term *discipline* is too narrow and refers primarily only to teachers' reactions to undesired student behavior. We can better understand methods of managing student behavior when we look at the totality of what goes on in classrooms, with teacher responses to student behavior as a part of that totality. Teachers have tremendous responsibility for the emotional climate that is set in a classroom. Whether students feel secure and safe and whether they want to learn depend to an enormous extent on the psychological frame of mind of the teacher. Teachers must be able to manage their own selves first in order to manage effectively the development of a humane and caring classroom environment.

Teachers bear moral and ethical responsibilities for being witnesses to and examples of responsible social behavior in the classroom. There are many models of observing life in classrooms. When one speaks of life in classrooms, arranging the total physical environment of the room is a very important part of the teacher's planning for learning activities. Teachers need to expect the best work and behavior from students that they are capable of achieving. Respect and caring are attitudes that a teacher must communicate to receive them in return. Open lines of communication between teachers and students enhance the possibility for congenial, fair dialogical resolution of problems as they occur.

Developing a high level of task orientation among students and encouraging cooperative learning and shared task achievement will foster camaraderie and self-confidence among students. Shared decision making will build an *esprit de corps,* a sense of pride and confidence, which will feed on itself and blossom into high-quality performance. Good class morale, well-managed, never hurts academic achievement. The importance of emphasizing quality, helping students to achieve levels of performance they can feel proud of having attained, and encouraging positive dialogue among them leads them to take ownership in their individual educative efforts. When that happens, they literally empower themselves to do their best.

When teachers (and prospective teachers) discuss what concerns them about their roles (and prospective roles) in the classroom, the issue of discipline, how to manage student behavior, will usually rank near or at the top of their lists. A teacher needs a clear understanding of what kinds of learning environments are most appropriate for the subject matter and ages of the students. Any person who wants to teach must also want his or her students to learn well, to acquire basic values of respect for others, and to become more effective citizens.

There is considerable debate among educators regarding certain approaches used in schools to achieve a form of order in classrooms that also develops respect for self and others. The dialogue about this point is spirited and informative. The bottom line for any effective and humane approach to discipline in the classroom, the necessary starting point, is the teacher's emotional balance and capacity for self-control. This precondition creates a further one—that the teacher wants to be in the classroom with his or her students in the first place. Unmotivated teachers cannot motivate students.

Helping young people learn the skills of self-control and motivation to become productive, contributing, and knowledgeable adult participants in society is one of the most important tasks that good teachers undertake. These are teachable and learnable skills; they do not relate to heredity or social conditions. They can be learned by any human being who wants to learn them and who is cognitively able to learn them. We know also that these skills are learnable by virtually all but the most severely cognitively disabled persons. There is a large knowledge base on how teachers can help students learn self-control. All that is required is the willingness of teachers to learn these skills themselves and to teach them to their students. No topic is more fundamentally related to any thorough examination of the social and cultural founda-

Unit 5

on the emotional tone and ethical principles implied by their own behaviors. To optimize their chances of achieving the classroom atmosphere that they wish, teachers must strive for emotional balance within themselves; they must learn to be accurate observers; and they must develop just, fair strategies of intervention to aid students in learning self-control and good behavior. To repeat, a teacher is a good model of courtesy, respect, tact, and discretion. Children learn by observing how other persons behave and not just by being told how they are to behave. There is no substitute for positive, assertive teacher interaction with students in class.

This unit addresses many of the topics covered in basic foundations courses. The selections shed light on classroom management issues, teacher leadership skills, the legal foundations of education, and the rights and responsibilities of teachers and students. In addition, the articles can be discussed in foundations courses involving curricula and instruction. This unit falls between the units on moral education and equal opportunity because it can be directly related to either or both of them.

Looking Ahead: Challenge Questions

What are some things that can be done to help students and teachers to feel safe in school?

What is a good technique for learning self-control?

What should be the behavioral standards in schools? On what factors should they be based?

Does peer mediation seem like a workable approach? Why, or why not?

What ethical issues may be raised in the management of student behavior in school settings?

What reliable information is available on the extent and severity of school discipline problems in North America? What sources contain such information?

What civil rights do students have? Do public schools have fewer rights than private schools in controlling student behavior problems? Why, or why not? What are the rights of a teacher in managing student behavior?

Do any coercive approaches to behavioral management in schools work better than noncoercive ones?

Why is teacher self-control a major factor in just and effective classroom management strategies?

—F. S.

tions of education. There are many sound techniques that new teachers can use to achieve success in managing students' classroom behavior, and they should not be afraid to ask colleagues questions and to develop peer support groups with whom they can work with confidence and trust.

Teachers' core ethical principles come into play when deciding what constitutes defensible and desirable standards of student conduct. As in medicine, realistic preventive techniques combined with humane but clear principles of procedure seem to be most effective. Teachers need to realize that before they can control behavior, they must identify what student behaviors are desired in their classrooms. They need to reflect, as well,

Conflict Resolution and Peer Mediation

Pathways to Safer Schools

Aline M. Stomfay-Stitz

Aline M. Stomfay-Stitz is Associate Professor, Education Department, Christopher Newport University, Newport News, Virginia.

Most educators will agree that finding ways to resolve conflict peaceably in America's schools may be our primary challenge. As waves of violence and incidents of racial and societal unrest spill over into our classrooms, we must take a closer look at the process for building safer, more harmonious schools.

Conflict Resolution and Peer Mediation Defined

Conflict resolution is a method or strategy that enables people to interact with each other in positive ways in order to resolve their differences. Peer mediation programs are based on a foundation of applied conflict resolution. Such programs empower students to share responsibility for creating a safe, secure school environment. Mediators help their peers to summarize the main points of their dispute and puzzle out possible solutions. Schoolchildren learn essential skills, such as intervention and conflict prevention.

Those who study conflict resolution generally identify its origin with Mary Parker Follett's research in the 1920s. Follett concentrated on "problem solving as integration of the needs of the bargainers" (Follett, 1941; Fogg, 1985). Since that time, the field of conflict resolution has expanded as a tool for business management, intergroup and community mediation, divorce, juvenile justice, civil courts and international negotiations.

A Theoretical or Research Base

The research base for conflict resolution and peer mediation includes the theories of Jean Piaget, Lev Vygotsky, Albert Bandura and Kurt Lewin. Morton Deutsch, David and Roger Johnson and others conducted research on the effects of cooperative and competitive classroom settings.

During middle childhood, children continually assess, weigh and judge their experiences in school, absorbing new behaviors into their existing knowledge. Piaget's cognitive development theory states that children will assimilate and accommodate new experiences into ones previously learned. The added context of social interaction, especially with one's peers, enhances the cognitive development process. Essentially, children need to watch adults think through problems so that they can practice those newly observed skills themselves (Seifert, 1993). Students hone these skills when they verbally and mentally work their way through the problem-solving process.

Vygotsky's theories on children's thinking emphasized a process in which children shared problem-solving experiences with a teacher, parent or peer. As a result, children's own language and thought intermingled and served as the vehicle for their own development (Vygotsky, 1962).

Social learning theorists, particularly Albert Bandura and Kurt Lewin, contributed to the research base. Bandura emphasized that children are essential actors and agents in their own learning and behavior as they model, observe and duplicate responses to a social situation (Seifert, 1993; Catron & Allen, 1993). Furthermore, those who observe conflict resolution or peer mediation confirm that an intellectual and emotional impact results when a potentially dangerous conflict is resolved and disputants "save face" and continue with their school lives.

Kurt Lewin's field theory is of special interest. Specifically, Lewin warned that "one has to face the education situation with all its social and cultural implications as one concrete dynamic whole . . . analysis must be a 'gestalt-theoretical' one" (Maruyama, 1992). Lewin believed that the individual in a school setting is affected by personal and environmental variables that have an impact on student behavioral outcomes (Maruyama, 1992). Equally important is the way that authority figures structure the environment and reward the system—what Lewin calls the "social climate" (Maruyama, 1992). Accordingly, Lewin delineated the concept of conflict as a situation in which forces acting on the individual move in opposite directions.

From *Childhood Education*, Vol. 70, No. 5, Annual Theme Issue, 1994, pp. 279-282. Reprinted by permission of the Association for Childhood Education International, 11501 Georgia Avenue, Suite 315, Wheaton, MD. © 1994.

For several decades, Morton Deutsch (Deutsch, 1949, 1973, 1991) and David and Roger Johnson (Johnson & Johnson, 1979, 1989, 1991) have emphasized that cooperative, rather than competitive, relationships within the classroom's social milieu create the constructive, positive environment that fosters true learning and conflict resolution. The Johnsons believe that students can learn to respect others' viewpoints through controversy experiences. The structured controversy approach can enhance and open students' minds to differing or opposing views (Johnson & Johnson, 1991).

Used as a corequisite with conflict resolution, cooperative learning permits students to practice skills, communicate and solve problems. Their social/emotional skills are likewise enhanced as they learn to listen to the ideas of others and to clarify, summarize, gather and analyze data. Such skills encourage reflective listening, compromise and an honest expression of feelings (Nattiv, Render, Lemire & Render, 1989).

One current education model has been described as a peace education curriculum; that is, it helps children understand and learn to resolve conflicts in peaceful ways. A multi-disciplinary group of researchers (Spodek & Brown, 1993) recommends that peace education curriculum teach children skills in negotiating, conflict resolution and problem-solving. An interrelated focus would include cooperative learning, conflict resolution and education for peace (Deutsch, 1991). The concept of peace education is multifaceted and cross-disciplinary, including peace and social justice, economic well-being, political participation, nonviolence, conflict resolution and concern for the environment (Stomfay-Stitz, 1993).

Objectives for Peer Mediation
A peer mediation program's first objective is to ensure that *all* students have learned the basic skills required to resolve conflicts. Usually, a guidance counselor or teacher supervises 15-20 hours of training. Peer mediators may be nominated by teachers or chosen by peers. Johnson and Johnson suggest that *all* students serve as peer mediators after mastering the basic skills. Peer mediators are assigned specific days and hours during which they are "on call" to handle conflicts that arise throughout the school (Johnson & Johnson, 1991).

Complementary goals would include teaching respect for the differences of others and encouraging attitudes and values required for a harmonious classroom. In Montgomery County, Maryland, the basic program emphasizes sensitivity to cultural diversity and provides mediation services for students fluent in Spanish and Vietnamese. A federal court order to desegregate schools in Westchester County, New York, sparked interest in peer mediation in that community. Their middle schools and high schools instituted such programs in 1987 (National Peace Foundation, 1991).

Basic Skills for Peer Mediation
One model program, Peace Works, developed by the Peace Education Foundation, provides a student mediation manual that carefully explains the basic skills for peer mediation. The program urges students to listen carefully, be fair, ask how each disputant feels, keep what they are told confidential and mediate in private. At the same time, they should not try to place blame, ask who started it, take sides or give advice (Schmidt, Friedman & Marvel, 1991).

Benefits of Peer Mediation
Strategies to prevent conflicts and identify situations that could provoke violence often include students, parents and school personnel—truly the entire school community. New York City's Project SMART teaches alternatives to violence, focusing on student/teacher conflicts. The program resulted in fewer incidents of vandalism and calls to police (National Peace Foundation, 1991).

Peer mediation may also include intervention strategies for situations with the potential for conflict, such as play behavior and playground disputes. Researchers criticized school staffs' lack of concern in fully addressing bullying as a widespread problem (Hazler, Hoover & Oliver, 1992). An older study revealed that victimization by bullies reaches its highest level during the middle school years (Hazler, Hoover & Oliver, 1991). In a videotape describing the Conflict Manager Program, a former bully describes how, as a peer mediator, he slowly came to understand his victims' viewpoints and how his behavior harmed the weaker and smaller students (Community Board of San Francisco, 1992). Bullying should receive wider attention in school peer mediation programs.

Students, faculty and administrators who participated in a detailed program at Greer Elementary School in Charlottesville, Virginia, reported positive results. Teachers reported that "pressure on teachers to serve as disciplinarians" decreased as a result of the program. The 5th-grade students themselves reported using "creative solutions when given the opportunity." They came to show greater respect for each other as they grew more adept at using their communication and problem-solving skills. The researcher recommended that peer mediation and conflict resolution skills be infused or "embedded in the entire curriculum and philosophy of a school." In cases where "the decision-making in the class is teacher-dictated, the program would be ineffective" (Stuart, 1991).

In a second study at a rural elementary school in West Virginia, the school counselor taught conflict resolution and peer mediation skills to 80 5th-graders. Results showed a decrease in behavior problems in the classroom, on the playground and in referrals to the principal's office (Messing, 1992).

Schools continue to report their success with conflict resolution and individual peer mediation programs. While many results are based on anecdotal evidence, several are based on data collected from students, faculty and administrators. A pilot program in Minnesota that was based on the Peacemaker Program reported that the "frequency of student-student conflicts . . . dropped 80 percent" while conflicts referred to the principal were reduced to zero (Johnson, Johnson, Dudley & Burnett, 1992). A Wisconsin middle school reported that 189 successful student disputes were mediated during the first six months of its program (Koch & Miller, 1987).

One researcher described a "ripple effect" from the programs. Parents and students indicated that they were resolving their home conflicts "in new and more productive ways" (Lane & McWhirter, 1991) and with noticeable benefits to sibling relationships (Gentry & Benenson, 1993).

Peer relationships are powerful ones, based on social interactions that can help others to learn, share and help each other. Each year of development makes the process more complex and inclusive. Peer relationships will eventually supplant the influence of family for children. Thus, autonomy, achievement and social skills are all influenced by peer relationships (Benard, 1990).

Success of System-wide and State-wide Programs

In recent years, entire school systems have adopted detailed plans for conflict resolution and peer mediation. The school system in Ann Arbor, Michigan, has included the Conflict Manager Program in all schools and summer neighborhood community centers (National Peace Foundation, 1991).

Several national organizations are helping to disseminate instructional and training materials, and also are serving as clearinghouses and networks for those interested in conflict resolution and peer mediation. Educators for Social Responsibility (ESR) reported greater demand for training in their Resolving Conflict Creatively Program (RCCP). Education organizations have also joined the effort. Phi Delta Kappa and the Association for Supervision and Curriculum Development have planned professional development institutes. The National Association for Mediation in Education (NAME), the Consortium for Peace, Research, Education and Development (COPRED), the National Institute for Dispute Resolution (NIDR) and the Children's Creative Response to Conflict (CCRC) all work to enhance knowledge and research on conflict resolution and peer mediation.

Ohio deserves attention as a leader in the creation of community and school-based projects under a model known as the Ohio Commission on Dispute Resolution and Conflict Management (OCDRCM). A three-year data collection and evaluation project is currently underway to assess the effect of pilot programs in mediation and conflict resolution in 17 schools throughout the state (OCDRCM, 1993). In New Mexico, a state-wide model included over 60 schools (K-12), in addition to juvenile justice, family and victim offender mediation programs (New Mexico Center for Dispute Resolution, 1993).

Conclusion

Peer mediation programs in the schools offer alternatives to violence. Instead of physical fights, threats and verbal abuse, students are taught specific communications and conflict resolution skills. These skills lead students and their peer mediators through a process of critical thinking and problem-solving in order to arrive at a mutually beneficial solution. Susan Schultz of the Ann Arbor Public Schools

assessed the benefits that accrued from their system-wide initiative:

Teaching conflict management skills is good. For the children to see adults around them using conflict management skills is better. For both the children and the adults to use these skills at school, at home, at work, and at play is best. (National Peace Foundation, 1991)

Clearly, conflict resolution and peer mediation offer viable opportunities for an entire school community to create a safer, more harmonious world. At the same time, growing numbers of educators have recognized that, through such programs, students are learning skills that have wider applications. These skills have the potential to create safer and more peaceful homes, schools and communities.

References

Benard, B. (1990). *The case for peers.* Portland, OR: Northwest Regional Educational Laboratory. ED 327-755.

Catron, C. E., & Allen, J. (1993). *Early childhood curriculum.* Columbus, OH: Merrill.

Community Board of San Francisco. (1992). Conflict Manager Program, videotape.

Deutsch, M. (1949). A theory of cooperation and competition. *Human Relations, 2,* 129-152.

Deutsch, M. (1973). *The resolution of conflict.* New Haven, CT: Yale University Press.

Deutsch, M. (1991). Educating beyond hate. *Peace, Environment, and Education, 2*(4), 3-19.

Fogg, R. W. (1985). Dealing with conflict: A repertoire of creative, peaceful approaches. *Journal of Conflict Resolution, 29*(2), 330-358.

Follett, M. P. (1941). *The collected papers of Mary Parker Follett.* London: Pittman.

Gentry, D. B., & Benenson, W. A. (1993). School-to-home transfer of conflict management skills among school-age children. *Families in Society: The Journal of Contemporary Human Services, 4*(2), 67-73.

Hazler, R., Hoover, J. H., & Oliver, R. (1991). Student perceptions of victimization by bullies in school. *Journal of Humanistic Education and Development, 29,* 143-150.

Hazler, R., Hoover, J. H., & Oliver, R. (November, 1992). What kids say about bullying. *Executive Educator, 14*(11), 20-22.

Johnson, D., & Johnson, R. (1979). *Circles of learning.* Edina, MN: Interaction Book.

Johnson, D., & Johnson, R. (1989). *Cooperation and competition: Theory and research.* Edina, MN: Interaction Book.

Johnson, D., & Johnson, R. (1991). *Teaching students to be peacemakers.* Edina, MN: Interaction Book.

Johnson, D. W., Johnson, R. T., Dudley, B., & Burnett, R. (1992). Teaching students to be peer mediators. *Educational Leadership, 50*(1), 10-13.

Koch, M. S., & Miller, S. (1987). Resolving student conflicts with student mediators. *Principal, 66,* 59-61.

Lane, P. S., & McWhirter, J. J. (1992). A peer mediation model: Conflict resolution for elementary and middle school children. *Elementary School Guidance and Counseling, 27,* 15-23.

Maruyama, G. (1992). Lewin's impact on education: Instilling cooperation and conflict management skills in school children. *Journal of Social Issues, 48*(2), 155-159.

Messing, J. K. (1992). *Impact of conflict resolution curriculum on elementary school students' perception of conflict and problem solving.* Charleston, WV: Appalachia Educational Laboratory.

National Peace Foundation (1991, Fall). Where does peace education stand today? *Peace Reporter,* 1-12.

Nattiv, A., Render, G. F., Lemire, D., & Render, K. R. (1989). Conflict resolution and interpersonal skill building through the use of cooperative learning. *Journal of Humanistic Education and Development, 28,* 96-101.

New Mexico Center for Dispute Resolution. (1993). Brochure and Publications. Albuquerque, NM: Author.

Ohio Commission on Dispute Resolution and Conflict Management. (1993). *Model school program in conflict resolution and peer mediation.* Columbus, OH: Author.

Schmidt, F., Friedman, A., & Marvel, J. (1992). *Mediation for kids: Kids in dispute settlement.* Miami, FL: Peace Education Foundation.

Seifert, K. L. (1993). Cognitive development and early childhood education. In B. Spodek (Ed.), *Handbook of research on the education of young children* (pp. 9-23). New York: Macmillan.

Spodek, B., & Brown, P. C. (1993). Curriculum alternatives in early childhood education. In B. Spodek (Ed.), *Handbook of research on the education of young children* (pp. 91-104). New York: Macmillan.

Stomfay-Stitz, A. (1993). *Peace education in America 1828-1990. Sourcebook for education and research.* Metuchen, NJ: Scarecrow Press.

Stuart, L. A. (1991). *Conflict resolution using mediation skills in the elementary schools.* Charlottesville, VA: University of Virginia. ED 333 258.

Vygotsky, L. (1962). *Thought and language.* Cambridge, MA: MIT Press.

CONFLICT RESOLUTION PROGRAMS

FOUR LEADING MODELS FOR CONFLICT RESOLUTION IN THE SCHOOLS, Community Board of San Francisco, 149 Ninth St., San Francisco, CA 94103
Students are trained as conflict managers or mediators. The program can be used in elementary, middle and secondary schools. Curriculum guide, videotapes and training materials for students and teachers are available.

TEACHING STUDENTS TO BE PEACEMAKERS, David and Roger Johnson, 7208 Cornelia Dr., Edina, MN 55435
Designed for grades K-12, this program is based on the cooperative learning approach and can be integrated into the curriculum. All students receive training in direct negotiation and mediation skills. All students eventually serve as peer mediators, learn to resolve conflicts with their peers and serve as "official mediators" on the playground and in the lunchroom. They are also available to mediate conflicts during the day.

CHILDREN'S CREATIVE RESPONSE TO CONFLICT, Fellowship of Reconciliation, Box 271, Nyack, NY 10960
This approach is based on a series of activities for K-12 classrooms that stress cooperation, communication, affirmation and conflict resolution. The program is used widely at the elementary level and with children with special needs.

PEACE WORKS, Peace Education Foundation, 2627 Biscayne Blvd., Miami, FL 33137-4532
This model develops positive interpersonal and communication skills with special respect for human diversity. It teaches conflict resolution strategies to students at all grade levels (K-12). Peer mediators are specially chosen and trained. The middle school guide is based on Martin Luther King's principles of nonviolence and is accompanied by a video that includes events and speeches from the Civil Rights era. Complete school program with guides, workbooks, videos, cassettes and posters is available.

Middle-Schoolers "Do Justice" by Their Classmates

Suzanne Miller
From *Update on Law-Related Education*

Suzanne Miller is Assistant Principal, Gifford Elementary School, Racine, Wisconsin.

IN the Spring of 1985, Gilmore Middle School staffers were invited by me, their assistant principal, to meet and discuss ways to make Gilmore a safer, more pleasant place. Almost 20 staff members responded for the "Project Safe" group, which felt that, most often, peace and harmony were disrupted by unresolvable disputes between two students. All problems named resulted from people not knowing how to handle relationships which have gone amiss, not knowing how to manage conflicts.

Drawing on experiences of cities such as San Francisco and New York, the group decided to learn conflict-resolution skills and train Gilmore students as mediators, with the goal of having many students, teachers, and parents trained in conflict resolution and mediation. Those trained would be better able to handle their own conflicts and help others solve theirs before they exploded into fights.

The first step was to ally the group with the Dispute Settlement Center of Racine County, whose professional mediators held eight two-hour conflict-resolution training sessions for teachers in the fall of 1985. Gilmore teachers then trained 21 students to be mediators, examining training manuals and plans from other places

and then tailoring the curriculum for Gilmore students.

Assemblies were held to explain to all students that, in mediation, a third party helps resolve a dispute so that nobody loses—and everybody wins. During this assembly, students presented a skit that illustrated the successful resolution of a dispute.

Finally, students were encouraged to apply for the training offered after school. Of over 50 who applied, 21 were chosen, with the mix reflecting the racial make-up of the school—and including students who had a history

> **Students liked settling their own problems with the help of other students instead of teachers or principals.**

of conflicts as well as students who didn't. We took care not to overlook fighters or students with latent leadership abilities. We wanted to turn street fighters around.

Students were trained in five afternoon sessions and one all-day session. Afterward, the 21 students were given special "mediator" T-shirts. They were ready to mediate student conflicts. It had been just a year since the Project Safe committee first met.

The newly trained mediators made announcements advertising their ser-

vices on the public address system. Teachers were given forms and encouraged to recommend feuding students for mediation. Students were encouraged to request mediation on forms in the counseling office.

Word got around, and the mediation business picked up. Mediators had a really good feeling about themselves and what they were doing. The students who had their conflicts mediated liked settling their own problems with the help of other students rather than having a teacher or principal step in.

Two years after the program began, over 50 student mediators had been trained, over 500 mediations had taken place, and the effects of Gilmore's peacemaker program had been far-reaching. An elderly lady in the community said, "Whenever we have trouble in the neighborhood, we call for one of your mediators." Other mediators are also called on in their homes, churches, and neighborhoods to help resolve conflicts.

At a public meeting discussing conflict resolution, one person said, "They must have a conflict resolution program at Gilmore. I used to substitute there and stopped because there was so much arguing and fighting. I substituted there again this year, and it is so different. Instead of fighting, kids are talking about contracts and mediation."

The Gilmore program has continued, and extended to help train stu-

Reprinted with permission from *The Education Digest*, Vol. 59, No. 3, November 1993, pp. 13-16. © 1995 by Prakken Publications, Inc., Ann Arbor, MI.

dent mediators from other schools in the area. By the 1992-93 school year, there was such demand for training that it became more practical to train teachers, counselors, and administrators who, in turn, would train their own students. Programs have also sprouted up throughout Wisconsin, Minnesota, and Illinois.

There are many other models for these programs. Most start with one person and a small group of students, and the idea is so successful that others become interested and the idea spreads. The first ingredient is a spark of interest. One person or a group can have it. But then what?

1. Join the National Association for Mediation in Education (NAME, 205 Hampshire House, UMASS, Amherst, MA 01003; phone: 413-545-2462). Order a publication list and membership directory from this major umbrella organization for school programs.

2. Contact a professional mediator. NAME is a resource. Colleges often have courses in mediation. The local bar association is another resource.

3. Publicize the concept of student mediation in assemblies, newsletters, and over the school P.A. system so interested students, teachers, and parents can get involved.

4. Form an advisory council of teachers, counselors, administrators, parents, and students to form policies and make decisions.

5. Decide on adults to be trained and involved.

6. Engage a professional mediator to train teachers and staff. This will take about 20 hours. Often, credit can be arranged through a local college. NAME has a directory of mediators who will present training institutes around the country. Training can be on weekends or on school days if substitute teachers can be provided.

7. Purchase or write a curriculum for training students.

8. Advertise for student trainees and have each fill out an application form including these questions: Why do you want to be a mediator? How do you think student mediators will be helpful to this school? When you disagree with someone, how do you usually resolve the dispute? In what ways have you shown leadership?

Include a contract for students to sign agreeing to attend all training sessions and a paragraph asking parental permission. Allow a section for a teacher to recommend the student for mediator training.

9. Select the trainees. This is the most difficult part because it's subjective and unscientific. Get the advisory committee involved in the selection. In a school of 1,000 a good number of mediators to train is 21. (Numbers divisible by three make for good role-playing.) You might want 6 or 12. Some schools train a whole room of students, knowing all will benefit from it but not all will want to be active mediators.

Select a group that reflects the racial and ethnic makeup of your school. Balance males with females and honor roll kids with average students and streetwise negative leaders. Often, the biggest "troublemakers" are the most effective mediators. A good question as you select is, "Who will benefit most from being a mediator?"

10. Train the student mediators. Set aside 17 to 20 hours for mediator training. After school usually works better, with late or activity buses governing the length of each session. An ideal way to train is to offer conflict resolution as a summer class.

Set a limit on absences allowed in training. Since 20 hours is not really enough time as it is, two absences should be the maximum allowed. Training should end with a longer session in which professional or trained adult mediators critique the trainees as they role-play mediations. At the end of training, mediators can be awarded certificates, arm bands, badges, or T-shirts identifying them as mediators.

11. Start the program. Publicize it in the newspaper, in newsletters, in assemblies, and over the P.A. system. Distribute forms to teachers, parents, bus drivers, and students to be used to request or recommend a mediation. (The bulk of mediations are requested by disputants themselves.)

Decide whether mediators will work solo or in teams of two. (The team approach has worked well in many school districts.) Decide where and when mediations will be held and which adult will be nearby during them. Create a duty roster, put-

ting two or more mediators "on duty" each day during each mediation time (recess, lunch, during study centers or home room periods).

12. Keep the program going. On daily P.A. announcements, thank by name the mediators who conducted mediations that day, and remind students they can request mediations. Hold monthly meetings with mediators to discuss problems, strengths, and questions. Provide some inservice at each meeting; remember, a mediator is never "done." Each year, train a few new mediators with "old" mediators assisting. Give frequent reports to staff, parents, and community through press releases sent to bulletins and newspapers. At award ceremonies, give mediators a certificate or other form of recognition.

As for program costs, the Gilmore program started and operated for several years with no money. Later, a mediation program was written into the Gilmore budget for $300 because the program meets needs of at-risk students and ones talented in the area of leadership.

Local businesses might underwrite brochures and other printed materials. Some programs are funded by the local bar association, service clubs, the county or city, the school district, foundation grants, or a combination of these. Business-school partnerships are growing; perhaps a business partner might join the school in starting a program.

Educators involved with student mediation programs feel they are the most beneficial programs they've been associated with. They realize the programs are teaching life skills which will serve all the students all their lives. They know this is both law-related and life-related education.

For all their variety, school-based conflict-resolution programs share a common goal: to show young people they have many choices, besides passivity or aggression, for dealing with conflict and to give them the skills to make those choices real in their own lives. The beauty is that student mediators, even third- and fourth-grade mediators, will tell you without being taught or prompted, that there can't be world peace until there's one-to-one peace right in their own school and neighborhood.

How to Create Discipline Problems

M. MARK WASICSKO and STEVEN M. ROSS

M. Mark Wasicsko is provost at Texas Wesleyan College in Fort Worth, Texas. Steven M. Ross is professor of education at Memphis State University.

Creating classroom discipline problems is easy. By following the ten simple rules listed you should be able to substantially improve your skill at this popular teacher pastime.

1. *Expect the worst from kids.* This will keep you on guard at all times.
2. *Never tell students what is expected of them.* Kids need to learn to figure things out for themselves.
3. *Punish and criticize kids often.* This better prepares them for real life.
4. *Punish the whole class when one student misbehaves.* All the other students were probably doing the same thing or at least thinking about doing it.
5. *Never give students privileges.* It makes students soft and they will just abuse privileges anyway.
6. *Punish every misbehavior you see.* If you don't, the students will take over.
7. *Threaten and warn kids often.* "If you aren't good, I'll keep you after school for the rest of your life."
8. *Use the same punishment for every student.* If it works for one it will work for all.
9. *Use school work as punishment.* "Okay, smarty, answer all the questions in the book for homework!"
10. *Maintain personal distance from students.* Familiarity breeds contempt, you know.

We doubt that teachers would deliberately follow any of these rules, but punishments are frequently dealt out without much thought about their effects. In this article we suggest that many discipline problems are caused and sustained by teachers who inadvertently use self-defeating discipline strategies. There are, we believe, several simple, concrete methods to reduce classroom discipline problems.

Expect the Best from Kids

That teachers' expectations play an important role in determining student behavior has long been known. One author remembers two teachers who, at first glance, appeared similar. Both were very strict, gave mountains of homework, and kept students busy from the first moment they entered the classroom. However, they differed in their expectations for students. One seemed to say, "I know I am hard on you, but it is because I know you can do the work." She was effective and was loved by students. The other conveyed her negative expectations, "If I don't keep these kids busy they will stab me in the back." Students did everything they could to live up to each teacher's expectations. Thus, by conveying negative attitudes toward students, many teachers create their own discipline problems.

A first step in reducing discipline problems is to demonstrate positive expectations toward students. This is relatively easy to do for "good" students but probably more necessary for the others. If you were lucky, you probably had a teacher or two who believed you were able and worthy, and expected you to be capable even when you presented evidence to the contrary. You probably looked up to these teachers and did whatever you could to please them (and possibly even became a teacher yourself as a result). Now is the time to return the favor. Expect the best from *each* of your students. Assume that *every* child, if given the chance, will act properly. And, most important, if students don't meet your expectations, *don't give up!* Some students will require much attention before they will begin to respond.

Make the Implicit Explicit

Many teachers increase the likelihood of discipline problems by not making their expectations about proper behavior clear and explicit. For example, how many times have you heard yourself saying, "Now class, BEHAVE!"? You assume everyone knows what you mean

This article originally appeared in the December 1982 issue of The Clearing House.

From *The Clearing House*, Vol. 67, No. 5, May/June 1994, pp. 248-251. Published by Heldref Publications, 1319 Eighteenth Street, NW, Washington, DC 20036-1802. Reprinted by permission of the Helen Dwight Reid Educational Foundation. © 1994.

by "behave." This assumption may not be reasonable. On the playground, for example, proper behavior means running, jumping, throwing things (preferably balls, not rocks), and cooperating with other students. Classroom teachers have different notions about proper behavior, but in few cases do teachers spell out their expectations carefully. Sad to say, most students must learn the meaning of "behave" by the process of elimination: "Don't look out the window. . . . Don't put hands on fellow students. . . . Don't put feet on the desk . . . don't . . . don't . . . don't . . . ."

A preferred approach would be to present rules for *proper* conduct on the front end (and try to phrase them positively: "Students should . . ."). The teacher (or the class) could prepare a poster on which rules are listed. In that way, rules are clear, explicit, and ever present in the classroom. If you want to increase the likelihood that rules will be followed, have students help make the rules. Research shows that when students feel responsible for rules, they make greater efforts to live by them.

Rewards, Yes! Punishments, No!

A major factor in creating classroom discipline problems is the overuse of punishments as an answer to misbehavior. While most teachers would agree with this statement, recent research indicates that punishments outweigh rewards by at least 10 to 1 in the typical classroom. The types of punishments identified include such old favorites as The Trip to the Office and "Write a million times, 'I will not. . . . ' " But punishments also include the almost unconscious (but frequent) responses made for minor infractions: the "evil eye" stare of disapproval and the countless pleas to "Face front," "Stop talking," "Sit down!" and so on.

Punishments (both major and minor) have at least four consequences that frequently lead to increased classroom disruption: (1) Punishment brings attention to those who misbehave. We all know the adage, "The squeaky wheel gets greased." Good behavior frequently leaves a student nameless and unnoticed, but bad behavior can bring the undivided attention of the teacher before an audience of classmates! (2) Punishment has negative side effects such as aggression, depression, anxiety, or embarrassment. At the least, when a child is punished he feels worse about himself, about you and your class, or about school in general. He may even try to reduce the negative side effects by taking it out on another child or on school equipment. (3) Punishment only temporarily suppresses bad behavior. The teacher who rules with an iron ruler can have students who never misbehave in her presence, but who misbehave the moment she leaves the room or turns her back. (4) Punishment disrupts the continuity of your lessons and reduces the time spent on productive learning. These facts, and because punishments are usually not premeditated (and frequently do not address the real problems of misbehavior such as boredom, frustration,

or physical discomfort), usually work to increase classroom discipline problems rather than to reduce them.

In view of these factors, the preferred approach is to use rewards. Rewards bring attention to *good* behaviors: "Thank you for being prepared." Rewards provide an appropriate model for other students, and make students feel positive about themselves, about you, and about your class. Also, reinforcing positive behaviors reduces the inclination toward misbehavior and enhances the flow of your lesson. You stay on task, get more student participation, and accentuate the correct responses.

Let the Punishment Fit the Crime

When rewards are inappropriate, many teachers create discipline problems by using short-sighted or ineffective punishments. The classic example is the "whole class punishment." "Okay, I said if anyone talked there would be no recess, so we stay in today!" This approach frustrates students (especially the ones who were behaving properly) and causes more misbehavior.

Research indicates that punishments are most effective when they are the natural consequences of the behavior. For example, if a child breaks a window, it makes sense to punish him with clean-up responsibilities and by making him pay for damage. Having him write 1,000 times, "I will not break the window," or having him do extra math problems(!) does little to help him see the relationship between actions and consequences.

In reality, this is one of the hardest suggestions to follow. In many cases, the "natural consequences" are obscure ("Okay Steve, you hurt Carlton's feelings by calling him fat. For your punishment, you will make him feel better"). So, finding an appropriate punishment is often difficult. We suggest that after racking your brain, you consult with the offenders. They may be able to come up with a consequence that at least appears to them to be a fit punishment. In any case, nothing is lost for trying.

If You Must Punish, Remove Privileges

In the event that there are no natural consequences that can serve as punishments, the next best approach is to withdraw privileges. This type of punishment fits in well with the actual conditions in our society. In "real life" (located somewhere outside the school walls) privileges and responsibilities go hand in hand. People who do not act responsibly quickly lose freedoms and privileges. Classrooms provide a great opportunity to teach this lesson, but there is one catch: *There must be privileges to withdraw!* Many privileges already exist in classrooms and many more should be created. For example, students who finish their work neatly and on time can play an educational game, do an extra credit math sheet, work on homework, or earn points toward fun activities and free time. The possibilities are limitless. The important point, however, is that those who break the rules lose out on the privileges.

5. MANAGING LIFE IN CLASSROOMS

"Ignor"ance Is Bliss

One of the most effective ways to create troubles is to reward the very behaviors you want to eliminate. Many teachers do this inadvertently by giving attention to misbehaviors. For example, while one author was observing a kindergarten class, a child uttered an expletive after dropping a box of toys. The teachers quickly surrounded him and excitedly exclaimed, "That's nasty! Shame! Shame! Don't ever say that nasty word again!" All the while the other kids looked on with studied interest. So by lunch time, many of the other students were chanting, ". . . (expletive deleted) . . ." and the teachers were in a frenzy! Teachers create similar problems by bringing attention to note passing, gum chewing, and countless other minor transgressions. Such problems can usually be avoided by ignoring minor misbehaviors and, at a later time, talking to the student individually. Some minor misbehavior is probably being committed by at least one student during every second you teach! Your choice is to spend your time trying to correct (and bring attention to) each one *or* to go about the business of teaching.

Consistency Is the Best Policy

Another good way to create discipline problems is to be inconsistent with rules, assignments, and punishments. For example, one author's daughter was given 750 math problems to complete over the Christmas holidays. She spent many hours (which she would rather have spent playing with friends) completing the task. As it turned out, no one else completed the assignment, so the teacher extended the deadline by another week. In this case, the teacher was teaching students that it is all right to skip assignments. When events like this recur, the teacher loses credibility and students are taught to procrastinate, which they may continue to do throughout their lives.

Inconsistent punishment has a similar effect. By warning and rewarning students, teachers actually cultivate misbehavior. "The next time you do that, you're going to the office!" Five minutes pass and then, "I'm warning you, one more time and you are gone!" And later, "This is your last warning!" And finally, "Okay, I have had it with you, go stand in the hall!" In this instance, a student has learned that a punishment buys him/her a number of chances to misbehave (she/he might as well use them all), and that the actual punishment will be less severe than the promised one (not a bad deal).

To avoid the pitfalls of inconsistency, mean what you say, and, when you say it, follow through.

Know Each Student Well

Discipline problems can frequently be caused by punishing students we intended to reward and vice versa. When a student is told to clean up the classroom after school, is that a reward or punishment? It's hard to tell. As we all know, "One person's pleasure is another's poison."

One author remembers the difficulty he had with reading in the fourth grade. It made him so anxious that he would become sick just before reading period in the hope that he would be sent to the clinic, home, or anywhere other than to "the circle." One day, after helping the teacher straighten out the room before school, the teacher thanked him with, "Mark, you've been so helpful, you can be the first to read today." The author made sure he was never "helpful" enough to be so severely punished again.

The opposite happens just as often. For example, there are many class clowns who delight in such "punishments" as standing in the corner, leaving the room, or being called to the blackboard. The same author recalls having to stand in the school courtyard for punishment. He missed math, social studies, and English, and by the end of the day had entertained many classmates with tales of his escapades.

The key to reducing discipline problems is to know your students well; know what is rewarding and what is punishing for each.

Use School Work as Rewards

One of the worst sins a teacher can commit is to use school work as punishments. There is something sadly humorous about the language arts teacher who punishes students with, "Write 1,000 times, I will not. . . . " or the math teacher who assigns 100 problems as punishment. In cases like these we are actually punishing students with that which we want them to use and enjoy! Teachers can actually reduce discipline problems (and increase learning) by using their subjects as rewards. This is done in subtle and sometimes indirect ways, through making lessons meaningful, practical, and fun. If you are teaching about fractions, bring in pies and cakes and see how fast those kids can learn the difference between 1/2, 1/4, and 1/8. Reading teachers should allow free reading as a reward for good behavior. Math teachers can give extra credit math sheets (points to be added to the next test) when regular assignments are completed. The possibilities are endless and the results will be less misbehavior and a greater appreciation for both teacher and subject.

Treat Students with Love and Respect

The final suggestion for reducing discipline problems is to treat students kindly. It is no secret that people tend to respond with the same kind of treatment that they are given. If students are treated in a cold or impersonal manner, they are less likely to care if they cause you grief. If they are treated with warmth and respect they will want to treat you well in return. One of the best ways to show you care (and thus reduce discipline problems) is to surprise kids. After they have worked particularly hard, give them a treat. "You kids have worked so hard you may have 30 minutes extra recess." Or have a party one day for no good reason at all. Kids will come to think, "This school stuff isn't so bad after all!'' Be careful to keep the surprises unexpected. If kids come to expect them, surprises lose their effectiveness. Recently, one author heard a student pay a teacher the highest tribute. He said, ''She is more than just a teacher; she is our friend.'' Not surprisingly, this teacher is known for having few major discipline problems.

Final Thoughts

When talking about reducing discipline problems, we need to be careful not to suggest that they can or should be totally eliminated. When children are enthusiastic about learning, involved in what they are doing, and allowed to express themselves creatively, ''discipline problems'' are apt to occur. Albert Einstein is one of numerous examples of highly successful people who were labeled discipline problems in school. It was said of Einstein that he was ''the boy who knew not merely which monkey wrench to throw in the works, but also how best to throw it.'' This led to his expulsion from school because his ''presence in the class is disruptive and affects the other students.'' For dictators and tyrants, robot-like obedience is a major goal. For teachers, however, a much more critical objective is to help a classroom full of students reach their maximum potential as individuals.

The theme of this article has been that many teachers create their own discipline problems. Just as we teach the way we were taught, we tend to discipline with the same ineffectual methods that were used on us. By becoming aware of this and by following the simple suggestions presented above, learning and teaching can become more rewarding for all involved.

A Lesson Plan Approach for Dealing with School Discipline

JOHN R. BAN

John R. Ban is professor of education and coordinator of administrative programs at Indiana University Northwest in Gary, Indiana.

Teaching school poses no more formidable challenge than managing student behavior. Over the years, a cavalcade of devices has been marshalled by educators to discipline unruly students. Sometimes with inspiration, often times in desperation, teachers have resorted to a wide assortment of discipline methods—ranging from the hickory stick and dunce caps to bribery and capitulation. Whatever the tactic, it has not completely tamed the land of unsavory behavior.

Teacher remedies for discipline problems today can be grouped into two categories. One can be labeled reactive discipline. A fly-by-the-seat approach, it is the most common form of discipline used in the public schools. Teachers react when infractions occur by deciding what to do on the spot to handle them. Misbehavior is not anticipated; nor is the response planned to deal with it. With reactive disciplines, similar behavior outbursts merit different reactions depending on the individual student. By dealing with problem students on an individual basis, teachers demonstrate an inconsistency that undermines their credibility and authority. Presently, teachers resort to a mixture of reaction practices, most varying from day-to-day, from student to student, and from circumstance to circumstance. Reactive discipline is improvisation and impromptu classroom management. It is a form of free-lancing that may work fine in show business but is fraught with hidden dangers in dealing with aberrant children.

Proactive Discipline

An approach that offers better prospect for success is a proactive design of classroom management. Proactive discipline is predicated on the necessity for forethought, anticipation, preparation, and consistency with regard to teacher behavior and the consequences occasioned by student misbehavior. It is a system approach to discipline problems. Like any system, proactive discipline consists of components that can be learned. It rests on the belief that the surest road to resolving classroom management problems is through the establishment of a comprehensive system that can be activated when problems arise.

Several excellent proactive discipline systems have been developed for teachers and schools around the country. These include Canter's Assertive Discipline, Glasser's Reality Therapy, Gill and Heller's Diagnostic Discipline, Duke's Systematic Management Plan, and Alschuler's Social Literacy.

Most of these discipline plans argue for changes in school organization. Furthermore, they urge that the entire school staff follow the same discipline format. Admittedly, a system-wide discipline plan enjoys the best chance of success since it would reduce inconsistencies in teacher management techniques and lead to collaborative efforts on the part of all educators. A system-wide approach, however, may not be realizable in many schools.

While system-wide discipline plans have been implemented around the country, they have not been without problems. It is exceedingly difficult to convince all educators to adopt lock, stock, and barrel a single system of school discipline. The reason is that schools differ, classrooms differ, and so do teachers and students—making the typical school heterogeneous and unsusceptible to a uniform discipline approach.

Many teachers can be expected to feel uncomfortable with a mandated set of rules that circumscribes widely diverse elements of classroom organization. Their anxieties can be further compounded by a wide spectrum of idiosyncrasies in their instructional style. Dissimilarities in the learning habits of students present an additional problem in implementing universal behavior decrees.

One may inquire why teachers cannot accept a standardized discipline system when they willingly follow

This article originally appeared in the April 1982 issue of The Clearing House.

From *The Clearing House,* Vol. 67, No. 5, May/June 1994, pp. 257-260. Published by Heldref Publications, 1319 Eighteenth Street, NW, Washington, DC 20036-1802. Reprinted by permission of the Helen Dwight Reid Educational Foundation. © 1994.

other school-wide requirements. The response to such an inquiry is that certain institutional requirements pertain to mechanics of operation, deal with things, and make organizational sense. Others do not. The directive of using one kind of report card or using a specific student attendance form, for instance, does not interfere with the infinite complexities of student conduct. Nor does it have a bearing on the fluid personal relationships between teacher and student.

Because a system-wide discipline plan may not be workable in many schools, a lesson plan approach to discipline is proposed here. This plan can be used either on a school-wide basis, which is preferable, or simply in a class-to-class situation. The lesson plan is a familiar instructional tool to all teachers. It is one in which they are skilled and which they employ daily. These features alone make it a palatable mechanism for strengthening discipline both within and outside the classroom.

Becoming involved in lesson planning for effective discipline can persuade teachers to employ a proactive approach in dealing with misbehavior. Just as teachers court trouble when they do not plan for instruction, they run the same risk when they do not prepare to handle discipline problems. If there is a chief weakness among teachers in dealing with discipline problems, it is their failure to design a synoptic strategy that addresses misbehavior before it happens.

Making the Lesson Plan

A lesson plan approach to discipline is predicated on several propositions: behavior in school should be an object for study in the classroom; instruction during the first week of school should center on conduct and its consequences; there should be a lesson plan prepared for this purpose; students should be involved in determining classroom rules; peer influence should be used as a force in molding conduct in school; a proper record-keeping system for misbehavior should comprise an essential part of a teacher's discipline system.

A lesson plan approach to discipline requires that the teacher set aside the teaching of subject matter during the first week of school. Instead, one should devote that time to "comportment training," teaching about not only behavior in general but also, more specifically, about behavior in educational institutions. One of the best sources for this lesson is the school's student conduct manual. Another is local school board policy relative to pupil behavior. Students should be encouraged to study in detail what the school system's student conduct code says about behavior, corporal punishment, suspension, expulsion, due process, student responsibilities, specific behavior offenses, and consequences for breaking certain rules. Students should be given the opportunity to explore the reasons behind these rules and express their reactions to them.

Understanding the role of rules or law in society is closely tied to any effective discipline system. Teachers should help students understand what schools are and why they need rules. Schools are institutions that handle, organize and are responsible for the learning of young people. They are learning communities made up of distinct groups (teachers, students, administrators, etc.) that are bound together by a common goal. Like other institutions, schools need rules to accomplish their goals. School rules have these functions: they guide behavior toward a particular end; ensure orderly processes; promote the common good; protect the rights of everyone; spell out responsibilities of all parties; provide lessons in living; and prepare youngsters for life in a society of law.

Central to a lesson plan on school discipline is involving students in assisting the teacher in instituting classroom rules. Classroom communities are stronger when all their members participate in designing rules for behavior. Substantial research indicates that people are more inclined to obey rules when they have had a significant part in determining them. Many authorities in school discipline are insisting that educators and students share in this function.

Student Involvement

In keeping with the points above, teachers should ask students to identify common behavior problems in school. In addition, the reasons for and consequences of these problems should be discussed. The students should formulate a behavior statement or rule that deals with these identified misbehaviors. To do this, teachers can divide students into committees that would report back to the class on their deliberations. Once these rules are amply debated and approved by the entire class, they should be promulgated. Promulgation can take the form of being posted on a bulletin board where they can serve as a constant reminder to students or prepared in a memo distributed to each student to take home for parental perusal and signature.

In too many classrooms student behavior is regulated solely by teacher authority, which students are eager to challenge. In classrooms where students have had a part in shaping the rules of behavior, the power of peer pressure will work to ensure student compliance with these rules.

A close companion to behavior restraints is temper management. How can one study proper conduct without examining measures for temper control? Yet few teachers treat this topic in a systematic way. Fewer still rally youngsters to establish temper management plans.

The first step in a temper management plan is student identification of those situations that cause a loss of temper. Students should be encouraged to monitor their angry responses during the day and acknowledge ways others handle hostility and aggression. Following this, students should make a value judgment of their temper loss, whether it was beneficial/harmful (good/bad) to them or others. It is important, too, that students associate consequences with unbridled anger.

Above all, students should have the opportunity to explore how exemplary people control their tempers. Teachers can then steer students to study, and even practice, suggested techniques of self-control, ranging from deep muscle relaxation to fantasizing pleasant scenes.

A basic feature of a lesson plan on discipline is to focus on behavior required of students outside the classroom. Some authorities on discipline point out that most of the unruly behavior in school occurs outside the classroom—in the halls, cafeteria, playground, washroom, and on school buses. This is the case in some schools but not all. Regardless, it is imperative that students know school rules regarding the behavior expected of them in extra-class areas. These rules should be studied in terms of their rationale, their place in the organization of the school, and their relationship to classroom rules.

Keeping records of student misbehavior is a necessary element in any effective classroom discipline system. Given the legal climate surrounding the schools and the rules of evidence inherent in student due process proceedings, teachers should establish a simple, easily retrievable log on discipline incidents in their classes. Once a discipline record plan is determined for the class, the teacher should notify students about it, explaining its purpose and rationale.

A discipline record form need not be sophisticated nor time consuming, but it should contain at least five categories that supply information sufficient for legal use. On a small note card, teachers could record the following: (a) *incident*—identifying the specific misbehavior; (b) *description*—specifying items like frequency, location or any unusual circumstance; (c)*impact*—shorthanding the effect of the misbehavior on students, learning, teacher, or school; (d) *corrective ac-*

tion—recording action taken by the teacher to deal with misbehavior; (e) *follow-up*—monitoring the conduct of an unruly child over a period of time and assessing the effectiveness of the remedy employed. An example of this record form is shown in figure 1.

In conjunction with the lesson plan approach to school discipline, teachers should schedule a private five-minute conference every three weeks with each student in class. These can be called HAT meetings (for How Are Things?). They are brief, time-out periods where the teacher demonstrates concern for youngsters through inquiring about how things are going for them in and out of class, where the teacher can volunteer assistance with personal or behavior problems, and where the teacher delivers an unmistakable message that he or she cares. Research at the University of Wisconsin Research and Development Center indicated that both the behavior and performance of students improved with the use of periodic conferences between teacher and students.

Teacher Attitude

In the final analysis, the key to any effective discipline system is teacher attitude. A lesson plan on discipline merely establishes the structure and substance for managing student behavior. Teacher style supplies the essential ingredient for its successful implementation. If discipline is important to learning, and few would deny that it is, then the teacher must take time not only to preplan a classroom management system but also to convey an enthusiasm and disposition for making it work.

Substantial research has been done on teacher behaviors that hold down the incidence of student misbehavior. These behaviors afford valuable guidelines for teachers in becoming effective classroom managers. They include extensive planning for instruction, teaching classroom rules, helping students learn proper behavior in school, employing praise and positive reinforcement, sending out cues that the teacher cares, giving greater structure and focus to assignments, providing opportunities for students in on-task activities, monitoring regularly student performance, supplying continuous feedback to students regarding their work, and allowing a high degree of student participation in classroom affairs.

Teachers have to project a caring attitude, a deep concern for youngsters and a willingness to be fair but firm. They have to place heavy reliance on praise, trust, and encouragement. They have to demonstrate control over their own temper if they expect students to control theirs. In the delicate art of interpersonal relations, they have to model proper behavior in front of students. Above all, teachers must sharpen their skills in classroom management since success in their trade hinges on

---

FIGURE 1
Sample Discipline Record Form

Student: Johnny Doe
Date: February 12, 1981
Time: 1:30 p.m.
Location: in class

Incident—Vandalism; ripping textbook

Description—Johnny tore a textbook twice in back of classroom. He said it was an accident, but he was seen deliberately vandalizing the book.

Impact—Johnny's action showed disrespect for property and set a bad example for the class.

Corrective action—He was made to pay for the book.

Follow-up—Johnny has not damaged books since he made restitution for the one vandalized.

this simple fact. To expect teachers to survive in a classroom without behavior management skills is like expecting an artist to paint without a brush.

The problem of student discipline is a painful thorn in the flesh of public education. It appears that everyone is waiting for teachers to perform the extraction that supplies relief. Yet teachers are caught in a squeeze between rising expectation of their control of student behavior and organizational and community forces that make this a difficult task. Without waiting for outside help, teachers can address the discipline problem on their own. Discipline can be learned from studying it. The lesson plan approach comprises a convenient and effective instrument to promote responsible behavior among students. Even more, it is a teaching medium that all teachers could comfortably use.

Equality of Educational Opportunity

The "equity agenda," or social justice agenda, in the field of education is a complex matrix of gender- and culture-related issues aggravated by incredibly wide gaps in the social and economic opportunity structures available to citizens. We are each situated by cultural, gender-based, and socioeconomic factors in society; this is true of all persons, everywhere. We have witnessed a great and glorious struggle for human rights in our time and in our nation. The struggle continues to deal more effectively with educational opportunity issues related to cultural diversity and gender.

The effort to improve equality of opportunity in the field of education relates to a wide range of both cultural and gender issues still confronting our society. Although there has been a great, truly historic, effort to achieve social justice in American society, that effort must continue. We need to see our social reality in the context of our "wholeness" as a culturally pluralistic society in which there remain unresolved issues in the field of education for both cultural minorities and women. Women's issues and concerns have historically been part of the struggle for civil liberties. An overview of the executive summary of the American Association of University Women's (AAUW) report, "How Schools Shortchange Girls" (1992), is published in this unit to identify what can be done to treat girls and women more fairly in the educational system.

The "Western canon" is being challenged by advocates of multicultural perspectives in school curriculum development. Multicultural educational programming, which will reflect the rapidly changing cultural demographics of North American schooling, is being fiercely advocated by some and strongly opposed by others. This controversy centers around several different issues regarding what it means to provide equality of opportunities for culturally diverse students. This debate is reflected in the essays in this unit. The traditional Western cultural content of general and social studies and language arts curricula is being challenged as Eurocentric.

Helping teachers to broaden their cultural perspectives and to take a more global view of curriculum content is something the advocates of culturally pluralistic approaches to curriculum development would like to see integrated into the entire elementary and secondary school curriculum structure. North America is as multicultural a region of the world as exists anywhere. Our enormous cultural diversity encompasses populations from many indigenous "First Americans" as well as peoples from every European culture, plus many peoples of Asian, African, and Latin American nations and the Cen-

tral and South Pacific Island groups. There is spirited controversy over how to help *all* Americans to better understand our collective multicultural heritage. There are spirited defenders and opponents to the traditional Eurocentric curriculum.

The problem of inequality of educational opportunity is of great concern to American educators. One in four American children do not have all of their basic needs met and live under poverty conditions. Almost one in three live in single-parent homes, which in itself is no disadvantage—but under conditions of poverty, it often is. More and more concern is expressed over how to help children of poverty. The equity agenda of our time has to do with many issues related to gender, race, and ethnicity. All forms of social deprivation and discrimination are aggravated by great disparities in income and accumulated wealth. How can students be helped to have an equal opportunity to succeed in school? We have wrestled with this dilemma in educational policy development for decades. How can we advance the just cause of the educational interests of our young people more effectively?

Some of us are still proud to say that we are a nation of immigrants. As we became a new nation, powerful demographic and economic forces impacted upon the makeup of our population. In addition to the traditional minority-majority group relationships that evolved in the United States, new waves of immigrants today are again making concerns for achieving equality of opportunity in education as important as ever. In light of these vast sociological and demographic changes, we must ensure that we will remain a multicultural democracy.

The social psychology of prejudice is something that psychiatrists, social psychologists, anthropologists, and sociologists have studied in great depth since the 1930s. Tolerance, acceptance, and a valuing of the unique worth of every person are teachable and learnable attitudes. A just society must be constantly challenged to find meaningful ways to raise human aspirations, to heal human hurt, and to help in the task of optimizing every citizen's potential. Education is a vital component to that end. Teachers can incorporate into their lessons an emphasis on acceptance of difference, toleration of and respect for the beliefs of others, and the skills of reasoned debate and dialogue.

We must remain alert to keep our constitutional promises. Although it is not easy to maintain fair opportunity structures in a culturally pluralistic society, we must continually try.

The struggle for optimal best possible representation of

minority perspectives in the schools will be a matter of serious concern to educators for the foreseeable future. From the many court decisions upholding the rights of women and cultural minorities in the schools over the past 40 years has emerged a national consensus that we must strive for the greatest degree of equality in education as may be possible. The triumph of constitutional law over prejudice and bigotry must continue.

As we look with hope to our future, we seek compassion in the classroom for our respective visions of the world.

Looking Ahead: Challenge Questions

How do you respond to calls for the integration of more multicultural content into school studies?

What do you know about how it feels to be poor? How do you think it would feel in school? How would you respond?

If you are a female, have you ever felt that you were discriminated against or, at the least, ignored?

If you are a male, have you ever felt that you were being favored?

How can schools address more effectively the issue of gender bias?

How do children learn to be prejudiced? How can they learn tolerance?

What were the constitutional precedents for the school desegregation cases?

What academic freedoms should every teacher and student have?

—F. S.

The Canon Debate, Knowledge Construction, and Multicultural Education

JAMES A. BANKS

JAMES A. BANKS *is professor and director, Center for Multicultural Education, University of Washington, Seattle, WA 98195. He specializes in social studies education and multicultural education.*

I review the debate over multicultural education in this article, state that all knowledge reflects the values and interests of its creators, and illustrate how the debate between the multiculturalists and the Western traditionalists is rooted in their conflicting conceptions about the nature of knowledge and their divergent political and social interests. I present a typology that describes five types of knowledge and contend that each type should be a part of the school, college, and university curriculum.

Educational Researcher, Vol. 22, No. 5, pp. 4-14.

A heated and divisive national debate is taking place about what knowledge related to ethnic and cultural diversity should be taught in the school and university curriculum (Asante, 1991a; Asante & Ravitch, 1991; D'Souza, 1991; Glazer, 1991; Schlesinger, 1991; Woodward, 1991). This debate has heightened ethnic tension and confused many educators about the meaning of multicultural education. At least three different groups of scholars are participating in the canon debate: the Western traditionalists, the multiculturalists, and the Afrocentrists. Although there are a range of perspectives and views within each of these groups, all groups share a number of important assumptions and beliefs about the nature of diversity in the United States and about the role of educational institutions in a pluralistic society.

The Western traditionalists have initiated a national effort to defend the dominance of Western civilization in the school and university curriculum (Gray, 1991; Howe, 1991; Woodward, 1991). These scholars believe that Western history, literature, and culture are endangered in the school and university curriculum because of the push by feminists, ethnic minority scholars, and other multiculturalists for curriculum reform and transformation. The Western traditionalists have formed an organization called the National Association of Scholars to defend the dominance of Western civilization in the curriculum.

The multiculturalists believe that the school, college, and university curriculum marginalizes the experiences of people of color and of women (Butler & Walter, 1991; Gates, 1992; Grant, 1992; Sleeter, personal communication, October 26, 1991). They contend that the curriculum should be reformed so that it will more accurately reflect the histories and cultures of ethnic groups and women. Two organizations have been formed to promote issues related to ethnic and cultural diversity. Teachers for a Democratic Culture promotes ethnic studies and women studies at the university level. The National Association for Multicultural Education focuses on teacher education and multicultural education in the nation's schools.

The Afrocentrists maintain that African culture and history should be placed at the "center" of the curriculum in order to motivate African Americans students to learn and to help all students to understand the important role that Africa has played in the development of Western civilization (Asante, 1991a). Many mainstream multiculturalists are ambivalent about Afrocentrism, although few have publicly opposed it. This is in part because the Western traditionalists rarely distinguish the Afrocentrists from the multiculturalists and describe them as one group. Some multiculturalists may also perceive Afrocentric ideas as compatible with a broader concept of multicultural education.

The influence of the multiculturalists within schools and universities in the last 20 years has been substantial. Many school districts, state departments of education, local school districts, and private agencies have developed and implemented multicultural staff development programs, conferences, policies, and curricula (New York City Board of Education, 1990; New York State Department of Education, 1989, 1991; Sokol, 1990). Multicultural requirements, programs, and policies have also been implemented at many of the nation's leading research universities, including the University of California, Berkeley, Stanford University, The Pennsylvania State University, and the University of Wisconsin system. The success that the multiculturalists have had in implementing their ideas within schools and universities is probably a major reason that the Western traditionalists are trying to halt multicultural reforms in the nation's schools, colleges, and universities.

The debate between the Western traditionalists and the multiculturalists is consistent with the ideals of a democratic society. To date, however, it has resulted in little productive interaction between the Western traditionalists and the multiculturalists. Rather, each group has talked primarily to audiences it viewed as sympathetic to its ideologies and visions of the present and future (Franklin, 1991; Schlesinger, 1991). Because there has been little productive dialogue and exchange between the Western traditionalists and the multiculturalists, the debate has been polarized, and writers have frequently not conformed to the established rules of scholarship (D'Souza, 1991). A kind of forensic social science has developed (Rivlin, 1973), with each side stating briefs and then marshaling evidence to support its

From *Educational Researcher*, June/July 1993, pp. 4-14. © 1993 by the American Educational Research Association. Reprinted by permission of the publisher.

position. The debate has also taken place primarily in the popular press rather than in academic and scholarly journals.

Valuation and Knowledge Construction

I hope to make a positive contribution to the canon debate in this article by providing evidence for the claim that the positions of both the Western traditionalists and the multiculturalists reflect values, ideologies, political positions, and human interests. Each position also implies a kind of knowledge that should be taught in the school and university curriculum. I will present a typology of the kinds of knowledge that exist in society and in educational institutions. This typology is designed to help practicing educators and researchers to identify types of knowledge that reflect particular values, assumptions, perspectives, and ideological positions.

Teachers should help students to understand all types of knowledge. Students should be involved in the debates about knowledge construction and conflicting interpretations, such as the extent to which Egypt and Phoenicia influenced Greek civilization. Students should also be taught how to create their own interpretations of the past and present, as well as how to identify their own positions, interests, ideologies, and assumptions. Teachers should help students to become critical thinkers who have the knowledge, attitudes, skills, and commitments needed to participate in democratic action to help the nation close the gap between its ideals and its realities. Multicultural education is an education for functioning effectively in a pluralistic democratic society. Helping students to develop the knowledge, skills, and attitudes needed to participate in reflective civic action is one of its major goals (Banks, 1991).

I argue that students should study all five types of knowledge. However, my own work and philosophical position are within the transformative tradition in ethnic studies and multicultural education (Banks, 1988, 1991; Banks & Banks, 1989). This tradition links knowledge, social commitment, and action (Meier & Rudwick, 1986). A transformative, action-oriented curriculum, in my view, can best be implemented when students examine different types of knowledge in a democratic classroom where they can freely examine their perspectives and moral commitments.

The Nature of Knowledge

I am using knowledge in this article to mean the way a person explains or interprets reality. *The American Heritage Dictionary* (1983) defines knowledge as "familiarity, awareness, or understandings gained through experience or study. The sum or range of what has been perceived, discovered or inferred" (p. 384). My conceptualization of knowledge is broad and is used the way in which it is usually used in the sociology of knowledge literature to include ideas, values, and interpretations (Farganis, 1986). As postmodern theorists have pointed out, knowledge is socially constructed and reflects human interests, values, and action (Code, 1991; Foucault, 1972; S. Harding, 1991; Rorty, 1989). Although many complex factors influence the knowledge that is created by an individual or group, including the actuality of what occurred, the knowledge that people create is heavily influenced by their interpretations of their experiences and their positions within particular social, economic, and political systems and structures of a society.

In the Western empirical tradition, the ideal within each academic discipline is the formulation of knowledge without the influence of the researcher's personal or cultural characteristics (Greer, 1969; Kaplan, 1964). However, as critical and postmodern theorists have pointed out, personal, cultural, and social factors influence the formulation of knowledge even when objective knowledge is the ideal within a discipline (Cherryholmes, 1988; Foucault, 1972; Habermas, 1971; Rorty, 1989; Young, 1971). Often the researchers themselves are unaware of how their personal experiences and positions within society influence the knowledge they produce. Most mainstream historians were unaware of how their regional and cultural biases influenced their interpretation of the Reconstruction period until W. E. B. DuBois published a study that challenged the accepted and established interpretations of that historical period (DuBois, 1935/1962).

Positionality and Knowledge Construction

Positionality is an important concept that emerged out of feminist scholarship. Tetreault (1993) writes:

> Positionality means that important aspects of our identity, for example, our gender, our race, our class, our age . . . are markers of relational positions rather than essential qualities. Their effects and implications change according to context. Recently, feminist thinkers have seen knowledge as valid when it comes from an acknowledgment of the knower's specific position in any context, one always defined by gender, race, class and other variables. (p. 139)

Positionality reveals the importance of identifying the positions and frames of reference from which scholars and writers present their data, interpretations, analyses, and instruction (Anzaldúa, 1990; Ellsworth, 1989). The need for researchers and scholars to identify their ideological positions and normative assumptions in their works—an inherent part of feminist and ethnic studies scholarship—contrasts with the empirical paradigm that has dominated science and research in the United States (Code, 1991; S. Harding, 1991).

The assumption within the Western empirical paradigm is that the knowledge produced within it is neutral and objective and that its principles are universal. The effects of values, frames of references, and the normative positions of researchers and scholars are infrequently discussed within the traditional empirical paradigm that has dominated scholarship and teaching in American colleges and universities since the turn of the century. However, scholars such as Mydral (1944) and Clark (1965), prior to the feminist and ethnic studies movements, wrote about the need for scholars to recognize and state their normative positions and valuations and to become, in the apt words of Kenneth B. Clark, "involved observers." Myrdal stated that valuations are not just attached to research but permeate it. He wrote, "*There is no device for excluding biases in social sciences than to face the valuations and to introduce them as explicitly stated, specific, and sufficiently concretized value premises*" (p. 1043).

Postmodern and critical theorists such as Habermas (1971) and Giroux (1983), and feminist postmodern theorists such as Farganis (1986), Code (1991), and S. Harding (1991), have developed important critiques of empirical knowledge. They argue that despite its claims, modern science is not value-free but contains important human interests and normative assumptions that should be identified, discussed, and examined. Code (1991), a feminist epistemologist, states that academic knowledge is both subjective and objective and that both aspects should be recognized and discussed. Code states that we need to ask these kinds of questions: "Out of whose subjectivity has this ideal [of objectivity] grown? Whose standpoint, whose values does it represent?" (p. 70). She writes:

> The point of the questions is to discover how subjective and objective conditions together produce knowledge, values, and epistemology. It is neither to reject objectivity nor to glorify subjectivity in its stead. Knowledge is neither value-free nor value-neutral; the processes that produce it are themselves value-laden; and these values are open to evaluation. (p. 70)

In her book, *What Can She Know? Feminist Theory and the Construction of Knowledge*, Code (1991) raises the question, "Is the sex of the knower epistemologically significant?" (p. 7). She answers this question in the affirmative because of the ways in which gender influences how knowledge is constructed, interpreted, and institutionalized within U.S. society. The ethnic and cultural experiences of the knower are also epistemologically significant because these factors also influence knowledge construction, use, and interpretation in U.S. society.

Empirical scholarship has been limited by the assumptions and biases that are implicit within it (Code, 1991; Gordon, 1985; S. Harding, 1991). However, these biases and assumptions have been infrequently recognized by the scholars and researchers themselves and by the consumers of their works, such as other scholars, professors, teachers, and the general reader. The lack of recognition and identification of these biases, assumptions, perspectives, and points of view have frequently victimized people of color such as African Americans and American Indians because of the stereotypes and misconceptions that have been perpetuated about them in the historical and social science literature (Ladner, 1973; Phillips, 1918).

Gordon, Miller, and Rollock (1990) call the bias that results in the negative depiction of minority groups by mainstream social scientists "communicentric bias." They point out that mainstream social scientists have often viewed diversity as deviance and differences as deficits. An important outcome of the revisionist and transformative interpretations that have been produced by scholars working in feminist and ethnic studies is that many misconceptions and partial truths about women and ethnic groups have been viewed from different and more complete perspectives (Acuña, 1988; Blassingame, 1972; V. Harding, 1981; King & Mitchell, 1990; Merton, 1972).

More complete perspectives result in a closer approximation to the actuality of what occurred. In an important and influential essay, Merton (1972) notes that the perspectives of both "insiders" and "outsiders" are needed to enable social scientists to gain a complete view of social reality. Anna Julia Cooper, the African American educator, made a point similar to Merton's when she wrote about how the perspectives of women enlarged our vision (Cooper, 1892/1969, cited in Minnich, 1990, p. viii).

> The world has had to limp along with the wobbling gait and the one-sided hesitancy of a man with one eye. Suddenly the bandage is removed from the other eye and the whole body is filled with light. It sees a circle where before it saw a segment.

A Knowledge Typology

A description of the major types of knowledge can help teachers and curriculum specialists to identify perspectives and content needed to make the curriculum multicultural. Each of the types of knowledge described below reflects particular purposes, perspectives, experiences, goals, and human interests. Teaching students various types of knowledge can help them to better understand the perspectives of different racial, ethnic, and cultural groups as well as to develop their own versions and interpretations of issues and events.

I identify and describe five types of knowledge (see Table 1): (a) personal/cultural knowledge; (b) popular knowledge; (c) mainstream academic knowledge; (d) transformative academic knowledge; and (e) school knowledge. This is an ideal-type typology in the Weberian sense. The five categories approximate, but do not describe, reality in its total complexity. The categories are useful conceptual tools for thinking about knowledge and planning multicultural teaching. For example, although the categories can be conceptually distinguished, in reality they overlap and are interrelated in a dynamic way.

Since the 1960s, some of the findings and insights from transformative academic knowledge have been incorporated into mainstream academic knowledge and scholarship. Traditionally, students were taught in schools and universities that the land that became North America was a thinly populated wilderness when the Europeans arrived in the 16th century and that African Americans had made few contributions to the development of American civilization (mainstream academic knowledge). Some of the findings from transformative academic knowledge that challenged these conceptions have influenced mainstream academic scholarship and have been incorporated into mainstream college and school textbooks (Hoxie, no date; Thornton, 1987). Consequently, the relationship between the five categories of knowledge is dynamic and interactive rather than static (see Figure 1).

The Types of Knowledge

Personal and Cultural Knowledge

The concepts, explanations, and interpretations that students derive from personal experiences in their homes, families, and community cultures constitute personal and cultural

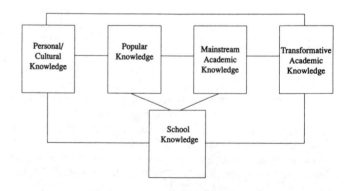

FIGURE 1. *The interrelationship of the types of knowledge. This figure illustrates that although the five types of knowledge discussed in this article are conceptually distinct, they are highly interrelated in a complex and dynamic way.*

Table 1
Types of Knowledge

Knowledge Type	Definition	Examples
Personal/cultural	The concepts, explanations, and interpretations that students derive from personal experiences in their homes, families, and community cultures.	Understandings by many African Americans and Hispanic students that highly individualistic behavior will be negatively sanctioned by many adults and peers in their cultural communities.
Popular	The facts, concepts, explanations, and interpretations that are institutionalized within the mass media and other institutions that are part of the popular culture.	Movies such as *Birth of a Nation, How the West Was Won,* and *Dances With Wolves.*
Mainstream academic	The concepts, paradigms, theories, and explanations that constitute traditional Western-centric knowledge in history and the behavioral and social sciences.	Ulrich B. Phillips, *American Negro Slavery;* Frederick Jackson Turner's frontier theory; Arthur R. Jensen's theory about Black and White intelligence.
Transformative academic	The facts, concepts, paradigms, themes, and explanations that challenge mainstream academic knowledge and expand and substantially revise established canons, paradigms, theories, explanations, and research methods. When transformative academic paradigms replace mainstream ones, a scientific revolution has occurred. What is more normal is that transformative academic paradigms coexist with established ones.	George Washington Williams, *History of the Negro Race in America;* W. E. B. DuBois, *Black Reconstruction;* Carter G. Woodson, *The Mis-education of the Negro;* Gerda Lerner, *The Majority Finds Its Past;* Rodolfo Acuña, *Occupied America: A History of Chicanos;* Herbert Gutman, *The Black Family in Slavery and Freedom 1750–1925.*
School	The facts, concepts, generalizations, and interpretations that are presented in textbooks, teacher's guides, other media forms, and lectures by teachers.	Lewis Paul Todd and Merle Curti, *Rise of the American Nation;* Richard C. Brown, Wilhelmena S. Robinson, & John Cunningham, *Let Freedom Ring: A United States History.*

knowledge. The assumptions, perspectives, and insights that students derive from their experiences in their homes and community cultures are used as screens to view and interpret the knowledge and experiences that they encounter in the school and in other institutions within the larger society.

Research and theory by Fordham and Ogbu (1986) indicate that low-income African American students often experience academic difficulties in the school because of the ways that cultural knowledge within their community conflicts with school knowledge, norms, and expectations. Fordham and Ogbu also state that the culture of many low-income African American students is oppositional to the school culture. These students believe that if they master the knowledge taught in the schools they will violate fictive kinship norms and run the risk of "acting White." Fordham (1988, 1991) has suggested that African American students who become high academic achievers resolve the conflict caused by the interaction of their personal cultural knowledge with the knowledge and norms within the schools by becoming "raceless" or by "ad hocing a culture."

Delpit (1988) has stated that African American students are often unfamiliar with school cultural knowledge regarding power relationships. They consequently experience academic and behavioral problems because of their failure to conform to established norms, rules, and expectations. She recommends that teachers help African American students learn the rules of power in the school culture by explicitly teaching them to the students. The cultural knowledge that many African American, Latino, and American Indian students bring to school conflict with school norms and values, with school knowledge, and with the ways that teachers interpret and mediate school knowledge. Student cultural knowledge and school knowledge often conflict on variables related to the ways that the individual should relate to and interact with the group (Hale-Benson, 1982; Ramírez & Castañeda, 1974; Shade, 1989), normative communication styles and interactions (Heath, 1983, Labov, 1975; Philips, 1983; Smitherman, 1977), and perspectives on the nature of U.S. history.

Personal and cultural knowledge is problematic when it conflicts with scientific ways of validating knowledge, is oppositional to the culture of the school, or challenges the main tenets and assumptions of mainstream academic knowledge. Much of the knowledge about out-groups that students learn from their home and community cultures consists of misconceptions, stereotypes, and partial truths (Milner, 1983). Most students in the United States are socialized within communities that are segregated along racial, ethnic, and social-class lines. Consequently, most American youths have few opportunities to learn firsthand about the cultures of people from different racial, ethnic, cultural, religious, and social-class groups.

The challenge that teachers face is how to make effective instructional use of the personal and cultural knowledge of students while at the same time helping them to reach beyond their own cultural boundaries. Although the school should recognize, validate, and make effective use of student personal and cultural knowledge in instruction, an important goal of education is to free students from their cultural and ethnic boundaries and enable them to cross cultural borders freely (Banks, 1988, 1991/1992).

In the past, the school has paid scant attention to the personal and cultural knowledge of students and has concentrated on teaching them school knowledge (Sleeter & Grant, 1991a). This practice has had different results for most White middle-class students, for most low-income students, and for most African American and Latino students. Because school knowledge is more consistent with the cultural experiences of most White middle-class students than for most other groups of students, these students have generally found the school a more comfortable place than have low-income students and most students of color—the majority of whom are also low income. A number of writers have described the ways in which many African American, American Indian, and Latino students find the school culture alienating and inconsistent with their cultural experiences, hopes, dreams, and struggles (Hale-Benson, 1982; Heath, 1983; Ramírez & Castañeda, 1974; Shade, 1989).

It is important for teachers to be aware of the personal and cultural knowledge of students when designing the curriculum for today's multicultural schools. Teachers can use student personal cultural knowledge as a vehicle to motivate students and as a foundation for teaching school knowledge. When teaching a unit on the Westward Movement to Lakota Sioux students, for example, the teacher can ask the students to make a list of their views about the Westward Movement, to relate family stories about the coming of the Whites to Lakota Sioux homelands, and to interview parents and grandparents about their perceptions of what happened when the Whites first occupied Indian lands. When teachers begin a unit on the Westward Movement with student personal cultural knowledge, they can increase student motivation as well as deepen their understanding of the schoolbook version (Wiggington, 1991/1992).

Popular Knowledge

Popular knowledge consists of the facts, interpretations, and beliefs that are institutionalized within television, movies, videos, records, and other forms of the mass media. Many of the tenets of popular knowledge are conveyed in subtle rather than obvious ways. Some examples of statements that constitute important themes in popular knowledge follow: (a) The United States is a powerful nation with unlimited opportunities for individuals who are willing to take advantage of them. (b) To succeed in the United States, an individual only has to work hard. You can realize your dreams in the United States if you are willing to work hard and pull yourself up by the bootstrap. (c) As a land of opportunity for all, the United States is a highly cohesive nation, whose ideals of equality and freedom are shared by all.

Most of the major tenets of American popular culture are widely shared and are deeply entrenched in U.S. society.

However, they are rarely explicitly articulated. Rather, they are presented in the media and in other sources in the forms of stories, anecdotes, news stories, and interpretations of current events (Cortés, 1991a, 1991b; Greenfield & Cortés, 1991).

Commercial entertainment films both reflect and perpetuate popular knowledge (Bogle, 1989; Cortés, 1991a, 1991b; Greenfield & Cortés, 1991). While preparing to write this article, I viewed an important and influential film that was directed by John Ford and released by MGM in 1962, *How the West Was Won*. I selected this film for review because the settlement of the West is a major theme in American culture and society about which there are many popular images, beliefs, myths, and misconceptions. In viewing the film, I was particularly interested in the images it depicted about the settlement of the West, about the people who were already in the West, and about those who went West looking for new opportunities.

Ford uses the Prescotts, a White family from Missouri bound for California, to tell his story. The film tells the story of three generations of this family. It focuses on the family's struggle to settle in the West. Indians, African Americans, and Mexicans are largely invisible in the film. Indians appear in the story when they attack the Prescott family during their long and perilous journey. The Mexicans appearing in the film are bandits who rob a train and are killed. The several African Americans in the film are in the background silently rowing a boat. At various points in the film, Indians are referred to as *hostile Indians* and as *squaws*.

How the West Was Won is a masterpiece in American popular culture. It not only depicts some of the major themes in American culture about the winning of the West; it reinforces and perpetuates dominant societal attitudes about ethnic groups and gives credence to the notion that the West was won by liberty-loving, hard-working people who pursued freedom for all. The film narrator states near its end, "[The movement West] produced a people free to dream, free to act, and free to mold their own destiny."

Mainstream Academic Knowledge

Mainstream academic knowledge consists of the concepts, paradigms, theories, and explanations that constitute traditional and established knowledge in the behavioral and social sciences. An important tenet within the mainstream academic paradigm is that there is a set of objective truths that can be verified through rigorous and objective research procedures that are uninfluenced by human interests, values, and perspectives (Greer, 1969; Kaplan, 1964; Sleeter, 1991). This empirical knowledge, uninfluenced by human values and interests, constitute a body of objective truths that should constitute the core of the school and university curriculum. Much of this objective knowledge originated in the West but is considered universal in nature and application.

Mainstream academic knowledge is the knowledge that multicultural critics such as Ravitch and Finn (1987), Hirsch (1987), and Bloom (1987) claim is threatened by the addition of content about women and ethnic minorities to the school and university curriculum. This knowledge reflects the established, Western-oriented canon that has historically dominated university research and teaching in the United States. Mainstream academic knowledge consists of the theories and interpretations that are internalized and accepted by most university researchers, academic societies, and organizations such as the American Historical Association, the American Sociological Association, the American Psychological Association, and the National Academy of Sciences.

It is important to point out, however, that an increasing number of university scholars are critical theorists and postmodernists who question the empirical paradigm that dominates Western science (Cherryholmes, 1988; Giroux, 1983; Rosenau, 1992). Many of these individuals are members of national academic organizations, such as the American Historical Association and the American Sociological Association. In most of these professional organizations, the postmodern scholars—made up of significant numbers of scholars of color and feminists—have formed caucuses and interest groups within the mainstream professional organizations.

No claim is made here that there is a uniformity of beliefs among mainstream academic scholars, but rather that there are dominant canons, paradigms, and theories that are accepted by the community of mainstream academic scholars and researchers. These established canons and paradigms are occasionally challenged within the mainstream academic community itself. However, they receive their most serious challenges from academics outside the mainstream, such as scholars within the transformative academic community whom I will describe later.

Mainstream academic knowledge, like the other forms of knowledge discussed in this article, is not static, but is dynamic, complex, and changing. Challenges to the dominant canons and paradigms within mainstream academic knowledge come from both within and without. These challenges lead to changes, reinterpretations, debates, disagreements and ultimately to paradigm shifts, new theories, and interpretations. Kuhn (1970) states that a scientific revolution takes place when a new paradigm emerges and replaces an existing one. What is more typical in education and the social sciences is that competing paradigms coexist, although particular ones might be more influential during certain times or periods.

We can examine the treatment of slavery within the mainstream academic community over time, or the treatment of the American Indian, to identify ways that mainstream academic knowledge has changed in important ways since the late 19th and early 20th centuries. Ulrich B. Phillips's highly influential book, *American Negro Slavery*, published in 1918, dominated the way Black slavery was interpreted until his views were challenged by researchers in the 1950s (Stampp, 1956). Phillips was a respected authority on the antebellum South and on slavery. His book, which became a historical classic, is essentially an apology for Southern slaveholders. A new paradigm about slavery was developed in the 1970s that drew heavily upon the slaves' view of their own experiences (Blassingame, 1972; Genovese, 1972; Gutman, 1976).

During the late 19th and early 20th centuries, the American Indian was portrayed in mainstream academic knowledge as either a noble or a hostile savage (Hoxie, 1988). Other notions that became institutionalized within mainstream academic knowledge include the idea that Columbus discovered America and that America was a thinly populated frontier when the Europeans arrived in the late 15th

century. Frederick Jackson Turner (Turner, 1894/1989) argued that the frontier, which he regarded as a wilderness, was the main source of American democracy. Although Turner's thesis is now being highly criticized by revisionist historians, his essay established a conception of the West that has been highly influential in American mainstream scholarship, in the popular culture, and in schoolbooks. The conception of the West he depicted is still influential today in the school curriculum and in textbooks (Sleeter & Grant, 1991b).

These ideas also became institutionalized within mainstream academic knowledge: The slaves were happy and contented; most of the important ideas that became a part of American civilization came from Western Europe; and the history of the United States has been one of constantly expanding progress and increasing democracy. African slaves were needed to transform the United States from an empty wilderness into an industrial democratic civilization. The American Indians had to be Christianized and removed to reservations in order for this to occur.

Transformative Academic Knowledge

Transformative academic knowledge consists of concepts, paradigms, themes, and explanations that challenge mainstream academic knowledge and that expand the historical and literary canon. Transformative academic knowledge challenges some of the key assumptions that mainstream scholars make about the nature of knowledge. Transformative and mainstream academic knowledge is based on different epistemological assumptions about the nature of knowledge, about the influence of human interests and values on knowledge construction, and about the purpose of knowledge.

An important tenet of mainstream academic knowledge is that it is neutral, objective, and was uninfluenced by human interests and values. Transformative academic knowledge reflects postmodern assumptions and goals about the nature and goals of knowledge (Foucault, 1972; Rorty, 1989; Rosenau, 1992). Transformative academic scholars assume that knowledge is not neutral but is influenced by human interests, that all knowledge reflects the power and social relationships within society, and that an important purpose of knowledge construction is to help people improve society (Code, 1991, S. Harding, 1991; hooks & West, 1991; King & Mitchell, 1990; Minnich, 1990). Write King and Mitchell: "Like other praxis-oriented Critical approaches, the Afrocentric method seeks to enable people to understand social reality in order to change it. But its additional imperative is to transform the society's basic ethos" (p. 95).

These statements reflect some of the main ideas and concepts in transformative academic knowledge: Columbus did not discover America. The Indians had been living in this land for about 40,000 years when the Europeans arrived. Concepts such as "The European Discovery of America" and "The Westward Movement" need to be reconceptualized and viewed from the perspectives of different cultural and ethnic groups. The Lakota Sioux's homeland was not the West to them; it was the center of the universe. It was not the West for the Alaskans; it was South. It was East for the Japanese and North for the people who lived in Mexico. The history of the United States has not been one of continuous progress toward democratic ideals. Rather, the nation's history has been characterized by a cyclic quest for democracy and by conflict, struggle, violence, and exclusion (Acuña, 1988; Zinn, 1980). A major challenge that faces the nation is how to make its democratic ideals a reality for all.

Transformative academic knowledge has a long history in the United States. In 1882 and 1883, George Washington Williams (1849–1891) published, in two volumes, the first comprehensive history of African Americans in the United States, *A History of the Negro Race in America From 1619 to 1880* (Williams, 1982–1983/1968). Williams, like other African American scholars after him, decided to research and write about the Black experience because of the neglect of African Americans by mainstream historians and social scientists and because of the stereotypes and misconceptions about African Americans that appeared in mainstream scholarship.

W. E. B. DuBois (1868–1963) is probably the most prolific African American scholar in U.S. history. His published writings constitute 38 volumes (Aptheker, 1973). DuBois devoted his long and prolific career to the formulation of new data, concepts, and paradigms that could be used to reinterpret the Black experience and reveal the role that African Americans had played in the development of American society. His seminal works include *The Suppression of the African Slave Trade to the United States of America, 1638–1870*, the first volume of the Harvard Historical Studies (DuBois, 1896/1969). Perhaps his most discussed book is *Black Reconstruction in America: An Essay Toward a History of the Part Which Black Folk Played in the Attempt to Reconstruct Democracy in America, 1860–1880*, published in 1935 (1935/1962). In this book, DuBois challenged the accepted, institutionalized interpretations of Reconstruction and emphasized the accomplishments of the Reconstruction governments and legislatures, especially the establishment of free public schools.

Carter G. Woodson (1875–1950), the historian and educator who founded the Association for the Study of Negro Life and History and the *Journal of Negro History*, also challenged established paradigms about the treatment of African Americans in a series of important publications, including *The Mis-education of the Negro*, published in 1933. Woodson and Wesley (1922) published a highly successful college textbook that described the contributions that African Americans have made to American life, *The Negro in Our History*. This book was issued in 10 editions.

Transformative Scholarship Since the 1970s

Many scholars have produced significant research and theories since the early 1970s that have challenged and modified institutionalized stereotypes and misconceptions about ethnic minorities, formulated new concepts and paradigms, and forced mainstream scholars to rethink established interpretations. Much of the transformative academic knowledge that has been produced since the 1970s is becoming institutionalized within mainstream scholarship and within the school, college, and university curricula. In time, much of this scholarship will become mainstream, thus reflecting the highly interrelated nature of the types of knowledge conceptualized and described in this article.

Only a few examples of this new, transformative scholarship will be mentioned here because of the limited scope of this article. Howard Zinn's *A People's History of the United States* (1980): *Red, White and Black: The Peoples of Early America* by Gary B. Nash (1982): *The Signifying Monkey: A Theory of African-American Literacy Criticism* by Henry Louis Gates, Jr.

(1988); *Occupied America: A History of Chicanos* by Rodolfo Acuña (1988); *Iron Cages: Race and Culture in 19th-Century America* by Ronald T. Takaki (1979); and *The Sacred Hoop: Recovering the Feminine in American Indian Traditions* by Paul Gunn Allen (1986) are examples of important scholarship that has provided significant new perspectives on the experiences of ethnic groups in the United States and has helped us to transform our conceptions about the experiences of American ethnic groups. Readers acquainted with this scholarship will note that transformative scholarship has been produced by both European-American and ethnic minority scholars.

I will discuss two examples of how the new scholarship in ethnic studies has questioned traditional interpretations

---

Students should be given opportunities to investigate and determine how cultural assumptions, frames of references, perspectives, and the biases within a discipline influence the ways knowledge is constructed.

---

and stimulated a search for new explanations and paradigms since the 1950s. Since the pioneering work of E. Franklin Frazier (1939), social scientists had accepted the notion that the slave experience had destroyed the Black family and that the destruction of the African American family continued in the post–World War II period during Black migration to and settlement in northern cities. Moynihan (1965), in his controversial book, *The Negro Family in America: The Case for National Action*, used the broken Black family explanation in his analysis. Gutman (1976), in an important historical study of the African American family from 1750 to 1925, concluded that "despite a high rate of earlier involuntary marital breakup, large numbers of slave couples lived in long marriages, and most slaves lived in double-headed households" (p. xxii).

An important group of African and African American scholars have challenged established interpretations about the origin of Greek civilization and the extent to which Greek civilization was influenced by African cultures. These scholars include Diop (1974), Williams (1987), and Van Sertima (1988, 1989). Cheikh Anta Diop is one of the most influential African scholars who has challenged established interpretations about the origin of Greek civilization. In *Black Nations and Culture*, published in 1955 (summarized by Van Sertima, 1989), he sets forth an important thesis that states that Africa is an important root of Western civilization. Diop argues that Egypt "was the node and center of a vast web linking the strands of cultures and languages; that the light that crystallized at the center of this early world had been energized by the cultural electricity streaming from the heartland of Africa" (p. 8).

Since the work by Diop, Williams, and Van Sertima, traditional interpretations about the formation of Greek civilization has been challenged by Bernal (1987–1991), a professor of government at Cornell University. The earlier challenges to established interpretations by African and African Americans received little attention, except within the African American community. However, Bernal's work has received wide attention in the popular press and among classicists.

Bernal (1987–1991) argues that important aspects of Greek civilization originated in ancient Egypt and Phoenicia and that the ancient civilization of Egypt was essentially African. Bernal believes that the contributions of Egypt and Phoenicia to Greek civilization have been deliberately ignored by classical scholars because of their biased attitudes toward non-White peoples and Semites. Bernal has published two of four planned volumes of his study *Black Athena*. In Volume 2 he uses evidence from linguistics, archeology and ancient documents to substantiate his claim that "between 2100 and 1100 B.C., when Greek culture was born, the people of the Aegean borrowed, adapted or had thrust upon them deities and language, technologies and architectures, notions of justice and polis" from Egypt and Phoenicia (Begley, Chideya, & Wilson, 1991, p. 50). Because transformative academic knowledge, such as that constructed by Diop, Williams, Van Sertima, and Bernal, challenges the established paradigms as well as because of the tremendous gap between academic knowledge and school knowledge, it often has little influence on school knowledge.

School Knowledge

School knowledge consists of the facts, concepts, and generalizations presented in textbooks, teachers' guides, and the other forms of media designed for school use. School knowledge also consists of the teacher's mediation and interpretation of that knowledge. The textbook is the main source of school knowledge in the United States (Apple & Christian-Smith, 1991; Goodlad, 1984; Shaver, Davis, & Helburn, 1979). Studies of textbooks indicate that these are some of the major themes in school knowledge (Anyon, 1979, 1981; Sleeter & Grant, 1991b): (a) America's founding fathers, such as Washington and Jefferson, were highly moral, liberty-loving men who championed equality and justice for all Americans; (b) the United States is a nation with justice, liberty, and freedom for all; (c) social class divisions are not significant issues in the United States; (d) there are no significant gender, class, or racial divisions within U.S. society; and (e) ethnic groups of color and Whites interact largely in harmony in the United States.

Studies of textbooks that have been conducted by researchers such as Anyon (1979, 1981) and Sleeter and Grant (1991b) indicate that textbooks present a highly selective view of social reality, give students the idea that knowledge is static rather than dynamic, and encourage students to master isolated facts rather than to develop complex understandings of social reality. These studies also indicate that textbooks reinforce the dominant social, economic, and power arrangements within society. Students are encouraged to accept rather than to question these arrangements.

In their examination of the treatment of race, class, gender, and disability in textbooks, Sleeter and Grant (1991b) concluded that although textbooks had largely eliminated sexist language and had incorporated images of ethnic minorities into them, they failed to help students to develop an understanding of the complex cultures of ethnic groups, an understanding of racism, sexism and classism in American society, and described the United States as a nation that had largely overcome its problems. Sleeter & Grant write:

The vision of social relations that the textbooks we analyzed for the most part project is one of harmony and equal opportunity—anyone can do or become whatever he or she wants; problems among people are mainly individual in nature and in the end are resolved. (p. 99)

A number of powerful factors influence the development and production of school textbooks (Altbach, Kelly, Petrie, & Weis, 1991; FitzGerald, 1979). One of the most important is the publisher's perception of statements and images that might be controversial. When textbooks become controversial, school districts often refuse to adopt and to purchase them. When developing a textbook, the publisher and the authors must also consider the developmental and reading levels of the students, state and district guidelines about what subject matter textbooks should include, and recent trends and developments in a content field that teachers and administrators will expect the textbook to reflect and incorporate. Because of the number of constraints and influences on the development of textbooks, school knowledge often does not include in-depth discussions and analyses of some of the major problems in American society, such as racism, sexism, social-class stratification, and poverty (Anyon, 1979, 1981; Sleeter & Grant, 1991b). Consequently, school knowledge is influenced most heavily by mainstream academic knowledge and popular knowledge. Transformative academic knowledge usually has little direct influence on school knowledge. It usually affects school knowledge in a significant way only after it has become a part of mainstream and popular knowledge. Teachers must make special efforts to introduce transformative knowledge and perspectives to elementary and secondary school students.

Teaching Implications

Multicultural education involves changes in the total school environment in order to create equal educational opportunities for all students (Banks, 1991; Banks & Banks, 1989; Sleeter & Grant, 1987). However, in this article I have focused on only one of the important dimensions of multicultural education—the kinds of *knowledge* that should be taught in the multicultural curriculum. The five types of knowledge described above have important implications for planning and teaching a multicultural curriculum.

An important goal of multicultural teaching is to help students to understand how knowledge is constructed. Students should be given opportunities to investigate and determine how cultural assumptions, frames of references, perspectives, and the biases within a discipline influence the ways the knowledge is constructed. Students should also be given opportunities to create knowledge themselves and identify ways in which the knowledge they construct is influenced and limited by their personal assumptions, positions, and experiences.

I will use a unit on the Westward Movement to illustrate how teachers can use the knowledge categories described above to teach from a multicultural perspective. When beginning the unit, teachers can draw upon the students' personal and cultural knowledge about the Westward Movement. They can ask the students to make a list of ideas that come to mind when they think of "The West." To enable the students to determine how the popular culture depicts the West, teachers can ask the students to view and analyze the film discussed above, *How the West Was Won*. They can also ask them to view videos of more recently made films about the West and to make a list of its major themes and images. Teachers can summarize Turner's frontier theory to give students an idea of how an influential mainstream historian described and interpreted the West in the late 19th century and how this theory influenced generations of historians.

Teachers can present a transformative perspective on the West by showing the students the film *How the West Was Won and Honor Lost*, narrated by Marlon Brando. This film describes how the European Americans who went West, with the use of broken treaties and deceptions, invaded the land of the Indians and displaced them. Teachers may also ask the students to view segments of the popular film *Dances With Wolves* and to discuss how the depiction of Indians in this film reflects both mainstream and transformative perspectives on Indians in U.S. history and culture. Teachers can present the textbook account of the Westward Movement in the final part of the unit.

The main goals of presenting different kinds of knowledge are to help students understand how knowledge is constructed and how it reflects the social context in which it is created and to enable them to develop the understandings and skills needed to become knowledge builders themselves. An important goal of multicultural education is to transform the school curriculum so that students not only learn the knowledge that has been constructed by others, but learn how to critically analyze the knowledge they master and how to construct their own interpretations of the past, present, and future.

Several important factors related to teaching the types of knowledge have not been discussed in this article but need to be examined. One is the personal/cultural knowledge of the classroom teacher. The teachers, like the students, bring understandings, concepts, explanations, and interpretations to the classroom that result from their experiences in their homes, families, and community cultures. Most teachers in the United States are European American (87%) and female (72%) (Ordovensky, 1992). However, there is enormous diversity among European Americans that is mirrored in the backgrounds of the teacher population, including diversity related to religion, social class, region, and ethnic origin. The diversity within European Americans is rarely discussed in the social science literature (Alba, 1990) or within classrooms. However, the rich diversity among the cultures of teachers is an important factor that needs to be examined and discussed in the classroom. The 13% of U.S. teachers who are ethnic minorities can also enrich their classrooms by sharing their personal and cultural knowledge with their students and by helping them to understand how it mediates textbook knowledge. The multicultural classroom is a forum of multiple voices and perspectives. The voices of the teacher, of the textbook, of mainstream and transformative authors—and of the students—are important components of classroom discourse.

Teachers can share their cultural experiences and interpretations of events as a way to motivate students to share theirs. However, they should examine their racial and ethnic attitudes toward diverse groups before engaging in cultural sharing. A democratic classroom atmosphere must also be created. The students must view the classroom as a forum where multiple perspectives are valued. An open and demo-cratic classroom will enable students to acquire the skills and abilities they need to examine conflicting knowledge claims and perspectives. Students must become critical consumers of knowledge as well as knowledge producers if they are to acquire the understandings and skills needed to function in the complex and diverse world of tomorrow. Only a broad and liberal multicultural education can prepare them for that world.

Notes

This article is adapted from a paper presented at the conference "Democracy and Education," sponsored by the Benton Center for Curriculum and Instruction, Department of Education, The University of Chicago, November 15–16, 1991, Chicago, Illinois. I am grateful to the following colleagues for helpful comments on an earlier draft of this article: Cherry A. McGee Banks, Carlos E. Cortés, Geneva Gay, Donna H. Kerr, Joyce E. King, Walter C. Parker, Pamela L. Grossman, and Christine E. Sleeter.

References

Acuña, R. (1988). *Occupied America: A history of Chicanos* (3rd ed.). New York: Harper & Row.

Alba, R. D. (1990). *Ethnic identity: The transformation of White America*. New Haven, CT: Yale University Press.

Allen, P. G. (1986). *The sacred hoop: Recovering the feminine in American Indian traditions*. Boston: Beacon Press.

Altbach, P. G., Kelly, G. P., Petrie, H. G., & Weis, L. (Eds.). (1991). *Textbooks in American Society*. Albany, NY: State University of New York Press.

The American heritage dictionary. (1983). New York: Dell.

Anyon, J. (1979). Ideology and United States history textbooks. *Harvard Educational Review, 49*, 361–386.

Anyon, J. (1981). Social class and school knowledge. *Curriculum Inquiry, 11*, 3–42.

Anzaldúa, G. (1990). Haciendo caras, una entrada: An introduction. in G. Anzaldúa (Ed.), *Making face, making soul: Haciendo caras* (pp. xv–xvii). San Francisco: Aunt Lute Foundation Books.

Apple, M. W., & Christian-Smith, L. K. (Eds.). (1991). *The politics of the textbook*. New York: Routledge.

Aptheker, H. (Ed.). (1973). *The collected published works of W. E. B. Dubois* (38 Vols.). Millwood, NY: Kraus.

Asante, M. K. (1991a). The Afrocentric idea in education. *The Journal of Negro Education, 60*, 170–180.

Asante, M. K. (1991b, September 23). Putting Africa at the center. *Newsweek, 118*, 46.

Asante, M. K., & Ravitch, D. (1991). Multiculturalism: An exchange. *The American Scholar, 60*, 267–275.

Banks, J. A. (1988). *Multiethnic education: Theory and practice* (2nd ed.). Boston: Allyn & Bacon.

Banks, J. A. (1991). *Teaching strategies for ethnic studies* (5th ed.). Boston: Allyn & Bacon.

Banks, J. A. (1991/1992). Multicultural education: For freedom's sake. *Educational Leadership, 49*, 32–36.

Banks, J. A., & Banks, C. A. M. (Eds.). (1989). *Multicultural education: Issues and perspectives*. Boston: Allyn & Bacon.

Begley, S., Chideya, F., & Wilson, L. (1991, September 23). Out of Egypt, Greece: Seeking the roots of Western civilization on the banks of the Nile. *Newsweek, 118*, 48–49.

Bernal, M. (1987–1991). *Black Athena: The Afroasiatic roots of classical civilization* (Vols. 1–2). London: Free Association Books.

Blassingame, J. W. (1972). *The slave community: Plantation life in the Antebellum South*. New York: Oxford University Press.

Bloom, A. (1987). *The closing of the American mind*. New York: Simon & Schuster.

Bogle, D. (1989). *Toms, coons, mulattoes, mammies & bucks: An interpretative history of Blacks in American films* (new expanded ed.). New York: Continuum.

Butler, J. E., & Walter, J. C. (1991). (Eds.). *Transforming the curriculum: Ethnic studies and women studies*. Albany, NY: State University of New York Press.

Cherryholmes, C. H. (1988). *Power and criticism: Poststructural investigations in education*. New York: Teachers College Press.

Clark, K. B. (1965). *Dark ghetto: Dilemmas of social power.* New York: Harper & Row.

Code, L. (1991). *What can she know? Feminist theory and the construction of knowledge.* Ithaca, NY: Cornell University Press.

Cooper, A. J. (1969). *A voice from the South.* New York: Negro Universities Press. (Original work published 1982)

Cortés, C. E. (1991a). Empowerment through media literacy. In C. E. Sleeter (Ed.), *Empowerment through multicultural education.* Albany: State University of New York Press.

Cortés, C. E. (1991b). Hollywood interracial love: Social taboo as screen titillation. In P. Loukides & L. K. Fuller (Eds.), *Beyond the stars II: Plot conventions in American popular film* (pp. 21–35). Bowling Green, OH: Bowling Green State University Press.

Delpit, L. D. (1988). The silenced dialogue: Power and pedagogy in educating other people's children. *Harvard Educational Review, 58,* 280–298.

Diop, C. A. (1974). *The African origin of civilization: Myth or reality?* New York: Lawrence Hill.

D'Souza, D. (1991). *Illiberal education: The politics of race and sex on campus.* New York: Free Press.

DuBois, W. E. B. (1962). *Black reconstruction in America 1860–1880: An essay toward a History of the part which Black folk played in the attempt to reconstruct democracy in America, 1860–1880.* New York: Atheneum. (Original work published 1935)

DuBois, W. E. B. (1969). *The suppression of the African slave trade to the United States of America, 1638–1870,* Baton Rouge, LA: Louisiana State University Press. (Original work published 1896)

Ellsworth, E. (1989). Why doesn't this feel empowering? Working through the repressive myths of critical pedagogy. *Harvard Educational Review, 59,* 297–324.

Farganis, S. (1986). *The social construction of the feminine character.* Totowa, NJ: Russell & Russell.

FitzGerald, F. (1979). *America revised: History schoolbooks in the twentieth century.* New York: Vintage.

Foucault, M. (1972). *The archaeology of knowledge and the discourse on language.* New York: Pantheon.

Fordham, S. (1988). Racelessness as a factor in Black students' school success: Pragmatic strategy or Pyrrhic victory? *Harvard Educational Review, 58,* 54–84.

Fordham, S. (1991). Racelessness in private schools: Should we deconstruct the racial and cultural identity of African-American adolescents? *Teachers College Record, 92,* 470–484.

Fordham, S., & Ogbu, J. (1986). Black students' school success: Coping with the burden of 'acting White.' *The Urban Review, 18,* 176–206.

Franklin, J. H. (1991, September 26). Illiberal education: An exchange. *New York Review of Books, 38,* 74–76.

Frazier, E. F. (1939). *The Negro family in the United States.* Chicago: University of Chicago Press.

Gates, H. L., Jr. (1988). *The signifying monkey: A theory of African-American literary criticism.* New York: Oxford University Press.

Gates, H. L., Jr. (1992). *Loose canons: Notes on the culture wars.* New York: Oxford University Press.

Genovese, E. D. (1972). *Roll Jordan roll: The world the slaves made.* New York: Pantheon.

Giroux, H. A. (1983). *Theory and resistance in education.* Boston: Bergin & Garvey.

Glazer, N. (1991, September 2). In defense of multiculturalism. *The New Republic,* 18–21.

Goodlad, J. I. (1984). *A place called school: Prospects for the future.* New York: McGraw-Hill.

Gordon, E. W. (1985). Social science knowledge production and minority experiences. *Journal of Negro Education, 54,* 117–132.

Gordon, E. W., Miller, F., & Rollock, D. (1990). Coping with communicentric bias in knowledge production in the social sciences. *Educational Researcher, 14(3),* 14–19.

Grant, C. A. (Ed.). (1992). *Research and multicultural education: From the margins to the mainstream.* Washington, DC: Falmer.

Gray, P. (1991, July 8). Whose America? *Time, 138,* 12–17.

Greenfield, G. M., & Cortés, C. E. (1991). Harmony and conflict of intercultural images: The treatment of Mexico in U.S. feature films and K–12 textbooks. *Mexican Studies/Estudios Mexicanos, 7,* 283–301.

Greer, S. (1969). *The logic of social inquiry.* Chicago: Aldine.

Gutman, H. G. (1976). *The Black family in slavery and freedom 1750–1925.* New York: Vintage.

Habermas, J. (1971). *Knowledge and human interests.* Boston: Beacon.

Hale-Benson, J. E. (1982). *Black children: Their roots, culture, and learning styles* (rev. ed.). Baltimore: John Hopkins University Press.

Harding, S. (1991). *Whose science? Whose knowledge? Thinking from women's lives.* Ithaca, NY: Cornell University Press.

Harding, V. (1981). *There is a river: The Black struggle for freedom in America.* New York: Vintage.

Heath, S. B. (1983). *Ways with words: Language, life and work in communities and classrooms.* New York: Cambridge University Press.

Hirsch, E. D., Jr. (1987). *Cultural literacy: What every American needs to know.* Boston: Houghton Mifflin.

hooks, b., & West, C. (1991). *Breaking bread: Insurgent Black intellectual life.* Boston: South End Press.

Howe, I. (1991, February 18). The value of the canon. *The New Republic,* 40–47.

Hoxie, F. E. (Ed.). (1988). *Indians in American history.* Arlington Heights, IL: Harlan Davidson.

Hoxie, F. E. (no date). *The Indians versus the textbooks: Is there any way out?* Chicago: The Newberry Library, Center for the History of the American Indian.

Kaplan, A. (1964). *The conduct of inquiry: Methodology for behavioral science.* San Francisco: Chandler.

King, J. E., & Mitchell, C. A. (1990). *Black mothers to sons: Juxtaposing African American literature with social practice.* New York: Lang.

Kuhn, T. S. (1970). *The structure of scientific revolutions* (2nd ed.). Chicago: University of Chicago Press.

Labov, W. (1975). *The study of nonstandard English.* Washington, DC: Center for Applied Linguistics.

Ladner, J. A. (Ed.). (1973). *The death of White sociology.* New York: Vintage.

Meier, A., & Rudwick, E. (1986). *Black history and the historical profession 1915–1980.* Urbana, IL: University of Illinois Press.

Merton, R. K. (1972). Insiders and outsiders: A chapter in the sociology of knowledge. *The American Journal of Sociology, 78,* 9–47.

Milner, D. (1983). *Children and race.* Beverly Hills, CA: Sage.

Minnich, E. K. (1990). *Transforming knowledge.* Philadelphia: Temple University Press.

Moynihan, D. P. (1965). *The Negro family in America: A case for national action.* Washington, DC: U.S. Department of Labor.

Myrdal, G. (with the assistance of R. Sterner & A. Rose). (1944). *An American dilemma: The Negro problem in modern democracy.* New York: Harper.

Nash, G. B. (1982). *Red, White and Black: The peoples of early America.* Englewood Cliffs, NJ: Prentice-Hall.

New York City Board of Education. (1990). *Grade 7, United States and New York state history: A multicultural perspective.* New York: Author.

New York State Department of Education. (1989, July). *A curriculum of inclusion* (Report of the Commissioner's Task Force on Minorities: Equity and excellence). Albany, NY: The State Education Department.

New York State Department of Education. (1991, June). *One nation, many peoples: A declaration of cultural interdependence.* Albany, NY: The State Education Department.

Ordovensky, P. (1992, July 7). Teachers: 87% White, 72% women. *USA Today,* p. 1A.

Philips, S. U. (1983). *The invisible culture: Communication in classroom and community on the Warm Springs Indian Reservation.* New York: Longman.

Phillips, U. B. (1918). *American Negro slavery.* New York: Appleton.

Ramírez, M., III, & Castañeda, A. (1974). *Cultural democracy, bicognitive development and education.* New York: Academic Press.

Ravitch, D., & Finn, C. E., Jr. (1987). *What do our 17-year-olds know? A report on the first national assessment of history and literature.* New York: Harper & Row.

Rivlin, A. M. (1973). Forensic social science. *Harvard Educational Review, 43,* 61–75.

Rorty, R. (1989). *Contingency, irony, and solidarity.* New York: Cambridge University Press.

Rosenau, P. M. (1992). *Post-modernism and the social sciences: Insights, inroads, and intrusions.* Princeton, NJ: Princeton University Press.

Schlesinger, A., Jr. (1991). *The disuniting of America: Reflections on a multicultural society.* Knoxville, TN: Whittle Direct Books.

Shade, B. J. R. (Ed.). (1989). *Culture, style and the educative process.* Springfield, IL: Thompson.

Shaver, J. P., Davis, O. L., Jr., & Helburn, S. W. (1979). The status of social studies education: Impressions from three NSF studies. *Social Education, 43,* 150–153.

Sleeter, C. E. (1991). (Ed.). *Empowerment through multicultural education.* Albany: State University of New York Press.

Sleeter, C. E., & Grant, C. A. (1987). An analysis of multicultural education in the United States. *Harvard Educational Review, 57,* 421–444.

Sleeter, C. E., & Grant, C. A. (1991a). Mapping terrains of power: Student cultural knowledge versus classroom knowledge. In C. E. Sleeter (Ed.), *Empowerment through multicultural education* (pp. 49–67). Albany: State University of New York Press.

Sleeter, C. E., & Grant, C. A. (1991b). Race, class, gender and disability in current textbooks. In M. W. Apple & L. K. Christian-Smith (Eds.), *The politics of textbooks* (pp. 78–110). New York: Routledge.

Smitherman, G. (1977). *Talkin and testifyin: The language of Black America.* Boston: Houghton Mifflin.

Sokol, E. (Ed.). (1990). *A world of difference: St. Louis metropolitan region, preschool through grade 6, teacher/student resource guide.* St. Louis: Anti-Defamation League of B'nai B'rith.

Stampp, K. M. (1956). *The peculiar institution: Slavery in the ante-bellum South.* New York: Vintage.

Takaki, R. T. (1979). *Iron cages: Race and culture in 19th-century America.* Seattle, WA: University of Washington Press.

Tetreault, M. K. T. (1993). Classrooms for diversity: Rethinking curriculum and pedagogy. In J. A. Banks & C. A. M. Banks (Eds.), *Multicultural education: Issues and perspectives* (2nd ed.) (pp. 129–148). Boston: Allyn & Bacon.

Thornton, R. (1987). *American Indian holocaust and survival: A population history since 1492.* Norman: University of Oklahoma Press.

Turner, F. J. (1989). The significance of the frontier in American history. In C. A. Milner II (Ed.), *Major problems in the history of the American West* (pp. 2–21). Lexington, MA: Heath. (Original work published 1894)

Van Sertima, I. V. (Ed.). (1988). *Great Black leaders: Ancient and modern.* New Brunswick, NJ: Rutgers University, Africana Studies Department.

Van Sertima, I. V. (Ed.). (1989). *Great African thinkers: Vol. 1. Cheikh Anta Diop.* New Brunswick, NJ: Transaction Books.

Wiggington, E. (1991/1992). Culture begins at home. *Educational Leadership, 49,* 60–64.

Williams, G. W. (1968). *History of the Negro Race in America from 1619 to 1880: Negroes as slaves, as soldiers, and as citizens* (2 vols.). New York: Arno Press. (Original work published 1892 & 1893)

Williams, C. (1987). *The destruction of Black civilization: Great issues of a race from 4500 B.C. to 2000 A.D.* Chicago: Third World Press.

Woodson, C. G. (1933). *The Mis-education of the Negro.* Washington, DC: Associated Publishers.

Woodson, C. G., & Wesley, C. H. (1922). *The Negro in our history.* Washington, DC: Associated Publishers.

Woodward, C. V. (1991, July 18). Freedom and the universities. *The New York Review of Books, 38,* 32–37.

Young, M. F. D. (1971). An approach to curricula as socially organized knowledge. In M. F. D. Young (Ed.), *Knowledge and control* (pp. 19–46). London: Collier-Macmillan.

Zinn, H. (1980). *A people's history of the United States.* New York: Harper & Row.

Investing in Our
CHILDREN:
A Struggle for America's Conscience and Future

"Too many young people of all races and classes are growing up unable to handle life, without hope or steady compasses to navigate a world that is reinventing itself technologically and politically at a kaleidoscopic pace."

Marian Wright Edelman

Ms. Edelman is president of the Children's Defense Fund, Washington, D.C.

THE 1990S' STRUGGLE is about the U.S.'s conscience and future. Many of the battles will not be as dramatic as Gettysburg or Vietnam or Desert Storm, but they are going to shape this nation's place in the 21st century. Every American in this last decade of the last century of this millennium must struggle to redefine success in the U.S., asking not "How much can I get?," but "How much can I do without and share?"; not "How can I find myself?," but "How can I lose myself in service to others?"; not just how I can take care of me and mine, but how I can help as one American to strengthen family and community values and help this great nation regain her moral and economic bearings at home and abroad.

When I was growing up, service was as essential as eating and sleeping and going to church and school. Caring black adults were buffers against the segregated outside world which told me that, as a black girl, I wasn't worth anything and was not important. However, I didn't believe it because my parents, teachers, and preachers said it wasn't so. The childhood message I internalized, despite the outside segregation and poverty all around, was that, as God's child, no man or woman could look down on me, and I could look down on no man or woman.

I couldn't play in segregated playgrounds or sit at drugstore lunch counters, so my father, a Baptist minister, built a playground and canteen behind our church. Whenever he saw a need, he tried to respond. There were no black homes for the aged in South Carolina at that time, so my parents began one across the street, and our entire family had to help out. I didn't like it a whole lot of the time, but that is how I learned that it was my responsibility to take care of elderly family members and neighbors, and that everyone was my neighbor.

I went everywhere with my parents and the members of my church and community who were my watchful extended family. The entire black community took responsibility for protecting its children. They reported on me when I did wrong, applauded me when I did well, and were very clear as adults about what doing well meant. It meant being helpful to others, achieving in school, and reading. We all finally figured out that the only time our father wouldn't give us a chore was when we were reading, so we all read a lot.

Children were taught, by example, that nothing was too lowly to do and that the work of our heads and hands were both valuable. As a child, I went with an older brother—I was eight or nine or 10 and remember the debate between my parents as to whether I was too young to go help clean the bedsores of a poor, sick woman— but I went and learned just how much the smallest helping hands can mean to a lonely person in need.

Our families, churches, and community made kids feel useful and important. While life often was hard and resources scarce, we always knew who we were and that the measure of our worth was inside our heads and hearts, not outside in material possessions or personal ambition. We were taught that the world had a lot of problems; that black people had an *extra* lot of problems, but that we could struggle and change them; that extra intellectual and material gifts brought with them the privilege and responsibility of sharing with others less fortunate; and that service is the rent each of us pays for living—the very purpose of life and not something you do in your spare time or after you have reached your personal goals.

I am grateful for these childhood legacies of a living faith reflected in daily service, the discipline of hard work, and stick-to-itiveness—a capacity to struggle in the face of adversity. Giving up, despite how bad the world was outside, simply was not a part of my childhood lexicon. You got up every morning and did what you had to do, and you got up every time you fell down and tried as many times as you had to until you got it right. I was 14 the night my father died. He had holes in his shoes, but he had two children who graduated from college, one in college, another in divinity school, and a vision that he was able to convey to me even as he was dying in an ambulance—that I, a young black girl, could be and do anything, that race and gender are shadows, and that character, self-discipline, determination, attitude, and service are the substance of life.

What kind of vision are we conveying to our children today as parents, political and business leaders, and professionals? Our children are growing up in an ethically polluted nation where instant sex without responsibility, instant gratification without effort, instant solutions without sacrifice, getting rather than giving, and hoarding rather than sharing are the too frequent signals of our mass media, popular culture, and political life.

The standard of success for far too many Americans has become personal greed, rather than common good. The standard for striving and achievement has become getting, rather than making an extra effort or service to others. Truth-telling and moral example have become devalued commodities. Nowhere is the paralysis of public or private conscience more evident than in the neglect and abandonment of millions of our shrinking pool of youngsters, whose futures will determine our nation's ability to compete economically and lead morally as much as any child of privilege and as much as any other issue.

We need to understand that investing in our children is not investing in a special interest group or helping out somebody else—it is absolutely essential to every American's well-being and future. Only two out of every 10 new labor force entrants in this decade will be white males born in the U.S. As an aging population with a shrinking pool of kids, we don't have a child to waste—we need every one of them. We either can decide to invest in them up front and give them a sense of nurturing and caring adults that are part of a community and a society that guarantees them a future, or we can continue to fear them, build more and more prisons, and worry about them shooting at us. We don't have a choice about investing in our children, only when we are going to invest and whether it's going to be positive or negative investment.

Every 16 seconds of every school day, as we talk about a competitive workforce in the future, one of our children drops out of school. Every 26 seconds of every day, an American child runs away from home. These are not just poor or black children—they are all of our children. This is not something affecting just a few families—these are national problems. Every 47

seconds, a youngster is abused. Every 67 seconds, a teenager has a baby. We produce the equivalent of the city of Seattle each year with children having children. Every seven minutes, a child is arrested for a drug offense. Every 30 minutes, one of our children is charged with drunken driving. Every 53 minutes, in the richest land on Earth, an American child dies because of poverty.

It is disgraceful that children are the poorest Americans and that, in the last year alone, 840,000 youngsters fell into poverty and that there has been a 26% increase since 1979 in poverty among children. The majority of poor youngsters in America are not black and not in inner cities. They are in rural and suburban areas and in working and two-parent families. A lot of folk who were middle class last year around the country are now in poverty and on food stamps. It can happen to any of us.

We are in a sad state when the American Dream for many middle-class young people has become a choice between a house and a child. They are worrying about how their offspring are going to make it through college, pay off their higher education loans, and get off the ground and form families. We have to begin investing in all of our kids and all of our families. I believe we have lost our sense of what is important as a people. Too many children of all races and classes are growing up unable to handle life, without hope or steady compasses to navigate a world that is reinventing itself technologically and politically at a kaleidoscopic pace. Too many are growing up terribly uncertain and fearful about the future.

Despite the global realities the nation faces and a lot of the economic and moral uncertainty of the present, there are some enduring values we have lost sight of. I agree with poet Archibald MacLeish that there is only one thing more powerful than learning from experience and that is *not* learning from experience. It is the responsibility of every adult—parent, teacher, preacher, professional, and political leader—to make sure that youngsters hear what adults have learned from the lessons of life. Author James Baldwin wrote some years back that children really don't ever do what we tell them to do, but they almost always do what we do.

Americans have to move away from the idea of being entitled to something because they are men, or wealthy, or white, or black. It is time to come together to work quietly and systematically toward building a more just America and ensuring that no child is left behind. We should resist quick-fix, simplistic answers and easy gains that disappear as fast as they come. I am sick of people talking big and making great promises, then not following up and getting it done. Too often, we get bogged down

in our ego needs and lose sight of deeper community and national needs.

Family values vs. hypocrisy

As a nation, we mouth family values we do not practice. Seventy countries provide medical care and financial assistance to all pregnant women and to children—the U.S. is not one of them. Seventeen industrialized nations have paid maternity/paternity leave programs—the U.S. is not one of them. In 1992, Pres. George Bush vetoed an unpaid leave bill that would have allowed parents to stay at home when a child is sick or disabled. We need to stop the hypocrisy of talking about families when all our practices are the opposite. It is time for parents to have a real choice about whether to remain at home or work outside the home without worrying about the safety of their children.

Many families have had to put a second parent into the workforce in order to make ends meet. Even when both parents work, a vast number are not able to meet their basic housing and health care needs.

The new generation of young people must share and stress family rituals and values and be moral examples for their children, just as this generation must try even harder to be. If people cut corners, their children will too. If they are not honest, their children will not be either. If adults spend all of their money and tithe no portion of it for colleges, synagogues or churches, and civic causes, their children won't either. If they tolerate political leaders who don't tell the truth or do what they say, their children will lose faith as too many are doing in the political process.

If we snicker at racial and gender jokes, another generation will pass on the poison that our generation still has not had the will to snuff out. Each of us must counter the proliferating voices of racial, ethnic, and religious division that separates us as Americans. It's important for us to face up to, rather than ignore, our growing racial problems, which are America's historic and future Achilles' heel. Whites didn't create black or brown people; men didn't create women; Christians didn't create Jews—so what gives anybody the right to feel entitled to diminish another?

We need to ask ourselves as Americans—how many potential Martin Luther King, Jrs. or Colin Powells, Sally Rides or Barbara McClintocks our nation is going to waste before it wakes up and recognizes that its ability to compete in the new century is as inextricably intertwined with poor and non-white children as with its white and privileged ones, with girls as well as its boys? As Rabbi Abraham Heschel put it, "We may not all be equally guilty for the problems that we face, but we are all equally responsible" for building a decent and just

America and seeing that no child is left behind.

People who are unwilling or unable to share and make complicated and sometimes hard choices may be incapable or taking courageous action to rebuild our families and community and nation. Nevertheless, I have great hopes about America and believe we can rebuild community and begin to put our children first as a nation. It is going to require that each of us figure out what we're going to be willing to sacrifice and share.

Many whites favor racial justice as long as things remain the same. Many voters hate Congress, but love their own Congressman as long as he or she takes care of their special interests. Many husbands are happier to share their wives' added income than share the housework and child care. Many Americans deny the growing gap between the rich and the poor, and they are sympathetic and concerned about escalating child suffering as long as somebody else's program is cut.

Americans have to grow up beyond this national adolescence. Everybody wants to spend, but nobody wants to pay. Everybody wants to lower the deficit, but also to get everything that they can. We have to ask ourselves how we're going to come together as a people to begin to make sure that the necessities of the many are taken care of and that every child gets what he or she needs to achieve a healthy start in life. If we're not too poor to bail out the savings and loan institutions, if we're not too poor to build all those B-2 bombers, we're not too poor to rescue our suffering children and to ensure that all youngsters get what they need.

In a time of economic uncertainty and fear about the future, of rising crime, rising costs, and rising joblessness, we must never give in to the urge to give up, no matter how hard it gets. There's an old proverb that says, "When you get to your wits end, remember that God lives there." Harriet Beecher Stowe once said that, when you get into a "tight place and everything goes against you, till it seems as though you could not hang on for a minute longer, never give up then, for that is just the place and the time when the tide will turn."

We can not continue as a nation to make a distinction between our children and other people's kids. Every youngster is entitled to an equal share of the American Dream. Every poor child, every black child, every white child—every child living everywhere—should have an equal shot. We need every one of them to be productive and educated and healthy.

Let me end this article with a prayer, written by a schoolteacher in South Carolina.

She urges us to pray and accept responsibility for children who sneak popsicles before supper, erase holes in math workbooks, and never can find their shoes, but let's also pray and accept responsibility for children who can't bound down the street in a new pair of sneakers, who don't have any rooms to clean up, whose pictures aren't on anybody's dresser, and whose monsters are real. Let each of us commit to praying and accepting responsibility for children who spend all their allowance before Tuesday, throw tantrums in the grocery store, pick at their food, shove dirty clothes under the bed, never rinse out the tub, squirm in church or temple, and scream in the phone, but let's also pray and accept responsibility for those children whose nightmares come in the daytime, who will eat anything, who have never seen a dentist, who aren't spoiled by anybody, who go to bed hungry and cry themselves to sleep all over this rich nation. Let's commit to praying and accepting responsibility for children who want to be carried and for those who must be carried. Let's commit to protecting those children whom we never give up on, but also those children who don't get a second chance. Let each of us commit to praying and voting and speaking and fighting for those children whom we smother, but also for those who will grab the hand of anybody kind enough to offer it.

Concerns About Teaching Culturally Diverse Students

Patricia L. Marshall

Patricia L. Marshall is Assistant Professor at North Carolina State University where she teaches courses in multicultural education and elementary school curriculum. Her current research interests involve cognitive developmental theory within multicultural education in teacher education programs. Dr. Marshall is a member of Omicron Rho Chapter.

The one word that best describes contemporary students, curricula, and school philosophies is *diverse*. A 1991 report conducted by the College Board and Western Interstate Commission for Higher Education report indicated that diverse student populations in the United States are expected to increase dramatically by the year 1994. Specifically, Asian and Pacific Islander student populations are predicted to increase by 70 percent, Hispanic by 54 percent, and African-American by 13 percent. While this diverse climate presents challenges, undoubtedly it also creates concerns among school personnel. Teachers may feel a definite need to develop a heightened sensitivity and cross-cultural awareness for teaching today's student populations.

The professional concerns that teachers hold about student diversity may potentially affect how teachers approach teaching tasks as well as how they interact with students. An examination of teachers' concerns about working with diverse students and ways they can address these concerns follows.

Identifying Concerns

Research (Fuller 1969; Gehrke 1987; Katz 1972; Marshall et al. 1990) suggests that teachers have varying levels of concern about working in classrooms. Heretofore, the research literature has not explicitly addressed the nature of teachers' concerns about working with diverse student populations. The phrase *multicultural teaching concern* refers to those concerns teachers have about working in contemporary culturally diverse school settings. Such teaching concerns are distinctive because they are held about students whose cultural backgrounds differ most from the teacher's background. Most multicultural teaching concerns are related to teacher and student racial or ethnic differences. Some concerns may reflect differences between individuals of the same racial or ethnic background but different socioeconomic backgrounds.

Surveying Concerns

Groups of teachers and university juniors and seniors were recently invited to respond to an open-ended questionnaire about multicultural education. They were asked to submit concerns they or their peers hold about teaching in diverse or "multicultural" school environments. More than 300 concerns were collected from this survey. Because the professional experiences with multicultural student populations varied among the groups, it was expected the concerns identified would also differ. However, the teachers and university students identified similar professional concerns about working—or the prospect of working—with culturally diverse students.

A group of multicultural education specialists analyzed the open-ended surveys and organized the original 300 concerns into a 64-item instrument called

Questions on the MTCS survey are presented in four categories. Within each category, samples are provided.

Multicultural Teaching Concerns Survey

Familial or Group Knowledge	Strategies and Techniques	Interpersonal Competence	School Bureaucracy
Concerns about the completeness of teachers' knowledge about diverse students' familial/group culture and background.	Concerns about utilizing appropriate techniques and including the most appropriate and inclusive content in curriculum and general school program.	Concerns about the impact of personal attitudes, actions, and/or beliefs on interactions with diverse student populations.	Concerns about whether the structure of schools (e.g., grouping patterns) and the actions of other school personnel impact efforts to effectively address school issues related to student diversity.
Examples:	*Examples:*	*Examples:*	*Examples:*
▼ How will I learn about the family culture of students and how it affects performance and attitudes toward school?	▼ How should I vary my teaching techniques when teaching culturally diverse students?	▼ Will my students be prejudiced against me?	▼ How do I combat school district policies that are inequitable for diverse students?
▼ How do I differentiate student values and behavior patterns that are culturally based?	▼ How should I go about selecting materials and resources to incorporate multicultural perspectives into the existing curricula?	▼ Will students perceive me as biased simply because my background is different from theirs?	▼ How do I deal with intolerance among my colleagues?
▼ In what ways do parent expectations impact or dictate behaviors exhibited in my class?		▼ Will I be able to be myself when working with culturally diverse students without appearing uncaring and aloof?	▼ What can I do when my classroom actually reflects the community in which I teach?

the *Multicultural Teaching Concerns Survey* (MTCS)[1]. Each item within the MTCS corresponds to one of four concern categories, which are outlined in the table above.

Ways to Address Concerns in the Classroom

Teachers who have concerns about teaching diverse student populations are often apprehensive about not being able to meet the needs of their students. Selecting the most appropriate teaching techniques and strategies involves constant vigilance on the part of every professional educator. Similar to other professionals, classroom teachers must constantly stay abreast of the latest interpretations of content and teaching techniques. One of the greatest tragedies is that many teachers simply have not had a formal professional opportunity to explore techniques and strategies more appropriate for their work with diverse student populations. In addition, the basic content knowledge that many teachers may have studied while training to become teachers may not have been comprehensive to the extent that it included varying cultural perspectives. Consequently, these teachers should work to lessen or eliminate multicultural teaching concerns. When this is done, teachers can redirect their attention toward those aspects of classroom interaction that will allow them to meet the needs of all students. Below are ways multicultural teaching concerns can be addressed:

✔ Make a concerted effort to learn more about the family structure of your students.

✔ Personalize contacts with students' parents by visiting homes and neighborhoods.

✔ Enroll in classes or workshops devoted to the past and more recent history of the ethnic or racial groups of students in your classes.

✔ Visit community centers, places of worship, civic events, or cultural or religious celebrations of members of nonmajority cultures.

---

[1]Pilot testing for Phase I of the MTCS included a survey of 300 teachers and university education majors. Analysis of the results revealed high construct validity and promising reliability coefficients. Currently in Phase II of its development, the MTCS is being refined using a larger, more diverse population of classroom teachers. For more information about the study, contact the author at North Carolina State University; Department of Curriculum and Instruction; 402 Poe Hall, Box 7801; Raleigh, NC 27695-7801.

6. EQUALITY OF EDUCATIONAL OPPORTUNITY

✔ Begin a self-study project to read contemporary literature written by authors from diverse backgrounds.

✔ Subscribe to or borrow from a library monthly magazines published for ethnic populations.

✔ Explore research on individual learning styles.

✔ Involve students in unit planning.

✔ Enroll in a race awareness or cross-cultural sensitivity workshop.

✔ Form professional collaborations with colleagues of a different race or ethnicity and with whom you can share concerns and questions about working with diverse students.

The MTCS offers opportunities to explore a new dimension of teachers' concerns about working in classrooms. It examines the nature of teachers' concerns as they relate to diversity in contemporary schools. Cultural diversity in schools will continue to increase, resulting in significant changes in the way schools operate. These changes need not cause major anxiety for teachers. Instead, diversity can be viewed as an opportunity for teachers to engage in analyzing their professional selves. These changes can also be perceived as opportunities for professional—and perhaps personal—growth.

Recommended Reading on Multicultural Education

Presently, multicultural education is the major schooling innovation that challenges teachers to explore their own attitudes and behaviors toward culturally diverse students. The following books are excellent sources of information on this growing field of study.

Banks, J. A., and C. McGee Banks, eds. 1993. *Multicultural education: Issues and perspectives.* Boston: Allyn and Bacon. Exploration of various dimensions of multicultural education including teaching about women, ethnic/racial minorities, and exceptionalities. Includes resources section and glossary list of culturally sensitive terminology.

Bennett, C. I. 1990. *Comprehensive multicultural education: Theory and practice.* Boston: Allyn and Bacon. Examines multicultural education as a "movement, curriculum approach, process and teacher commitment." Includes chapters on the role of individual learning styles on teaching and learning.

Grant, C. A. and C. E. Sleeter, 1989. *Turning on learning: Five approaches for multicultural teaching plans for races, class, gender, and disability.* Columbus: Merrill Publishing Company. Provides a collection of lesson plans for various subjects (including art and mathematics) and grade levels using five different approaches to multicultural education.

Gollnick, D. M., and P.C. Chinn, 1992. *Multicultural education in a pluralistic society.* Columbus: Merrill Publishing Company. Excellent introductory text on multicultural education. Includes one of the best all-around discussions on the basic tenets of multicultural education and the dominant culture in the United States.

Tiedt, P. L., and I. M. Tiedt, 1992. *Multicultural education teaching: A handbook of activities, information, and resources.* Boston: Allyn and Bacon. Collection of activities and ideas for incorporating multicultural education into existing curricula. Especially appropriate for elementary school teachers.

References

Fuller, F. F. 1969. Concerns of teachers: A developmental conceputalization. *American Educational Research Journal,* 6(2): 207–26.

Gehrke, N. 1987. *On Being A Teacher.* West Lafayette, Ind.: Kappa Delta Pi.

Katz, L. G. 1972. Developmental stages of preschool teachers. *Elementary School Journal,* 73(1): 50–54.

Marshall, P., S. Fittinghoff, and C. O. Cheney. 1990. Beginning teacher developmental stages: implications for creating collaborative internship programs. *Teacher Education Quarterly,* 17(3):25–35.

School Guides Students to Goals and Self-Respect

Shoshana Gilbert

Shoshana Gilbert writes for World Media Coordination in Paris

Adriana's run-down neighborhood is ruled by a deadly combination of apathy and violence. At 13, she is the leader of a group of adolescent girls, decked out in hair spray and heavy makeup, whose social life revolves around the parties and territorial wars of Modesto, Calif., gangs.

A few months ago, Adriana's best friend was brutally murdered when her boyfriend left the girl at one of these parties. The girl remains immortalized in the spray-painted graffiti that commemorates her name.

Modesto's largely Hispanic population of 172,000 is home to 43 identified gangs. Some of the primary centers for gang-related violence are schoolyards, where youths come armed with knives and guns. The schools are used by gangs as fertile recruiting grounds for adolescents coming from broken homes and living in communities with high unemployment, who are desperately looking for a sense of belonging.

Under such circumstances, academic success is not a priority, and the drop-out rate among Hispanics is 60 percent before the age of 15. Adriana currently attends the Evelyn Hanshaw Middle School, for 11-to-13-year-olds, which has undertaken one of the city's boldest attempts to keep disadvantaged children in school. While most public schools perpetuate academic failure by neglecting to consider the backgrounds of the children they are trying to teach, Hanshaw defies the traditional textbook approach to education by creating an environment that responds to the specific needs of its children—in this case a school that offers its students safety, a sense of self-worth, and a feeling of belonging.

Located across the street from the Salvation Army building, the school is built and fenced in protective concrete. Standing at the entrance, with a pocketful of pencils and a walky-talky, is principal Charles Vidal. He and two security guards are wearing burgundy jackets. They carefully monitor the students as they walk to class. One guard writes down the license number of a suspicious-looking car that slowly cruises by.

"When we first opened, I used to have groups of guys standing on the other side of the street watching. I made sure we had enough policemen to let them know who this school belongs to. Territory is important here," Mr. Vidal says.

When Adriana and her friends see their principal, they immediately cluster around him. "Hey, Mr. Vidal, I'm being my personal best," she says.

"Glad to hear it, Adriana. Need a pencil?"

"Yeah, thanks," she responds.

A boy with slicked-back hair struts by with a University of California at Los Angeles sweatshirt. "Hey Carlos, I like your shirt, good job," Vidal calls out. As 900 students walk to their classes, this continues to happen. Vidal greets many of them by name with a smile and occasionally a warm pat on the back, more like that of a concerned parent than an authority figure.

In a curious ritual, adolescents with don't-mess-with-me attitudes voluntarily approach their principal, smile and repeat the Hanshaw slogan—"I'm being my personal best"—for which they receive a yellow pencil. Vidal is an ardent believer that academic success starts with the way these kids see themselves.

"Our school mascot is the Titan—an all-powerful person known for greatness of achievement," he says. "We're trying to tell these kids that they all have sleeping Titans within them, and it is our job to wake them up."

"We are the only dependable routine in these children's lives," he explains. "They have no adults who are motivating them, and it is our job to give them the hope and a sense of purpose which promote success and personal achievement. This particular school is often the best thing in these kids' lives. I have to counsel some of them before they will get on the buses to go home on Fridays."

For the students here, school has become much more than an obligation; it's a haven. Adriana refers to her school as a "fairy-tale land."

"On the streets you're respected because you are big and bad, but school is our own world," she says. "It's like we can be kids and they respect us. Everyone is so sweet and nice that it makes you feel good."

Before Vidal opened the school in 1991, he interviewed hundreds of dropouts to find out why they had left school. He discovered that there was a huge gap between what schools generally evaluate as important for students and what was specifically relevant to these children.

"The kids I spoke to could not understand how what they were learning applied to their lives on a daily basis," he says. "It did not make sense to stay in school."

Hoping to keep them in school, Vidal decided that the priority was to build an environment that took into account the needs of these street-smart kids from turbulent families and gang-plagued neighborhoods by creating a school that offered them the sense of community they were searching for.

The students are strictly forbidden to dress all in one color or wear parapher-

nalia that imply gang membership, such as red or blue shoelaces. Even sports-team shirts or baseball caps are forbidden.

But colors, handshakes, and slogans—all of which are used by gangs to symbolize membership and "belonging" on the streets—are adopted by the students for one purpose: their school and their future college education. The youths are praised and rewarded for wearing burgundy, the school color, and T-shirts with college emblems. They have their own handshake, which is supposed to represent receiving their future diplomas.

Hanshaw Middle School tries to get them to start imagining what it would be like to go to college, not by telling them how important it is, but by making them feel as if they are already there. The students are divided into seven "neighborhoods," each named after one of California's state universities. The highlight of the students' year is a trip to "their"

college, where they meet students with similar backgrounds who have stayed in school and made it to college.

"Only 3 percent of California state graduates are Hispanic. Most [of our Hispanic students] have never seen a university. You have to at least show them one, and make them feel like they can be part of one if you ever want them to get there," Principal Vidal says.

"Most of the parents of these children have never completed high school, and often the only books in their home are the Bible and Playboy [magazine]," says Barbara Hickman, the science and math teacher for the "Sonoma University" group of students. "And yet after one year, these kids are scoring above grade level in math and science because of the encouragement they are given and the way they are taught. The idea is to wrap what is found in textbooks around a classroom experience, something that relates to their own lives. We talk about questions such as authority and identity and then find the science, history, and English to teach it," Ms. Hickman says.

Vidal and the other adults at Hanshaw call themselves "community leaders," not teachers. Students are referred to as "citizens." Vidal has hand-picked "community leaders" whom students can "borrow character from."

Jeff Albritton's history and English class of seventh graders has been doing projects on watershed decisions in history and is discussing how to make decisions in their own lives.

"If your parents get divorced, how do you choose which one to live with?" Mr. Albritton asks. A shy girl answers, "I don't know." Adriana says from across the classroom, "You have to choose or else you'll end up in a foster home. Choose the one you have a better relationship with," she tells the girl.

"No, choose your father; he has to pay for you so you might as well live with him anyway," advises another student.

Albritton says that "70 percent of these children come from single-parent families. The key is to trick these kids into learning by empowering them to learn in a way that brings in relevant issues in their lives and gets them socially active."

Hanshaw has set up "university clubs" in various high schools so that former students can keep in touch with each other and their teachers. But Vidal knows that the real test for these children will come later.

"School is not neutral with regard to success," he says. "Children from this kind of social background must be told by someone, at some point, what they are capable of doing, to get them curious about life. We have had over 50 school districts coming to look at our school. What worries me is that so many find this revolutionary. It seem like common sense. But few schools are doing it," Vidal says.

Adriana says she wants to go to college, but her fragile confidence relies on the personal dedication of her teachers and the nurturing environment they have succeeded in creating—conditions that are not easily sustained.

The gender machine

Congress is looking for ways to remove old barriers to girls' success

Most adults still remember the prefeminist ditty about little girls being made of "sugar and spice and everything nice." And most who remember have long since dismissed it as an archaic old saw, a vestige of sexism long since eradicated. But while Americans have been busy celebrating their own sexual enlightenment over the past decades, scientists have continued to examine the nuances of gender and sex roles in the classroom, on the playing field and at home, and the latest research is far from encouraging. Despite the 20-year-old federal mandate for gender equity in schools, despite feminism's many effects and despite Hillary Rodham Clinton's ground-breaking activism in the White House, society's gender-sorting machinery still grinds away, steering girls forcefully into outdated female roles. Its grumblings can be heard throughout a girl's everyday world; at playtime, in television programming, even in the guiding words of well-intentioned parents and teachers. Its damage can be seen in the way girls hush up as they age, in the crisis of confidence most face as teens and in the often-diminished career aspirations of even the brightest young women.

Renewed crusade. This unsettling news from social scientists has left a generation of feminists aghast, and it is now spawning a massive national movement aimed at dismantling the gender-sorting machine and ensuring that girls have the opportunities everyone assumed they already had. Universities, foundations and women's groups have all joined the crusade, formulating programs to counter old stereotypes, foster self-esteem and encourage girls to venture into nontraditional fields. At the forefront of the drive is a nine-part piece of legislation entitled the Gender Equity in Education Act, cosponsored by more than 70 members of the House of Representatives and poised to move through Congress this fall. The bill is a response to various social forces working against girls, ranging from teacher indifference and discouragement to debilitating sexual harassment. While the measure has drawn the scorn of some critics who see it transforming girls and young women into a new class of victims, so far the bill has not met with a trace of opposition inside the halls of Congress.

Advocates of the legislation are adamant that their efforts have less to do with altruism than they do with a productive citizenry. "It's not only that these girls need us, it's that we absolutely need them," says Jane Daniels, head of a National Science Foundation effort to bring more girls into math and science. "How can we imagine, in this highly technical world, that our economy won't collapse if we fail to fully develop half our nation's brainpower?" The future awaiting today's schoolgirl not only will be devoid of many of the low-skilled jobs that 60 percent of women now hold, but it will demand three times the current number of women scientists, according to NSF projections.

Against such prospects, current findings on the typical girl's development look grim indeed. Girls participate in class discussions at only an eighth the rate that boys do, and researchers find links between this silence and the depression and suicidal feelings that strike girls three or four times more often than boys. Although the old myth that boys are more capable and interested in math and science has been disproved time and time again, many girls nevertheless believe they can't handle the subjects and drop out of those classes, even after earning exceptional grades. By the time high-school graduation approaches, young women are a minority in all advanced math and science courses; they are outnumbered 2 to 1 in computer classes and score 50 points lower than boys on the math portion of the Scholastic Aptitude Test. With the 21st century in sight, secretary and nurse still often top the list of girls' career aspirations.

Some efforts to chip away at girls' disincentives are already paying off. Through training efforts that include classroom videotapes, teachers have been able to spot how they inadvertently overlook or discourage their female students. With simple adjustments of style, teachers find that the girls in their classrooms change from silent witnesses into involved hand-raisers virtually overnight and that the 8-to-1 gender gap in participation simply vanishes. At least a few schools in all 50 states have hired gender-equity trainers, and the Gender Equity in Education Act would provide more federal dollars for such training.

A key factor in capturing and maintaining girls' interest and proficiency in science, math and computer classes appears to be a cooperative learning environment. In trying to find out why girls shied away from the classes, educators discovered that boys typically monopolize the computer monitors, science equipment and math contests, leaving even the brightest girls to lurk about in the corners of the classroom. By focusing on group projects, teachers were able to keep girls involved and enthusiastic. The NSF is currently funding 15 model programs, and the new legislation calls for added funds to encourage new ways of teaching math and science.

Spreading the word. The broader purpose of the Gender Equity Act is to institutionalize the idea of gender equity in the nation's public schools. An Office of Women's Equity at the education department, for example, would disseminate information on programs that work for girls throughout the nation's schools and mandate that schools follow certain equity policies. "The law would put gender issues firmly in the mind of every school administrator," says Alicia Coro, head of the department's school-improvement programs. The Clinton administration is expected to declare its support for the proposal within the next few weeks.

Yet for all the signs of progress, a close look at girls' lives hints that many of the forces that inhibit them will not be easily countered with a new law or an experimental program. A landmark study by human development scholars Carol Gilligan of Harvard University and Lyn Mikel Brown of Colby College shows that even girls with "all the right" circumstances suffer a traumatic loss of confidence as they grow up. Gilligan's and Brown's recent book, "Meeting at the Crossroads," details a five-year study of 100 girls between 7 and 18 at a private, all-girls school in Ohio. Even though these girls had professional mothers as role models and did well academically, at the age of 11 or 12 their psychological development stalled. The girls began to repress emotions and opinions; they grew confused and uncertain, unable to speak their minds and were paralyzed at the thought of even minor conflict.

Extensive interviews revealed the source of such symptoms. The girls described poignantly how they had learned, even from mothers and female teachers, that a "good girl" attempts to please everyone, is too nice to express anger or cause conflict, politely lets the other person have the upper hand and thoughtfully puts her own needs last. As the girls left childhood and entered puberty, these messages intensified. To conform to the ideal, the girls explained how they silenced themselves, went through mental dissociations and even remained in harmful or abusive situations. Many girls spoke of "not really feeling like myself."

It is this pervasive cultural image of the "good girl" that is perhaps the most powerful gear of the gender-sorting machine, and the one that will undoubtedly prove hardest to shut down. Studies of a girl's first years of life show that from the day she is born, she is inundated with old-fashioned toys, clothes and rules of conduct. Child-development scholars Kay Bussey and Albert Bandura published a report in *Child Development* last fall showing that kids learn and internalize such stereotypes between the ages of 2 and 5, and that despite current applause for gender equality, children in the study "seem to be as stereotypically sex-typed as those of yesteryear."

Although the traditional feminine ideal, the sugar and spice, may seem innocuous enough, it is in fact potent, deterministic and harmful, psychologists are now saying. It is this ideal that keeps girls from studying "male" subjects even when the doors are opened to them, that leads girls to hide their intellect when around boys and that discourages girls from taking risks or mastering new challenges. "The very behaviors adults praise in girls—compliance, selflessness, silence—are the same behaviors that are going to drop them out of the competition in the work force," says Brown. "Virtually all the qualities needed to thrive in life—strength, courage, independence—also happen to be the stereotypic 'male' attributes."

But society's gender norms can change, and the legal and institutional efforts afoot may speed that process. "There was a time when long, flowing hair and cooking skills were the antithesis to masculinity," notes Heather Johnston Nicholson, research director for the nonprofit group Girls Inc. "Those days are gone." New fairy tales are crafted almost daily, featuring girl heroes and leaders. As they take root in popular culture, the idea of the damsel in distress may lose its allure and so, too, the notion that there are some things girls just can't do.

The AAUW Report: How Schools Shortchange Girls — Overview —

— Why a Report on Girls? —

The invisibility of girls in the current education debate suggests that girls and boys have identical educational experiences in school. Nothing could be further from the truth. Whether one looks at achievement scores, curriculum design, or teacher-student interaction, it is clear that sex and gender make a difference in the nation's public elementary and secondary schools.

The educational system is not meeting girls' needs. Girls and boys enter school roughly equal in measured ability. Twelve years later, girls have fallen behind their male classmates in key areas such as higher-level mathematics and measures of self-esteem. Yet gender equity is still not a part of the national debate on educational reform.

Research shows that policies developed to foster the equitable treatment of students and the creation of gender-equitable educational environments can make a difference. They can make a difference, that is, if they are strongly worded and vigorously enforced.

V. Lee, H. Marks and T. Knowles, "Sexism in Single-Sex and Coeducational Secondary School Classrooms," paper presented at the American Sociological Association annual meeting, Cincinnati, OH, August 1991; S. Bailey and R. Smith, *Policies for the Future,* Council of Chief State School Officers, Washington, DC, 1982.

Neither the *National Education Goals* issued by the National Governors Association in 1990 nor *America 2000,* the 1991 plan of the President and the U.S. Department of Education to "move every community in America toward these goals" makes any mention of providing girls equitable opportunities in the nation's public schools. Girls continue to be left out of the debate—despite the fact that for more than two decades researchers have identified gender bias as a major problem at all levels of schooling.

Schools must prepare both girls and boys for full and active roles in the family, the community, and the work force. Whether we look at the issues from an economic, political, or social perspective, girls are one-half of our future. We must move them from the sidelines to the center of the education-reform debate.

A critical step in correcting educational inequities is identifying them publicly. The *AAUW Report: How Schools Shortchange Girls* provides a comprehensive assessment of the status of girls in public education today. It exposes myths about girls and learning, and it supports the work of the many teachers who have struggled to define and combat gender bias in their schools. The report challenges us all—policymakers, educators, administrators, parents, and citizens—to rethink old assumptions and act now to stop schools from shortchanging girls.

Our public education system is plagued by numerous failings that affect boys as negatively as girls. But in many respects girls are put at a disadvantage simply because they are girls. *The AAUW Report* documents this in hundreds of cited studies.

When our schools become more gender-fair, education will improve for all our students—boys as well as girls—because excellence in education cannot be achieved without equity in education. By studying what happens to girls in school, we can gain valuable insights about what has to change in order for each student, every girl and every boy, to do as well as she or he can.

What Do We Teach Our Students?

• The contributions and experiences of girls and women are still marginalized or ignored in many of the textbooks used in our nation's schools.

• Schools, for the most part, provide inadequate education on sexuality and healthy development despite national concern about teen pregnancy, the AIDS crisis, and the increase of sexually transmitted diseases among adolescents.

• Incest, rape, and other physical violence severely compromise the lives of girls and women all across the country. These realities are rarely, if ever, discussed in schools.

Curriculum delivers the central messages of education. It can strengthen or decrease student motivation for engagement, effort, growth, and development through the images it gives to students about themselves and the world. When the curriculum does not reflect the diversity of students' lives and cultures, it delivers an incomplete message.

Studies have shown that multicultural readings produced markedly more favorable attitudes toward nondominant groups than did the traditional reading lists, that academic achievement for all students was linked to use of nonsexist and multicultural materials, and that sex-role stereotyping was reduced in students whose curriculum portrayed males and females in non-stereotypical roles. Yet during the 1980s, federal support for reform regarding sex and race equity dropped, and a 1989 study showed that of the ten books most frequently assigned in public high school English courses only one was written by a woman and none by members of minority groups.

The "evaded" curriculum is a term coined in this report to refer to matters central to the lives of students that are touched on only briefly, if at all, in most schools. The United States has the highest rate of teenage childbearing in the Western indus-trialized world. Syphilis rates are now equal for girls and boys, and more teenage girls than boys contract gonorrhea. Although in the adult population AIDS is nine times more prevalent in men than in women, the same is not true for young people. In a District of Columbia study, the rate of HIV infection for girls was almost three times that for boys. Despite all of this, adequate sex and health education is the exception rather than the rule.

Adolescence is a difficult period for all young people, but it is particularly difficult for girls, who are far more likely to develop eating disorders and experience depression. Adolescent girls attempt suicide four to five times as often as boys (although boys, who choose more lethal methods, are more likely to be successful in their attempts).

Despite medical studies indicating that roughly equal proportions of girls and boys suffer from learning disabilities, more than twice as many boys are identified by school personnel as in need of special-education services for learning-disabled students.

U.S. Department of Education, Office for Civil Rights, 1988.

Perhaps the most evaded of all topics in schools is the issue of gender and power. As girls mature they confront a culture that both idealizes and exploits the sexuality of young women while assigning them roles that are clearly less valued than male roles. If we do not begin to discuss more openly the ways in which

ascribed power—whether on the basis of race, sex, class, sexual orientation, or religion—affects individual lives, we cannot truly prepare our students for responsible citizenship.

These issues are discussed in detail and the research fully annotated in Part 4/Chapters 1 and 3 of The AAUW Report.

How Do Race/Ethnicity and Socioeconomic Status Affect Achievement in School?

• Girls from low-income families face particularly severe obstacles. Socioeconomic status, more than any other variable, affects access to school resources and educational outcomes.
• Test scores of low-socioeconomic-status girls are somewhat better than for boys from the same background in the lower grades, but by high school these differences disappear. Among high-socioeconomic-status students, boys generally outperform girls regardless of race/ethnicity.
• Girls and boys with the same Math SAT scores do not do equally well in college—girls do better.

In most cases tests reflect rather than cause inequities in American education. The fact that groups score differently on a test does not necessarily mean that the test is biased. If, however, the score differences are related to the validity of the test—for example, if girls and boys know about the same amount of math but boys' test scores are consistently and significantly higher—then the test is biased.

A number of aspects of a test—beyond that which is being tested—can affect the score. For example, girls tend to score better than boys on essay tests, boys better than girls on multiple-choice items. Even today many girls and boys come to a testing situation with different interests and experiences. Thus a reading-comprehension passage that focuses on baseball scores will tend to favor boys, while a question testing the same skills that focuses on child care will tend to favor girls.

These issues are discussed in detail and the research fully annotated in Part 3 of The AAUW Report.

Why Do Girls Drop Out and What Are the Consequences?

• Pregnancy is not the only reason girls drop out of school. In fact, less than half the girls who leave school give pregnancy as the reason.
• Dropout rates for Hispanic girls vary considerably by national origin: Puerto Rican and Cuban American girls are more likely to drop out than are boys from the same cultures or other Hispanic girls.
• Childhood poverty is almost inescapable in single-parent families headed by women without a high school diploma: 77 percent for whites and 87 percent for African Americans.

In a recent study, 37 percent of the female drop-outs compared to only 5 percent of the male drop-outs cited "family-related problems" as the reason they left high school. Traditional gender roles place greater family responsibilities on adolescent girls than on their brothers. Girls are often expected to "help out" with caretaking responsibilities; boys rarely encounter this expectation.

There has been little change in sex-segregated enrollment patterns in vocational education: girls are enrolled primarily in office and business-training programs, boys in programs leading to higher-paying jobs in the trades.

U.S. Department of Education, 1989.

However, girls as well as boys also drop out of school simply because they do not consider school pleasant or worthwhile. Asked what a worthwhile school experience would be, a group of teenage girls responded, "School would be fun. Our teachers would be excited and lively, not bored. They would act caring and take time to understand how students feel. . . . Boys would treat us with respect. If they run by and grab your tits, they would get into trouble."*

Women and children are the most impoverished members of our society. Inadequate education not only limits opportunities for women but jeopardizes their children's—and the nation's—future.

These issues are discussed in detail and the research fully annotated in Part 2/Chapters 4 and 6 of The AAUW Report.

The research reviewed in this report challenges traditional assumptions about the egalitarian nature of American schools. Young women in the United States today are still not participating equally in our educational system. Research documents that girls do not receive equitable amounts of teacher attention, that they are less apt than boys to see themselves reflected in the materials they study, and that they often are not expected or encouraged to pursue higher level mathematics and science courses. The implications are clear; the system must change.

We now have a window of opportunity that must not be missed. Efforts to improve public education are under way around the nation. We must move girls from the sidelines to the center of educational planning. The nation can no longer afford to ignore the potential of girls and young women. Whether one looks at the issues from an economic, political, or social perspective, girls are one-half of our future.

Significant improvements in the educational opportunities available to girls have occurred in the past two decades. However, twenty years after the passage of Title IX, the achievement of sex- and gender-equitable education remains an elusive dream. The time to turn dreams to reality is now. The

current education-reform movement cannot succeed if it continues to ignore half of its constituents. The issues are urgent; our actions must be swift and effective.

— The Recommendations —

Strengthened Reinforcement of Title IX Is Essential.

1. Require school districts to assess and report on a regular basis to the Office for Civil Rights in the U.S. Department of Education on their own Title IX compliance measures.
2. Fund the Office for Civil Rights at a level that permits increased compliance reviews and full and prompt investigation of Title IX complaints.
3. In assessing the status of Title IX compliance, school districts must include a review of the treatment of pregnant teens and teen parents. Evidence indicates that these students are still the victims of discriminatory treatment in many schools.

Teachers, Administrators and Counselors Must Be Prepared and Encouraged to Bring Gender Equity and Awareness to Every Aspect of Schooling.

4. State certification standards for teachers and administrators should require course work on gender issues, including new research on women, bias in classroom-interaction patterns, and the ways in which schools can develop and implement gender-fair multicultural curricula.
5. If a national teacher examination is developed, it should include items on methods for achieving gender equity in the classroom and in curricula.
6. Teachers, administrators, and counselors should be evaluated on the degree to which they promote and encourage gender-equitable and multicultural education.
7. Support and released time must be provided by school districts for teacher-initiated research on curricula and classroom variables that affect student learning. Gender equity should be a focus of this research and a criterion for awarding funds.
8. School-improvement efforts must include a focus on the ongoing professional development of teachers and administrators, including those working in specialized areas such as bilingual, compensatory, special, and vocational education.
9. Teacher-training courses must not perpetuate assumptions about the superiority of traits and activities traditionally ascribed to males in our society. Assertive and affiliative skills as well as verbal and mathematical skills must be fostered in both girls and boys.
10. Teachers must help girls develop positive views of themselves and their futures, as well as an understanding of the obstacles women must overcome in a society where their options and opportunities are still limited by gender stereotypes and assumptions.

---

*As quoted in *In Their Own Voices: Young Women Talk About Dropping Out,* Project on Equal Education Rights (New York, National Organization for Women Legal Defense and Education Fund, 1988), p. 12.

6. EQUALITY OF EDUCATIONAL OPPORTUNITY

The Formal School Curriculum Must Include the Experiences of Women and Men From All Walks of Life. Girls and Boys Must See Women and Girls Reflected and Valued in the Materials They Study.

11. Federal and state funding must be used to support research, development, and follow-up study of gender-fair multicultural curricular models.

12. The Women's Educational Equity Act Program (WEEAP) in the U.S. Department of Education must receive increased funding in order to continue the development of curricular materials and models, and to assist school districts in Title IX compliance.

13. School curricula should deal directly with issues of power, gender politics, and violence against women. Better-informed girls are better equipped to make decisions about their futures. Girls and young women who have a strong sense of themselves are better able to confront violence and abuse in their lives.

14. Educational organizations must support, via conferences, meetings, budget deliberations, and policy decisions, the development of gender-fair multicultural curricula in all areas of instruction.

15. Curricula for young children must not perpetuate gender stereotypes and should reflect sensitivity to different learning styles.

Girls Must Be Educated and Encouraged to Understand That Mathematics and the Sciences Are Important and Relevant to Their Lives. Girls Must Be Actively Supported in Pursuing Education and Employment in These Areas.

16. Existing equity guidelines should be effectively implemented in all programs supported by local, state, and federal governments. Specific attention must be directed toward including women on planning committees and focusing on girls and women in the goals, instructional strategies, teacher training, and research components of these programs.

17. The federal government must fund and encourage research on the effect on girls and boys of new curricula in the sciences and mathematics. Research is needed particularly in science areas where boys appear to be improving their performance while girls are not.

18. Educational institutions, professional organizations, and the business community must work together to dispel myths about math and science as "inappropriate" fields for women.

19. Local schools and communities must encourage and support girls studying science and mathematics by showcasing women role models in scientific and technological fields, disseminating career information, and offering "hands-on" experiences and work groups in science and math classes.

20. Local schools should seek strong links with youth-serving organizations that have developed successful out-of-school programs for girls in mathematics and science and with those girls' schools that have developed effective programs in these areas.

Continued Attention to Gender Equity in Vocational Education Programs Must Be a High Priority at Every Level of Educational Governance and Administration.

21. Linkages must be developed with the private sector to help ensure that girls with training in nontraditional areas find appropriate employment.

22. The use of a discretionary process for awarding vocational-education funds should be encouraged to prompt innovative efforts.

23. All states should be required to make support services (such as child care and transportation) available to both vocational and prevocational students.

24. There must be continuing research on the effectiveness of vocational education for girls and the extent to which the 1990 Vocational Education Amendments benefit girls.

Testing and Assessment Must Serve as Stepping Stones Not Stop Signs. New Tests and Testing Techniques Must Accurately Reflect the Abilities of Both Girls and Boys.

25. Test scores should not be the only factor considered in admissions or the awarding of scholarships.

26. General aptitude and achievement tests should balance sex differences in item types and contexts. Tests should favor neither females nor males.

27. Tests that relate to "real life situations" should reflect the experiences of both girls and boys.

Girls and Women Must Play a Central Role in Educational Reform. The Experiences, Strengths, and Needs of Girls From Every Race and Social Class Must Be Considered in Order to Provide Excellence and Equity for All Our Nation's Students.

28. National, state, and local governing bodies should ensure that women of diverse backgrounds are equitably represented on committees and commissions on educational reform.

29. Receipt of government funding for in-service and professional development programs should be conditioned upon evidence of efforts to increase the number of women in positions in which they are underrepresented. All levels of government have a role to play in increasing the numbers of women, especially women of color, in education-management and policy positions.

30. The U.S. Department of Education's Office of Educational Research and Improvement (OERI) should establish an advisory panel of gender-equity experts to work with OERI to develop a research and dissemination agenda to foster gender-equitable education in the nation's classrooms.

31. Federal and state agencies must collect, analyze, and report data broken down by race/ethnicity, sex, and some measure of socioeconomic status, such as parental income or education. National standards for use by all school districts should be developed so that data are comparable across district and state lines.

32. National standards for computing dropout rates should be developed for use by all school districts.

33. Professional organizations should ensure that women serve on education-focused committees. Organizations should utilize the expertise of their female membership when developing educational initiatives.

34. Local schools must call on the expertise of teachers, a majority of whom are women, in their restructuring efforts.

35. Women teachers must be encouraged and supported to seek administrative positions and elected office, where they can bring the insights gained in the classroom to the formulation of education policies.

A Critical Goal of Education Reform Must Be to Enable Students to Deal Effectively with the Realities of Their Lives, Particularly in Areas Such as Sexuality and Health.

36. Strong policies against sexual harassment must be developed. All school personnel must take responsibility for enforcing these policies.

37. Federal and state funding should be used to promote partnerships between schools and community groups, including social service agencies, youth-serving organizations, medical facilities, and local businesses. The needs of students, particularly as highlighted by pregnant teens and teen mothers, require a multi-institutional response.

38. Comprehensive school-based health- and sex-education programs must begin in the early grades and continue sequentially through twelfth grade. These courses must address the topics of reproduction and reproductive health, sexual abuse, drug and alcohol use, and general mental and physical health issues. There must be a special focus on the prevention of AIDS.

39. State and local school board policies should enable and encourage young mothers to complete school, without compromising the quality of education these students receive.

40. Child care for the children of teen mothers must be an integral part of all programs designed to encourage young women to pursue or complete educational programs.

The AAUW Report: How Schools Shortchange Girls

A startling examination of how girls are disadvantaged in America's schools, grades K–12. Prepared by the Wellesley College Center for Research on Women, the book includes recommendations for educators and policymakers, as well as concrete strategies for change. 128 pages/1992. $14.95 AAUW members/$16.95 nonmembers. Bulk prices available.

Serving Special Needs and Concerns

Providing educational services to one's fellow human beings is the primary mission of a teacher. People learn under many different sets of circumstances. There are many categories of concern relating to the education of persons, both within schools and in other alternative learning contexts. Each year we include in this section of this volume several articles on a variety of special topics that we believe our readers will find to be interesting and relevant. The range of topics represented by the essays is broad; this year we look at articles on home schooling, social violence as it affects the lives of children and youth, violence in schools, a classic quality essay on local school politics in New England, tracking students by ability in schools, assumptions to avoid in sex education courses, and some very creative insights relating to vocational preparation and how we should go about developing a "smarter," better prepared workforce.

Home schooling is a major alternative educational phenomenon in the United States. Although less than one percent of American elementary and secondary school students are taught in their homes, the commitment and dedication to the idea of educating children at home on the part of those parents who choose to do so are amazing. And these home schoolers are very well organized; they have active national and state organizations, and they frequently link up with other home schoolers at the local community level to socialize, carry out field trips for their children, and share expertise in and questions on the challenges of educating them. Furthermore, these parents have access to several home school service organizations that provide books, lesson plans, inquiry and experiment packages, testing services, and support materials for assisting parents in the instruction of their children from kindergarten through twelfth grade. This correspondence school organization enables parents to offer great breadth and depth to their children's education.

Joycelyn Elders, the former U.S. surgeon general, has contributed an excellent article on how violence in society becomes a health hazard to children and youth. Young persons who are poor and who live in economically marginal and multiproblematic neighborhoods are at great risk of physical injury and even death. How violence in society spills over into violence in school and how school violence affects learning and behavior are discussed in an essay by Jackson Toby. Toby discusses how the disorder created in schools by violent incidents within them leads to a decline in students' ability to learn academically and encourages them to learn antisocial, counterproductive behavior. Elders and Toby point out how social violence increases greatly the risks to the health and safety of our youth. The rates of occurrence of several types of social violence in the United States are several times higher than in other industrialized nations.

The article on poverty, rape, and adult/teenage sex explodes many myths about how teenage pregnancies and rapes occur; the author, Mike Males, provides demographic data to demonstrate the high level of adult male involvement with teenage females in the United States. This is a phenomenon that all educators should know about because it is one that is usually not discussed in the preservice preparation of teachers. Many inservice teachers already know it well and argue that school policy reforms intended to reduce rates of teenage pregnancy are foiled by the high levels of adult male sexual involvement with teenage girls. This essay should spark some interesting discussion.

"Blowing up the Tracks," by Patricia Kean, is a criticism of ability grouping in schools. The author is clearly in favor of inclusion of all students into a heterogeneous pattern of scheduling their classes in school without regard to traditional ways of defining ability. She supports optimum levels of inclusivity of students. One major movement toward a more inclusive scheduling of students—and away from ability grouping—is really an offshoot of the "mainstreaming" concept of the 1970s and 1980s, when all physically and cognitively handicapped students were required to be integrated into regular classes based on the criterion of "the least restrictive environment" possible for each child. This movement, in turn, has been a controversial issue since the United States made its commitment to mass universal secondary education in the teens of this century; that issue is the controversy over "heterogeneous versus homogeneous" grouping (ability "tracking") of students. Advocates of inclusion today favor heterogeneously scheduling students in schools without regard to ability on the primary premise that all students will learn from one another. Academically, they will benefit from being in classes with fellow students representing a broad range of abilities and interests.

The next topic addressed deals with certain assumptions that teachers should try to avoid in sex education or wherever discussion of sex and sexual orientation develops in school. Mary Krueger makes some very valuable observations in her essay on human sexual exceptionality.

Finally, the essay by Ray Marshall and Marc Tucker explores ways in which we could more effectively provide vocational training in the United States to produce a more

proficient and talented future workforce. They offer several very original, creative proposals for helping young people to be better prepared to participate in the national workforce while not necessarily foreclosing on their post-secondary educational opportunities.

Since first issued in 1973, this ongoing anthology has sought to provide discussion of special social or curriculum issues affecting the teaching-learning conditions in schools. Fundamental forces at work in our culture during the past several years have greatly affected millions of students. The social, cultural, and economic pressures on families have produced several special problems of great concern to teachers. Serving special needs and concerns requires greater degrees of individualization of instruction and greater attention paid to the development and maintenance of healthier self-concepts by students.

Looking Ahead: Challenge Questions

What are the strengths of home schooling? Why do parents do it? What are the disadvantages, if any, to it?

How does social violence affect youth? Why are children at risk?

What happens when violence breaks out at school? How would you react to having to attend a school plagued with violent incidents? Did you? How would you respond to violent behavior in school?

What are the pros and cons of inclusion in the scheduling of students in schools?

What does it mean to say everyone is an exception when it comes to sex? What assumptions should we avoid?

How can we develop a better prepared workforce?

—F. S.

THE CASE FOR HOMESCHOOLING

Roy Lechtreck

Mr. Lechtreck is Associate Professor of Political Science at the University of Montevallo in Alabama.

I f it is not broken, don't fix it.
    If it is broken, fix it.

But if it cannot be fixed, replace it.

The public schools are beyond repair. If it is not practical to replace the current system, then at least let those alone who wish to homeschool. Hassle them not. Instead, encourage them and help them.

That may sound pretty revolutionary and, some will say, un-American. But more and more parents are homeschooling their children. The best-seller *Megatrends* states that a million children are being taught at home, but that is probably an exaggeration. Yet several authors estimate that 250,000 families engage in homeschooling.

Advocates of homeschooling argue that all past attempts at reforming the public school have failed. Decentralization, open classrooms, a return to the basics, values clarification, and an emphasis on counseling and programs directed toward the potential dropout, are but a few of the recent attempts to put Humpty-Dumpty together again. Schools were even turned over to private corporations without any appreciable changes.

Parents who homeschool their children have three basic complaints against public schools: the lack of academic rigor, the number of maladjusted graduates, and the anti-religious atmosphere. Homeschool advocates claim that homeschooling overcomes these problems. They argue that no matter whether the educational philosophy one holds is that schooling prepares for life or schooling is life, the homeschooled do better. Proponents also claim that private schools are nearly always similar to public schools, so the fundamental criticisms of public schools apply to private schools also, although to a lesser degree.

There are two ways to look at the arguments for homeschooling: by personal case histories[1] and by scholarly analysis. Although the true merit of homeschooling probably is best told as a series of case histories, this paper will examine the many studies done on various aspects of homeschooling.

Before we do so, however, we ought to look at the legal situation. Almost every state permits some type of homeschooling. The stringent rules against it have usually fallen when challenged in court, unless the challenge was based on the claim that the state may impose no regulations whatsoever on any homeschool. Existing state laws generally demand that homeschool children have a certain number of hours of schooling per year, and require parents to keep records of what is being done. These records are to be inspected by the public school authorities.

Academic Performance

Let us now see how homeschooling compares to the public schools in academic performance. According to a study in Alabama, elementary-age homeschooled children performed at comparable levels to public school children. Furthermore, the level of education of the teacher-parent was not related to the performance of the children, and children of parents without teacher certification did as well as those who had a certified teacher-parent.[2]

Borg Hendrickson, in *Home School: Taking the First Step* points out other studies which say basically the same thing:

• Home-tutored children scored higher on standardized achievement tests than did their peers in the Los Angeles public schools and also made significant gains in maturation and social growth.

• A survey showed that the majority of 2,000 homeschooled children from various backgrounds achieved notable academic, attitudinal, and motivational progress.

• Homeschooled children in Arizona scored at above-average levels on standardized achievement tests in the mid-1980s.

• During the first half of the 1980s homeschooled children in Alaska consistently outscored their public school peers on standardized achievement tests.

• 76.1 percent of Oregon's homeschooled students scored above average on achievement tests in 1986.

• A 1987 comparison of Western Washington homeschooled students' achievement test scores with national norms showed that, with the exception of grade 1 math scores at the 49th percentile, the homeschooled students at each grade level scored above the 50th percentile in all subjects.

• In 1986, homeschooled students in grades 2, 3, 6, and 8 in Tennessee outscored public school students consistently. In national comparisons, the homeschooled students scored in the top 3% in math, top 4% in spelling, top 1% in listening skills, and top 6% in environmental knowledge.

• Documentation by the Washington Public Instruction Department showed across the board higher performance by homeschooled students over public school students.[3]

These successes usually occur with only three hours of instruction each day. The teacher-parent, of course, has numerous texts, workbooks, videos, and materials to choose from, and when several families form a support group, an inexperienced parent can usually find answers to problems from other members of the group. The children have the almost undivided attention of the teacher without the distractions of a classroom. Homeschooled children also are much more likely to go to libraries, art, history, and science museums, and attend lectures and special events. (Several families which homeschool will often engage in these activities together.)

The suggestions of educational reformers that teachers be better prepared, that classes be smaller, and that more money be spent will not bring about any substantial improvement in academic achievement, according to George Leonard. He says that the cause of poor education is the nature of the public school today, and only drastic restructuring will work.

One argument of Leonard's that can be used to promote homeschooling is that human beings learn at different rates. Individualized education then can be much more effective than group education.

A second argument is that "a certain amount of self-confidence and self-respect is an essential precondition to learning. Yet by and large, school is set up to humiliate publicly those who, for whatever reason, are unable to come up with the right answer when called upon."[4]

A third premise of his is that "the effectiveness of any learning experience depends on the frequency, variety, quality, and intensity of that interaction."[5] Homeschooling would obviously be the best form of interaction.

The child, Leonard continues, is a "learning animal, sure and simple. . . . By the time our children start to school, almost all of them have completed one of the most spectacular learning tasks on this planet: The mastery of spoken language with no formal instruction whatever. . . . They have enjoyed a feast of high-intensity interaction with their teaching environment, which in this case comprises all the adults and other children around them."[6]

Social Adjustment

None of the above comes at the expense of good social adjustment. Negative, not positive, socialization is the end product of most regular schooling, according to home-school advocates. The drastic increase in crimes perpetrated by pupils against teachers, pupils against pupils, and teachers against pupils is an indication of a system that has lost sight of its goals or cannot achieve them. How can children be properly socialized in an atmosphere of fear and chaos? Peer dependency is also an example of negative socialization. It often prevents students from maturing, developing their own individual personalities, developing a moral code separate from that of the group, becoming self-reliant, and developing an acceptable work ethic. One wonders about the viability of a system wherein most admit to cheating regularly and trying to get by with as little effort as possible.

Another aspect of negative socialization, according to many scholars and homeschool advocates, is the school's emphasis on competition. A student is not regularly encouraged to do his best, but just to be better than someone else. Nor is he encouraged to cooperate with others. It is impressed upon him daily that progress has come about by competition. Cooperation is considered utopian, cultish, or trivial. This, however, is a serious misinterpretation of history, free enterprise, and human nature, as very ably pointed out by Alfie Kohn in *No Contest: The Case Against Competition*.[7]

The glorification of sports in high school is another type of negative socialization. Sportsmanship is fine, but when students are given passing grades to stay on the football team and taught that winning is the only reason for playing, our priorities are misplaced. Also, the emphasis on attracting the opposite sex and having the latest in videos and cassettes places a premium on pleasure—a selfishness destructive of friendships and sound judgment. Many argue that the negative socialization in public schools produces a population lacking in those civic virtues necessary for the survival of a democracy.

After reviewing the literature on home-schooling and socialization, Brian Roy writes that "the available empirical data suggest that homeschooled youth are doing at least as well as those in conventional schools in terms of affective outcomes . . . . [In] values, attitudes, and socialization of home-schooled youth, no tangible evidence was identified that they are inferior to conventional school youth in these areas."[8]

Religious Beliefs

Regarding the third complaint against public schools, that they are anti-religion, homeschool advocates take the position that they cannot bring up their children in their own faith and send them to public schools where that faith is challenged or mocked. If adults have a hard time keeping a faith in the face of ridicule, how much more difficult will it be for a child?

Schools can be said to be anti-religion in at least two ways: by attacking religion directly, in history, literature, psychology, and biology textbooks and library books, or by ignoring religion and thereby letting children think it is unimportant. It is interesting that schools are more willing to allow a student to pass a biology course without dissecting a frog than they are willing to allow a student to substitute some other assignment for a chapter of a textbook promoting the idea that man is different from an ape only in the number of nerve endings in the brain and its chemistry. Sex education is also a big problem, for many such courses say or imply that being sexually active is nothing to be ashamed of and everything is okay as long as one practices "safe sex." As for history, there is little about the positive role religion has played at times in world affairs. In psychology books, sin is often presented simply as sickness. (Hitler was not evil, just insane!) The anti-religion of some literature is more subtle. Many fundamentalists object to certain four-letter words, but that is minor compared to the glorification or acceptance of evil portrayed in some novels, essays, or poems.

Courses in values clarification implicitly deny that there are moral guideposts which we ought to follow. Instead of pointing out what moral codes are necessary for society to function, and the demands placed on us by the requirements that we observe others' rights (as, for instance, spelled out in the Declaration of Independence), the values-clarification approach looks at everything from the viewpoint of a child's supposed need for self-satisfaction. The question "What must you do to be a good citizen?"

has been replaced by "What personal desires do you need to fulfill to be happy?"

Parents vs. Bureaucracy

Homeschool advocates are *not* conducting an assault against the public schools. All they ask is that the public school system recognize that they are sincere in their beliefs and to leave them alone as much as possible. Their number will never be large enough to pose a threat to any regular school teacher's job or education budgets. Homeschoolers say, "Our students are as well educated and as well adjusted as yours, if not more so. So just let us be."

In many cases, in fact, homeschooling may be the only sensible way of educating children. This is especially true of families who move around a lot and families with children with exceptional abilities or disabilities.

The defense of homeschooling is not necessarily an attack on public school teachers. Most homeschoolers would probably argue that it is not the teachers but the system that is at fault.

In the recent book *Politics, Markets, and American Schools*, John Chubb and Terry Moe claim that public school bureaucracy is the major culprit. After making allowances for tax revenues, size of school, economic and social background of the pupils, and many other factors, Chubb and Moe argue that the most effective schools are the less constrained schools. Too many supervisors and too many rules spoil the process.[9]

In preparing this article, I was fortunate to meet a lower-middle income, homeschooling couple from central Alabama, who have been homeschooling their two children (now 14 and 11 years of age) for six years. Both children have traveled alone to visit relatives in Germany. The elder had a $500 bank account at the age of 12. Both have won numerous prizes in local contests. In a letter to me, the mother mentioned what is probably her greatest satisfaction as a homeschool parent: "I feel that if anything . . . were to happen to my husband and myself, John and Angela would be left with the basics of survival and enough sense to make it through life knowing what hard work is. . . . They are happy children and know how to make the best of just about every situation."

1. David Williams, Larry Arnoldsen, and Peter Reynolds, *Understanding Home Education: Case Studies in Home Schools*—Conference Paper, April 1984 (New Orleans, La.: American Educational Research Association, 1984).

2. C. J. Daane and Jennie Rakestraw, "Home Schooling: A Profile and Study of Achievement Test Results in Alabama," *ERS Spectrum*, Spring 1989.

3. Borg Hendrickson, *Home School: Taking the First Step* (Kooskia, Idaho: Mountain Meadow Press, 1989), pp. 10–11.

4. George Leonard, "The End of School," *The Atlantic*, May 1992, p. 26.

5. *Ibid.*

6. *Ibid.*

7. Alfie Kohn, *No Contest: The Case Against Competition* (Boston, Mass.: Houghton Mifflin, 1986).

8. Brian D. Roy, *A Comparison of Home Schooling and Conventional Schooling with a Focus on Learner Outcomes* (Corvallis, Ore.: Oregon State University, 1986), doctoral dissertation.

9. John Chubb and Terry Moe, *Politics, Markets, and American Schools* (Washington, D.C.: Brookings Institution, 1990).

Violence as a Public Health Issue for Children

Joycelyn Elders

Joycelyn Elders is [a former] Surgeon General of the United States. The statistics in this article were based on data collected by the Centers for Disease Control and Prevention.

The Surgeon General's primary role is to make the people of the United States aware of serious health threats. One does not have to look far into the home, school or community to realize that a major threat to our health is violence. I would like to share with *Childhood Education* readers my views on the public health consequences of violence, and to discuss prevention efforts and the implications for health and child care professionals.

The problem of violence in this country has increased markedly in recent years, including extraordinary increases in homicide and suicide rates among our young people. Since the 1950s, suicide rates among our youth have almost quadrupled. Homicide rates among young men are 20 times as high as most other industrialized countries. Concurrently, the average age of perpetrators and victims has fallen. We now have the problem of children killing children. On the day you read this, 14 children in America under the age of 19 will die in suicides, homicides or accidental shootings and many more will be injured.

The violence has spilled over into the schools. In increasing numbers and proportions, kids are carrying guns to school. In 1989, an estimated 430,000 students took a weapon to school to protect themselves from attack or harm at least once during a six-month period.

Also, much of today's violence occurs in the home. In 1990, there were over 500,000 reported and confirmed cases of child abuse (physical and sexual) in the U.S. Evidence suggests that this figure may be only one-third the actual incidence—much of which results from drug and alcohol abuse. Furthermore, research shows that approximately 30 percent of the adult population experiences some form of spousal violence. Twenty to 30 percent of emergency room visits by women are the result of domestic violence.

Our children are learning to use violence to solve problems. Violent behavior is being modeled in our homes, schools, neighborhoods and in the media. If we are to have confidence in health care reform, we must restore security in our homes, our schools, our streets and our nation. It is time for us to roll up our sleeves and rid this country of the hideous, highly infectious, yet preventable problem of violence.

Public Health Consequences

The costs of violence to this country are clearly too great to ignore:

- Firearm injuries represent nearly $3 billion a year. The cost of firearm injuries alone to our health care system is nearly $3 billion a year.
- The vast majority (85 percent) of the hospital costs for treatment of firearm injuries is unreimbursed care.
- In the District of Columbia, the cost to hospitals of criminal violence totaled $20.4 million in 1989.

- The total medical cost of all violence in the U.S. was $13.5 billion in 1992—$3 billion due to suicides and suicide attempts and $10.5 billion due to interpersonal violence.
- In 1988, one out of six pediatricians nationwide treated a young gunshot victim.

The public health toll, however, is not just financial. We can clearly document the immediate adverse psychological and physical consequences of violence, including family violence and rape. The long-term effects of such violence include trauma-related disorders (including post-traumatic stress disorder, especially for rape victims), personality disorders, addictive disorders and even physical disorders. We also know that many violent individuals were victims themselves of child abuse.

Drug use is a leading cause of America's crime and violence. Research suggests that 40 percent of all homicides are related to drugs. In Washington, D.C., 80 percent of homicide victims had evidence of cocaine in their bodies. Likewise, in 65 percent of all homicides, the perpetrator and/or the victims had been drinking. Alcohol is a factor in at least 55 percent of all domestic disputes.

An estimated 1.2 million elementary-age children have access to guns in their homes. Having a handgun in the home constitutes a very real and serious threat. A recent study in the *New England Journal of Medicine* reported that if you have a gun at home:

From *Childhood Education*, Vol. 70, No. 5, Annual Theme Issue, 1994, pp. 260-262. Reprinted by permission of the Association for Childhood Education International, 11501 Georgia Avenue, Suite 315, Wheaton, MD. © 1994.

- You are eight times more likely to be killed by, or to kill, a family member or intimate acquaintance.
- You are three times more likely to be killed or to kill someone in your home.
- You or a family member are five times more likely to commit suicide.

With its roots in poverty, violence has a disproportionately greater effect on racial and ethnic minorities. One of two African American children is poor and one out of three Hispanic children is poor. Up to 90 percent of all Native American children live in poverty. The violence exhibited in our society is not, however, the result of any racial or ethnic risk factor. Rather, it reflects an association between violence and poverty.

Although African Americans constitute 12 percent of the population, 50 percent of murder victims are African American. This is not interracial violence. In 1990, 93 percent of African American murder victims were killed by other African Americans. The vast majority of violence committed in this country is between people who know each other.

The media depiction of violence weaves its way throughout these factors. By portraying violence as the normal means of conflict resolution, the media gives youth the message that violence is socially acceptable and the best way to resolve problems. After more than 10 years of research, we know that a correlation exists between violence on television and aggressive behavior by children.

Perhaps even more important than the violence children view on television is the violence that they see in their own homes and communities and on the streets. I believe that this "real" violence is even more frightening and disruptive and leaves scars that can last a lifetime.

Let me now turn to what we in public health can do to help solve

this enormous threat. We can't call out the military, we can't enforce gun control laws, we can't go on foot patrols in our neighborhoods. What we can do is help *prevent violence before it starts!*

Prevention Efforts

As President Clinton has said, one of the things our health care reform package and the anti-crime and anti-drug initiatives have in common is a focus on prevention. Although I want to focus primarily upon the role of public health in preventing violence, I also want to assure you that the Department of Health and Human Services is working on this problem at all levels with other Cabinet agencies—particularly the Departments of Justice, Education, HUD, Labor and the Office of National Drug Control Policy. Collectively, we are looking at five aspects of violence—family violence, youth violence, sexual assault, media violence and firearms.

Violence prevention, from a public health perspective, means two things: reducing our children's risk of facing violence in the future and preventing the *immediate* threat of violence to our adolescents and young children. Let me add that we must deal not only with the individual child, but also with the family, the social environment and the community in a coordinated fashion. Furthermore, what we do must be *long-term*—since violent behavior is persistent throughout adolescence and young adulthood.

Violence prevention means offering prenatal parenting classes and guidance, particularly to teen mothers and other parents at risk. *It means starting early.* That is why we must fully fund early childhood education programs like Head Start. Children who successfully complete Head Start are less likely as adults to be incarcerated or to be on welfare and more likely to have high school diplomas.

I am convinced that school offers us the best and easiest way to reach

as many children as possible. That is why I personally have supported comprehensive school health education in junior and senior high school as an element of the health care reform package. I add my voice to those calling for passage of the Safe Schools Act, an act that would provide schools the means to choose their own "weapons" against drugs and violence. Obviously, such an effort requires a violence prevention curriculum as an integral part of a comprehensive health curriculum.

Since I became Surgeon General last spring, I have worked with the Department of Education to put together a plan for health care reform that would first provide funds for comprehensive health education in schools of highest need. Later, we hope we can do the same in all schools. Research has shown that comprehensive school health education is effective in influencing youths' behaviors and establishing a pattern of healthy behavior in the future.

Comprehensive school health education means, in part, a focus on safety and the prevention of injuries every day, in every grade and in age-appropriate ways. The most effective interventions with young children involve shaping their attitudes, imparting knowledge and modifying behaviors while the children are still open to positive influences. *We must teach children how to resolve conflicts peacefully*, especially those children at highest risk. We must work especially hard with young minority males in the inner cities.

It is also important to support families by providing parenting classes and helping parents become part of their communities. We know that individuals and families who feel connected to their communities are less likely to be abusive.

We must develop programs to train young people and make jobs available for them. Adolescents must become part of our society with clear, positive roles to perform. I am concerned that children today are not learning the skills they need to be employable and productive in today's modern work force. I am worried because one quarter of all African American males ages 20 to 29 are incarcerated, on probation or on parole, and only one fifth are enrolled in higher education.

This type of violence prevention education must be available for families in order to break the so-called "intergeneration cycle" of violence. When children regularly witness abuse and violence and know that they are likely victims, they often grow up to become violent themselves. We know that men who witness parental violence as children are much more likely to physically abuse their partners than men who have not. We must break that cycle.

Violence prevention means revitalizing our neighborhoods and making them safe and cohesive places. Communities should collectively share the burden of raising children by providing social structure and positive, peaceful role models. Violence prevention also means understanding why gangs flourish in our cities—what needs do they fill, and what security do they offer young people? We need to understand what kind of guidance these youth are seeking and what they will accept from their elders.

Violence prevention means removing the tools of violence and providing opportunities for our children to make the transition into adulthood. We can prevent violence and offer a hopeful future by providing community support, realistic role models, education and training, and the knowledge that jobs will be available. I fervently hope that the media will become part of the solution by airing prosocial programming, helping with public service announcements, showing the true conse-

quences of violence and giving us all hope that we can turn this around.

Implications for Health and Child Care Professionals

I join with my predecessor Surgeon Generals in urging our colleagues to recognize violence as a public health threat. When I talk about "health and child care professionals," I am speaking in the broadest sense to include physicians, school nurses, social workers, psychologists, mental health workers and, especially, teachers.

On a day-to-day basis, these professionals can:

- Become familiar with the AMA's effort to train health care professionals to identify and report domestic violence. A key part of this training is learning to refer patients to appropriate social service agencies and shelters.

- Use the emergency room as a place to intervene by identifying persons who are victims or perpetrators of violence and referring them to needed services such as conflict resolution training, family counseling, problem-solving training, substance abuse counseling and treatment and other mental health and social services.

- Become trained in and offer expectant parents prenatal counseling and guidance about early childhood growth and development.

- Participate with schools to develop curricula designed to promote healthful behaviors and prevent violence and other destructive behaviors.

- Recognize and determine the immediate risk factors facing students—with questions about gun storage at home, safety at school, aggressive be-

havior patterns at home or in school, and substance abuse.

- Become a credible source of information for students about preventing these problems.

Conclusion

Violence does not have to be a fact of life. Although it is now an epidemic, we can prevent it. We need to focus on the *prevention* of violence. To do this, we need to focus our efforts on children and teach them carefully at school and at home. We need to provide them with education and job opportunities, mentors and a chance to grow up without access to alcohol and other drugs. We can revitalize our neighborhoods.

By the time this issue is published, we will have announced details for establishing "empowerment zones" and "enterprise communities" in which designated communities receive cash assistance, federal tax incentives and coordinated economic and human development services. We need to concentrate less on fixing the results of violence, and more on preventing it. Violence is a complex problem that will not yield to simple solutions. Violence prevention will require all of us to work together—doctors and judges, teachers and police officers, scientists and community organizers.

Finally, I want to tell you that there is hope and there *is* a solution to this problem. We must not retreat behind locked doors. We must become even more involved with our children and our communities. We must empower ourselves to make needed changes. To do anything else is to sit back and let our children die. As Surgeon General, I know that this is a preventable problem and I am committed to help lead us to the solution.

Editor's note: Joycelyn Elders served 15 months as U.S. Surgeon General in the Clinton administration. She resigned in December 1994.

EVERYDAY SCHOOL VIOLENCE: HOW DISORDER FUELS IT

JACKSON TOBY

Jackson Toby, professor of sociology and director of the Institute of Criminological Research at Rutgers University, is writing a book, Everyday Violence at School.

IN JANUARY 1989, an alcoholic drifter named Patrick Purdy walked onto the playground of the Cleveland Elementary School in Stockton, California, and, without warning, began spraying bullets from his AK-47 assault rifle. Five children died and 29 persons were wounded, some critically. In January 1992, two students at Thomas Jefferson High School in Brooklyn, New York, were fatally shot by an angry 15-year-old classmate. In April 1993, three teenagers armed with a baseball bat, a billy club, and a buck knife invaded an American Government class at Dartmouth High School, in Dartmouth, Massachusetts, a small town six miles southwest of New Bedford. They were looking for a boy they had fought with the previous Sunday. When 16-year-old Jason Robinson stood up and asked why they were looking for his friend, one of the youths fatally stabbed him in the stomach. That same month a 17-year-old Long Island high school student who had been reprimanded by her teacher poured nail polish into the teacher's can of soda. The teacher was taken to Good Samaritan Hospital; the student was arrested for second-degree assault.

The public is outraged when dramatic murders and attempted murders—as well as assaults and rapes—in or around schools are widely reported in the press and on television. Parents fear for the safety of their children and for the integrity of the educational process. People ask, "Why is there so much more school violence now than when I was in school?"

School violence is often blamed on a violence-prone society. Some urban schools *are* located—as Thomas Jefferson High School is—in slum neighborhoods where drug sellers routinely kill one another, as well as innocent bystanders, on the streets surrounding the school. More than 50 Thomas Jefferson students died in the past five years, most of them in the neighborhood, a few in the school itself. Some violence erupts inside schools like Thomas Jefferson when intruders import neighborhood violence to the schools or when students—themselves products of the neighborhood—carry knives and guns to school in order "to protect themselves." But the other three violent incidents—in Stockton, California; Dartmouth, Massachusetts; and Deer Park, Long Island—did not occur in particularly violent communities.

The most frightening cases of school violence, those of insanely furious armed intruders such as Patrick Purdy, are, like floods or tornadoes, not easy to predict or to prevent. Although these dramatically violent acts occur at schools, the acts cannot be blamed on anything the schools did or failed to do. Such unusual cases of school violence differ from *everyday* school violence: a group of students beating up a schoolmate, one student forcing another to surrender lunch money or jewelry. Mundane non-lethal, everyday school violence is more common in big-city schools than in suburban and rural ones, but it can be found in these schools as well.

Everyday school violence is more predictable than the sensational incidents that get widespread media attention, because everyday school violence is caused at least in part by educational policies and procedures governing schools and by how those policies are implemented in individual schools. This article addresses the causes of everyday school violence and the educational policies that might be changed to reduce it.

STATISTICAL FACTS ABOUT EVERYDAY SCHOOL VIOLENCE

Partly in response to alarming newspaper, magazine, and television reports of violence and vandalism in American public schools—not just occasionally or in the central cities, but chronically and all over the United States—the 93rd Congress decided in 1974 to require the Department of Health, Education, and Welfare to conduct a survey to determine the extent and seriousness of school crime.

In January 1978, the National Institute of Education published a 350-page report to Congress, *Violent Schools—Safe Schools,* which detailed the findings of an elaborate study. Principals in 4,014 schools in large cities, smaller cities, suburban areas, and rural areas filled out questionnaires. Then, 31,373 students and 23,895 teachers in 642 junior and senior high schools throughout the country were questioned about their experiences with school crime—in particular whether they themselves had been victimized and, if so, how. From among these 31,373 students who filled out anonymous questionnaires, 6,283 were selected randomly for individual inter-

From *American Educator,* Vol. 17, No. 4, Winter 1993/1994, pp. 4-9, 44-48. Reprinted by permission of *American Educator,* the quarterly journal of the American Federation of Teachers. © 1993.

views on the same subject. Discrepancies between questionnaire reports of victimization and interview reports of victimization were probed to find out exactly what respondents meant when they answered that they had been attacked, robbed, or had property stolen from their desks or lockers. Finally, intensive field studies were conducted in 10 schools that had experienced especially serious crime problems in the past and had made some progress in overcoming them.

The results of this massive study are still worth paying attention to even though the data are nearly 20 years old. Because the study was conducted in schools, it remains the only large-scale national study of school violence that probed a broad range of questions about the school milieu. The other national surveys of school violence, one (McDermott, 1979) based on data collected at about the same time as the Safe Schools study, the other in 1989 (Bastian and Taylor, 1991), were based on a few questions about school victimizations in the interview schedule of the National Crime Survey—too few to throw light on why some schools seemed unable to control violent students.

The statistical picture of crime and violence in public secondary schools that emerged from these three studies placed the sensational media stories in the broader context of everyday school violence.

The report, *Violent Schools—Safe Schools,* was not mainly concerned with mischief or with foul language—although it mentioned in passing that a majority of American junior high school teachers (and about a third of senior high school teachers) were sworn at by their students or were the target of obscene gestures within the month preceding the survey. The report was concerned mainly with illegal acts and with the fear those acts aroused, not with language or gestures. Both on the questionnaires and in personal interviews, students were asked questions designed to provide an estimate of the amount of theft and violence in public secondary schools:

In [the previous month] did anyone steal things of yours from your desk, locker, or other place at school?

Did anyone take money or things directly from you by force, weapons, or threats at school in [the previous month]?

At school in [the previous month] did anyone physically attack and hurt you?

Eleven percent of secondary-school students reported in personal interviews having something worth more than a dollar stolen from them in the past month. A fifth of these nonviolent thefts involved property worth $10 or more. One-half of 1 percent of secondary-school students reported being robbed in a month's time—that is, having property taken from them by force, weapons, or threats. One out of nine of these robberies resulted in physical injuries to the victims. Students also told of being assaulted. One-and-one-third percent of secondary-school students reported being attacked over the course of a month, and two-fifths of these were physically injured. (Only 14 percent of the assaults, however, resulted in injuries serious enough to require medical attention.)

These percentages were based on face-to-face interviews with students. When samples of students were asked the same questions, by means of anonymous questionnaires, the estimates of victimization were about twice as high overall, and in the case of robbery four times as high. Methodological studies conducted by the school-crime researchers convinced them that the interview results were more valid than the questionnaire results for estimating the extent of victimization; some students might have had difficulty reading and understanding the questionnaire.

The report also contained data on the victimization of teachers, which were derived from questionnaires similar to those filled out by students. (There were no teacher interviews, perhaps because teachers were presumed more capable of understanding the questions and replying appropriately.) An appreciable proportion of teachers reported property stolen, but only a tiny proportion of teachers reported robberies and assaults. However, robberies of teachers in inner-city schools were three times as common as in rural schools, and assaults were nine times as common. Even in big-city secondary schools, less than 2 percent of the teachers surveyed cited assaults by students within the past month, but threats were more frequent. Some 36 percent of inner-city junior high school teachers reported that students threatened to hurt them, as did 24 percent of inner-city high school teachers. Understandably, many teachers said they were afraid of their students. Twenty-eight percent of big-city teachers reported hesitating to confront misbehaving students for fear of their own safety, as did 18 percent of smaller-city teachers, 11 percent of suburban teachers, and 7 percent of rural teachers.

Violence against teachers (assaults, rapes, and robberies) is more rare than violence against students. It is an appreciable problem only in a handful of inner-city schools, but, when it occurs, it has enormous symbolic importance. The violent victimization of teachers suggests that they are not in control of the school. In another segment of the Safe Schools study, principals were questioned about a variety of crimes against the school as a community: trespassing, breaking and entering, theft of school property, vandalism, and the like. Based on these reports as well as on data collected by the National Center for Educational Statistics in a survey of vandalism, *Violent Schools—Safe Schools* estimated the monetary cost of replacing damaged or stolen property at $200 million per year. Vandalism, called "malicious mischief" by the legal system, is a nuisance in most schools, not a major threat to the educational process. But vandalism of school property, especially major vandalism and firesetting, is a precursor of school violence because its existence suggests that school authorities are not in control and "anything goes."

Some of the statistics from the two national studies were reassuring. Both the 1978 Safe Schools study and the 1989 School Crime Supplement to the National Crime Survey studies showed that, in the aggregate, school crime consisted mostly of nonviolent larcenies rather than violent attacks or robberies, which were rare. In other words, the bulk of school crime is essentially

What would have been furtive larcenies in a well-ordered school can become robberies when the school authorities do not appear to be in control, just as angry words can turn into blows or stabbings.

furtive misbehavior—theft of unattended property of other students and teachers, fights between students that stop as soon as teachers loom into view, graffiti scrawled secretly on toilet walls. But schools differ in the mix of nonviolent and violent crime: In some schools, violence was appreciable—and frightening—both to students and to teachers. What apparently happens is that what would have been furtive larcenies in a well-ordered school can become robberies when the school authorities do not appear to be in control, just as angry words can turn into blows or stabbings. Under conditions of weak control, students are tempted to employ force or the threat of force to get property they would like or to hurt someone they dislike. Consequently, student-on-student shakedowns (robberies) and attacks occur, infrequently in most schools, fairly often in some inner-city schools.

Thus, school crime partly reflects weak control and is partly the cause of further disorder, which in turn leads to more crime.

HOW DISORDER PROMOTES EVERYDAY SCHOOL VIOLENCE

Everyday school violence is a visible threat to the educational process, but it's only the tip of the iceberg. Under the surface is what criminologist James Q. Wilson calls "disorder" (Wilson, 1985). Professor Wilson argues (in a more general analysis of the relationship between disorder and criminal violence) that neighborhoods ordinarily become vulnerable to the violent street crime that arouses so much fear among city dwellers only *after* they have first become disorderly. What makes a neighborhood "disorderly"? When panhandlers are able to accost passersby, when garbage is not collected often enough, when alcoholics drink in doorways and urinate in the street, when broken windows are not repaired or graffiti removed, when abandoned cars are allowed to disintegrate on the street—a sense of community is lost, even when the rate of statutory crimes is not particularly high. According to Wilson, "disorderly" means the violation of conventional expectations about proper conduct in "public places as well as allowing property to get run down" or broken. Wilson believes that the informal community controls effective in preventing crime cannot survive in a neighborhood where residents believe nobody cares:

> [M]any residents will think that crime, especially violent crime, is on the rise, and they will modify their behavior accordingly. They will use the streets less often, and when on the streets will stay apart from their fellows.... For some

residents, this growing atomization will matter little, because the neighborhood is not their "home" but "the place where they live." But it will matter greatly to other people, whose lives derive meaning and satisfaction from local attachments rather than from worldly affairs; for them, the neighborhood will cease to exist except for a few reliable friends whom they arrange to meet.

Such an area is vulnerable to criminal invasion. Though it is not inevitable, it is more likely that here, rather than in places where people are confident they can regulate public behavior by informal controls, drugs will change hands, prostitutes will solicit, and cars will be stripped. Drunks will be robbed by boys who do it as a lark, and the prostitutes' customers will be robbed by men who do it purposefully and perhaps violently. Muggings will occur.

Persuasive as Wilson's thesis is with regard to *neighborhood* crime rates, it seems even more relevant to *school* crime. A school in which students wander the halls during times when they are supposed to be in class, where candy wrappers and empty soft-drink cans have been discarded in the corridors, and where graffiti can be seen on most walls, invites youngsters to test further and further the limits of acceptable behavior. One connection between the inability of school authorities to maintain order and an increasing rate of violence is that—for students who have little faith in the usefulness of the education they are supposed to be getting—challenging rules is part of the fun. When they succeed in littering or in writing on walls, they feel encouraged to challenge other, more sacred, rules like the prohibition against assaulting fellow students. If the process goes far enough, students come to think they can do *anything*. The school has become a jungle.

The Significance of Disorder

Psychologists and sociologists long have recognized that families vary both in their cohesiveness and in their effectiveness at raising children; experts regard "dysfunctional families" as a factor in juvenile delinquency, substance abuse, and the personality pathologies of young people that lead to violence. The concept of "school disorder" suggests that schools, like families, also vary in their cohesiveness and effectiveness. What school disorder means in concrete terms is that one or both of two departures from normality exists: A significant proportion of students do not seem to recognize the legitimacy of the rules governing the school's operation and therefore violate them frequently; and/or a significant proportion of students defy the authority of teachers and other staff members charged with enforcing the rules.

Although disorder is never total, at some point in the deterioration process, students get the impression that the perpetrators of violent behavior will not be detected or, if detected, will not be punished. When that happens, the school is out of control. Even lesser degrees of school disorder demoralize teachers, who make weaker efforts to control student misbehavior, lose enthusiasm for teaching, and take "sick days" when they are not really sick. Some teachers, often the youngest and the most dynamic, consider leaving the profession or transferring to private or suburban schools. A disorderly atmosphere also demoralizes the most academically able students,

Verbal abuse of a teacher, because it prevents a teacher from maintaining classroom authority, or even composure, may interfere with education more than would larceny from a desk or locker.

and they seek escape to academically better, safer schools. For other students, a disorderly atmosphere presents a golden opportunity for class-cutting and absenteeism. The proportions of potentially violent students grow in the disorderly school, and thus the likelihood decreases that violence will meet with an effective response from justifiably fearful teachers.

Disorder leads to violence partly because it prevents meaningful learning from taking place. Thus, an insolent student who responds to his history teacher's classroom question about the Civil War: "I won't tell you, asshole," merely commits an offense against school order, not a criminal offense in the larger society. Nevertheless, verbal abuse of a teacher, because it prevents a teacher from maintaining classroom authority, or even composure, may interfere with education more than would larceny from a desk or locker. The disrespectful student challenges the norm mandating a cooperative relationship between teachers and students to promote education. Under conditions of disorder, a building may look and smell like a school, but an essential ingredient is missing. Punching a teacher is only a further stage on the same road.

SOCIAL TRENDS LEADING TO DISORDERLY SCHOOLS

Part of the explanation for the greater incidence of disorderly schools in central cities is that there is less consensus in inner cities that education is crucially important. Why? Because big cities tend to be the first stop of immigrants from less developed societies where, frequently, formal secular education is less valued. (Toby, 1957; Hawaii Crime Commission, 1980) Consequently, maintaining order is easier in rural and suburban schools than those in central cities. But the problem of school disorder is not solely a problem of central cities. Social trends in American society have tended greatly to reduce the effectiveness of adult controls over students in all public secondary schools. Some of these developments have simultaneously tempted enrolled students to be unruly. It is to these trends that I now turn.

The Separation of School and Community

Historically, the development of American public education increasingly separated the school from students' families and neighborhoods. Even the one-room schoolhouse of rural America represented separation of the educational process from the family. But the consolidated school districts in nonmetropolitan areas and the

jumbo schools of the inner city carried separation much further. Large schools developed because the bigger the school, the lower the per capita cost of education; the more feasible it was to hire teachers with academic specialties like art, music, drama, or advanced mathematics; and the more likely that teachers and administrators could operate according to professional standards instead of in response to local sensitivities—for example, in teaching biological evolution or in designing a sex-education curriculum. But the unintended consequence of large schools that operated efficiently by bureaucratic and professional standards was to make them relatively autonomous from the local community. While the advantages of autonomy were immediately obvious, the disadvantages took longer to reveal themselves.

The main disadvantage was that students developed distinctive subcultures only tangentially related to education. Thus, in data collected during the 1950s Professor James Coleman found that American high school students seemed more preoccupied with athletics and personal popularity than with intellectual achievement. Students were doing their own thing, and their thing was not what teachers and principals were mainly concerned about. Presumably, if parents had been more closely involved in the educational process, they would have strengthened the academic influence of teachers. Even in the 1950s, student subcultures at school promoted misbehavior; in New York and other large cities, fights between members of street gangs from different neighborhoods sometimes broke out in secondary schools. However, Soviet achievements in space during the 1950s drew more attention to academic performance than to school crime and misbehavior. Insofar as community adults were brought into schools as teacher aides, they were introduced not to help control student misbehavior but to improve academic performance.

Until the 1960s and 1970s, school administrators did not sufficiently appreciate the potential for disorder when many hundreds of young people come together for congregate instruction. Principals did not like to call in police, preferring to organize their own disciplinary procedures. They did not believe in security guards, preferring to use teachers to monitor behavior in the halls and lunchrooms. They did not tell school architects about the need for what has come to be called "defensible space," and as a result schools were built with too many ways to gain entrance from the outside and too many rooms and corridors where surveillance was difficult. Above all, principals did not consider that they had lost control over potential student misbehavior when parents were kept far away, not knowing how their children were behaving. The focus of PTAs was on the curriculum, and it was the better-educated, middle-class parents who tended to join such groups. In short, the isolation of the school from the local community always meant that, if a large enough proportion of students misbehaved, teachers and principals could not maintain order.

Conceivably, schools can exercise effective control even though parents and neighbors do not reinforce their values through membership in PTAs or through conferences with teachers. But social control is weakened by population mobility, which creates an atmosphere of anonymity. Consider how much moving around there is in the United States. Only 82 percent of persons were living in the same residential unit in 1990 as they were in 1989. Residential mobility was much greater in the central cities of metropolitan areas. Since cities have long been considered places to which people migrate from rural areas, from other cities, and indeed from foreign countries, it may come as no surprise that during a five-year period, a majority of the residents of American central cities move to a different house. Yet the anonymity generated by this atmosphere of impermanence can plausibly explain why American society is not very successful in imposing order in urban neighborhoods. Anonymity is not confined to central cities. High rates of mobility are typical, creating the anonymity that complicates problems of social control. Schools vary of course in their rates of student turnover. In some big-city schools less than half the students complete an academic year; in some small-town schools, on the other hand, the bulk of students are together for four years of high school.

The Relentless Pressure to Keep Children In School Longer

The most important trend underlying school disorder is the rising proportion of the age cohort attending high school in all modern societies. The reason for raising the age of compulsory school attendance is excellent: Children need all the education they can get in order to work at satisfying jobs in an increasingly complex economy and to be able to vote intelligently. However, higher ages of compulsory school attendance mean that some enrolled youngsters hate school and feel like prisoners. Obviously, such youngsters don't respect the rules or the rule-enforcers as much as students who regard education as an opportunity.

Compulsory education laws vary from state to state. But they share an assumption that the state can compel not only school attendance but school achievement. In reality, compulsory education laws are successful only in keeping children *enrolled,* sometimes longer than the nominal age of compulsory school attendance. Parental consent was often written into the law as necessary for withdrawal from school before reaching 17 or 18 or a specified level of educational achievement. Parents have little incentive to consent, partly because they hold unrealistic educational aspirations even for academically marginal students, partly because they recognize the difficulties faced by adolescents in the labor market and do not want their children loitering on the streets, and partly because benefits are available from programs like Aid to Families with Dependent Children for children enrolled in school.

Like their parents, the disengaged students also have incentives to remain enrolled, although not necessarily to attend regularly. In addition to conforming to parental pressure, they are called "students" although they are not necessarily studious, and this status has advantages. The school is more pleasant than the streets in cold or rainy weather—it is an interesting place to be. Friends are visited; enemies attacked; sexual adventures begun; drugs

bought and sold; valuables stolen. There are material advantages also to being an enrolled student, such as bus passes and lunch tickets, which can be sold as well as used. Consequently, many remain enrolled although they are actually occasional or chronic truants. The existence of a large population of enrolled nonattenders blurs the line between intruders and students. School officials understand this all too well, but the compulsory school attendance laws prevent them from doing much about it. (Toby, 1983)

Keeping more children in school who do not want to be there interferes with traditional learning. Consequently, functional illiteracy has spread to more students, resulting not necessarily in the formal withdrawal from school of marginal students but, more usually, in "internal" dropouts. School systems are making strenuous efforts to educate such students whom they would have given up on in a previous generation. Such students used to be described as "lazy," and they were given poor grades for "conduct." It is perhaps not surprising that the public schools have had great difficulty providing satisfaction, not to mention success, to students whose aptitudes or attitudes do not permit them to function within the range of traditional standards of academic performance. One response is to "dumb-down" the curriculum with "relevant," intellectually undemanding courses that increase the proportion of entertainment to work.

The Extension of Civil Rights to Children

A third trend indirectly affecting school order is the increasing sensitivity of public schools to the rights of children. A generation ago it was possible for principals to rule schools autocratically, to suspend or expel students without much regard for procedural niceties. Injustices occurred; children were "pushed out" of schools because they antagonized teachers and principals. But this arbitrariness enabled school administrators to control the situation when serious misbehavior occurred. Student assaults on teachers were punished so swiftly that such assaults were almost unthinkable. Even disrespectful language was unusual. Today, as a result of greater concern for the rights of children, school officials are required to observe due process in handling student discipline. Hearings are necessary. Charges must be specified. Witnesses must confirm suspicions. Appeals are provided for. Greater due process for students accused of misbehavior gives unruly students better protection against teachers and principals; unfortunately, it also gives well-behaved students less protection from their classmates.

Related to the extension of civil rights in the school setting is the decreased ability of schools to get help with discipline problems from the juvenile courts. Like the schools, the juvenile courts also have become more attentive to children's rights. Juvenile courts today are less willing to exile children to a correctional Siberia. More than 20 years ago, the Supreme Court ruled that children could not be sent to juvenile prisons for "rehabilitation" unless proof existed that they had *done* something for which imprisonment was appropriate. The 1967 *Gault* decision set off a revolution in juvenile court procedures. For example, formal hearings with youngsters represented by attorneys became common practice for serious offenses that might result in incarceration.

Furthermore, a number of state legislatures restricted the discretion of juvenile court judges. In New York and New Jersey, for example, juvenile court judges may not commit a youngster to correctional institutions for "status offenses," that is, for behavior that would not be a crime if done by adults. Thus, truancy or ungovernable behavior in school or at home are not grounds for incarceration in these two states. The differentiation of juvenile delinquents from persons in need of supervision (PINS in New York nomenclature, JINS in New Jersey) may have been needed. However, one consequence of this reform is that the public schools can less easily persuade juvenile courts to help with school-discipline problems. In some cases, the juvenile court judge cannot incarcerate because the behavior is a status offense rather than "delinquency." In other cases the alleged behavior, such as slapping or punching a teacher, is indeed delinquency, but many judges will not commit a youngster to a correctional institution for this kind of behavior, because they have to deal with what they perceive as worse juvenile violence on the streets. Thus, for its own very good reasons, the juvenile justice system does not help the schools appreciably in dealing with disorder. Only when disorder results in violence will the juvenile courts intervene; their reponse is too little, too late.

Increased attention to civil rights for students, including students accused of violence, was also an unintended consequence of compulsory school attendance laws. The Supreme Court held in *Goss v. Lopez* not only that schoolchildren were entitled to due process when accused by school authorities of misbehavior and that greater due-process protections were required for students in danger of suspension for more than 10 days or for expulsion, than for students threatened with less severe disciplinary penalties. The Court held also that the state, in enacting a compulsory school attendance law, incurred an *obligation* to educate children until the age specified in the law, which implied greater attention to due process for youngsters still subject to compulsory attendance laws than for youngsters beyond their scope. Boards of education interpreted these requirements to mean that formal hearings were necessary in cases of youngsters in danger of losing the educational benefits the law required them to receive. Such hearings were to be conducted at a higher administrative level than the school itself, and the principals had to document the case and produce witnesses who could be cross-examined.

In Hawaii, for example, which has a compulsory education law extending to age 18, Rule 21, which the Hawaii Department of Education adopted in 1976 to meet the requirement of *Goss v. Lopez,* aroused unanimous dissatisfaction from principals interviewed in the Crime Commission's study of school violence and vandalism. They had three complaints. First, in cases where expulsion or suspension of more than 10 days might be the outcome, the principal was required to gather evidence, to file notices, and to participate in long adversarial hearings at the district superintendent's office in a prosecutorial capacity, which discouraged principals from initiating this procedure in serious cases. Thus principals down-

Part of the reason for the decline of homework in public secondary schools is the erosion of teacher authority.

graded serious offenses in order to deal with them expeditiously, by means of informal hearings. Second, Rule 21 forbade principals to impose a series of short suspensions of a student within one semester that cumulatively amounted to more than 10 days unless there was a formal hearing. Although intended to prevent principals from getting around the requirement for formal hearings in serious cases involving long suspensions, what this provision achieved was to prevent principals from imposing any discipline at all on multiple offenders. Once suspended for a total of 10 days in a semester, a student could engage in minor and not-so-minor misbehavior with impunity. Third, the principals complained that their obligation to supply "alternative education" for students expelled or suspended for more than 10 days was unrealistic in terms of available facilities.

The Blurring of the Line Between Disability And Misbehavior

"Special education" serves a heterogeneous group of students, some with physical handicaps, others with behavior problems from which emotional handicaps are inferred without independent psychiatric justification. Inferring personality disturbances from deviant behavior has a long, disreputable history in the criminal courts where defense attorneys have creatively described stealing and fire-setting as "kleptomania" and "pyromania" when the behavior had no intuitively plausible explanation. In 1975 Congress passed Public Law 94-142, the Education for All Handicapped Children Act, which provided "not only that every handicapped child is entitled to a free public education, but that such an education shall be provided *in the least restrictive educational setting.*" (Hewett and Watson, 1979) Thus the philosophy of mainstreaming handicapped children—exceptional children, as they are sometimes called—became national policy. Some of the handicaps are verifiable independent of classroom behavior: deafness, blindness, motor problems, speech pathologies, retardation. But learning disabilities and behavior disorders, especially the latter, are more ambiguous. Does a child who punches other children in his classroom have a behavior disorder for which he should be pitied, or does he deserve punishment for naughtiness?

The state of Hawaii ran into this dilemma in attempting to implement Public Law 94-142. The Hawaii Board of Education promulgated Rule 49.13, which asserted that "handicapped children in special education programs may not be seriously disciplined by suspensions for over 10 days or by dismissal from school for violating any of the school's rules." This meant that there were two standards of behavior, one for ordinary students and one for "handicapped" students. But students who were classified as handicapped because of a clinical judgment that they were "emotionally disturbed" (usually inferred from "acting out" behavior) seemed to be getting a license to commit disciplinary infractions.

According to a 1980 Hawaii Crime Commission report, *Violence and Vandalism in the Public Schools of Hawaii:*

> [I]t was the consensus of 14 principals from the Leeward and Central School Districts of Oahu that the special disciplinary section under Rule 49 created a "double standard" between regular students who were subject to varying degrees of suspensions and special education students who were not. These principals believe that such an alleged double standard fosters a belief among special education students that they are immune from suspension under regular disciplinary rules and, therefore, can engage in misconduct with impunity.

"Special education" students placed in that category because of supposed emotional disturbance may have violence-prone personalities. On the other hand, they may only be assumed to have such personalities because they have engaged in inexplicably violent behavior. They might be able to control their behavior if they had incentives to do so. In formulating Rule 49.13, the Department of Education of the state of Hawaii has been explicit about denying responsibility to special education youngsters, but the same heightened concern about the special needs of presumed emotionally disturbed students is common in other American public school systems. One result of not holding some children responsible for violent behavior is that they are more likely to engage in violence than they would otherwise be.

The Erosion of Teacher Authority

The social changes that have separated secondary schools from effective family and neighborhood influences and that have made it burdensome for school administrators to expel students guilty of violent behavior or to suspend them for more than 10 days partially explain the eroding authority of teachers. Social changes are not the entire explanation, however. There also have been *cultural* changes undermining the authority of teachers. There was a time when teachers were considered godlike, and their judgments went unquestioned. No more. Doubtless, reduced respect for teachers is part of fundamental cultural changes by which many authority figures—parents, police, government officials have come to have less prestige. In the case of teachers, the general demythologizing was amplified by special ideological criticism. Bestselling books of the 1960s portrayed teachers, especially middle-class teachers, as the villains of education—insensitive, authoritarian, and even racist.

Part of the reason for the decline of homework in public secondary schools is the erosion of teacher authority. When teachers could depend on all but a handful of students to turn in required written homework, they could assign homework and mean it. The slackers could be disciplined. But in schools where teachers could no longer count on a majority of students doing their homework, assigning it became a meaningless ritual, and many teachers gave up. Professor James Coleman and his research team found that private and parochial school sophomores in high school reported doing, on the average, at least two hours more of homework per week than public school sophomores. Many teachers felt they lacked authority to induce students to do *anything* they did not want to do: to attend classes regularly, to keep quiet so orderly recitation could proceed, to refrain from annoying a disliked classmate.

A charismatic teacher can still control a class. But the erosion of teacher authority meant that *run-of-the-mill* teachers are less effective at influencing behavior in their classes, in hallways, and in lunchrooms. What has changed is that the *role* of teacher no longer commands the automatic respect it once did from students and their parents. This means that less forceful, less experienced, or less effective teachers cannot rely on the authority of the role to help them maintain control. They are on their own in a sense that the previous generation was not.

WHAT CAN BE DONE

Faced with the worrisome problem of school violence, Americans look for simple solutions like hiring additional security guards or installing metal detectors. Security guards and metal directors *are* useful, especially in inner-city schools where invading predators from surrounding neighborhoods are a major source of violence. But dealing with *student* sources of everyday school violence requires more effective teacher control over the submerged part of the violence iceberg: disorder.

Teachers, not security guards, already prevent disorder in most American high schools. They do it by expressing approval of some student behavior and disapproval of other student behavior. This is tremendously effective in schools where the majority of students care about what teachers think of them. Expressing approval and disapproval is useless (and sometimes dangerous) in schools where students have contempt for teachers and teachers know it. In such schools, particularly those in inner cities, many teachers are too intimidated to condemn curses, threats, obscenities, drunkenness, and, of course, the neglect of homework and other academic obligations. It would help enormously if all families inculcated moral values before children started school and if all teachers motivated students better in the earliest grades so that they are hooked on education by the time they reach high school. But, unfortunately, many students arrive without these desirable formative experiences.

The problem is how to empower teachers in schools where they are now intimidated by students who are not as receptive to education as we would like them to be. Teachers cannot empower themselves. Ultimately, teachers derive their authority from student respect for education and the people who transmit it. Japan provides a classic illustration of what respect for teachers, inculcated in the family, can accomplish. Japanese high school

The age limit for high school entitlement should be raised from 21, the usual age at present, to 100.

teachers are firmly in control of their high schools without the help of security guards or metal detectors. No Japanese high school teacher is afraid to admonish students who start to misbehave, because the overwhelming majority of students will respond deferentially. Japanese high school teachers know that their students care about the grades they receive at school.

Students have good reason to care. Japanese teachers give grades that employers as well as colleges scrutinize; they also write letters of recommendation that prospective employers take seriously. In short, Japanese high school students are deeply concerned about the favorable attitudes of their teachers. As a result, Japanese teachers can require lots of homework. Homework is a major factor in the superior academic performance of Japanese students in international comparisons. But effective teacher control has consequences for school safety too. Japanese high school teachers never are assaulted by their students; on the contrary, high school students pay attention to their teachers and graduate from high school in greater proportions (93 percent) than American students. They *want* to go to school because they are convinced, correctly, that their occupational futures depend on educational achievement.

It is unlikely that American high school students will ever respect their teachers as much as Japanese students do theirs. Japan's culture is more homogeneous than American culture, and Japan's high schools have a closer connection with employers than American high schools do. Japanese employers as well as Japanese colleges want to see the grades that students receive in high school, and they pay attention to letters of recommendation from teachers. Furthermore, Japan's high schools have the advantage of containing only voluntary students. (Compulsory education ends in junior high school in Japan.) But there are several measures we can take that will greatly enhance teacher control in American high schools.

The first one is to break through the anonymous, impersonal atmosphere of jumbo high schools and junior highs by creating smaller communities of learning within larger structures, where teachers and students can come to know each other well. A number of urban school districts—New York and Philadelphia among them—are already moving ahead with this strategy of schools within schools or "house plans," as they are sometimes called. Such a strategy promotes a sense of community and encourages strong relationships to grow between teachers and students. Destructive student subcultures are less likely to emerge. Problems are caught before they get out of hand; students do not fall between the cracks. And teacher disapproval of student misbehavior carries more sting in schools where students and teachers are close.

The second measure we can take—one that would significantly empower teachers—is to have employers start demanding high school transcripts and make it known to students that the best jobs will go to those whose effort and learning earn them. This idea, which John Bishop and James Rosenbaum have written about, and which Al Shanker has devoted a number of his *New York Times* columns to, is an important one. Employers currently pay little or no attention to high school transcripts. Very few ask for them. They don't know what courses their job applicants took or what grades they got. The only requirement the typical employer has is that the applicant possess a high school diploma. Whether that diploma represents four years of effort, achievement, and good behavior—or four years of seat time and surliness—is a distinction not made.

And the students know it. Rosenbaum describes the consequences:

> Since employers ignore grades, it is not surprising that many work-bound students lack motivation to improve them. While some students work hard in school because of personal standards or parental pressure or real interest in a particular subject, students who lack these motivations have little incentive since schoolwork doesn't affect the jobs they will get after graduation, and it is difficult for them to see how it could affect job possibilities ten years later.
>
> The consequences are far reaching . . . . Many kinds of motivation and discipline problems are widespread: absenteeism, class cutting, tardiness, disruptive behavior, verbal abuse, failure to do homework assignments, and substance abuse. . . .
>
> While employers ask why teachers don't exert their authority in the classroom, they unwittingly undermine teachers' authority over work-bound students. Grades are the main direct sanction that teachers control. When students see that grades don't affect the jobs they will get, teacher authority is severely crippled.

Employers, of course, would have to hold up their end of the bargain: good jobs for good grades. Once the system was credible, significant numbers of students would take heed, and teachers would be re-armed—not with hardware, but with the authority to command serious attention to the work of school.

Third, we should show that American society takes education seriously by insisting that it is not enough for a youngster to be on the school rolls and show up occasionally. Dropout prevention is not an end in itself; perhaps a youngster who does not pay attention in class and do homework *ought* to drop out. Our policy in every high school, including inner-city high schools with traditionally high dropout rates, should be that excellence is not only possible, it is expected. Those who balk at giving prospective dropouts a choice between a more onerous school experience than they now have and leaving school altogether should keep in mind that students would make the choice in consultation with parents or other relatives. Most families, even pretty demoralized ones, would urge children to stay in school when offered a clear choice. The problem today is that many families don't get a clear choice; the schools attended by their children unprotestingly accept tardiness, class cutting, inattention in class, and truancy. A child can drop out of such a school psychologically, unbeknownst to his family, because enrollment doesn't even mean regular attendance. In effect, prospective dropouts choose whether to fool around inside school or outside school. That is why making schools tougher academically, with substantial amounts of homework, might have the paradoxical effect of persuading a higher proportion of families to encourage their kids to opt for an education. Furthermore, education, unlike imprisonment, depends on cooperation from the beneficiaries of the opportunities offered. Keeping internal dropouts in school is an empty victory.

A fourth measure will demonstrate that we really meant it when we said we would welcome dropouts back when they are ready to take education seriously. School boards should encourage community adults to come into high schools, not as teachers, not as aides, not as counselors, not as security guards, but as students. A recent front-page story in the *New York Times* (November 28, 1993) illustrated the practicality of this proposal. Dropouts from an impoverished neighborhood not only hungered for a second chance at a high school education but became role models for younger students. At Chicago's DuSable High School, an all-black school close to a notorious public housing project, a 39-year-old father of six children, a 29-year-old mother of a 14-year-old son, who, like his mother is a freshman at DuSable, a 39-year-old mother of five children—returned to high school. They had come to believe that dropping out a decade or two earlier was a terrible mistake. Some of these adult students are embarrassed to meet their children in the hallways; some of their children are embarrassed that their parents are schoolmates; some of the teachers at the high school were initially skeptical about mixing teenagers and adults in classes. But everyone at DuSable High School agrees that these adult students take education seriously, work harder than the teenage students, and, by their presence, set a good example.

Adult students are not in school to reduce school violence. But an incidental byproduct of their presence is improved order. For example, it is less easy to cut classes or skip school altogether when your mother or even your neighbor is attending the school. The principal at DuSable High School observed one mother marching her son off to gym class, which he had intended to cut. Unfortunately, most school systems do not welcome adult students except in special adult school programs or G.E.D. classes. Such age-segregated programs will continue to enroll most of the high school dropouts who later decide they want a high school diploma because work or child-care responsibilities will keep all but the most deter-

mined in these age-segregated programs. But education laws should not *prevent* persons over 21 from re-enrollment in high school. The age limit for high school entitlement should be raised from 21, the usual age at present, to 100. Especially in inner-city high schools, much can be gained by encouraging even a handful of adult dropouts to return to regular high school classes. Teachers who have an adult student or two in their classes are not alone with a horde of teenagers. They have adult allies during the inevitable confrontations with misbehaving students. Even though the adults say nothing, their presence bolsters the will of teachers to maintain order.

Teenage students who feel a stake in educational achievement and adult students who have lived to regret dropping out and are eager to return to high school both empower teachers in the struggle against disorder. These secret weapons against violence are less expensive—and probably more effective—than additional security guards. Teachers need all the help they can get.

It is important also to remind ourselves that plenty of schools—including ones in the worst crime-ridden neighborhoods—are oases in the midst of despair, where teachers have managed, against all odds, to maintain a good environment for learning. America's goal must be nothing short of making all schools safe havens where children can come to learn and grow.

REFERENCES

Bastian, Lisa D. and Bruce M. Taylor, *School Crime: A National Crime Victimization Survey Report.* Washington: Bureau of Justice Statistics, 1991.

Hawaii Crime Commission, *Violence and Vandalism in the Public Schools of Hawaii. Vol. 1.* Honolulu: Mimeographed Report to the Hawaii State Legislature, September 1980.

Hewett, Frank M. and Philip C. Watson, "Classroom Management and the Exceptional Learner." In *Classroom Management,* Daniel L. Duke, ed. Chicago: University of Chicago Press, 1979.

McDermott, M. Joan, *Criminal Victimization in Urban Schools.* Washington, D.C.: U.S. Government Printing Office, 1979.

Rosenbaum, James, E., "What If Good Jobs Depended on Good Grades?" *American Educator,* Winter 1989.

Toby, Jackson, "Hoodlum or Business Man: An American Dilemma." In *The Jews: Social Patterns of an American Group,* ed. Marshall Sklare, Glencoe, Ill. Free Press, 1957.

Toby, Jackson, "Violence in School," from *Crime and Justice: An Annual Review of Research,* Vol. 4, Michael Tonry and Norval Morris, eds., 1983.

U.S. Department of Health, Education and Welfare, *Violent Schools— Safe Schools: The Safe Schools Report to the Congress.* Washington, D.C.: U.S. Government Printing Office, 1978.

Wilson, James Q., *Thinking About Crime,* pp. 75–89. New York: Vintage, 1985.

Poverty, Rape, Adult/Teen Sex: Why 'Pregnancy Prevention' Programs Don't Work

Mr. Males responds with new data to support his central point — that teenage and adult sexual behaviors are so intertwined at both the personal and the societal levels that there is, in reality, no distinct "teenage pregnancy" phenomenon amenable to school intervention.

MIKE MALES

MIKE MALES is a freelance writer and a graduate student in psychology at Occidental College, Los Angeles.

STEPHEN CALDAS presents a cogent argument for expanding school programs of sexual and contraceptive education in order to prevent what we call "teenage" pregnancy. Unfortunately, he does not address the points in my March 1993 article regarding the monumental difficulties confronting the school-based measures he advocates.[1]

We begin with a fundamental disagreement: Caldas assumes that modern "teenage" sex and pregnancy are deviant behaviors that schools can isolate and address separately from socially acceptable "adult" sex and pregnancy. But the point of my previous article was that teenage and adult sexual behaviors are so intermixed at both the personal and the societal levels that there is, in reality, no distinct teenage phenomenon amenable to school intervention. I now offer an update of crucial, rarely mentioned facts in support of my argument:

1. *The large majority of all "teenage" pregnancies are caused by adults.* A 1990 tabulation of 60,000 births among both married and unmarried teenage mothers in California (85% of all teen births in the state that year — the most comprehensive sample yet assembled) details the overwhelming adult role in "teen" pregnancy.[2]

• Men older than high school age account for 77% of all births among girls of high school age (ages 16-18) and for 51% of births among girls of junior high school age (15 and younger).

• Men over age 25 father twice as many "teenage" births as do boys under age 18.

• Men over age 20 father five times more births among junior high school age girls than do junior high school age boys and 2.5 times more births among senior high school age girls than do senior high school age boys.

• Junior high school age boys account for just 7% of the births among junior high school age girls. Senior high school age boys father only 24% of births among all school-age girls.

• Additionally, adult women over age 20 account for 14% of the births fathered by school-age boys.

A less complete national tabulation of 309,819 "teen" births reported in the most recent *Vital Statistics of the United States* (1988) confirms the pattern found in California: only 89,509 births (29%) involved two teenage partners; 220,310 (71%) involved a teenage partner and an adult partner over age 20.[3]

California figures show that the age gap between male and female partners is much larger than is generally assumed. Indeed, the younger the mother, the greater the age gap. When the mother is 12 years old or younger, the father averages 22 years of age; for mothers of junior high age, fathers average nearly five years older; for mothers of high school age, fathers average nearly four years older. These adult/youth sex patterns have profound implications for the spread of sexually transmitted disease (STD) and AIDS as well. STD and AIDS rates are 2.5 times higher among females under age 20 than can be predicted from rates among males under age 20 — a "surplus" pointing strongly to transmission from older men.[4]

By denying the definitive reality of adult/teen sex, school prevention programs, in effect, assign girls as young as junior high school age the responsibility of preventing pregnancies typically involving much older adult partners. Such an approach is fraught with troubling real-life implications, both practical and philosophical, which are exacerbated by the special problems of girls who are at risk of becoming pregnant.

2. *A large majority of all pregnant teenagers have histories of rape, sexual abuse, and physical abuse.* A 1985 *Los Angeles Times* survey showed that 27% of all women and 16% of all men were sexually abused as children — nearly all by adults and half by "someone in authority."[5] In a 1992 study of 500 adolescent mothers, Washington researchers Debra Boyer and David Fine found that two-thirds of them had been sexually victimized in the past by men whose ages averaged 27 years. Some 5% of all "teen" births are caused by rape, their figures show.[6]

From *Phi Delta Kappan*, Vol. 76, No. 1, January 1994, pp. 41-56. © 1994 by Phi Delta Kappa, Inc. Reprinted by permission.

Attempting to preach "values" that contradict the values adults practice is an exercise in futility.

This landmark study found that, compared to nonabused mothers, abused mothers report younger sexual initiation, sex with much older partners, and riskier, more frequent, and promiscuous sex. Victims of abuse are the population that school programs most need to reach, yet the effects of sexual abuse and rape are ignored by Caldas and most prevention programs. Why is the decisive adult role in both voluntary and involuntary sex with school-age youth exempt from discussion?

3. *What we call "teenage" sexual behavior is virtually identical to "adult" sexual behavior.* Caldas cites one measure and time period (unwed childbearing since 1970) to bolster his claim that modern "teenage" pregnancy is a deviant behavior. But a comprehensive analysis of multiple measures over longer periods of time shows that this argument is flawed. Correlational analyses of rates of birth, unwed birth, abortion, STD, and AIDS for teenagers (under age 20) and adults (over age 20) over the longest periods since 1940 for which national statistics are available show that adult behaviors explain nearly all "teenage" behaviors (r values ranging from .88 to .99, p < .0001).[7] Separate calculations by race or for the period before 1970 versus the period after 1970 also show near one-to-one adult/teen associations. Efforts, then, to portray "teenage sex" as deviant or as radically different from "adult sex" are completely unwarranted. The behavior and values systems associated with teenage sex and adult sex are, at the individual and societal levels, the same. Prevention programs that continue to deny this fact are likely to remain ineffective.

Caldas further argues that the "conflicting" messages American teens receive regarding sex contribute to early sexual activity. This does not seem to be the case: teenagers receive highly consistent sexual messages from adults. Not only are adults involved in most "teen" pregnancy, but many adults model unhealthy sexual behaviors. Among Americans over age 20 during the decade of the 1980s,

there were 100 million cases of STD, 25 million unplanned pregnancies, 12 million abortions, and eight million births to unwed mothers — the latter including two million with teenage partners.[8] These are the highest rates of any industrial country.[9]

Again, consider the enormous challenge school programs face: convincing young, abused adolescents to resist the active examples that adults set. Attempting to contrive and preach "values" that contradict the values adults practice is an exercise in futility. The problem is not that teenagers are confused or that they reject the values of adults around them, but that they copy them only too well.

4. *Poverty is the key predictor of early pregnancy.* In Caldas' state, Louisiana, 12,381 teenage girls gave birth in the most recent comparative year (1988). During that same year in similarly populated Minnesota, 4,857 teenage girls gave birth.[10] Differences in exposure to sex in the media, conflicting messages, and school programs are insufficient to explain why Louisiana's rate is 2.5 times higher than Minnesota's. However, the percentage of young people living below the federal poverty level in Louisiana (31.2%) is also 2.5 times higher than the comparable figure in Minnesota (12.4%).[11] Correlation of youth poverty and "teen" childbearing rates over the 50 states and the District of Columbia yields an r value of .812 (49 dof, p < .0001), a powerful association.

Caldas further notes the low teenage birthrate in France — only one-third as high as that in the U.S. There is nothing miraculous about this: France's youth poverty rate is only one-third that of the U.S.[12] American locales with youth poverty rates similar to France's (i.e., Marin County, California) have teenage pregnancy rates similar to France's.[13]

Lately, the argument has arisen that "teen" parenting causes poverty, which Caldas suggests contributes to America's global economic decline. This argument strikes me as similar to blaming minority groups for creating their own poverty. For both the young and minority

groups, larger social forces are the real culprits. Whether we compare specific areas (e.g., the tenfold higher rate of teenage childbearing in Louisiana versus Marin County) or eras (e.g., the 47% decrease in teenage birthrates from 1958 to 1986),[14] the fact is that high rates of youth poverty *precede* high rates of teenage childbearing. The U.S. is only now — a dozen years later — experiencing the rising rates of teenage childbearing (up 20% from 1986 through 1990) predicted by the rise in youth poverty that began in the mid-1970s. The key to an ameliorative strategy lies in creating policies — such as the "social insurance" common to Western Europe — that channel a greater share of resources to families with children,[15] thereby preventing the cycles of child poverty that force young girls into alliances with much older partners as a means of escape.

As noted in my previous article, the studies of the "social cost" of teenage childbearing cited by Caldas represent orange/apple comparisons. First, they ignore the most important cause of the rising social costs of both teenage and adult childbearing: the increasing failure of fathers (nearly all of whom are adults) to support their children financially.[16] Second, Caldas' estimate of the cost of teenage childbearing fails to reflect the fact that the same amount of childbearing by adult mothers generates 60% as many public costs.[17] Third, while analyses of more comparable teen and adult populations narrow the gap between the groups even further,[18] key variables, such as the mother's history of sexual or physical victimization, continue to be omitted.

Fourth, studies of social costs are irrelevant. "Teenage" childbearing is not now, and never has been during its long history, a distinct social phenomenon amenable to separate analysis. Decreeing it a post-1970 "problem" does not make it one any more than would declaring all childbearing by minority groups a "social problem" because of its much higher "social costs."

Fifth, recent large-scale studies, such as that of 2,000 youths by Arlene Stiffman and her colleagues, show that "the adolescent mother, in contrast with the sexually active adolescent who is not a mother, feels better about herself and engages in fewer overt undesirable behaviors." She shows "significantly lower rates of symptoms of substance abuse/dependence, conduct disorder, post-traumatic stress, suicide ideation, and depression."[19] These are benefits that neither prevention programs nor enormously costly mental health treatments have been able to achieve among at-risk youth, and they are important ones for schools to work with to prevent teenage mothers from dropping out.

Finally, Caldas contends that "teenage" childbearing has become unacceptable because of changing economic trends and expanded career opportunities for women. Yet in reality, the last two decades have brought deteriorating economic conditions and restricted career opportunities for low-income youths, the population most likely to be involved in early pregnancies.

Since 1973, during a time in which Americans over age 40 became our richest generation in history, the percentage of American youths living below the federal poverty level rose by 51%.[20] Four million more young people grow up in poverty today than 20 years ago. Despite a decade of concern over high rates of physical and sexual abuse of children and adolescents, the U.S. has no coherent ameliorative strategy. Rapidly rising rates of violence and childbearing among teenagers and their adult partners in the late 1980s and 1990s are inevitable and predictable results of America's nightmarish war of attrition against the young over the past two decades.

Caldas and I agree that schools should be freed to educate students as to the full array of options for responsible sexual behavior, from abstinence to contraceptive use. But this is only one drop in a very large bucket. The critical social problems of school-age youths and adults most likely to be involved in "teen" pregnancies cannot be mitigated by pedagogy, preaching, or devices.[21] For educators to insist that schools can solve young people's problems provides policy makers with a tempting cure-all and diverts

> *The fact is that high rates of youth poverty precede high rates of teenage childbearing.*

attention away from painful, long-overdue reforms in economic and family policy.

I propose the opposite stance: that educators frankly and publicly declare at every opportunity that schools have no magic wand with which to rescue the nation from 20 years of expedient anti-youth policies. Education lobbies are in a position to vigorously impress on policy makers the fact that reducing the incidence of early pregnancy requires comprehensive increases in support for impoverished families, for the prevention of child abuse, for the enforcement of laws governing payment of child support, and for investment in opportunities for young people. Pending major reforms in national policies toward youth, the best role that schools can play is to provide supportive services that will give pregnant and parenting students the best chance to remain in school.

1. Mike Males, "Schools, Society, and 'Teen' Pregnancy," *Phi Delta Kappan*, March 1993, pp. 566-68.
2. California Vital Statistics Section, "California Resident Live Births, 1990, by Age of Mother, Age of Father, Race, Marital Status," California Department of Health Services, Sacramento, 1992 printout.
3. National Center for Health Statistics, *Vital Statistics of the United States, Vol. 1, Natality* (Hyattsville, Md.: Public Health Services, 1988).
4. Centers for Disease Control, *STD Statistics* (Washington, D.C.: U.S. Department of Health and Human Services, No. 134, 1985); and idem, *HIV/AIDS Surveillance Report* (Washington, D.C.: U.S. Department of Health and Human Services, May 1993).
5. Lois Timnick, "22% in Survey Were Victims of Abuse," *Los Angeles Times*, 25 August 1985, pp. 1, 34.
6. Debra Boyer and David Fine, "Sexual Abuse as a Factor in Adolescent Childbearing and Child Maltreatment," *Family Planning Perspectives*, vol. 24, 1992, pp. 4-11, 19.
7. National Center for Health Statistics, op. cit.; Centers for Disease Control, *STD Statistics*; and idem, *HIV/AIDS Report*.
8. National Center for Health Statistics, op. cit.; and Centers for Disease Control, *STD Statistics*.
9. Jeannie I. Rosoff, "Not Just Teenagers," *Family Planning Perspectives*, vol. 20, 1988, p. 52.
10. National Center for Health Statistics, op. cit.
11. *Poverty in the United States: 1991* (Washington, D.C.: U.S. Bureau of the Census: Current Population Reports, Series P-60, No. 181, 1993).
12. Elise F. Jones et al., "Teenage Pregnancy in Developed Countries: Determinants and Policy Implications," *Family Planning Perspectives*, vol. 17, 1985, pp. 53-63.
13. California Vital Statistics Section, op. cit.
14. National Center for Health Statistics, op. cit.
15. Jones et al., op. cit.
16. Barbara D. Whitehead, "Dan Quayle Was Right," *Atlantic*, April 1993, pp. 47-84.
17. Martha Burt, "Estimating the Public Costs of Teenage Childbearing," *Family Planning Perspectives*, vol. 18, 1986, pp. 221-26.
18. Saul D. Hoffman, E. Michael Foster, and Frank F. Furstenberg, Jr., "Reevaluating the Costs of Teenage Childbearing," *Demography*, February 1993, pp. 1-13.
19. Arlene R. Stiffman et al., "Pregnancies, Childrearing, and Mental Health Problems in Adolescents," *Youth & Society*, vol. 21, 1990, pp. 483-93.
20. *Poverty in the United States*, op. cit.
21. Stiffman et al., op. cit.

Blowing up the Tracks

Stop segregating schools by ability and watch kids grow

Patricia Kean

Patrician Kean is a writer in New York City.

It's morning in New York, and some seventh graders are more equal than others.

Class 7-16 files slowly into the room, prodded by hard-faced men whose walkie-talkies crackle with static. A pleasant looking woman shouts over the din, "What's rule number one?" No reply. She writes on the board. "Rule One: Sit down."

Rule number two seems to be an unwritten law: Speak slowly. Each of Mrs. H's syllables hangs in the air a second longer than necessary. In fact, the entire class seems to be conducted at 16 RPM. Books come out gradually. Kids wander about the room aimlessly. Twelve minutes into class, we settle down and begin to play "O. Henry Jeopardy," a game which requires students to supply one-word answers to questions like: "O. Henry moved from North Carolina to what state— Andy? Find the word on the page."

The class takes out a vocabulary sheet. Some of the words they are expected to find difficult include popular, ranch, suitcase, arrested, recipe, tricky, ordinary, humorous, and grand jury.

Thirty minutes pass. Bells ring, doors slam.

Class 7-1 marches in unescorted, mindful of rule number one. Paperbacks of Poe smack sharply on desks, notebooks rustle, and kids lean forward expectantly, waiting for Mrs. H. to fire the first question. What did we learn about the writer?

Hands shoot into the air. Though Edgar Allen Poe ends up sounding a lot like Jerry Lee Lewis—a booze-hound who married his 13-year-old cousin—these kids speak confidently, in paragraphs. Absolutely no looking at the book allowed.

We also have a vocabulary sheet, drawn from "The Tell-Tale Heart," containing words like audacity, dissimulation, sagacity, stealthy, anxiety, derision, agony, and supposition.

As I sit in the back of the classroom watching these two very different groups of seventh graders, my previous life as an English teacher allows me to make an educated guess and a chilling prediction. With the best of intentions, Mrs. H. is teaching the first group, otherwise known as the "slow kids," as though they are fourth graders, and the second, the

honors group, as though they are high school freshmen. Given the odds of finding a word like "ordinary" on the SAT's, the children of 7-16 have a better chance of standing before a "grand jury" than making it to college.

Tracking, the practice of placing students in "ability groups" based on a host of ill-defined criteria— everything from test scores to behavior to how much of a fuss a mother can be counted on to make—encourages even well-meaning teachers and administrators to turn out generation after generation of self-fulfilling prophecies. "These kids know they're no Einsteins," Mrs. H. said of her low-track class when we sat together in the teacher's lounge. "They know they don't read well. This way I can go really slowly with them."

With his grades, however, young Albert would probably be hanging right here with the rest of lunch table 7-16. That's where I discover that while their school may think they're dumb, these kids are anything but stupid. "That teacher," sniffs a pretty girl wearing lots of purple lipstick. "She talks so slow. She thinks we're babies. She takes a year to do anything." "What about that other one?" a girl named Ingrid asks, referring to their once-a-week student teacher. "He comes in and goes like this: Rail (pauses) road. Rail (pauses) road. Like we don't know what railroad means!" The table breaks up laughing.

Outside the walls of schools across the country, it's slowly become an open secret that enforced homogeneity benefits no one. The work of researchers like Jeannie Oakes of UCLA and Robert Slavin of Johns Hopkins has proven that tracking does not merely reflect differences—it causes them. Over time, slow kids get slower, while those in the middle and in the so-called "gifted and talented" top tracks fail to gain from isolation. Along the way, the practice resegregates the nation's schools, dividing the middle from the lower classes, white from black and brown. As the evidence piles up, everyone from the Carnegie Corporation to the National Governors Association has called for change.

Though some fashionably progressive schools have begun to reform, tracking persists. Parent groups, school boards, teachers, and administrators who hold the power within schools cling to the myths and wax apocalyptic about the horrors of heterogeneity. On their side is the most potent force known to man: bureaucratic inertia. Because tracking puts kids in boxes, keeps the lid on, and shifts responsibility for mediocrity and failure away from the schools themselves, there is little incentive to change a nearly-century old tradition. "Research is research," the principal told me that day, "This is practice."

Back track

Tracking has been around since just after the turn of the century. It was then, as cities teemed with immigrants and industry, that education reformers like John Franklin Bobbitt began to argue that the school and the factory shared a common mission, to "work up the raw material into that finished product for which it was best adapted." By the twenties, the scientific principles that ruled the factory floor had been applied to the classroom. They believed the IQ test—which had just become popular—allowed pure science, not the whims of birth or class, to determine whether a child received the type of education appropriate for a future manager or a future laborer.

It hasn't quite worked out that way. Driven by standardized tests, the descendants of the old IQ tests, tracking has evolved into a kind of educational triage premised on the notion that only the least wounded can be saved. Yet when the classroom operates like a battleground, society's casualties mount, and the results begin to seem absurd: Kids who enter school needing more get less, while the already enriched get, well, enricher. Then, too, the low-track graduates of 70 years ago held a distinct advantage over their modern counterparts: If tracking prepared them for mindless jobs, at least those jobs existed.

The sifting and winnowing starts as early as pre-K. Three-year old Ebony and her classmates have won the highly prized "gifted and talented" label after enduring a battery of IQ and psychological tests. There's nothing wrong with the "regular" class in this Harlem public school. But high expectations for Ebony and her new friends bring tangible rewards like a weekly field trip and music and computer lessons.

Meanwhile, regular kids move on to regular kindergartens where they too will be tested, and where it will be determined that some children need more help, perhaps a "pre-first grade" developmental year. So by the time they're ready for first grade reading groups, certain six-year-olds have already been marked as "sparrows"—the low performers in the class.

In the beginning, it doesn't seem to matter so much, because the other reading groups—the robins and the eagles—are just a few feet away and the class is together for most of the day. Trouble is, as they toil over basic drill sheets, the sparrows are slipping farther behind. The robins are gathering more challenging vocabulary words, and the eagles soaring on to critical thinking skills.

Though policies vary, by fourth grade many of these groups have flown into completely separate class-

rooms, turning an innocent three-tier reading system into three increasingly rigid academic tracks—honors, regular, and remedial—by middle school.

Unless middle school principals take heroic measures like buying expensive software or crafting daily schedules by hand, it often becomes a lot easier to sort everybody by reading scores. So kids who do well on reading tests can land in the high track for math, science, social studies, even lunch, and move together as a self-contained unit all day. Friendships form, attitudes harden. Kids on top study together, kids in the middle console themselves by making fun of the "nerds" above and the "dummies" below, and kids on the bottom develop behavioral problems and get plenty of negative reinforcement.

> **It's easier for educators to tinker with programs and make cosmetic adjustments than it is to ask them to do what bureaucrats hate most: give up one method of doing things without having another to put in its place. Tracking is a system; untracking is a leap of faith.**

By high school, many low-track students are locked out of what Jeannie Oakes calls "gatekeeper courses," the science, math, and foreign language classes that hold the key to life after twelfth grade. Doors to college are slamming shut, though the kids themselves are often the last to know. When researcher Anne Wheelock interviewed students in Boston's public schools, they'd all insist they were going to become architects, teachers, and the like. What courses were they taking? "Oh, Keyboarding II, Earth Science, Consumer Math. This would be junior year and I'd ask, 'Are you taking Algebra?' and they'd say no."

Black marks

A funny thing can happen to minority students on the way to being tracked. Even when minority children score high, they often find themselves placed in lower tracks where counselors and principals assume they belong.

In Paula Hart's travels for The Achievement Council, a Los Angeles-based educational advocacy group, she comes across district after district where black and Latino kids score in the 75th percentile for math, yet never quite make it into Algebra I, the classic gatekeeper course. A strange phenomenon occurs in inner city areas with large minority populations—high track classes shrink, and low track classes expand to fit humble expectations for the entire school population.

A few years ago, Dr. Norward Roussell's curiosity got the best of him. As Selma, Alabama's first black school superintendent, he couldn't help but notice that "gifted and talented" tracks were nearly lily white in a district that was 70 percent black. When he looked for answers in the files of high school students, he discovered that a surprising number of low track minority kids had actually scored higher than their white top track counterparts.

Parents of gifted and talented students staged a full-scale revolt against Roussell's subsequent efforts to establish logical standards for placement. In four days of public hearings, speaker after speaker said the same thing: We're going to lose a lot of our students to other schools. To Roussell, their meaning was clear: Put black kids in the high tracks and we pull white kids out of the system. More blacks and more low-income whites did make it to the top under the new criteria, but Roussell himself was left behind. The majority-white school board chose not to renew his contract, and he's now superintendent in Macon County, Alabama, a district that is overwhelmingly black.

Race and class divisions usually play themselves out in a more subtle fashion. Talk to teachers about how their high track kids differ from their low track kids and most speak not of intelligence, but of motivation and "family." It seems that being gifted and talented is hereditary after all, largely a matter of having parents who read to you, who take you to museums and concerts, and who know how to work the system. Placement is often a matter of who's connected. Jennifer P., a teacher in a Brooklyn elementary school saw a pattern in her class. "The principal put all the kids whose parents were in the PTA in the top tracks no matter what their scores were. He figures that if his PTA's happy, he's happy."

Once the offspring of the brightest and the best connected have been skimmed off in honors or regular tracks, low tracks begin to fill up with children whose parents are not likely to complain. These kids get less homework, spend less class time learning, and are often taught by the least experienced teachers, because avoiding them can become a reward for seniority in a profession where perks are few.

With the courts reluctant to get involved, even when tracking leads to racial segregation and at least the appearance of civil rights violations, changing the system becomes an arduous local battle fought school by school. Those who undertake the delicate process of untracking need nerves of steel and should be prepared to find resistance from every quarter, since, as Slavin notes, parents of high-achieving kids will fight this to the death. One-time guidance counselor Hart learned this lesson more than a decade ago when she and two colleagues struggled to introduce a now-thriving college curriculum program at Los Angeles' Banning High. Their efforts to open top-track classes to all students prompted death threats from an unlikely source—their fellow teachers.

Off track betting

Anne Wheelock's new book, *Crossing the Tracks*, tells the stories of schools that have successfully untracked or never tracked at all. Schools that make the transition often achieve dramatic results. True to its name, Pioneer Valley Regional school in Northfield, Massachusetts was one of the first in the nation to untrack. Since 1983, the number of Pioneer Valley seniors going on to higher education jumped from 37 to 80 percent. But, the author says, urban schools continue to lag behind. "We're talking about unequal distribution of reform," Wheelock declares. "Change is taking place in areas like Wellesley, Massachusetts and Jericho, Long Island. It's easier to untrack when kids are closer to one another to begin with."

It's also easier for educators to tinker with programs and make cosmetic adjustments than it is to ask them to do what bureaucrats hate most: give up one method of doing things without having another to put in its place. Tracking is a system; untracking is a leap of faith. When difficult kids can no longer be dumped in low tracks, new ways must be found to deal with disruptive behavior: early intervention, intensive work with families, and lots of tutoring. Untracking may also entail new instructional techniques like cooperative group learning and peer tutoring, but what it really demands is flexibility and improvisation.

It also demands that schools—and the rest of us—admit that some kids will be so disruptive or violent that a solution for dealing with them must be found *outside* of the regular public school system. New York City seems close to such a conclusion. Schools Chancellor Joseph Fernandez is moving forward with a voluntary "academy" program, planning separate schools designed to meet the needs of chronic troublemakers. One of them, the Wildcat Academy, run by a non-profit group of the same name, plans to enroll 150 students by the end of the year. Wildcat kids will attend classes from nine to five, wear uniforms, hold part-time jobs, and be matched with mentors from professional fields. Districts in Florida and California are conducting similar experiments.

Moving away from tracking is not about taking away from the gifted and talented and giving to the poor. That, as Wheelock notes, is "political suicide." It's not even about placing more black and Latino kids in their midst, a kind of pre-K affirmative action. Rather, it's about raising expectations for everyone. Or, as Slavin puts it: "You can maintain your tracking system. Just put everyone into the top track."

That's not as quixotic as it sounds. In fact, it's

long been standard practice in the nation's Catholic schools, a system so backward it's actually progressive. When I taught in an untracked parochial high school, one size fit all—with the exception of the few we expelled for poor grades or behavior. My students, who differed widely in ability, interest, and background, nevertheless got Shakespeare, Thoreau, and Langston Hughes at the same pace, at the same time—and lived to tell the tale. Their survival came, in part, because my colleagues and I could decide if the cost of keeping a certain student around was too high and we had the option of sending him or her elsewhere if expulsion was warranted.

The result was that my honor students wrote elegant essays and made it to Ivy League schools, right on schedule. And far from being held back by their "regular" and "irregular" counterparts, straight-A students were more likely to be challenged by questions they would never dream of asking. "Why are we studying this?" a big-haired girl snapping gum in the back of the room wondered aloud one day. Her question led to a discussion that turned into the best class I ever taught.

In four years, I never saw a single standardized test score. But time after time I watched my students climb out of whatever mental category I had put them in. Tracking sees to it that they never get that chance. Flying directly in the face of Yogi Berra's Rule Number One, it tells kids it's over before it's even begun. For ultimately, tracking stunts the opportunity for growth, the one area in which all children are naturally gifted.

Everyone Is an Exception: Assumptions to Avoid in the Sex Education Classroom

More often than not, the teachers who are assigned to teach courses in sex education have little or no professional preparation to do so. Taking account of the difficulties inherent in the situation, Ms. Krueger provides helpful advice about how not *to proceed.*

Mary M. Krueger

MARY M. KRUEGER is the director of health education and an adjunct professor of public health at Emory University, Atlanta.

Illustration by Joe Lee

UNFORTUNATE though it may be, most public school teachers rarely have the opportunity (or luxury) to devote significant time to students as individuals. Such is the nature of our work — the classroom is made up of *groups* of people, and the moments in a school day when we can interact with our students one-to-one are infrequent at best. As a result, and in order to function with some degree of consistency, teachers usually develop and act on a set of generalizations and assumptions regarding students.

However, the unique nature of sex education — a field of growing importance as more and more states mandate its incorporation into the public school curriculum — necessitates a reexamination of some of these assumptions. To date 34 states have passed legislation requiring sex education in the schools, and additional state mandates are pending.[1] Nonetheless, there are no undergraduate degree-granting programs in the discipline, nor do any state boards of education certify teachers in sex education; most frequently, in fact, sex education courses are assigned to teachers with little or no professional training in the area.[2] Such teachers — who have been, in effect, *dumped* into the sex education classroom — are not only undertrained in methodology and curriculum design but expected to facilitate activities and discussions in an exquisitely sensitive area. It is truly ironic that the sex education issues that are the most difficult for teachers (particularly undertrained teachers) to address are those in which teachers' assumptions have the potential to do the greatest disservice to students.

Regardless of their personal awkwardness or inexperience, sex education teachers have a special responsibility to avoid causing students embarrassment or pain. Above all, they have a duty to remember that their students are *individuals* with varying family backgrounds, experiences, and values.

During more than 12 years of experience in sex education, I have learned that sex education efforts are more effective when teachers respect students' individuality and interact with students in ways that make them feel unique and special. I have also become familiar with the most common (and dangerous) assumptions that teachers of sex education hold about students. I list them here, along with suggestions about how to avoid them. If teachers refrain from making these assumptions, their students will feel that their individuality is being honored and will thus be more willing to participate fully in and gain from lesson activities.

ASSUMPTIONS TO AVOID

1. *All students come from traditional nuclear families.* This misconception is especially relevant to the sex education classroom, with its (one hopes) frequent references to and encouragement of family communication about sexuality. Teachers who automatically refer to students' families with such phrases as "mom and dad" deny the experience of the majority of their students, as well as the realities of modern American culture.

In almost every region of the U.S., two-parent, traditionally structured families are now the exception.[3] Families no longer consist solely of nuclear groupings of heterosexual married couples and their biological children. Students' families may comprise such aggregations as single parents with children; married parents with children from the current and previous marriages; single or married parents with foster or adopted children; or cohabiting heterosexual or homosexual couples with biological, adopted, or foster children. If teachers are successfully to facilitate the full participation of students in activities that involve parent/child communication and the clarification and validation of family values, we owe it to our students to remember that daily access to "mom and dad," in the traditional sense, is a fact of life for less than 20% of today's children.[4]

2. *All students are heterosexual.* Ten percent of students are *not* heterosexual, regardless of whether they have consciously internalized the fact yet.[5] It is common, yet potentially alienating to gay and lesbian students, to make unthinking references to male students' "girlfriends" or female students' "boyfriends." Such practices send a clear message to gay students that their sexual orientation is, at best, to be hidden and, at worst, abnormal and shameful.

In addition to promoting inclusive language with regard to sexual orientation, the field of sex education has an ethical obligation to condemn homophobic harassment and intimidation of gay, lesbian, and bisexual students. As one of society's most potent agents of socialization, schools are duty-bound to take a stand against hatred and ignorance and to allow all students to learn in a safe and nurturing environment. The denial of such an environment in the past has contributed to a suicide rate for gay and lesbian teenagers that is two to six times higher than that of heterosexual teens.[6] Gay and lesbian teens are also more likely than their heterosexual peers to drop out of school, become runaways, and abuse alcohol and other drugs.[7] Such self-destructive behavior is often the result of feeling overwhelmed by the challenge of learning to like oneself in a hostile world. Much of the self-doubt and inner turmoil that too often diminish the quality of life for these students can be averted by early and consistent messages of acceptance from adult authority figures. Sex education teachers are in a position to take significant steps toward that end.

3. *All students are sexually involved.* Many students are not sexually involved, and they need support for that decision. While we adults frequently wring our hands in concern over (and probably disapproval of) the percentage of "sexually active" teens, we must keep in mind that, in certain age groups and in many parts of the country, students who are not sexually involved are in the majority. However, they (like us) have been profoundly influenced by television, films, and the popular press, all of which send the message that "everyone" is having sex. Because adolescence is a stage of life that so strongly emphasizes conformity, young people may respond to these societal pressures by feeling that virginity is something to be hidden — a source of embarrassment. In an environment that bombards teens at every turn with incentives to become involved with sex, the decision to resist — when one wants above all else to "fit in" — is difficult indeed.

In classroom presentations that address sexual behavior, teachers may unwittingly reflect this "of-course-all-teenagers-are-having-sex" mindset by, for example, phrasing references in the second person ("when you have sex, you need to be responsible"). Training oneself to speak almost exclusively in the third person when presenting lessons will allow students who choose abstinence to feel supported, normal, and comfortable with their decision (and respected for their courage in resisting peer pressure and acting in accordance with their own values).

4. *No students are sexually involved.* Despite all efforts to the contrary on the part of parents, teachers, and other concerned adults, students are becoming involved in sexual behavior with partners at increasingly younger ages. They need the skills to clarify their decisions and to protect their health. Surveys of American teenagers have found that the average age of first intercourse is 16. More than half of high school students have had intercourse at least once, and many participate in intercourse on a regular basis.[8]

With regard to these students, sex education teachers face another dilemma. While generally preferring that students avoid premature sexual involvement, with all its concomitant emotional and medical risks, savvy teachers realize that their preferences are irrelevant to the fact that significant numbers of young people are already involved in sexual behavior that was formerly considered the exclusive domain of adults. No truly caring teacher can choose to ignore the realities that accompany a young person's decision to be involved in sexual activity simply because the teacher is unwilling to face the fact that it is happening.

Teachers best serve the needs of sexually involved students by helping them to clarify their decisions and improve their decision-making skills, rather than making decisions for them; by educating them regarding the risks of early sexual activi-

> More than half of high school students have had intercourse at least once, and many participate in intercourse on a regular basis.

ty, without excluding the positive aspects of human sexual expression; and by expressing concern for their students' welfare, rather than standing in judgment of their behavior.

5. *All students' sexual involvements are consensual.* The faces we see in our classrooms every day include, by even the most rudimentary statistical calculations, more than one victim of sexual violence. It is estimated that 27% of girls and 16% of boys are sexually abused before they reach age 18.[9] Among adolescents, sexual abuse is the most common form of child abuse.[10] In addition, 50% of all rape victims are between the ages of 10 and 19, with half of that number under the age of 16.[11] Up to one-fourth of all college women report having experienced acquaintance rape.[12] (We must extrapolate from that figure to reflect the experience of junior high and high school girls, since the vast majority of research on acquaintance rape has focused on university populations.) Indeed, young people are being sexually exploited with frightening regularity.

Perhaps the best service a teacher can provide to students who have been sexually victimized is to be approachable, and certainly a sex education class offers a natural venue for students to approach a caring adult with questions and concerns. Among adolescents who have been sexually abused, 27% disclose the fact on their own initiative[13] — a figure that tells us that few adults are diligently looking for indicators of abuse or assertively seeking information from survivors. By remembering that, for many students, sexual experience is, in fact, rape experience, sex education teachers can help students begin the necessary healing process, perhaps by putting students in touch with intervention services.

6. *Students who are "sexually active" are having intercourse.* A large number of young people are participating in sexual behaviors other than penis/vagina intercourse, thus rendering moot the overused and ill-defined catch phrase "sexually active." The most common expression of sexuality among teens is solo masturbation;[14] thus class discussions of sexual behavior that focus only on the risk of pregnancy or disease transmission exclude those students who are "sexually active" but not involved in behavior that puts them at medical risk.

Other nonintercourse behaviors, such as oral sex, partner masturbation, variations of "petting," and even such benign activities as kissing and hugging are part of the sexual repertoire of most adolescents. Ninety-seven percent of teenagers have kissed someone by the time they are 15; by age 13, 25% of girls have had their breasts touched by a partner. At least 40% of teens participate in partner masturbation.[15] By age 17, 41% of girls have performed fellatio on a partner, and 33% of boys have performed cunnilingus on a partner. Overall, 69% of young people who are sexually involved with a partner include oral sex in their behavior.[16]

When adults deny the full range of human sexual expression and regard only intercourse as "sex," students are denied an important educational opportunity. Many young people believe that there is no acceptable form of sexual behavior other than intercourse.[17] Operating under that assumption, students may put themselves at risk for unwanted pregnancy or sexually transmitted disease by engaging in intercourse when less risky sexual behavior would have been equally fulfilling. The myth that intercourse is the only way to act on one's sexual feelings has surely contributed significantly to such negative phenomena as premature pregnancy and the spread of sexually transmitted diseases (including AIDS). Clearly, ignorance is anything but bliss where sexual health is concerned. Teachers who help young people learn that intercourse is not required to enjoy one's sexuality not only broaden their students' horizons, but also impart knowledge that may help lower rates of adolescent pregnancy and sexually transmitted disease by lowering the rate of adolescent intercourse.

SCHOOLS ARE increasingly expected to address social problems that were formerly the province of the family, religious organizations, and social agencies. Understandably, teachers often feel overwhelmed by the prospect of dealing with sexuality, pregnancy, sexual abuse, and other complex issues facing young people. Complicating matters further are teachers' fears that sex education curricula are necessarily controversial, that they will incite negative community reaction, and that the majority of parents will disapprove. Indeed, both prospective and current sex education teachers are vociferous in expressing doubts about their ability to deal with potential objections to their curricula.[18]

Since the likelihood of avoiding all controversy when operating a school-based sex education program is slim, the best approach may be to expect and accept diversity of opinion among members of the community, to respect well-intentioned questioning of curricula and methodology, and to operate with unflagging vigor despite any limitations that may result from controversy.[19] Teachers' primary concern, however, *must* remain the well-being of the students, and the work of sex educators needs to be steeped in an awareness of the unique manner in which sexuality and well-being interact. If teachers know their material, believe in the importance of the program, and have clearly defined goals and objectives (one of which is the best possible quality of life for students), then they will be able to comfortably defend those curricular approaches that protect students' health, life, and individuality.

The sweeping alterations in American lifestyles, family structures, and interpersonal mores that have marked recent decades have been mind-boggling indeed. Precisely because modern society is so complicated, family organization so tenuous, and support systems so capricious, students need more than ever to be viewed as individuals. As teachers dealing with topics of an especially personal and sensitive nature, let us remember that, in one way or another, each of our students is an exception. Let us celebrate and respect the uniqueness of our stu-

7. SERVING SPECIAL NEEDS AND CONCERNS

dents — because, when we do, we earn for ourselves the right to expect the same kind of treatment in return.

1. Debra Haffner, "1992 Report Card on the States: Sexual Rights in America," *SIECUS Report*, February/March 1992, pp. 1-7.
2. Mary M. Krueger, "Sex Education by State Mandate: Teachers' Perceptions of Its Impact" (Doctoral dissertation, University of Pennsylvania, 1990).
3. Steven Mintz and Susan Kellogg, *Domestic Revolutions: A Social History of American Family Life* (New York: Free Press, 1988); and Mary S. Calderone and Eric W. Johnson, *The Family Book About Sexuality* (New York: Harper & Row, 1985).
4. Calderone and Johnson, op. cit.
5. A. Damien Martin, "Learning to Hide: The Socialization of the Gay Adolescent," *Adolescent Psychiatry*, vol. 10, 1982, pp. 52-64.
6. "Suicide Major Cause of Death for Homosexual Youth," *Contemporary Sexuality*, September 1989, p. 3.
7. Laura Pender, "Growing Up Gay," *Cincinnati Magazine*, February 1990, pp. 26-29.
8. Mark O. Bigler, "Adolescent Sexual Behavior in the Eighties," *SIECUS Report*, October/November 1989, pp. 6-9.
9. Calderone and Johnson, op. cit.
10. Janet Eckenrode et al., "The Nature and Substantiation of Official Sexual Abuse Reports," *Child Abuse and Neglect*, vol. 13, 1988, pp. 311-19.
11. Donald E. Greydanus and Robert B. Shearin, *Adolescent Sexuality and Gynecology* (Philadelphia: Lea and Febiger, 1990).
12. Robin Warshaw, *I Never Called It Rape* (New York: Harper & Row, 1988); and Jean Hughes and Bernice Sandler, *Friends Raping Friends: Could It Happen to You?* (Washington, D.C.: Project on the Status and Education of Women, Association of American Colleges, 1987).
13. Warshaw, op. cit.
14. Kenneth R. Sladkin, "Counseling Adolescents About Sexuality," *Seminars in Adolescent Medicine*, vol. 1, 1985, pp. 223-30.
15. Robert Coles and Geoffrey Stokes, *Sex and the American Teenager* (New York: Harper & Row, 1985).
16. Susan F. Newcomer and J. Richard Udry, "Oral Sex in an Adolescent Population," *Archives of Sexual Behavior*, vol. 14, 1985, pp. 41-46.
17. Sladkin, op. cit.
18. Ione J. Ryan and Patricia C. Dunn, "Sex Education from Prospective Teachers' View Poses a Dilemma," *Journal of School Health*, vol. 49, 1979, pp. 573-75; and Krueger, op. cit.
19. Peter Scales, *The Front Lines of Sexuality Education* (Santa Cruz, Calif.: Network Publications, 1984).

Building a Smarter Work Force

Vocational education in the U.S. must be expanded and modernized, in the manner of other industrialized countries, to help build high-performance work organizations.

Ray Marshall and Marc Tucker

Ray Marshall, formerly secretary of labor under President Jimmy Carter, is a professor of economics and public affairs at the University of Texas at Austin. Marc Tucker is president of the National Center on Education and the Economy (based in Washington, D.C., and Rochester, N.Y.).

American enterprise has been organized on the principle that most workers do not need to know much, or be able to do much, beyond what's necessary to perform narrowly defined tasks. The high productivity growth that the United States enjoyed until recently was made possible by giving our workers the most advanced equipment on the market. Today, however, the same equipment is available to low-wage countries that can sell their products all over the world—including here in the United States—at prices way below ours. If we continue to compete with them on wages and hours, as we are now doing, real wages will continue the decline that began in the 1970s and hours will increase until they match the low-wage competition. In short, the U.S. standard of living will plummet.

The alternative is to join the ranks of countries such as Germany, Japan, Sweden, and Denmark that promote high-performance work organizations. In such businesses, highly skilled, well-paid front-line workers are given many of the responsibilities of managers—tasks such as scheduling production, ordering parts, and attending to quality control.

The advantages of this form of work organization are enormous. The ranks of middle management and many support functions are thinned out, creating a large productivity gain. Quality improves dramatically. There is better coordination of the myriad functions involved in manufacturing a product, and far fewer mistakes. Improvements in design and construction are made constantly, instead of waiting for new model introductions,

creating a strong market advantage. It becomes possible to go after small market segments, because success no longer depends on producing thousands or millions of identical products. Worker motivation and morale are greatly enhanced, because workers take real pride in their work. Taken together, these changes give firms a decisive edge over low-wage, low-skill competitors.

Unfortunately for the United States, high-performance work organizations hinge on a well-educated work force. The U.S. system of educating and training workers has been shaped around the meager demands of "scientific management," where employers design the jobs of their front-line workers so that they require little knowledge or ability. U.S. skill requirements look more like those of Third World countries than those of the leading industrial nations.

Third World skills are fine for companies that choose to compete with South Korea, Mexico, and the Philippines. But firms that want to take on Germany and Japan are finding themselves at a disadvantage. The scant minority—fewer than 5 percent—of American firms that are embracing high-performance forms of work organization report that they are experiencing or expect to face a shortage of skilled labor. If the vast majority of employers were to adopt high-performance organization, there would be a skilled-labor shortage of epic proportions.

The economic future of the United States depends mainly on the skills of the front-line work force, the people whose jobs will not require a baccalaureate degree. Success, then, depends on developing a program to prepare close to three-quarters of our work force to take on tasks in restructured workplaces that, up to now, have been assigned mainly to the college educated. The idea that Americans just turning 19 or 20 would come to the job equipped for such tasks might sound like the stuff of fantasy, but it is increasingly common in many European countries. If it does not happen here, the United States will simply be unable to attain the rates of productivity growth and deliver the quality that it must achieve.

From *Technology Review*, October 1992, pp. 52-60. Adapted from *Thinking for a Living: Education and the Wealth of Nations* by Ray Marshall and Marc Tucker. © 1992 by BasicBooks, a division of HarperCollins Publishers, Inc. Reprinted by permission.

So far, our record on educating workers has been grim. More than a quarter of American students—perhaps as much as half our future front-line workers—drop out of school. We do virtually nothing to recover them. We spend an average of about $4,300 a year on our high-school students, but only $235 a year trying to give those who drop out the education and job skills they will need to survive in our economy.

Half of our high-school students, and a much higher fraction of our future front-line workers, are in the "general" curriculum, enrolled neither in the academic track for the college-bound nor in the vocational track. Most of them emerge from school—with or without a diploma—with eighth-grade academic skills or worse. And they do no better with respect to vocational skills. Twenty-five percent of the vocational courses in the United States are taken by the general-curriculum students. The result is that most of our future front-line workers leave school with academic and vocational skills that fall below those of virtually all mature industrialized countries and many newly industrialized countries. In other words, they leave school with Third World skills.

U.S. employers spend about $30 billion a year to educate and train their workers. But two-thirds of that sum goes to college-educated employees, and 90 percent of it is paid out by only one-half of one percent of the nation's firms. Therefore the vast majority of American front-line workers get no further formal education or training after they leave school.

HOW OTHER COUNTRIES TRAIN STUDENTS

The extent of our failure can best be seen by comparing what we do with the job-training systems common in other countries. The methods by which Japan, Germany, Sweden, and Denmark arrange for a high level of vocational competence among their front-line workers differ greatly, but the result is the same: all four nations boast work forces that are among the most highly skilled in the world.

In Japan, the best vocational education occurs in companies. The country's well-known system of lifetime employment in the large firms, combined with the Japanese practice of shifting workers from one job to another, makes employers more than willing to pay for job training; they know that the investment will be recovered. By 1992, for example, Toyota plans to put all new high-school graduates it hires for the front line through a two-year full-time course in digital electronics and "mechatronics." The company's assembly-line workers will then have roughly the same qualifications as junior engineers in the United States.

Schools still play an important role. They are closely linked with employers and typically provide their graduates with a smooth transition to the workplace. Japanese firms look at the schools as they look at any other supplier, cultivating close relations and demanding the highest possible quality.

The process by which young people enter the work force takes place in stages. First, firms send literature—and even videotapes—about themselves to schools at all levels. Recruiters stay in touch with high-school teachers, taking them to lunch, inquiring about the quality of their students, and urging them to encourage their best students to consider employment at their firm. Just before the students graduate, the big firms ask the principals of schools with which they have a special relationship to select the most qualified students for the available jobs on the basis of their academic performance as judged by the school staff.

The Japanese system provides a powerful motivation to all non-college-bound Japanese youth to do well in school, because the judgment of one's teachers is crucial. It also gives teachers far more authority than those of the non-college-bound in the United States have ever dreamed of having. Most important, it provides a swift, dependable entry for Japanese youth into real careers in the labor market.

In Germany, work is built on a centuries-old craft tradition, where workers tend to identify less with a particular company than with the trade or occupation in which they apprentice, become journeymen, and achieve—or hope to achieve—master status.

Germany's apprenticeship system provides the superb worker preparation that is a key factor in the country's economic success.

The German skills-development system begins early in school with the *Arbeitslehrer*, a formal program about industry that is compulsory for all grade-school students except those in a *Gymnasium*, a secondary school for college-bound students. Then, at age 15 or 16, most students not going on to college become apprentices with an employer in one of 480 trades and occupations.

Apprentices typically spend one day a week at a *Berufschule* (state vocational school) specializing in the student's trade and four days in a structured program of training at the employer's work site, guided by a master. In their two to three years of training, the apprentices receive a training wage, which gradually increases. At the end of the contract period, the apprentice faces a pencil-and-paper exam and a careful review of selected work samples. Apprentices who pass are awarded a certificate honored by employers all over Germany that attests to their having the skills required to assume journeyman status in their trade or occupation.

Given the costs that must be borne by the firms and the detailed regulations they must follow, one wonders why they don't just let the competition train future workers and then hire them away, much as U.S. firms would. But the companies view apprenticeship as a profitable investment. Since 90 percent of the apprentices remain employed by the firm that trains them, companies can tailor training to their specific needs. Many managers came up through the apprenticeship system and take great pride in continuing the tradition. And because all the large firms train, none are afraid that a nonparticipating firm will take unfair advantage.

These German apprenticeships constitute a national mentoring system, resulting in the superb preparation of the front-line worker that is a key factor in German economic success.

In Sweden, work experience begins at age seven, in first grade. Swedish students spend from one to several weeks a year in various kinds of workplaces, finding out what people do and how they do it. Representatives of employers visit schools as these kids are growing up, describing their industries and the careers within them.

When Swedish students are 16 and about to enter upper secondary school, they choose from among 27 courses of study within 6 divisions: arts and social sciences, care professions, economics and commerce, technology and science, technology and industry, and agriculture, horticulture, and forestry. All these programs include core courses in Swedish, English, and mathematics.

For the 75 percent of Swedish students who do not plan to go to college, 10 to 20 percent of their first and second years, and as much as 60 percent of their third year, are spent in the workplace. School vocational counselors, advised by industry committees, are responsible for organizing the "work-life" experiences of these students. Through the three years of upper secondary school, the student's field of vision narrows from familiarization with the occupational requirements of a broad industry group to the development of strong skills in a particular job. But the Swedish system, unlike the German, is designed *not* to commit youth to a narrow specialization for life. By exposing young people to a wide range of occupations, Swedish authorities hope to enable citizens to shift occupations with relative ease.

By guiding out-of-school youth into job-training programs, Sweden's Youth Centers put most dropouts back on track toward productive careers.

In stark contrast to the United States, Sweden also has a national dropout recovery program. In 1980, the Swedish Parliament enacted legislation holding every municipality responsible for locating disadvantaged and disaffected out-of-school youth between the ages of 16 and 18, recruiting them into a job-training program, and securing

work opportunities for them. The result is the country's system of Youth Centers, which has been highly successful in putting the vast majority of dropouts back on track toward productive careers.

Denmark goes even further than Sweden in ensuring that its non-college-bound students will be able to apply their skills in a range of trades. As in Germany and Sweden, most Danish youth not going on to university participate in a three-year program of combined work and study after they complete the tenth grade. Periods of work alternate with time spent in study at a technical college. But the Danes also try to impart generic "work skills"—such as self-motivation, communication, organization, and creativity—that employers value in high-performance settings.

In a large company, the work-study program begins with a few days of orientation, followed by 6 to 12 months of training in teamwork and the functioning of self-governing groups. Then comes a brief period of formal individual training. The rest of the program, about two years long, consists of project-based, self-directed learning. Groups of trainees who intend to specialize in different but complementary areas are given complex long-term projects that require the skills of everyone in the group. The teams are expected to organize themselves and to reach their goal without supervision. They have access to any member of the firm and to any of its information sources, but they must locate the people and information on their own.

Team members keep diaries recording the problems they encounter, the approaches they are taking to address them, and the progress they make on acquiring the skills they need to meet the standards set by the employers. Each trainee meets regularly with his or her teachers to evaluate progress. The students are expected to constantly assess their learning; the teachers act like mentors and coaches but do not engage in direct instruction. This scheme has become a paradigm of the work environment in a high-performance organization.

Another appealing feature of the Danish vocational system is that it leaves the door open to higher education. As Danish youth progress through the job-training system, they are free to take courses that, if passed, qualify them for admission to university. In this way, the Danes have made explicit provisions for a no-dead-end system, one where people can always advance to the level of opportunity that more education affords.

REVAMPING VOCATIONAL EDUCATION

In describing what other countries do to ensure a successful transition from school to work, we do not mean to imply that nothing of value goes on in the United States. We know of secondary vocational schools, for-profit technical schools, and community colleges that prepare their students well for challenging and rewarding careers, that have strong ties to employers, that are responsive to shifting industry requirements, and that have the latest equipment on which their students can train. We know of good grade-school programs that acquaint students with a wide range of careers, dropout recovery programs that plainly do what they were intended to do, and curricula that are explicitly designed to help students develop generic work skills.

But these are all isolated occurrences, running against the grain of a system that produces, overall, dismal results. What the country sorely lacks is a system that embraces the great majority of our students and prepares them to become productive members of a highly capable front-line work force.

It is doubtful that we would serve this country well by replicating any of the systems of other industrialized nations. We can certainly learn from their successes, but we must keep in mind their different cultural contexts—and outright shortcomings. For example, the Germans are themselves concerned about the rigidity of their system of narrow lifelong specialization in trades and occupations. What's more, the strong pride in the ancient German craft system that motivates employers to invest large sums in vocational education voluntarily is wholly lacking in the American experience.

The Japanese system, where the schools are responsible for producing graduates with a high level of "general intelligence," would appear to be much better adapted to a world of changing job requirements. But this system, too, has liabilities. Although large employers make massive efforts to provide first-rate vocational skills to their new hires, these firms employ only about a third of Japanese workers, leaving the others to depend on a weak backup network of state-run vocational schools. The other drawback of the Japanese system is the lack of any formal national system for recognizing vocational qualifications. In a highly mobile country like the United States, such a system is essential if individuals are to invest in themselves and have the opportunity to realize that investment when they move.

The United States must construct its own system for developing strong technical and professional skills in high-school students not going directly to a four-year college—a system that builds on the best practices of the leading industrial nations. Specifically, that means:

Setting aside several weeks each year for grade-school students to visit work sites and learn about the range of career opportunities.

All students need this exposure, not just those headed for the workplace right out of school. Most of our children learn about what goes on at work from movies and television, which give a highly distorted picture. The problem is particularly severe for poor and minority children, but it applies in some measure to almost everyone. There is no substitute for visiting workplaces and talking to the people who work in them.

No nation in which a quarter of the students fail to complete secondary education can hope to have a world-class work force.

Many U.S. educators reject the idea that schools exist in part to prepare people for work. This view partly accounts for the primacy of college as the only goal worth working for in school—but this has to change. Teachers themselves will have to be persuaded that work not requiring a college degree can be challenging, rewarding, and the source of real status. That task should become easier as the number of high-performance work organizations grows.

Creating a system of youth centers through which municipalities recover dropouts.

No nation in which a quarter of the students fail to complete secondary education can hope to have a world-class work force. South Korea's dropout rate is only 10 percent, and Sweden's rate—thanks to its Youth Center program—is even less. Every state should require its municipalities to operate alternative education and work-experience programs based on the Swedish model. Whenever a student dropped out of school, the school district would have to notify the nearest youth center, which would then actively recruit that student.

Many existing programs—ranging from the Job Corps to programs run by churches and community organizations—already have the capacity to do some or all of the functions we would assign to youth centers. The youth centers would contract with such organizations and with school districts to get the job done. The point is not so much to create new institutions as to designate one local agency to take sole responsibility for recovering every dropout.

How to fund such a program? Every local, state, and federal dollar earmarked for a student's education in a regular high school should follow the dropout to the youth center. While this will not be an easy requirement to meet for states and localities experiencing hard fiscal times, there is overwhelming evidence that the nation would save far more in reduced welfare and prison costs.

Building the vocational education system on a base of real academic accomplishment.

Without exception, the countries with the most successful vocational education systems realize that job training must be complemented by solid academic skills. In most U.S. school districts, one can get a high-school diploma if one shows up most of the time and does not cause any trouble. The states that do impose some sort of performance requirement rarely set the standard above seventh-grade equivalency.

We urge adoption of "certificates of initial mastery," to be awarded to most students around age 16 when they pass an appropriate examination. The subject matter would encompass reading, writing, listening, and speaking, as well as mathematics, the sciences, history, and the social sciences, the arts, and work skills, but the examinations would place a premium on the capacity to integrate knowledge from many of these disciplines in solving problems. Students would be able to take the performance exams as often as they liked until they passed them.

By setting a single standard for everyone, we break ranks with the Europeans, who use their exams to sort students out, dividing those who will go to college from those who will not. Students who get their certificate would be able to choose whether to begin a technical and professional certificate program, enroll in a college preparatory program, or go directly into the work force.

Providing access for all students who want it to a high-quality on-the-job learning experience leading to a universally recognized qualification.

The United States ought to create a system of technical and professional certificates covering most trades and occupations not requiring a four-year college degree. The certificates would be awarded when students completed a three-year program of combined schooling and structured on-the-job training and passed a written and practical examination. Programs could be offered by many kinds of institutions—high schools, vocational schools, employers, community colleges, and for-profit technical schools among them—working singly or in combination, but always teamed with employers offering the job-site component. These institutions would compete for students' tuition.

Much of the money required to meet this commitment would come from a repackaging of government funds now spent on the last two years of secondary school and the first two years of college. But other funding could come from employers, especially if—as we recommend below—firms are required to contribute to the continued education and training of their employees.

Each state and industry should have a strong voice in constructing the system and an equally strong role in administering it, but it must be a national system, with national standards, nationally recognized certificates, and a system of occupational classifications that do not vary by jurisdiction. Anything less will lead to a system that will reduce the mobility of our work force or lower individuals' incentive to train, or both. The country will almost surely begin to create this system industry by industry and state by state, but the aim from the start must be to make it truly national.

Designing the work-based portion of the program so it develops the qualities needed for high-performance work organizations.

The United States faces something of a dilemma. On the one hand, a system of technical and professional standards is urgently needed, and it is only common sense that these standards should be largely set by employers. On the other hand, most employers today would design standards around jobs that ask little of the people who have them.

Perhaps the United States should rely mainly on employers who are using advanced forms of work organization to formulate the new standards and then devise a curriculum, much like that of the Danes, explicitly to prepare our youth to function in the new work milieu. No doubt many young people will be employed at first by organizations that are not prepared to give them all the responsibility they have been trained to exercise or take advantage of all the skills they bring to the job. But these new employees can be powerful agents of change and can make it easier for forward-looking employers to restructure their workplaces.

Providing incentives to employers to invest in developing their employees.

Most advanced nations require companies to invest at least 1 percent of wages in continuing education and training. So should the U.S.

Most advanced nations and many newly industrialized countries require employers to invest a sum equal to at least 1 percent of salaries and wages for continuing education and training. The United States should require companies to do likewise—or, if they are unable or unwilling, to contribute to a government-operated Skills Development Fund, which would supply the education and training. Only expenditures on programs leading to state educational certificates, industry-wide training certificates, or recognized degrees would satisfy the requirement.

The situation is urgent. If we continue on our low-performance work track, real wages will fall much faster in the next 20 years than they have in the last 20. As that happens—and as the proportion of our population in the work force continues to drop—tax revenue will fall, and the investment capital required to educate and train our front-line workers will be increasingly hard to come by. Many states already find themselves in just such a bind. If we do not change course before 2010, when the baby boomers—77 million people—begin turning 65, and straining our pension and health resources, we could truly reach a point of no return.

If ever there was a time to make the choice for a high-skill work force, it is now.

The Profession of Teaching Today

We continue the dialogue over what makes a teacher "good." There are numerous external pressures on the teaching profession today from a variety of public interest groups. The profession continues to develop its knowledge base on effective teaching through ethnographic and empirical inquiry on classroom practice and teacher behavior in elementary and secondary classrooms across the nation. Concern continues as to how best to teach to enhance insightful, reflective student interaction with the content of instruction. We continue to consider alternative visions of literacy and the roles of teachers in fostering a desire for learning within their students.

All of us who live the life of a teacher are aware of those features that we associate with the concept of a good teacher. In addition, we do well to remember that the teacher-student relationship is both a tacit and an explicit one—one in which teacher attitude and emotional outreach are as important as student response to our instructional effort. The teacher-student bond in their assent into the teaching/learning process cannot be overemphasized; teaching is a two-way street. We must maintain an emotional link in the teacher-student relationship that will compel students to want to accept instruction and attain an optimal learning performance. What, then, constitute those most defensible standards for assessing good teaching?

The past decade has yielded much in-depth research on the various levels of expertise in the practice of teaching. We know much more now about specific teaching competencies and how they are acquired than in the 1970s. Expert teachers do differ from novices and experienced teachers in terms of their capacity to exhibit accurate, integrated, and holistic perceptions and analyses of what goes on when students try to learn in classroom settings. We can now pinpoint some of these qualitative differences.

As the knowledge base on our professional practice continues to expand, we will be able to certify with greater precision what constitute acceptable ranges of teacher performance based on more clearly defined procedures of practice, as we have, for example, in medicine and dentistry. Medicine is, after all, a practical art as well as a science—and so is teaching. The analogy in terms of setting standards of professional practice is a strong one. Yet the emotional pressure on teachers that theirs is also a performing art, and that clear standards of practice can be applied to that art, is a bitter pill to swallow for many of them. Hence, the intense reaction of many against external competency testing and any rigorous classroom observation standards. The writing, however, is on the wall: the profession cannot hide behind the tradition that teaching is a special art, unlike all others, which cannot be subjected to objective observational standards, aesthetic critique, or to a standard knowledge base. Those years are behind us. The public demands the same levels of demonstrable professional standards of practice as are demanded of those in the medical arts.

Likewise, we have identified certain approaches to working with students in the classroom that have been effective. Classroom practices such as cooperative learning strategies have won widespread support for inclusion in the knowledge base on teaching. The knowledge base of the social psychology of life in classrooms has been significantly expanded by collaborative research between classroom teachers and various specialists in psychology and teacher education. This has been accomplished by using anthropological field research techniques to ground theory of classroom practice into demonstrable phenomenological perspectives. Many issues have been raised—and answers found—by basic ethnographic field observations, interviews, and anecdotal record-keeping techniques to understand more precisely how teachers and students interact in the classroom. A rich dialectic is developing among teachers regarding the description of ideal classroom environments. The methodological insight from this research into the day-to-day realities of life in schools is transforming what we know about teaching as a professional activity and how to best advance our knowledge of effective teaching strategies.

Creative, insightful persons who become teachers will usually find ways to network their interests and concerns with other teachers and will make their own opportunities for creative teaching in spite of external assessment procedures. They acknowledge that the science of teaching involves the observation and measurement of teaching behaviors but that the art of teaching involves the humanistic dimensions of instructional activities, an alertness to the details of what is taught, and equal alertness to how students receive it. Creative, insightful teachers guide class processes and formulate questions according to their perceptions of how students are responding to the material.

To build their hope, as well as their self-confidence, teachers must be motivated to an even greater effort for professional growth in the midst of these fundamental revisions. Teachers need support, appreciation, and respect. Simply criticizing them while refusing to alter social and economic conditions that affect the quality of their

work will not solve their problems, nor will it lead to excellence in education. Not only must teachers work to improve their public image and the public's confidence in them but the public must confront its own misunderstandings of the level of commitment required to achieve teacher excellence—and their share of responsibility in that task. Teachers need to know that the public cares about and respects them enough to fund their professional improvement in a primary recognition that they are an all-important force in the life of this nation. The articles in this unit consider the quality of education and the status of the teaching profession today.

Looking Ahead: Challenge Questions

What is "expertise" in teaching?

What are some ways in which teacher-student classroom interaction can be studied?

Why has the knowledge base on teaching expanded so dramatically in recent years?

List by order of importance what you think are the five most vital issues confronting the teaching profession today. What criteria did you use in ranking these issues? What is your position on each of them?

What does gaining a student's assent to a teacher's instructional effort mean to you?

What are the most defensible standards to assess the quality of a teaching performance?

What is the role of creativity in the classroom?

What political pressures do teachers in the United States face today?

Can teachers be sufficiently imaginative in their teaching and still get students to meet standardized objective test requirements? What are the issues to be considered regarding assessment of student learning?

—F. S.

How To Recognize Good Teaching

*Use this research overview to assess
how well your school system is fulfilling its central mission:
successful teaching and learning*

ALLAN C. ORNSTEIN

Allan C. Ornstein is an education professor at Loyola University of Chicago.

What is an effective teacher? What kinds of behavior contribute to success (or the lack of it) in teaching?

These are important questions for your school board. How you answer will bear on the kinds of teachers your school system recruits and hires and will influence how your district evaluates teachers. In short, these questions cut to the heart of instructional excellence. As an education researcher, I suggest you use the following overview of research on effective teaching as a tool for assessing how your school district is fulfilling its central mission: successful teaching and learning.

Over the years, researchers have conducted thousands of studies to identify and analyze effective and ineffective teaching. The results are, to put it bluntly, confusing and contradictory. Often, the research findings seem simply to confirm the obvious. (For example, a friendly teacher is an effective teacher.) But this much is clear: Teaching is a complex act—both an art and a science. What works in some situations with some students might not work in different settings with different subjects, students, and schools. Some teachers break many of the rules of teaching procedure and methods yet are profoundly successful; others follow the rules to the letter and are unsuccessful. Distinguishing between "good" and "poor" or "effective" and "ineffective" teachers is so difficult that even the experts have trouble defining and measuring teacher competence.

Some researchers look at the results and conclude that teaching is so complex and unpredictable it's nearly impossible to make generalizations about successful teaching. Others contend it's possible to define appropriate and inappropriate kinds of teaching behavior—for example, the kinds of questions teachers ask, the ways they respond to students, their classroom management techniques, their teaching methods—and to measure the effect of these differences on students.

Basically, the research on teacher effectiveness falls into two groups: research on teacher styles and research on teacher competencies (see sidebar on page 185). Missing in both these approaches, as I'll discuss in a moment, is research into the human element in teaching.

The science of teaching

What does it mean to be a "competent" or "effective" teacher? Some researchers say an effective teacher is task-oriented and businesslike—in short, the image of an old-fashioned teacher. According to this definition, a competent teacher strives to meet academic goals, structures activities carefully and explicitly, covers content thoroughly, does lots of practice and review, explains concepts and procedures, monitors classroom progress, gives and checks homework regularly, and holds students accountable. This is the prototype of a no-nonsense teacher—the kind of teacher many of us remember well from our school years.

Research into this view of effective teaching confirms the basic principles and methods used by many experienced teachers. This body of research also helps provide a base of professional knowledge for teacher educators and teacher-training institutions. Indeed, if this knowledge base continues to develop and is used appropriately, advocates say it might guide decisions about when to use certain teaching techniques—even decisions about who should teach.

Education researcher Jere Brophy, at Michigan State University, goes so far as to maintain that this expanding body of knowledge empowers teachers because it allows them to act confidently on the basis of well-established principles rather than trial-and-error notions. Brophy compares the potential power of this information base with the way advancing scientific knowledge influences and upgrades the practice of medicine.

But I contend this approach to identifying good teaching falls short of the mark. Research that identifies teacher "competencies" amounts to little more than listing the principles and methods good teachers have known and used for many years. The product-oriented researchers who conduct this kind of research have summarized what we've known for a long time and often have passed on in the form of "tips for teachers" or "practical suggestions."

Indeed, considering what we know about the art of teaching, it's something of an overstatement to maintain an agreed-upon knowledge base exists to undergird the teaching profession. Instead of a defined knowledge base, we have a host of theories, models, and ideas that are analyzed and reanalyzed. Little of this "new" knowledge differs from the "old" knowledge—or from what teachers call "common sense."

A search for the human element

The trend to portray the effective teacher as task-oriented, organized, and structured—what I'll call the pro-

Research mulls teacher styles and competencies

RESEARCH on teacher effectiveness falls into two general categories: research on teacher styles and research on teacher competencies.

• **Research on teacher styles.** Studies of teaching style look at broad patterns or personality types, encompassing a teacher's stance, behavior pattern, mode of performance, and attitude toward self and others. Every teacher has a style that's reflected in how the teacher conducts the class and how students perform and interact with the teacher and with one another.

A teacher's pattern of behavior and methods is quite stable over time, even with different students and in different classroom situations. A teacher's preferred style is influenced by early teaching experiences and perceptions and by training as a beginning teacher. As years pass, a teacher's style becomes more ingrained, and changing it requires powerful stimuli and intense attention.

The research on teacher style tends to analyze classroom ecology, give detailed and descriptive accounts of classroom events, and conduct extensive interviews with teachers and students to shed light on what teachers do and how they do it. The recent trend is for researchers to take what I call a process/product approach—that is, they attempt to identify specific kinds of teacher behavior (the process) that have a direct relationship with and impact on specific student outcomes (the product).

But this approach has its limitations: Critics maintain it's impossible to pinpoint and quantify all the elements that directly affect the teacher-student relationship. A teacher's professional judgments, hunches, and intuitions can be as important as specific types of behavior or methods. Personality characteristics—such as empathy, enthusiasm, friendliness, and nurturing—might be more important than training in specific pedagogical methods.

The debate over how to define teacher style—whether in broad generalizations or in specific, measurable items—points to the limitations of this approach to understanding teacher effectiveness. Studies of teacher style are interesting and offer insights into good teaching, but either the conclusions are too broad to be applied to specific situations, or the attempt to quantify specific aspects of teaching excludes much of what constitutes teaching "style."

• **Research on teacher competencies.** Because of the problems in defining teacher styles, some researchers try to use more precise terms—what they call teacher competencies. Competencies deal mainly with what the teacher is doing while teaching, rather than with broad personality characteristics or teaching patterns. This research aims to define items of behavior with care and specificity—as if one were including them in an instruction manual or a teacher-appraisal system. This approach often results in long, specific lists, sometimes bordering on the esoteric or trivial.

One criticism of this approach is that the long lists of teacher competence usually identify minimum competencies. The utility of this approach, in other words, lies in identifying teacher *in*competence. Another criticism: The lists generally reflect a narrow and behaviorist view of a "good" teacher and ignore the humanistic or affective elements of good teaching.

Regardless of the limitations of this approach, the nationwide education reform movement has pushed for an appraisal system based on specific teacher competencies. A few words of caution for your school board: If your school district intends to use the teacher competency approach in making personnel decisions, those decisions should be based on multiple observations of teachers. To be valid—and to stand up to legal scrutiny—decisions about teacher-competence must be based on an adequate sampling of teacher performance.

One more important consideration: The most valid appraisal system based on teacher competencies is derived from the professionals being evaluated. Administrators and teachers should agree on goals, categories of behavior, and processes used in evaluation. Successful appraisal also requires a degree of willingness to give the teacher the benefit of the doubt and a chance to improve before being terminated. It calls for an open mind, so that competencies not listed can be incorporated into the appraisal system. And it calls for common sense—that is, the knowledge that more than one list of competencies or model of successful teaching is possible.—A.C.O.

cess/product approach—tends to overlook the friendly, warm, democratic teacher. It neglects the creative teacher who is stimulating and imaginative, the dramatic teacher who bubbles with energy and enthusiasm, the philosophical teacher who encourages students to play with ideas and concepts, and the problem-solving teacher who requires that students think out answers to questions.

In identifying and prescribing measurable and quantifiable behavior, process/product research fails to take into account the emotional, qualitative, and interpretive descriptions of classrooms and the joys of teaching. It takes little note of social and psychological factors in teaching, and it recommends few of these factors as effective. The generalizations and principles growing out of the process/product research tend to deal with techniques for structuring, controlling, and managing the classroom—perhaps because a good portion of the work has dealt with low-achieving and at-risk students.

It's important to note, however, that some leading researchers take a quite different point of view. Maxine Greene, of Columbia University, asserts that a good deal of teaching is not subject to empirical inquiry or to correlates of student achievement. For Greene, good teaching and learning involve values, experiences, insights, imagination, and appreciation—the "stuff" that cannot be easily observed or measured. As Greene describes it, teaching and learning are an existential encounter, a philosophical process involving ideas and creative inquiries that cannot be easily quantified.

Stanford University's Elliot Eisner posits that what is not measurable goes unnoticed in a process/product teaching model. According to Eisner, breaking down the teaching act into dimensions, competencies, and criteria that researchers can define and quantify neglects the hard-to-measure aspects of teaching—the personal, humanistic, and playful aspects. In Eisner's view, to say that excellence in teaching requires measurable behavior and outcomes is to miss a substantial part of teaching—what some educators refer to as artistry, drama, tone, and flavor. Indeed, the kinds of teacher behavior that correlate with measurable outcomes often lead to rote learning, drill, and automatic responses.

Process/product research pays close attention to subject-matter content in teaching and learning—what and how much teachers know, how they relate their subject knowledge to student understanding, how they teach content, and how content can be integrated with principles and methods of effective teaching. This research stresses narrow student outcomes based on knowledge-based achievement. But the researchers pay little attention to the thought processes involved in learning—especially the ability to think critically, solve problems, approach ideas creatively, and carry out other forms of high-level cognition.

The teaching models based on process/product research also seem to miss the moral and ethical results of teaching, as well as the social, personal, and developmental facets related to learning and life—in effect, the affective domain of learning and the psychology of being human. In attempting to observe and measure what teachers do—and to detail whether students improve their performance on reading or math tests—these models ignore the learner's imagination, fantasy, and artistic thinking. They miss out on students' dreams, hopes, and aspirations and on the impact teachers have on these hard-to-define but important aspects of a student's life.

The chief variable of process/product research, in short, is cognitive performance, followed closely by student control. Learning experiences that deal with character, spiritual outlook, and philosophy are absent. The personal and human dimension of teaching is usually ignored—a sad commentary for a helping profession.

What this means for your schools

Good teachers know—though they might not be able to prove it—that good teaching has a great deal to do with caring and sharing. Effective teachers have the capacity to accept, understand, and appreciate students on their terms and through their world. They can make students feel good about themselves. They're cheerful and positive, they set achievement goals, and they get fired up with enthusiasm.

These are basically fuzzy qualities that the scientific theories of teaching tend to overlook. Indeed, teachers who place high priority on humanistic and affective practices— on the personal and social development of their students— often are not much interested in teaching small pieces of information that can be measured and correlated with specific kinds of teaching behavior.

Interestingly, researchers Alan Hofmeister and Margaret Lubke of Utah State have found a direct relationship between student learning and teacher esteem. The higher the teacher's esteem, the more students learn. No one taught these teachers how to build their own self-esteem or the esteem of their students. Indeed, teachers who are confident about themselves usually are not overly concerned about

Selected references

Jere E. Brophy, "Classroom Management Techniques," *Education and Urban Society* (February 1986), pp. 182-194.

Marilyn Cochran-Smith and Susan L. Lytle, "Research on Teaching and Teacher Research: The Issues That Divide," *Educational Researcher* (March 1990), pp. 2-11.

Elliot W. Eisner, *The Educational Imagination*, 2nd ed. (New York: Macmillan, 1985).

N.L. Gage, "What Do We Know about Teaching Effectiveness?" *Phi Delta Kappan* (October 1984), pp. 87-90.

Maxine Greene, *The Dialectic of Teaching* (New York: Teachers College Press, Columbia University, 1988).

Maxine Greene, "Philosophy and Teaching," in *Handbook of Research on Teaching*, Merlin Wittrock, ed. New York: Macmillan, 1986.

Alan Hofmeister and Margaret Lubke, *Research into Practice: Implementing Effective Teaching Strategies* (Needham Heights, Mass.: Allyn & Bacon, 1991).

Allan C. Ornstein, "Teacher Effectiveness Research: Theoretical Considerations," in H.C. Waxman and H.J. Walberg, eds., *Effective Teaching* (Berkeley, Calif.: McCutchan, 1991), pp. 63-80.

Allan C. Ornstein, "A Look at Teacher Effectiveness: Research, Theory, and Practice," *NASSP Bulletin* (October 1990), pp. 78-88.

their evaluation ratings—or with what the research has to say about their teaching behavior.

Teaching is a people industry, and people (especially young people) perform best when they feel wanted and respected. It's quite possible for a teacher to disengage students from the learning process by belittling them, ignoring them, undercutting them, or even "yessing" them (failing to hold them accountable for the right answer) and still get high marks on the kinds of competencies associated with the teacher as technician: "The teacher came to class on time"; "The teacher checked homework regularly"; "The teacher graded quizzes on a timely basis."

Such checklists are quite common in research-based models of what constitutes a "good" teacher—and in school district evaluation instruments. But these lists ignore what it means to be a kind and generous teacher or to work with students so they develop their own unique strengths. Even worse, such lists trivialize teaching and highlight the technocratic aspect of teaching at the expense of the human dimension.

Teacher research and teacher evaluation, I believe, should focus on the learner, not on content. It should attend to the feelings and attitudes of students, not just knowledge and skills, because feelings and attitudes determine what knowledge and skills the student will seek and acquire. It should examine the long-term growth and development of students, not short-term objectives or specific tasks.

The trouble is, in most school districts, teachers who concentrate on the learner's feelings and attitudes and on the social or personal development of the student are likely to be penalized. Why? Because most school districts correlate cognitive outcomes—little pieces of information acquired by students—with teaching behavior. The more bits of information students can demonstrate they know on standardized tests, the "better" the teacher.

Students need to be encouraged and nurtured by their teachers. Parents and teachers need to help children and adolescents establish a source for true self-esteem by highlighting their strengths, supporting them, discouraging their negative feelings and attitudes, and helping them take control of their lives and live their own values.

Teachers need to create experiences in which kids learn to feel good about themselves. The more students learn to like themselves, the more they'll achieve. And the more they achieve, the more they'll like themselves. This takes time. It doesn't show up on standardized tests within a semester or a school year. And that doesn't help the teacher who is being evaluated by a content-driven or test-driven school administrator. It certainly does not benefit the teacher who is evaluated according to the number of department meetings attended or whether the shades on the classroom windows were evenly drawn.

The process/product research on teaching is concerned primarily with the present—with processes and products that are measured in one term or one year by standardized tests of cognitive results, not affective outcomes. This approach to teacher effectiveness misses the mark. The most effective teachers endow their students with a "can-do" attitude, with good feelings about themselves that are indirectly and eventually related to cognitive achievement. Every teacher should demand high academic standards and should teach content, to be sure. But we also need to acknowledge that students learn content through process. If

We're wrong to insist that all teachers must use certain methods and procedures. Instead, we must permit teachers to teach according to their own personalities, teaching philosophies, and goals

the process is humanistic, I believe, then students are more likely to learn the content.

What it boils down to is this: We're wrong to insist that all teachers use certain methods or procedures. Instead, we must permit teachers to teach according to their own personalities, teaching philosophies, and goals. Teachers should be able to pick and choose from a wide range of research and theory and to discard the kinds of teaching behavior and methods that conflict with their personal styles. They should be free to set aside the no-nonsense, heavily cognitive approach without being considered ineffective.

Quite likely, certain types of behavior contribute to good teaching. Trouble is, we can't agree on exactly which methods and kinds of behavior are most important. Some teachers know theoretically "what works," but they're unable to put those ideas into practice. Some teachers act effortlessly in the classroom, and others consider teaching a chore. All this suggests that teaching cannot be described in a checklist or precise model. It also suggests teaching is a holistic activity—not tiny competencies or slices of behavior—that deals with whole people and how they develop and behave in a variety of classroom and school settings.

Although the research on teacher competencies offers insight into good teaching, it can lead us to become too rigid in our view of effective teaching. Following this line of research alone can lead to an overemphasis on specific kinds of teaching behavior that can be easily measured or prescribed in advance.

As for teacher evaluation instruments, keep in mind that the human side of teaching is difficult to measure. As a result, it seldom shows up in teacher evaluations. In our attempts to be scientific—to predict and control behavior and assess group patterns—it's too easy to lose sight of the affective side of teaching and the individual differences among teachers. It's too easy to attend to specific types of behavior and cognitive results.

Teachers appreciate evaluation processes that help them improve their teaching—so long as the processes are honest and fair; so long as the evaluations are professionally planned and administered; so long as teachers are permitted to make and learn from their mistakes; and so long as more than one model of effectiveness is acceptable and teachers are free to adopt the styles that fit their personalities and teaching philosophies.

Needed: A New Literacy

Melvin E. Levison

Melvin E. Levison is professor emeritus of education at the City University of New York's Brooklyn College.

What is a school? It's a place where we blindfold the young, plug their ears, and encapsulate them in heavy plastic. Then we're perplexed when they behave like strangers in a strange and hostile world.

This problem, deeply rooted in the society as a whole, will not be resolved by resurrecting the educational goals and standards of the recent past, which themselves reenforce rather than solve the problem. We must look elsewhere, even to ancient roots, for guidance.

Here are three propositions that, if carried out, will provide an education in depth and breadth, drawing out students' inborn capacities to perceive keenly, reason critically, and grow increasingly more aware and respectful of self and others, and helping them to explore the world around them, to investigate in a rich and meaningful way their own and other societies and ages, and to become familiar with rich facets of their own personalities.

PROPOSITION I:
OPEN WIDE THE DOORS AND LET THE SENSES INTO THE CLASSROOM

Am I serious? In an age of instant gratification, where the jock reigns supreme, welcome the senses into the classroom? But of course! Not to censure or suppress but to *redirect* sensory energies into fruitful channels. Outside the classroom, they are uncontrolled and will continue to run wild.

Infants amaze parents and psychologists by the speed with which they develop new skills and constantly seek out new knowledge and new ways of acquiring them. The senses play a prominent role in this growth. No matter how you measure it, pre-school learning is prodigious. During those years, children learn to speak their mother tongue fluently, with a firm grasp of the basic grammar, picked up within the context of gesture, action, facial expression, the total environment. Their touching, tasting, and handling of objects is the indispensable preliminary to naming them; through movement, they gain that sense of

space and depth essential for thinking mathematically. As they acquire this vast range of knowledge and skills, they develop a sense of self.

They become remarkable observers. It is they, not their parents, who notice that the cat in the picture book hasn't the collar around its neck to be found in all the previous pictures; it is they who distinguish music by its sound, while their elders have to check the CD label. Within this context, we can understand Picasso's confession, "Once I drew like Raphael, but it takes me a lifetime to learn to draw like children."

When children first enter school, the goal is to move them from the sensory and concrete to the abstract and general. Is leaving behind the sensory and concrete and functioning on increasingly more abstract and generalized planes the mark of a superior education? Would it stunt intellectual growth to enhance the multisensory and to build organically on the way pre-school children learn?

The common answer to both is "yes." But there are critics who protest. There are those who feel that children's rich sensory experiences become too predigested and mechanical when they grow up and go to school. Joyce Cary laments that children are instructed to forget the colors, the fluffy feathers, the delightful chirping, the adroitness in flight, and simply remember the label *bird*. Paul Valéry offers an antidote, preaching that "seeing is forgetting the name of the thing one sees." Cézanne makes the astonishing observation: "The day is coming when a single carrot, freshly observed, will set off a revolution." Whitehead complains that, because of the narrow way language is taught, students fail to appreciate that "every phrase and word embodies some habitual idea of men and women as they plowed their fields, tended their homes, and built their cities."

It's not only literary and artistic figures and the stray philosopher-mathematician whose voices are heard in protest. Maslow and Kuhn tell us that, although there are a good number of run-of-the-mill scientists who accept theories "on the authority of teacher and text, not because of evidence," and who confuse technique for science and scientific formulation for reality, the picture changes radically when we turn to so many of the great creative geniuses, the bold eagles of science and math. Their words may scandalize those who insist that we think only in words. Whether we listen to Clerk-Maxwell, Galton, Kekulé, Hadamard, Medawar, Poincaré, or Einstein, they state that when a problem becomes difficult they prescind from words and turn to sensory imagery. Einstein is explicit: "The words or the language, as they are written or spoken, do not seem to play any role in my mechanism of thought." The "elements" he used in the primary stage of his work were "visual and some of muscular type. Conventional words or other signs have to be sought for laboriously only in a secondary state. . . ." Perhaps his experience as a violinist and boatman provided a rich source for the "muscular type." This would lend credence to recent arguments of phenomenologists that understanding and meaning don't originate in language but are experienced first as bodily states. Strange how we blot the obvious from our minds: that all human experience and endeavor—whether the crassly materialistic, the intellectually brilliant, or the spiritually sublime— occur in and through the body.

The autobiography of Herbert Simon, a father of artificial intelligence, gives us another stunning example. One would expect to hear him describe his invention as "an impersonal product of technological progress." Hardly so. As Sherry Turkle, herself an authority on the social impact of computers, concludes, readers "will come away seeing that" constructing thinking machines "is a deeply personal enterprise—an expression of the aesthetic of the people who work it and, more than that, a science of self-reflection, a way of thinking about one's thoughts."

Two distinguished teachers—one of science, the other of computers—also stress the importance of sensory imagery, the aesthetic, and the personal. In a freshman physics seminar at Harvard, William J. J. Gordon taught students to use metaphors and visual imagery as the key to solving highly abstract problems and as a means for gaining a gut understanding of "the image-formation that underlies great science. . . ." Students were highly pleased that their professors in the other, the regular science courses took their metaphors seriously; sometimes approving, sometimes preferring their own. At times, these conversations veered "from the stilted elements of science toward a discussion of aesthetic values. . . ."

In teaching the very young, Papert rejects what is likely the prevailing use of computers—"to *program* the child"—and presents his vision where the child programs the computer. He exults over his own good fortune that, by the age of two, he had become intensely involved with gears, which became for him the model for his understanding of advanced mathematical ideas. "You can be the gear, you can understand how it turns by projecting yourself into its place and turning with it." His ultimate goal: "to turn computers into instruments flexible enough so that many children can each create for themselves something like what gears were for me."

Perhaps you're now ready to open wide the doors and let the senses into the classroom. Good! Before you do, there's one more hurdle to clear.

"Seein's believin'," we say. But is it? In the August 17, 1990, *International Herald-Tribune,* through the use of a new computer-graphics technique, Groucho Marx and Sylvester Stallone are pictured with Franklin Delano Roosevelt and Winston Churchill at the 1945 Yalta conference. In the movie *Zelig,* Woody Allen, by similar "magic," is standing next to Hitler.

Believing is also a lot easier than smelling. The January 1981 issue of the *Progressive* reports that, at the MGM Hotel in Las Vegas, a man noticed and reported to hotel employees and a police officer that he smelled smoke. To no avail. Later, all hell broke loose. The fire was blamed on missing sprinklers, smoke detectors, and faulty alarms. The article concludes, "by extending our senses with artificial devices, we lose belief in what we see, hear, and smell for ourselves."

There's a need to improve the quality of our perceptions. We must strip away the set images behind our senses in order to overcome the tendency, as Gordon puts it, "to short-circuit the fullness of [our] experiences [by] settling for established ideas, cultural formulas, and the cliches of language and manners." It's for this reason that Aldous Huxley argues for education in "the nonverbal humanities," which would help reclaim or keep our innocence: the capacity to perceive the familiar as strange and the strange as familiar. Opening the doors to let the senses in is a first and crucial step in enriching the teaching-learning process and, of course, all aspects of daily living.

PROPOSITION II:
IDENTIFY AND TEACH READING AS A PROCESS APPLICABLE NOT ONLY TO PRINT BUT TO THE MESSAGES IN THE VISUAL, AURAL, OLFACTORY— INDEED, IN ALL—MEDIA

Only in the last 200 years has the verb *to read* come to refer only to written material. Originally, Thomas Wolfe points out, reading meant "giving counsel . . . explaining the obscure." Latin, Greek, Arabic, Hebrew, and Gothic sources substantiate this broader meaning. *Read* is also traced to the fourth stomach of a ruminant, linking reading to musing and cogitating.

Reading is but one subset of a complex human process of analyzing information in considerable depth—regardless of the medium.

There's more than etymology and history to support this view. One of the fathers of the Great Books tradition, Mortimer Adler, states that "the art of reading . . . applies to any kind of communication," that reading nature and reading books involve the same skills: "keenness of observation, readily available memory, range of imagination, and, of course, a reason trained in analysis and reflection." Thorndike goes even further, arguing that reading a paragraph and solving a math problem are "not unlike." And over 1,500 years ago, Chinese poet Tsung Ping explained: "The task of the painter consists in transposing nature onto silk from which the beholder will reexperience nature's grandeur as it has first affected the painter. Each, whether creator or beholder, seeks the fullness of life."

So reading as we usually identify it—involving decoding and understanding print—is *not* a unique process. It's but one subset of a complex human process of extracting, sorting, collating, analyzing, correlating, and evaluating information in considerable depth—regardless of the medium. The skilled reading of a painting, a dance, a perfume, a dump, X-rays, or wine is essentially the same process as the skilled reading of print. Arguably, all cognitive processes are reading processes, so that from birth, as newborns learn through touch, smell, hearing, seeing, and moving, they are reading media and learning.

What are media? Money as a medium of exchange and language as a medium of communication are not unfamiliar notions; and the mass media are, if anything, too familiar. There are many more: the individual arts, humanities, and sciences, media which we label "the higher manifestations of a society"; and the vast domain of anthropologists and other social scientists covering all the ways humans feed, clothe, house, worship, transport, mate, heal, and entertain. Lest I leave any medium out: media are any and all the "tracks" humans leave behind—knowingly and unknowingly—which reveal their presence some time, some where on Earth, on the moon, or wherever. It may not be immediately apparent when we look at our own society, but when we visit another and suffer culture shock, we come to see that, like print, all media are encoded. Nor should we overlook the media through which nature expresses itself.

Citizens must be able to read the media with sophistication if they are to fulfill their civic, as well as professional, responsibilities.

Two things should be apparent: first, that this education, based on reading media, grows organically out of the way the young learn during the exceedingly rich pre-school years; and second, that this method of teaching could have been carried out before the advent of the mass media, with the vast array of primary source materials to be found in museums of science and technology, natural history, art; at sites like Colonial Williamsburg; in the sky above and the earth below; and, of course, in libraries. This hardly means we should shun the mass media. *When properly used,* they become powerful educational tools. The crucial role of 81 seconds of videotape in both Rodney King beating trials makes it clear that citizens, in the future, must be able to read the mass media with sophistication if they are to fulfill their civic—as well as their personal and professional—responsibilities.

But reading the mass media is hardly enough. *Literacy for our age requires that students learn to read all media in order to be able to read all media to learn.* For where are the primary source materials of all the disciplines if not prismatized throughout the media? Eminent French historian Marc Bloch, repeating the thoughts of G. B. Vico, the father of the social sciences, muses: "What do we mean by document if not a 'track,' as it were, perceptible to the senses, which some phenomenon, in itself inaccessible, has left behind?"

When exploring the media, we must also make ourselves aware of what's *not* there, and ask why. Frederick Jackson Turner, who stressed the role of the frontier in the development of "the American," points out that, until recently, human history was pictured as male-centered. Why? Because males worked in durable materials that ended up in museums; females worked in straw, in leather, or in tilling the fields. "A wiser paleoanthropologist now tells us that the women were the culture-bearers, and they left a much more durable and complete legacy: us."

PROPOSITION III:
IDENTIFY AND TEACH WRITING AS A PROCESS APPLICABLE NOT ONLY TO THE VERBAL BUT TO EXPRESSION IN ALL MEDIA

Like reading, writing, too, hasn't always been limited to words. In Anglo-Saxon, for example, *writan* refers not only to drawing or forming letters, symbols, and words but also to composing and writing music and "forming by painting or drawing or sketching or designing."

Throughout Western history, there has been strong support for this proposition. Genesis is the source of the tradition that humans, whatever their vocation, should complete the Almighty's Creation in the way they perform their daily tasks. Thirteenth-century philosophers, including St. Bonaventure, stress the egalitarian nature of work, distinguishing the mechanical from the liberal arts not hierarchically "but upon the different processes employed"—a position hardly foreign to the thought of John Dewey and the American pragmatists.

In classical Greek education, the goal was *paideia,* the ideal fulfillment of all aspects of human potential. To attain this end, the word played the central role—but not the written word nor the abstract, impersonal, spoken word. Only too aware of the limitations of the written word, the Greeks idealized the oral word, profoundly interrelated with all the concomitants of oral expression. In literature, sculpture, architecture, painting, rhetoric, drama, poetry, music, and philosophy, they found the same principles of form, a universal pattern behind the helter-skelter of daily life.

There are many contemporary scholars in agreement with this broad view. Robert J. Wolff cites the tendency of liberal-arts students, in a basic design course, to seek rules and regulations—quotations, as it were, from Renoir or Picasso. Instead, they have to learn that their decisions in art are "a matter of personal discipline and judgment." For many, this is "the first breakaway from their inbred dependence on authority." Isadora Duncan put it so simply: "If I could tell you what it meant, there would be no point in dancing it." Like individuals, Kouwenhoven points out, not all societies have expressed themselves best through literature. The English did, but not the Dutch, Romans, or Germans. To date, Roebling's Brooklyn Bridge and mass production for the good of the many have been our forte. Cassirer, the philosopher of philosophic forms, maintains that the sensuous forms of our words and imagery in the arts, sciences, myth, and religion are "forms of [our] own self-revelation." And through market research, Gerald Zaltman has learned that "there are people who are not very articulate verbally but . . . are fluent with pictures, sounds, or smells."

Howard Gardner provides sound psychological footing for this proposition, maintaining that there are seven—not two—types of intelligence. Besides the linguistic and logical-mathematical, there are the spatial, musical, bodily kinesthetic, the interpersonal, and the intrapersonal, each with its own "special neurological organization." Even if he were wrong, achievement in any one of the latter five areas could spark students' self-confidence and enable them to return to the first two with new vigor, incentive, and perseverance.

These three propositions didn't spring full-blown from my head. I started with a simple, flexible, concrete method based on the assumption that the young have sensory acuity, the capacity to reason cogently and critically, and—in a "threat-free climate"—to grow in their ability to peek into the theater of their own minds, as they explore mainly nonverbal media. It's been most gratifying to see what graduate, undergraduate, and gifted secondary-school students achieve when using this method; and a delight, most recently, to note the utter fascination of groups of 70- and 80-year-olds over the insights and knowledge they garner using this method to analyze such simple things as cartoons and silhouettes.

But what about "at risk" elementary- and secondary-school children—the poorest that administrators would assign us? It's what these students achieve using the method to fulfill their regular curricular requirements that provokes me to labor long and hard to figure out the implications of the outcome. In their case, when the learning revolves around not remembering the textbook but exploring what they are seeing and hearing here and now, a remarkable transformation ensues. They discover that the skills they pick up on the street can be used to good advantage in school. Almost from the first day, they begin, as it were, to look in the mirror and to see that they can take justifiable pride in what they are accomplishing academically. They don't rest on their laurels but become increasingly more observant and notably articulate.

Here are a few results. First, sixth, and ninth grade students, on their own, transfer the skills they develop reading media to the reading of print—with the result showing up clearly on reading scores. Some of the first graders become interested in spelling and write little stories. The sixth grade students, in their analysis of the documentary *Medieval Images,* would, in President Clinton's words, "celebrate ideas" and in their continual struggle for just the right word, rival the search of a bald, bearded writer, in a *New Yorker* cartoon, pondering, " 'Yes,' she mumbled? . . . sighed? . . . muttered? . . . hissed? . . . growled? . . ." Tenth graders, at least three and a half years retarded in reading and many unable to write at all, in analyzing a series of antique dolls whose provenance they sought to determine, drew the following praise from a City University of New York professor: "I found especially noteworthy students' willingness to recognize and accept ambiguities and questions which could not be answered unless additional information could be found"—a trait, I must add, by no means universal among undergraduate and graduate students.

While John Dewey's vision of an ideal education grew out of his study of middle- and upper-middle-class kids, mine is based on what these inner-city youngsters—severely retarded in reading and all their academic subjects—accomplished using this method. Yet in both instances, the conclusions are notably the same: build on the riches the young bring with them to school. In Emerson's words, draw out, don't drain off their *"naturel."*

These propositions offer the young more incentive to develop their capabilities in our age, with the focus on *all* media rather than only on print and writing only with words. They enable them to cope better with the world in which they live. (Whether or not we cherish the idea, in the future traditional reading and writing may survive only because they are linked to the broader definitions offered here.)

Though I stress the achievements of "at risk" students, this is hardly a compensatory or remedial education. If anything, it's elitist, drawing out the most uncommon in the most common of us. If the goal is to so stimulate students intellectually, ethically, and aesthetically that they will strive to go over the top, then the three propositions are relevant for American society today. Simply to jack up the bottom by patching here and there will hardly suffice.

These propositions, moreover, are as relevant for adults as for the young. Emily, in Wilder's *Our Town,* decides to leave heaven and visit Grover's Corners, New Hampshire, as it was on her twelfth birthday. She comments: "I can't look at everything hard enough. . . . Oh! It goes so fast. We don't have time to look at one another. I didn't realize. So all that was going on and we never noticed. Take me back—up the hill—to my grave. But first—wait! One more look . . . "; then to the stage manager: "Do human beings ever realize while they live it—every, every minute?" The stage manager responds: "No . . . The saints and poets, maybe they do some."

Ngaio Marsh's detective, Roderick Alleyn, notes in *Death of a Peer* that "your brain is really rather like a camera. It takes a photograph of everything you see, only very often you never develop the photograph!" To relish relics of the past, to savor the present, to make for a richer future, the propositions enable adults to develop some of these photos, to discover what they've been missing, what may have influenced them unawares, and what registered on the periphery of their consciousness.

GIVING THEIR BEST

Grading and Recognition Practices That Motivate Students To Work Hard

DOUGLAS J. MAC IVER AND DAVID A. REUMAN

Douglas J. Mac Iver is a research scientist and associate director at the Johns Hopkins University Center for the Social Organization of Schools. David A. Reuman is associate professor of psychology at Trinity College in Hartford, Connecticut. Both are former members of the AFT.

WE LAMENT the lack of material resources—desks, textbooks, computers, laboratory equipment—in our underfunded inner-city and rural schools. However, the resource in shortest supply not only in these schools, but in virtually every American school, is not material in nature—it is concentrated, persistent student effort.

American middle and high school students readily admit they are not putting forth 100 percent effort to learn the subject matter in the courses they take and, as a result, are only working to a fraction of their potential. When asked "How much effort do you usually put forth in this [biology or social science] class?" the average high school student in one recent survey reported expending less then 70 percent effort on a scale ranging from 0 percent (I am not trying at all) to 100 percent (I am working to my highest potential).[1]

Not only do most students decline to do their very best, they also decline to support the effort and achievement of their peers. "Across the socioeconomic spectrum and among all racial and ethnic groups, the informal norms that develop among students are *not* norms that extol achievement, but are norms that scorn effort, and reward scholastic achievement only when it appears to be done without effort," observes James Coleman, a renowned sociologist at the University of Chicago. Students who violate these norms face "the kiss of death"—being labeled by their peers as a "nerd"—the worst fate imaginable to many a young adolescent.

Traditional assessment, grading, and student recognition practices are partly responsible for the anti-academic norms and low levels of student effort that pervade American schools. These practices fail to apply what psychologists and sociologists have learned about the enormous combined power of *specific assigned goals* that are challenging but reachable, individual *performance summaries* that clearly indicate whether or not a given goal was attained, and a system of *recognition* and commendation that is tied to goal attainment.[2]

In traditional grading and feedback practices, individual students are not assigned specific quantitative goals. As a result students often choose a goal that is unchallenging (to pass the course), or vague ("to do my best"). Extensive research involving more than 100 studies in work settings in business and industry has established that goals that are perceived to be challenging but reachable lead to better performance than easy goals, and that specific quantitative goals "consistently lead to better performance than the goal of 'doing one's best.' This is because, paradoxically, people do not do their best when they are trying to do their best! 'Doing your best' is a vague goal because the meaning of 'best' is not specified. The way to get individuals to truly do their best is to set a challenging, quantifiable goal that demands the maximum use of their skills and abilities."[3]

From *American Educator*, Vol. 17, No. 4, Winter 1993/1994, pp. 24-31. Reprinted by permission of *American Educator*, the quarterly journal of the American Federation of Teachers. © 1993.

Although many teachers and parents explicitly encourage students to strive for "a good grade," this generic assigned goal is not very effective in motivating high effort and performance, because the two most commonly used grading practices do not take into account students' starting points. In most middle and secondary school classrooms, teachers award desirable grades and positive recognition to those students who have the highest ranking performance regardless of students' starting levels of skill and understanding. The other common approach is to set "percent-correct" standards of mastery (e.g., to award A's to all those with an average at or above 90 percent, B's to all those with an average between 80 percent and 89 percent, and so on).

These traditional approaches usually are ineffective in motivating students because the approaches do little to ensure that each and every student faces a goal that is reachable yet challenging. For example, if grades and recognitions are based on the rank-in-classroom of one's performances, then students whose starting points are considerably above the classroom average find that even modest effort typically is sufficient to ensure them of scores near the top of the class in comparative terms. Furthermore, these top students receive little peer support for their achievement efforts, because their peers are afraid that the top students will "blow the curve" and make it harder for others to get a desirable grade. Thus, top students have little incentive or support for giving it their all.

Rank-in-classroom also gives little incentive to students whose starting point is considerably below the classroom average. These students quickly become frustrated in a class using rank-in-classroom grading because even substantial progress on their part still leaves them near the bottom of the class in comparative terms. As soon as these below-average students realize that their best efforts will not improve their grades, they become alienated and disengaged.

Unfortunately, "percent-correct" standards work as poorly as "rank-in-classroom" standards, because no matter where the standard is set, it will be overchallenging or underchallenging for some students and, thus, an ineffective goal.

These problems with traditional grading practices are most severe in classrooms having students of widely different abilities. Yet, schools increasingly are moving toward heterogeneous classrooms because of a growing recognition that: (1) tracking results in the unequal distribution of favorable learning conditions so that students in the lower tracks do not receive the learning opportunities, instructional resources, motivational settings, and academic climates they need in order to develop their talent, and (2) "we need to develop the talent of *all* our people if this nation is to be economically competitive and socially cohesive in the different world of the next century."[4]

The compelling body of evidence that the systematic use of assigned goals, feedback, and recognition results in higher effort and performance in the workplace has led some teachers in Maryland and Connecticut to seek a practical way to modify traditional grading practices so that each student in a heterogeneous class is assigned specific goals that are challenging but reasonable (neither too hard nor too easy). These teachers also have

> ## *The two most commonly used grading practices do not take into account students' starting points.*

sought an affordable and manageable way to modify traditional feedback and recognition practices so that students will always receive recognition for meeting these assigned goals. We will describe here two improvement-focused systems for student accountability and recognition that we have developed in collaboration with these teachers, and which the teachers have field-tested and refined. We also will show how these systems affect student norms, attitudes, effort, and performance.

A practical way to set goals—used extensively in the business world—is to use *previous performance* as the standard to beat.[5] Most people consider surpassing their average previous performance to be a fair and reasonable goal. The Incentives for Improvement Program (field-tested in several Baltimore middle schools) and the Challenge Program (field-tested in a Connecticut high school) both use students' average previous recent performance as the standard to beat; distribute feedback charts to students that show their attainment or nonattainment of various types of improvement goals; and provide official recognition and awards to all students who raise their performance levels across time. The two programs differ in many respects, however. For example, students in the Incentives for Improvement Program are assigned individual goals only; those in the Challenge Program are assigned both group and individual goals. These differences will be evident in the program descriptions that follow.

THE INCENTIVES FOR IMPROVEMENT PROGRAM

The Incentives for Improvement Program[6] has three major components: *base scores, improvement points*, and *awards*.

Base Scores. Each week, students are given a specific goal—to beat their current "base score" on the week's most important quiz, test, project, assignment, or performance task. This base score represents a student's average performance level in the class on recent assessments. As students improve, their individualized base scores also go up.

There are two ways to determine students' initial base scores: (1) assign initial base scores that are about five points lower than a student's grade in the same subject last year. For example, a student who got a final grade of 70 percent on his report card last year in math would be assigned an initial base score of 65 percent in math; or (2) give students a couple of *challenging* quizzes or tests before introducing the program, and then use each stu-

Table 1

HOW TO EARN IMPROVEMENT POINTS

If You . . .	You Earn
Beat your base score by more than 9 points	30 Improvement Points
Beat your base score by 5 to 9 points	20 Improvement Points
Score within 4 points of your base score	10 Improvement Points
Get a perfect paper	30 Improvement Points
Score within 5 points of a perfect paper	20 Improvement Points

dent's average score on these as his or her initial base score.

Improvement Points. The program features a modified version of an improvement-oriented scoring system that was first developed for use with cooperative learning techniques.[7] Students earn improvement points by beating their base scores, that is, by raising their performance levels. Students who already have reached a high level of performance also are awarded improvement points for maintaining that level.

Improvement points are earned in *rounds*. A round

Figure 1

SUBJECT U.S. History CLASS 703 TIME 9:10-9:55 NAME	BASE SCORE NO. 1	GRADE	IMPROVEMENT POINTS	GRADE	IMPROVEMENT POINTS	GRADE	IMPROVEMENT POINTS	BASE SCORE NO.
1. Gay Abravanel	74	50	0					
2. Avi Achenbach	78	80	10					
3. Terry Aebi	95	100	30					
4. Akhtar Ahmed	70	80	30					
5. Diane Bradford	65	70	20					

lasts about three weeks, during which students are given three opportunities to beat their current base score (to get—on an important performance assessment—a "percent-correct" score that is higher then their base score). After each assessment, the student's score is compared with his or her base score and 0, 10, 20, or 30 improvement points are awarded as shown in Table 1.

Thus, improvement points are given in relationship to past performance. A student whose current base score is a 65 percent and who gets a 70 percent on an assessment earns the same number of improvement points (20) as a student whose base score is a 75 percent and gets an 80 percent. Note that there is no danger of students "topping out" with too high a base score; students who have a base score above 90 percent receive 20 improvement points when they score 95 percent to 99 percent, and receive the maximum possible number of improvement points (30) if they get a perfect paper.

Figure 1 shows an enlarged portion of a page from a seventh-grade history teacher's gradebook, which lists initial base scores, first quiz scores, and improvement points earned on the first quiz for five students in a U.S. History class. The teacher is using the loose-leaf *Incentives for Improvement Program Gradebook* from the *Incentives for Improvement Resource Catalog* (see box on page 197). At the beginning of the year, the teacher assigned each student a base score five points lower than his or her final grade in sixth-grade social studies the previous year (see first column of Figure 1, "Base Score No. 1"). At the end of the first unit, students took a quiz. Students' grades on this quiz are recorded in the second column. The next column shows the number of improvement points earned.

Looking at the first four students we see that Gay Abravanel got only 50 percent of the items correct on the first quiz. Because she scored 24 percentage points below her base, she didn't win any improvement points. On the other hand, Avi Achenbach beat his base score by two percentage points, thus earning 10 improvement points. Terry Aebi and Akhtar Ahmed each won 30 improvement points on the first quiz. Terry won his improvement points by getting a perfect paper, while Akhtar earned his by beating his base score by more than nine points.[8]

End-of-Round Computations and Awards. At the end of each round, students are assigned an updated base score (the last three performances are averaged with the current base score). When a student's updated base score is higher than his or her previously highest base score, the student is awarded a Personal Best Base Score Award. And, every student who averages at least 20 improvement points on the three performances in a round receives a Rising Star Award. Thus, at the end of every round, students have two chances to obtain an award. Although the *Incentives for Improvement Resource Catalog* includes certificates and other types of small awards (a neon eraser for Personal Best Award winners with an "I erased my old record!" imprint; or a "Rising Star" pin), some teachers may prefer to use certificates they or their students create or other rewards that are already available at their school.

The *Incentives for Improvement Program Gradebook* provides designated columns for recording improvement points, base scores, and awards won, but any gradebook can be used with the program. For teachers having access to a computer and to a spreadsheet or database program, "electronic gradebook" shareware also is available.[9] To use the electronic gradebook, the teacher must first type in students' names and their initial base scores. Then, after every 'performance' (quiz, test, or major assignment), all the teacher has to do is type in students' scores—the computer automatically calculates improvement points. At the end of a round, the computer also automatically figures each student's improvement point average, new base score, and award eligibility. Although administering the Incentives for Improvement Program is not difficult or time-consuming, the electronic gradebook makes it easy even for teachers with a heavy student load.

Effects on Student Effort and Performance

The Incentives for Improvement Progam had a modest, but statistically significant, impact on students' assessment of their own efforts; students in the Incentives for Improvement Program reported working harder to master course content, studying harder for quizzes and tests, and working closer to their potential than did students in control classes. This moderate increase in student effort translated into a substantial increase in student performance; students in the Incentives for Improvement Program classes performed almost two-thirds of a standard deviation higher on fourth-quarter assessments than did students in the control classes.[10]

The program produced marginally significant increases in students' valuing of the subject matter (their interest and enthusiasm for what they were studying) and self-concept of ability. Because of its positive impact on student effort and performance, the Incentives for Improvement Program significantly increased the probability that at-risk students (those with very low preintervention performance levels) would pass the course (83 percent of the at-risk students passed the course in Incentives for Improvement Program classes compared with 71 percent of at-risk students in control classes).

Our evaluation confirmed that student effort and performance can be increased by a student accountability program that gives students specific improvement goals and provides them with recognition whenever they reach these goals. Next, we wanted to see whether a modified version of such a program might help a high school to successfully offer challenging, high-level coursework to a greater proportion of its students than it had been able do in the past.

THE WINDHAM CHALLENGE PROGRAM

Students entering Windham High School in Willimantic, Connecticut, are quite diverse in their skills and abilities. This is due in large part to differences in students' learning opportunities and attainments in the elementary and middle grades. As do most high schools, Windham High responds to this diversity by "tracking" students. For example, English 10 is offered at five levels of instruction: basic, standard, advanced, honors, and high honors.

In theory, tracking accommodates instruction to students' needs, interests, and the various career and educational choices they eventually will face, while ensuring that students face attainable requirements and receive lessons that are neither too difficult nor too easy. Because tracking assigns students in the "basic" and "standard" tracks to a dumbed-down curriculum, tracking is, in practice, partly responsible for the dismally low proficiency levels attained by these students. Students cannot learn content to which they are not exposed. Those in the lower tracks fall further and further behind their more advantaged peers partly because they are given fewer opportunities to learn advanced topics and develop higher-level thinking skills, and in part because they experience a slower instructional pace and fewer positive peer models.[11]

During the 1991-92 school year, the second author was invited to Windham High School to present a yearlong workshop series on "Practical Alternatives to Tracking." At one of those sessions, the first author made a presentation on assessment and evaluation practices designed for heterogeneous classrooms. Later that year, some of the teachers in the science and social science departments at Windham decided that *all* students needed and deserved a high-level understanding of the natural and social sciences. As they considered how to help all students become literate in these disciplines, they began

External standard-setting and performance assessment allow each teacher to function more like a coach.

questioning their school's tracking practices. The teachers requested our assistance in designing an alternative program in which all students would receive a high-level curriculum, students who had low initial levels of achievement would not become disheartened, and students who had high initial levels would not have their progress impeded. The teachers also asked for our help in combating anti-academic peer norms that might undermine even the best efforts to raise standards.

With these teachers, we developed a theory-based, multiple component "best-practice" program that eliminates low-track science and social science courses and replaces them with heterogeneous advanced-level classrooms. To make these heterogeneous classrooms work well, we instituted a departmental team approach to set standards and assess performance, a student-team learning approach to provide students with extra help and to combat anti-academic peer norms, and an improvement-focused system that would hold individual students as well as student teams accountable. This alternative program is being evaluated rigorously in a series of controlled field experiments with random assignment of students to either the traditional or alternative programs. The alternative program is being introduced into the high school gradually (only two or three courses per year are being de-tracked).

To illustrate what the Challenge Program and the research design look like in actual practice, we will describe how the program was implemented in Biology I in the 1992-93 school year (the first yearlong course that was de-tracked). In spring 1992, 119 students pre-registered for Biology I (about 30 percent of these students preregistered for the "basic-level" course, and 70 percent for the "advanced-level" course). We randomly selected 44 of the preregistrants to serve as a control group: These 44 students would receive just what they had signed up for—the traditional Biology I course at the level they had chosen. The remaining 75 students were assigned to heterogeneous Challenge Biology I classes taught at the advanced level but using innovative approaches to standard-setting, performance assessment, and student and group accountability.

External Standards Change the Student-Teacher Relationship

Individual teachers traditionally are given lots of flexibility in setting the academic requirements in their classrooms. Because teachers can raise or lower requirements at their discretion, students—especially those who feel overchallenged—expend great effort trying to "wear the teacher down" and negotiate a lessening of demands. Often these efforts at negotiation are successful and lead to subtle treaties or explicit classroom bargains between students and teachers that lower standards but keep the peace.[12]

Although this "battle of requirements"[13] occurs in virtually all secondary school classrooms, it becomes especially severe when departments decide—as the science and social science departments at Windham did—to offer a high-level curriculum to all students in heterogeneous classrooms. Even if improvement-focused grading and recognition are used, each heterogeneous class will have many students who feel overchallenged by the advanced topics and difficult assignments. This is especially true in the early years of a de-tracking plan, because many former low-track students will have had many years to become accustomed to the dumbed-down curriculum, texts, and standards of the lower track.

We—teachers and researchers—decided we could defuse this battle of requirements by applying external standard-setting and performance assessment, which would allow each teacher to function more like a coach. One advantage a coach has over the typical classroom teacher is that the coach seldom has to fight the battle of requirements with his or her players. The reason is simple: The coach's players face frequent external "tests." When athletes are faced with a challenging game or match in the near future, they realize it would be counterproductive to pressure the coach to lower standards and lessen demands during training and practice sessions. The athletes might grumble to themselves about how hard they have to work, but they still cooperate with the coach's agenda (if it is clearly designed to help them do well) and encourage their teammates to do likewise.

Similarly, one reason that advanced students work more and complain less in AP classes than in some of their other demanding courses is because the students know that the AP test is coming. They realize it's counterproductive to complain about being asked to master particularly difficult content, if that content is going to figure prominently on the test. In fact, the teacher is doing the students a favor by pushing them, and the students realize this.

Not only is it beneficial to have frequent external assessments (as long as they assess what is essential and important), it is also beneficial to have external graders because of the taboo against brownnosers. In most classrooms, when a student attempts to establish a close personal relationship with the teacher, the student's peers view this behavior with suspicion. Even such seemingly innocent actions as demonstrating alertness or responsiveness in class often are interpreted by other students as strategic behavior designed to bias the instructor's grading. As a result, student norms develop, tacitly stating that it's "cool" to appear bored in class and to exhibit only grudging cooperation with the teacher's agenda. One way to weaken this taboo against brownnosers and the anti-academic norms that accompany it is to redistribute grading responsibilities so that most of a student's grade is derived from evaluations made by external parties (e.g., other teachers who teach different sections of the same course) rather than by his or her own teacher.

The Challenge Program features standards, tests, and graders that are external to the classroom. Teams of teachers who have different sections of the same course serve as that course's standard-setters, exam-developers, and graders. The standards the team of teachers set are then embodied in performance exams, also written by the team. To write these exams, the teachers must reach consensus on the most important learning objectives for units the exam will cover. These exams are given three times a quarter with every section taking the same exam on about the same day. The exams feature performance tasks (authentic assessment) that are "essential, integrative, rich, engaging, active, and feasible."[14] Because teachers take turns grading the performance exams, a substantial portion of a student's grade is derived from evaluations made by teachers other than the student's own. For example, with three Challenge Biology teachers and three exams per quarter, each teacher grades only one exam per quarter.

It's not only the students who find the presence of external exams and external graders motivating, so do their teachers. They want to give students in their sections the very best possible opportunities to learn the skills and understandings that are going to be tested.

YOU DON'T HAVE TO START FROM SCRATCH

The Incentives for Improvement Resource Catalog is available from the dissemination office at the Center for the Social Organization of Schools. The dissemination office is a not-for-profit venture designed to encourage implementation of effective practices by offering affordable training and inexpensive materials (at cost plus shipping and handling charges). Write to: Dissemination Office, The Incentives for Improvement Program, Center for the Social Organization of Schools, 3505 N. Charles St., Baltimore, Maryland 21218. Or call Barbara Colton at (410) 516-0370.

They want the external grader (one of their colleagues) to be impressed by how much their students have mastered. They don't want their students to hit a section of the test that contains material to which they were never exposed. All this motivates teachers to be sure to cover all the important content and keep their sections going at a challenging pace.

Student Team Learning

Teachers in the Challenge Program receive extensive training in the use of Student Team Learning (see Reference 7) instructional methods, and teams of teachers develop lesson plans that use these methods to accommodate student diversity and to make classroom activities more meaningful and rewarding. The peer interactions in student team learning sessions can motivate students to work harder and help them process information more thoroughly, thereby improving their understanding of complex tasks.[15]

Student and Group Accountability

Challenge classes use a modified version of the Incentives for Improvement System to ensure that all students are challenged and have an equal opportunity for success—if they work hard—regardless of their individual starting points. In Biology, students' initial base scores are determined by their performance on a science literacy pretest. (We double-check the accuracy of these initial base scores by comparing them with students' past grades in science.) Students earn improvement points for beating their base scores on the demanding and authentic external exams. In the Challenge Program, students' base scores are recomputed after every external exam (about once every two-and-a-half weeks). Thirty percent of a student's semester grade in Biology is determined by his or her improvement point average on the six external exams for the semester.

After each external exam, students can earn two types of awards for individual improvement: Personal Best Base Score Awards (for setting personal base score records) and Personal High Exam Awards (for setting personal records on the external exams). And, each student's cooperative learning team can earn awards based on the average improvement points earned by team members. The team awards give students a reason to help one another, and the individual accountability ensures that each member of the team learns. Under these conditions, students interact to instruct one another rather than simply to provide answers to questions,[16] and the teacher can work more effectively to coach individual students and small groups of students to meet their specific needs.

Preliminary Findings

We recently completed preliminary analyses of end-of-year survey and test data collected in Biology I classes during the first year of the Challenge Program. The Challenge Program was highly successful in combating anti-academic norms. That is, students in the Challenge Program were significantly less likely than control students to endorse the following statements: "Sometimes I don't do as well in this class as I could so that I will fit in better with my friends," "My classmates don't think it is important to pay attention to the teacher in this class," "My friends would make fun of me if I did too well in this class," and "My classmates make fun of students who ask questions in this class." The size of the reduction in anti-academic norms in Challenge classes was quite large: almost one-half of a standard deviation.

Similarly, the Challenge Program had a positive effect on peer support for achievement; the Challenge students were more likely than control students to endorse statements like the following: "My classmates want me to be a good student," "My classmates want to help me to do my best work," "My classmates believe it is important to come to school every day," and even "If I don't do my best in this class, my classmates will be mad at me." Again the size of the program's effect on peer support for achievement was nearly one-half of a standard deviation.

The Challenge Program had no effect on students' overall performance on our most important measure of achievement in Biology: The National Association of Biology Teachers/National Science Teachers Association High School Biology Test. On the whole, Challenge students performed no better (and no worse) than control students on this test. This can be viewed as very positive: Our heterogeneously grouped Challenge students of all achievement levels are achieving as well academically as tracked control students and suffering none of tracking's stigmatizing social effects. And there are indications that strong implementation of the program may affect achievement—the Challenge section with the highest measured implementation of program components was significantly higher than the control group on the Genetics and Ecology subscales of the test.[17]

Finally, students in the Challenge Program were *not* more likely than control students to report test anxiety or the feeling of being overchallenged. Overall, the early evidence suggests that the Challenge Program is helping Windham High School successfully untrack its course offerings in Biology. The findings further confirm the positive benefits of improvement-focused student accountability systems. It appears that such systems are effective in encouraging students to hold up their end of the bargain in the classroom.

REFERENCES

[1] See Douglas J. Mac Iver and David A. Reuman, *Peace with Honor(s): Winning the "Battle of Requirements" through Externally-Established Standards and Value-Added Accountability.* Baltimore: Johns Hopkins University Center for Research on Effective Schooling for Disadvantaged Students, 1993.

[2] See Edwin A. Locke and Gary P. Latham, *Goal Setting: A Motivational Technique that Works!* Englewood Cliffs, N.J.: Prentice-Hall, 1984.

[3] Locke and Latham, op. cit., p. 23.

[4] Carnegie Task Force on Education of Young Adolescents, *Turning Points: Preparing American Youth for the 21st Century.* New York: Carnegie Council on Adolescent Development of the Carnegie Corporation, 1989., p. 14.

[5] Locke and Latham, op. cit., p. 31.

[6] This program description summarizes the current version of the program, which incorporates revisions suggested by teachers during field-testing.

[7] See R.E. Slavin, *Cooperative Learning: Theory, Research, and Practice.* Englewood Cliffs, N.J.: Prentice-Hall, 1990.

[8] Variations in task difficulty within a course can make it unusually easy or hard for students to earn improvement points on certain tasks. The improvement points system does not adjust for variations in task difficulty because such adjustments would make the system more difficult to implement and more difficult for students and parents to understand. According to the teachers who field-tested the program, students were able to cope with task difficulty variations in a productive manner (e.g., by increasing their effort when faced with unusually difficult tasks and by partially discounting improvement points earned on unusually easy tasks).

[9] If you would like a copy of the electronic gradebook, contact Barbara Colton in the Center for the Social Organization of Schools dissemination office at the address and phone number listed in the box on page 30.

[10] For a full report of the evaluation study, see Douglas Mac Iver, "Effects of Improvement-Focused Student Recognition on Young Adolescents' Performance and Motivation in the Classroom," in Martin Maehr and Paul Pintrich, *Advances in Motivation and Achievement: Volume 8, Motivation and Adolescent Development.* Greenwich, Conn.: JAI Press, 1993 (pp. 193-218).

[11] Jomills Braddock, "Tracking the Middle Grades: National Patterns of Grouping for Instruction," *Phi Delta Kappan,* vol. 71, 1990, pp. 450-57; Joyce Epstein and Douglas Mac Iver, *Opportunities to Learn: Effects on Eighth Graders of Curriculum Offerings and Instructional Approaches,* (Baltimore, Md.: Center for Research on Effective Schooling for Disadvantaged Students, 1992); Jeanie Oakes, *Keeping Track: How Schools Structure Inequality.* New Haven, Conn.: Yale University Press.

[12] Michael W. Sedlak, Christopher W. Wheeler, Diana C. Pullin, and Phillip A. Cusick. *Selling Students Short: Classroom Bargains and Academic Reform in American High Schools,* (N.Y.: Teachers College Press, 1986). Powell, A.G., Farrar, E., and Cohen, D.K. *The Shopping Mall High School: Winners and Losers in the Educational Marketplace.* Boston: Houghton Mifflin, 1985.

[13] Willard Waller, *Sociology of Teaching,* New York: Wiley, 1932.

[14] Patrick Forgione, *Accountability and Assessment: The Connecticut Approach.* Paper presented at the Public Education Forum, Baltimore, 1990.

[15] Nel Noddings and others, *What do individuals gain in small group problem solving?* Paper presented at annual meeting of American Educational Research Association, Montreal, 1983.

[16] Noreen Webb, "Student Interaction and Learning in Small Groups," In Robert Slavin and others (eds.) *Learning to Cooperate, Cooperating to Learn,* pp. 147-172. New York: Plenum, 1985.

[17] Sec Mac Iver and Reuman, op. cit for a full technical report of the controlled field experiment in Biology.

An Interview with Howard Gardner

Educating for Understanding

In this interview, Howard Gardner, a professor in the Graduate School of Education at Harvard University who is widely known for his views on intelligence, discusses his work, his current research interests, and the field of education.

JANNA SIEGEL AND
MICHAEL F. SHAUGHNESSY

JANNA SIEGEL is an assistant professor of special education at Eastern New Mexico University, Portales, where MICHAEL F. SHAUGHNESSY is an associate professor of psychology.

WIDELY known for his views on intelligence, as put forth in the highly acclaimed *Frames of Mind: The Theory of Multiple Intelligences* (Basic Books, 1983), Howard Gardner is a professor in the Graduate School of Education at Harvard University and a researcher at the Veterans Administration Medical Center in Boston. He has written on creativity and on the history of the study of cognition. In *The Unschooled Mind: How Children Think and How Schools Should Teach* (Basic Books, 1991), he describes some of the problems of contemporary American education and outlines some possible solutions for parents, teachers, and administrators. In this interview he discusses his work, his current research interests, and the field of education.

JS/MFS: In *The Unschooled Mind*, you criticized American schooling. What is your biggest concern?

Gardner: My biggest concern about American education is that even our better students in our better schools are just going through the motions of education. In *The Unschooled Mind*, I review ample evidence that suggests an absence of understanding — the inability of students to take knowledge, skills, and other apparent attainments and apply them successfully in new situations. In the absence of such flexibility and adaptability, the education that the students receive is worth little. I suspect that this problem exists in other countries as well, but our American fixation on the mastery of facts and the administration of short-answer instruments of assessment makes the problem particularly acute here.

JS/MFS: Should "deep understanding" be fostered across the curriculum and possibly across intelligences?

Gardner: Yes. I don't see how anyone could hold a different view. But just *how* to achieve understanding in different intelligences and across the disparate areas of curriculum is a difficult issue on which many scholars will need to work.

JS/MFS: For students with an I.Q. of say, 84 or lower, is a "deep understanding" realistic?

Gardner: I am not interested in a student's I.Q. I am interested in his or her current understanding and what can be done to enhance it. No human understands everything; every human being understands some things. Education should strive to improve understanding as much as possible, whatever the student's proclivities and potential might be.

JS/MFS: How can we best educate exceptional children — the mentally retarded, the learning disabled, and even the gifted?

Gardner: Obviously, there is no one best way to educate all children. Indeed, the biggest mistake of past centuries has been to treat all children as if they were variants of the same individual and thus to feel justified in teaching the same subjects in the same ways. We must discover areas of strength and characteristic approaches to learning. And, as much as possible, we must bring the teaching to where the child is. When a child does not learn, it is premature to blame the child, because, more often than not, the failure lies with the educator. When we educate better and when we can educate in a more personalized way, then children will learn better.

JS/MFS: Why do our schools fail to teach generalization, understanding, and transfer?

Gardner: Educators have simply not appreciated how difficult it is for students to transfer knowledge from one situation or domain to another. Unless one takes the "high road to transfer" and helps students to see explicitly the connections (and nonconnections) between domains, generalization and transfer will not occur with any reliability.

JS/MFS: What theories of learning might you suggest for teaching for understanding?

Gardner: In *The Unschooled Mind*, I develop an approach to learning that is built on a triangle: 1) Piaget's approach to cognitive development, 2) my own theory of multiple intelligences, and 3) recent research on the constraints that govern the ways in which young children master such domains of knowledge as language, number, and causality. Naturally, I am sympathetic to this view as a basis for teaching for understanding. However, to be an effective teacher, one also needs to have knowledge of the discipline and of pedagogy — what is sometimes called "pedagogical content knowledge."

JS/MFS: What can teachers who want to foster deeper understanding do today in their classrooms?

Gardner: They can decide what evidence there is that their students understand. They can look to see whether students are able to use knowledge in new ways. I can virtually promise that students will not be able to do so. And so teachers can begin to demonstrate to their students what it means to stretch their knowledge, and they can give them many opportunities to do so. Provide feedback on how students are doing and give them the chance to understand better, and before long they will insist that all instruction pursue that goal.

JS/MFS: Should colleges and universities assess the "deep understanding" of their entering freshmen? Of their graduating seniors?

Gardner: I am all in favor of assessing the understanding of college students, so long as it is done in a sensible way. But I can guarantee one thing: unless strong efforts are made to educate the understanding, there is no point in testing the graduating seniors. Their understanding will be no better than that of the entering freshmen. Conversely, if the teaching is done well and if student performance has been monitored throughout, final testing will not even be necessary.

JS/MFS: What advantages does portfolio assessment offer?

Gardner: Standardized tests that require only short answers present a situation that does not exist outside of school; life does not present itself in multiple-choice formats. Outside of school, individuals mostly carry out projects — either projects assigned to them or projects that they have had a hand in fashioning. I favor an education that features many projects in which students are engaged for significant periods of time and which lead to genuine products.

Portfolios are collections of such projects — both portfolios that represent the best that a student can do and those that represent other aspects of a student's work (for example, a favorite hobby or a problem one finds fascinating). Such portfolios are valuable in themselves, but they gain in value when they have been assessed and when students and others receive feedback about learning and understanding as it is manifested in the projects.

It takes time to collect and to assess a portfolio. But portfolios accomplish something of great importance: they draw attention to the work itself. Sometimes teachers say, "Portfolios are great, but I don't have time to look at them." To which I respond, "If you do not have time to look at your students' work, you should stop teaching. In fact, you have already stopped teaching." These are harsh words, but they do make one think about what one is trying to accomplish and how one determines whether one has had any success.

JS/MFS: How could portfolios be used to assess "deep understanding"?

Gardner: Portfolios provide opportunities for students to show what they know and what they can understand. If understanding is not revealed in the works collected in a portfolio, I would conclude that a student is not really understanding. Let me be concrete. If a student's essays in history or her lab reports in science are devoid of understanding, then we can assume that little understanding has been achieved. Remember that understanding is demonstrated when a student *uses* knowledge in new situations, such as writing essays or lab reports.

JS/MFS: You have visited China and written about that nation's system of education in your book *To Open Minds*. What is the single most important point you would like to make about Chinese education?

Gardner: I'd like to make two points about China. First, China showed me that students of all abilities and interests can gain from apprenticeships. Moreover, even if students work in domains and crafts for which they apparently do not have much talent, they will still gain immeasurably from participation in an apprenticeship.

Second, contrary to what many Westerners (including me) have thought, it is not necessary to have much opportunity for free exploration before any acquisition of basic skills takes place. China shows that individuals can move in creative directions after they have attained basic skills. The important point is that periods that stress one approach to knowledge (skill or creativity) need to be supplemented by periods that have the contrasting emphasis.

JS/MFS: How could apprenticeship programs help in the educational endeavor?

Gardner: Apprenticeships are one of two institutions — the children's museum being the other — that harbor important clues for an education geared toward understanding. In an apprenticeship, a learner spends significant periods of time over many months with an adult who is capable and who himself (or herself) can use knowledge and skills in varying contexts. The apprentice learns what it is like to be competent — to understand. As time goes on and skills accumulate, the apprentice proceeds to journeyman status and gradually becomes able to produce a "masterpiece." There is no need to administer separate tests to apprentices; they are being tested and assessed all the time. And at the end of the day, so to speak, the apprentice will be able to demonstrate genuine understanding.

A tragedy in American life today is that so few of our children have the opportunity to be apprentices, either in schools or in their lives outside of school. The impoverished children do not have the opportunity; the rich children flit from one activity to another, never achieving sufficient mastery of any. The greatest educational gift to any child is the opportunity to see that he or she can advance, can master skills, and can become competent. Apprenticeships are formidable catalysts in this process.

JS/MFS: What type of master teacher should student teachers be apprenticed to?

Gardner: It should be someone who is an excellent teacher and who knows how to work with individuals who have had no experience in teaching. So the person must be knowledgeable and yet able to sympathize with a novice. That's easy to say, but such teachers are hard to find.

JS/MFS: What is lacking in our teacher training programs?

Gardner: Too few of our teacher training programs demonstrate what it is like to teach well, to assess well, or to serve as an effective role model. Most teachers of college or graduate students see their job as transmitting the inert knowledge of their discipline. While experts need to have some of this inert knowledge, classroom teachers need to know how to coach and encourage their students, so that students can gain various literacies, come to love knowledge, know how to learn, and know how to assess their own growth. Unless candidate teachers have had such experiences in their own education, it is unreasonable to expect them to display these virtues to their students.

JS/MFS: Should developmental psychology courses be required for teacher training programs? And if so, should educators teach these courses?

Gardner: Certainly an understanding of human development is a prerequisite for any teacher, including a teacher of university students. Developmental psychology should be taught by someone who knows the discipline and knows how to teach. I could not care less what kind of a degree that person happens to hold. Indeed, my teacher — the great developmentalist Erik Erikson — never even went to college and never took a course in psychology.

JS/MFS: Many universities are apprehensive about rejecting students for teacher training programs for fear of lawsuits. How can we screen prospective teachers to insure quality instruction for our children in the future?

Gardner: I think that teachers are made, not born. And so I am not worried about the wrong students gaining entrance to a training program; I am worried about inadequate training for those who do enter.

JS/MFS: Could you discuss leadership — perhaps educational leadership specifically?

Gardner: I am interested in leadership that brings about change. In my view, leaders tell stories. The normal or routine leader is simply somewhat better than others at telling a story that already exists. A more innovative leader takes a story that has been latent in a setting and brings new attention to it. The truly innovative or visionary or transformational leader creates a new story and convinces individuals of its validity. He or she needs to embody that new story. One of the tragedies of American collegiate life is that the old stories no longer compel. The tragedy of precollegiate life is that there is no argument whatsoever on what the story should be. The paucity of educational leadership in this country is pathetic — particularly inasmuch as our last two presidents have claimed to be interested in providing educational leadership. The contrast with Lyndon Johnson or Thomas Jefferson could not be more compelling.

JS/MFS: What are your views on "nationalizing the curriculum" in America?

Gardner: I am not in favor of a national curriculum. But I do favor some kind of a national system of assessment of the sort being researched by the New Standards Project. In such a system students will take performance-based examinations and will also present their own exhibitions and portfolios for assessment. In such a system students will have the opportunity to demonstrate what they have learned. In the best of all possible worlds, we would pursue national *understanding*, and these assessments would tell us whether we are producing a nation of *understanders*.

JS/MFS: In *The Unschooled Mind* you give readers an assignment: to set up their own system of education. Given E. D. Hirsch's views with regard to cultural literacy and Allan Bloom's emphasis on the great books, where would *you* begin to establish a formal education system?

Gardner: I don't understand what you mean by a "formal education system." I do not believe that there should be a canon, but I do favor a focus on a limited number of ways over several years. This position is remote from what Hirsch says; it has some affinity with Bloom, except that Bloom feels that important knowledge has already been identified, whereas I am much more interested in the quest for new understanding.

JS/MFS: The 1980s saw a plethora of books and research about intelligence. Looking back, what have we accomplished?

Gardner: We do not yet have consensus on the right way to think about or to test intelligence, but there is certainly an emerging consensus that the standard view of intelligence and intelligence testing is inadequate. More attention is being paid to intelligences beyond the scholastic forms. And there are interesting efforts to assess capacities in new ways, ranging from the study of brain waves to the examination of portfolios. I think that the 1980s will be seen as a turning point in the study of intelligence, as much in the area of education as in the area of psychology or biology.

JS/MFS: You have recently been funded to study how children really learn in schools. What are some of your basic hypotheses?

Gardner: In our Spencer Foundation-supported project on understanding, we begin from the assumption that students form strong conceptions early in life and that these beliefs and theories are difficult to dislodge. To move from these stereotypical ways of thinking toward deeper understanding, it is necessary to do three things: 1) choose topics with great care and spend sufficient time on them; 2) approach topics in a number of ways and give students many opportunities to display their understandings; and 3) build directly into the regular curriculum many opportunities for assessment so that assessment can become a "habit of mind." We are now engaged in empirical research to determine the appropriateness of our analysis and to see whether we can actually demonstrate deeper understanding among high school students who are working in the major disciplines.

JS/MFS: What are you currently investigating?

Gardner: In addition to the Spencer project on understanding, I have recently completed a study of the nature of creativity. In a book titled *Creating Minds*, published last year by Basic Books, I analyze the creativity of seven important figures who lived around 1900. I put forth a model of what it means to be creative and what is the nature of a creative breakthrough. I hope that my method will prove useful to others. I expect to begin a similar study of leadership in the next year or so.

In addition to this research, I am deeply involved in efforts to determine how the theory of multiple intelligences can be applied usefully in school settings. I have described my current conclusions in a book titled *Multiple Intelligences: The Theory in Practice*, published in 1993. Our research group at Project Zero is joining forces with Theodore Sizer of the Coalition of Essential Schools, James Comer of the School Development Program, and Janet Whitla of the Education Development Center to try to create models of New American Schools as part of the New American Schools Development Corporation.

JS/MFS: What do you think education will be like in the year 2000?

Gardner: I cannot tell what education will be like in 2000, but in *The Unschooled Mind*, *To Open Minds*, and *Multiple Intelligences: The Theory in Practice*, I offer my own vision of what education *could be like* if we made it a national priority and pursued it with the same vigor and enthusiasm that we ordinarily reserve for wars, athletic events, and life in a consumer culture. Absent strong and selfless leadership, there is, alas, little chance that we will succeed.

Challenges to the Public School Curriculum: New Targets and Strategies

Conservative challenges to materials used in the public schools are no longer limited to isolated attacks against individual books. Ms. McCarthy alerts readers to the powerful tactics now being employed to influence all aspects of the curriculum.

MARTHA M. MCCARTHY

MARTHA M. McCARTHY is a professor of education at Indiana University, Bloomington.

EFFORTS to make fundamental changes in public schooling for the 21st century face a number of obstacles.[1] Among the significant threats to these efforts are challenges from conservative citizen groups objecting to particular instructional strategies and materials. Some of the best-known conservative groups are listed in the box on page 205.[2] Challenges by these groups to the public school curriculum are increasing dramatically; according to People for the American Way, the number of reported incidents was 50% higher in 1991-92 than in the previous school year.[3]

The conservative groups' most common complaint is that certain curricular materials or activities advance anti-Christian, anti-American doctrine, often referred to as "secular humanism" or, more recently, "New Age theology." Materials that encourage students to think critically, to examine alternatives, or to clarify values — in other words, to become more active learners — are alleged

to represent this anti-theistic belief.[4] The conservative groups contend that secular humanism and New Age theology are characterized by reliance on science and human nature instead of God and the Bible.[5] Humanistic, New Age materials and practices allegedly are founded on such doctrinal cornerstones as mysticism, occultism, globalism, moral relativism, internationalism, and hedonism.[6] "Secular humanism" and "New Age" have become catchall phrases, used by critics — much as "communism" was used in the 1950s and 1960s — to refer to everything that is considered a threat to traditional American values and institutions.[7]

Curriculum challenges are not a new phenomenon. However, recent efforts in this regard are particularly noteworthy, not only because of their increasing frequency, but also because of the shift in targets and the change in strategies used to influence the content of the public school curriculum.

NEW TARGETS

There have been subtle but important changes in the targets of curriculum challenges. Until the late 1970s the targets were usually individual books, such as *The Catcher in the Rye* and *Of Mice and Men*. Those making the charges were often parents acting on their own. While the list of individual books under attack continues to grow, recent protests — often orchestrated by national conservative groups — are more likely to focus on entire textbook series and components of the instructional program.

Currently, the most widely challenged textbook series is the Impressions reading series published by Harcourt Brace

Recent curriculum challenges are noteworthy for their frequency, new targets, and changed strategies.

Jovanovich. This 15-volume anthology for elementary grades contains selections by such noted authors as A. A. Milne, Maurice Sendak, and C. S. Lewis. The series, used by school districts in 34 states, embraces the whole-language approach to reading instruction. This approach is grounded in the belief that children learn to read as they learn to speak. Accordingly, the series focuses on reading for meaning, with selections that are believed to be of interest to children in the elementary grades. The conservative groups allege that the selections are depressing, morbid, and violent; invade students' privacy; attack traditional values; and promote Satanism, mysticism, and the occult.[8] Most of the challenges focus on the series' subject matter rather than on its pedagogical approach, but the controversy associated with Impressions may have implications for the future of whole-language instruction.

From *Phi Delta Kappan*, Vol. 75, No. 1, September 1993, pp. 55-56, 58-60. © 1993 by Phi Delta Kappa, Inc. Reprinted by permission.

Courts try to defer to local school boards, whether the boards are defending or restricting the curriculum.

Because of California's influence on the textbook market nationwide, it is not surprising that the conservative groups have focused their attacks on the Impressions series in this state. Two closely aligned groups, Citizens for Excellence in Education (CEE) and the National Association of Christian Educators (NACE), both based in Costa Mesa, have distributed statewide mailings condemning the Impressions series. One letter begins with the following passage: "Before you read this letter, I want to warn you that it contains shocking and graphic quotes from a children's reading series used in classrooms across America. The good news is that God is doing wonderful things through His committed people. . . ."[9] Approximately 100 California school districts have adopted the Impressions series, and the series was challenged in about one-fourth of these districts between 1989 and 1990.[10] One in five of the school districts that have experienced challenges no longer uses the series.

Another recent popular target of the conservative groups is the Lions-Quest drug prevention curriculum, developed by Quest International and the Lions Club International. Lions-Quest consists of programs for elementary grades (Skills for Growing) and middle school students (Skills for Adolescence). A program for high school students (Skills for Living) is currently being revised. The asserted purposes of the programs are to develop character, citizenship, responsibility, and positive social skills.[11] The programs encourage students to make positive commitments to their families and communities and to lead healthy, drug-free lives.

The materials emphasize parent involvement and include exercises designed for students to complete at home with their parents. However, the conservative groups allege that the materials teach relative values and encourage students to make their own decisions rather than to rely on parental authority. In a 1992 study of challenges to the curriculum in Indiana, the Lions-Quest program was by far the most popular target of attacks, with 28 school districts reporting challenges to this program within the previous four years.[12]

Also challenged by conservative groups has been the program Tactics for Thinking, developed by Robert Marzano and distributed by the Association for Supervision and Curriculum Development. This program is designed to improve students' higher-level thinking skills and their ability to address complex problems. This thinking-skills program has been attacked as undermining Christian values and promoting New Age theology through practices that allegedly include meditation and mental imagery.[13] Such exercises as having children focus all their energy on an object for one minute and then describe their concentration process have been challenged as encouraging students to enter into self-hypnotic trances.[14]

Moreover, many course offerings (e.g., sociology, psychology, health, and biology) as well as instruction pertaining to values clarification, self-esteem, multicultural education,[15] evolution, AIDS education, and global education are being contested as anti-Christian, anti-American, or otherwise inappropriate. Several instructional strategies currently touted in the education literature, such as collaborative learning and thematic instruction, are being challenged because they shift to students some of the responsibility that was formerly lodged with the teacher.[16] Outcome-based education (OBE), a popular reform strategy intended to focus attention on school results in terms of what students actually learn, is being attacked by conservative groups as replacing factual subject matter with subjective learning outcomes.[17] OBE initiatives often emphasize higher-order thinking skills, problem solving, and content integration across subject areas. In states such as Iowa, Ohio, Oklahoma, and Pennsylvania, OBE programs have been modified or dropped because of serious opposition from conservative citizen groups.[18]

These recent challenges to textbook series, pedagogical approaches, and think-

ing-skills programs call into question some of the basic assumptions of school restructuring initiatives (e.g., that students should examine alternatives critically and take responsibility for their learning). Thus they pose far more serious threats to efforts to improve the public school program than do challenges to individual novels.

INCREASING USE OF GRASSROOTS STRATEGIES

In their efforts to influence the content of the public school curriculum, the conservative groups are using a number of strategies, ranging from litigation to personal persuasion. Recently, these groups have experienced setbacks in their attempts to influence state textbook adoptions.[19] They have also been unsuccessful with their litigation alleging that certain materials unconstitutionally advance an anti-theistic creed.[20] Although courts have upheld school boards' decisions to implement challenged programs, they have also upheld board efforts to *restrict* the curriculum, as long as the boards followed their own adopted procedures and based their decisions on legitimate pedagogical concerns.[21] In short, courts try to defer to local school boards, whether the boards are defending or restricting the curriculum.

Consequently, the conservative groups have focused their recent efforts on influencing school boards. They have attempted to marshal grassroots support and have boasted considerable recent success in rallying communities behind their attacks on particular aspects of the public school program. Often the campaigns are initiated by a few individuals who go door-to-door telling parents that, if they care about their children, they will join the crusade against the targeted materials or activities. When enough support is garnered, pressure is applied to the school board to bar the materials and courses from the curriculum.

As noted above, local attacks on curriculum materials are often orchestrated or at least influenced by national conservative groups. CEE, which has more than a thousand chapters nationwide, has produced "Public School Awareness" kits, which are distributed for $195 and contain materials to use in convincing parents of the "danger" of particular instructional materials. The organization's goal is to have such kits available in all Christian churches across the nation and to establish "Public School Awareness" committees in all communities.

The national conservative groups have also distributed to a wide audience a number of books condemning the allegedly anti-theistic orientation of public school offerings. These include such titles as *Secular Humanism: The Most Dangerous Religion in America*, by Homer Duncan; *Your Child and the Occult: Like Lambs to the Slaughter*, by Johanna Michaelsen; *Globalism: America's Demise*, by William Bowen, Jr.; and *Dark Secrets of the New Age*, by Texe Marrs. In addition, the national organizations' newsletters alert parents to "warning signs" of the New Age world view, among them such symbols as rainbows and unicorns and such phrases as "human potential" and "impersonal force."[22] These materials are designed to alarm parents and motivate them to take action.

As a result of the conservative groups' increasing numbers and greater identification with the mainstream, they are having a more significant impact on school board elections.[23] CEE has claimed that its chapters helped to elect approximately 2,000 school board members from 1989 to 1991, and the organization's goal was to elect 3,500 members by 1993.[24] Skipp Porteous, president of the Institute for First Amendment Studies, has noted that these well-organized conservative groups can have an impact on school board elections because of general voter apathy: "The fundamentalists are a minority, but they're an active minority. This is where the power is."[25]

CEE and NACE have distributed a book, *How to Elect Christians to Public Office*, in which Robert Simonds asserts, "We need strong school board members who know right from wrong. The Bible, being the only true source on right and wrong, should be the guide of board members. Only godly Christians can truly qualify for this critically important position."[26] Simonds has voiced optimism regarding the Religious Right's potential to "gain complete control of all local school boards. This would allow us to determine all local policy, select good textbooks, good curriculum programs, superintendents, and principals."[27]

IMPLICATIONS

Without question, challenges to the public school curriculum are more widespread, well-organized, and complex than many educators have realized. Until the latter 1980s educators did not take such challenges very seriously. Those making the challenges were often viewed as the fundamentalist fringe, and courts consistently backed school boards in resisting censorship efforts. However, as noted above, current challenges to entire programs and textbook series are much more serious than isolated attacks on books. And the success rate of those initiating challenges has been rising.[28]

Educators have underestimated the political strength of those challenging the curriculum. Some of the conservative groups, viewing their activities as a divine crusade, sincerely believe that the materials and programs under attack pose a threat to the well-being of children. These groups have been effective in convincing parents that, if they are concerned about their children, they will not let them be exposed to the targeted "harmful" materials. Professional education associations have begun to recognize the magnitude of the challenges, but this professional awareness has come late. Many communities have become mobilized against particular instructional programs and materials, catching educators unprepared. Robert Marzano has asserted that "this movement is very powerful and growing at a geometric rate, and I don't think we realize what we have to lose as educators."[29]

Even if a school board does not remove a challenged program, the controversy itself can disrupt school operations and interfere with implementation of the program. Furthermore, challenges to the curriculum have a ripple effect, a fact that conservative organizations use to their advantage. When materials or programs are attacked in one school district, the controversy often affects other districts, as seen with the spreading challenges to the Impressions reading series in California.[30] Similarly, in the recent Indiana study, most of the reported challenges to the curriculum were geographically clustered.[31]

Moreover, a school board may be reluctant to adopt a specific program that has been challenged in a neighboring district. The board may decide that the educational benefits of the program are not worth the risk of a heated community controversy. Even without school board directives, educators may avoid materials they fear will offend influential conservative parent groups.[32] Such self-censorship by teachers and administrators in public schools is difficult to document be-

*W*hen materials are attacked in one school district, the controversy often affects other districts.

cause it is simply handled informally and not reported. Henry Reichman has noted:

> Where sound formal policies and procedures are lacking, censorship efforts may quietly succeed. In these types of situations, teachers, librarians, or administrators may accede to pressure without any "incident" being registered. Perhaps more ominously, school personnel may initiate removals on their own, either to deter perceived threats or to impose their own values and orthodoxies on the educational process. In some cases, potentially controversial materials simply are not acquired in the first place.[33]

School personnel need to become more assertive in involving parents in efforts to restructure the instructional program. When innovative materials or strategies are adopted without parental participation, it is not surprising that suspicions are aroused. Educators need to explain

Selected Conservative Citizen Groups

American Coalition for Traditional Values (Tim LaHaye)
Christian Coalition (Pat Robertson)
Christian Educators Association (Forrest Turpen)
Citizens for Excellence in Education; National Association of Christian Educators (Robert Simonds)
Concerned Women for America (Beverly LaHaye)
Eagle Forum (Phyllis Schlafly)
Educational Research Analysts (Mel and Norma Gabler)
Family Research Council (Gary Bauer)
Focus on the Family (James Dobson)

Educators
*and policy makers
need to take a
stand that some
content, attitudes,
and skills shouldn't
be compromised.*

to parents the pedagogical justification for programs and materials. If parents become knowledgeable about the rationale for specific programs, they will be less likely to be persuaded by groups that have a "hit list" of materials and programs. Often parents are simply confused and do not understand the educational rationale for the questioned programs.[34] Many have not personally reviewed the materials they are challenging; instead, they rely on information distributed by the national organizations.

School boards often find, when the curriculum is challenged, that they have no procedures in place to handle such complaints. It is imperative for boards to establish a review process *before* a controversy arises. Critics of the curriculum deserve a forum in which to be heard, and some complaints may be valid. Challenges to materials and programs certainly have a "legitimate function in a democratic educational system."[35] But decisions regarding the fate of the challenged materials or programs should be based on educational considerations rather than on emotion, religious zeal, or political expediency. It is too late to establish a process when parents are storming the school with their list of "objectionable" materials. Challenges are twice as likely to be turned back in school districts with explicit procedures for handling curriculum complaints.[36]

Policy makers and educators must recognize that public schools cannot appease all groups. Public schools are not value-free, and the argument that they are value-neutral is destined to fail. For example, if critical thinking is emphasized, that is a value judgment. We must accept

that, for some groups, any material or strategy that does not promote reliance on Biblical absolutes is offensive. Indeed, trying to convince some fundamentalist groups of the religious neutrality of public schools simply fuels their allegations that Christianity is being denounced, because "neutral" instruction is viewed as anti-Christian.[37]

Instead of arguing that the challenged instructional programs are value-neutral or trying to sanitize the curriculum so that no groups are offended, policy makers and educators need to take a stand that some content (e.g., science), attitudes (e.g., respect for racial diversity), and skills (e.g., critical thinking) should not be compromised. Such instruction is necessary to ensure an educated citizenry in our democratic society, and educators should not have to defend the merits of teaching children how to think or how to get along with others from diverse backgrounds. If policy makers do not take a stand against the mounting threats to the public school curriculum, many school restructuring efforts may be doomed before they get off the ground. And, more significantly, we may produce a generation of citizens who lack the skills necessary to address the vexing dilemmas that will confront our nation in the 21st century.

1. A range of groups, from civil rights organizations to consumer activists, are condemning various curricular materials for being racist or sexist or for promoting bad health habits for students. And, of course, public schools have not been immune to the current debate over "political correctness." But most of the recent challenges have been mounted by conservative citizen groups. See *Attacks on Freedom to Learn* (Washington, D.C.: People for the American Way, 1992).

2. The conservative citizen groups — fundamentalist or evangelical Protestant in orientation — emerged in the 1970s and "coalesced with the political right in the 1980s." For an analysis of this movement, see Richard Pierard, "The New Religious Right and Censorship," *Contemporary Education*, vol. 58, 1987, p. 131.

3. Arthur J. Kropp, press release, People for the American Way, 1 September 1992, p. 3. See also Dianne Hopkins, "Challenges to Materials in Secondary School Library Media Centers: Results of a National Study," *Journal of Youth Services in Libraries*, vol. 4, 1991, pp. 131-40; and "Schools Face Increased Censorship," *School Board News*, 27 September 1989, p. 4.

4. See Charles Kniker, "Accommodating the Religious Diversity of Public School Students: Putting the 'Carts' Before the House," *Religion and Public Education*, vol. 15, 1988, p. 316.

5. See Edward Jenkinson, "Secular Humanism, Elitist Humanoids, and Banned Books," paper presented at the National Education Association Leadership Conference, Washington, D.C., February 1985, p. 5; and Christy Macy and Ricki Seidman, "Attacks on 'Secular Humanism': The Real Threat

to Public Education," *Kappa Delta Pi Record*, vol. 23, 1987, p. 77.

6. See Johanna Michaelsen, *Your Child and the Occult: Like Lambs to the Slaughter* (Eugene, Ore.: Harvest House, 1989).

7. James Wood, "Religious Fundamentalism and the Public Schools," *Religion and Public Education*, vol. 15, 1988, p. 51.

8. See Robert Simonds, *President's Report* (Costa Mesa, Calif.: National Association of Christian Educators/Citizens for Excellence in Education, June 1990), pp. 1-2.

9. Ibid., p. 1.

10. Louise Adler and Kip Tellez, "Curriculum Challenge from the Religious Right: The *Impressions* Reading Series," *Urban Education*, July 1992, pp. 152-73.

11. *Frequently Asked Questions* (Granville, Ohio: Quest International, n.d.); and Sue Keister, Judy Graves, and Dick Kinsley, "Skills for Growing: The Program Structure," *Principal*, vol. 68, 1988, p. 24.

12. See Martha McCarthy and Carol Langdon, *Challenges to the Public School Curriculum in Indiana's Public Schools* (Bloomington, Ind.: Indiana Education Policy Center, 1993).

13. See Debra Viadero, "Christian 'Movement' Seen Trying to Influence Schools," *Education Week*, 15 April 1992, p. 8.

14. Edward Jenkinson, "The New Age of Schoolbook Protest," *Phi Delta Kappan*, September 1988, pp. 66-69.

15. Children of the Rainbow, a multicultural curriculum adopted in the New York City School District, sparked a volatile controversy over the component of the program promoting tolerance toward homosexuals. See Peter Schmidt, "Fernandez Ousted as School Chief in New York City," *Education Week*, 17 February 1993, pp. 1, 14.

16. See Pamela Klein, "New Age Lessons Put Educators, Parents at Odds," *Indianapolis Star*, 3 December 1991, pp. 1, 4.

17. Phyllis Schlafly, "What's Wrong with Outcome-Based Education?," *Phyllis Schlafly Report*, May 1993.

18. Diane Brockett, "Outcome-Based Education Faces Strong Opposition," *School Board News*, 8 June 1993, pp. 1, 6.

19. See Edwin Darden, "Texas Adopts Textbook List: Ripple Effect May Be Felt Nationwide," *Education Daily*, 28 November 1988, p. 2; Robert Rothman, "Scientist, Creationist Each Claim Victory in Texas Evolution Vote," *Education Week*, 22 March 1989, pp. 1, 14; and Kent Ashworth, "Texas Board Repeals Rule on Evolution in Textbooks," *Education Daily*, 18 April 1984, p. 3. See also Franklyn Haiman, "School Censors and the Law," *Communication Education*, vol. 36, 1987, p. 337.

20. See *Mozert* v. *Hawkins County Pub. Schools*, 827 F.2d 1058 (6th Cir. 1987), *cert. denied*, 484 U.S. 1066 (1988); *Smith* v. *School Comm'rs of Mobile County*, 827 F.2d 684 (11th Cir. 1987); and *Grove* v. *Mead School Dist. No. 354*, 753 F.2d 1528 (9th Cir. 1985), *cert. denied*, 474 U.S. 826 (1985).

21. See *Virgil* v. *School Bd. of Columbia County*, 862 F.2d 1517 (11th Cir. 1989); and *Zykan* v. *Warsaw Community School Corp.*, 631 F.2d 1300 (7th Cir. 1980).

22. Andrea Priolo, "Principals Claim Most Parental 'Impressions' Problems Are Resolved," *Dixon Tribune*, 11 May 1990, p. 3.

23. See Viadero, p. 8. See also Erica Sorohan, "School Leaders Grapple with 'New Age' Accusations," *School Board News*, 1 October 1991, p. 5.

24. Sonia Nazario, "Crusader Vows to Put God Back into Schools Using Local Elections," *Wall Street Journal*, 15 July 1992, pp. A-1, A-5.

25. Quoted in Del Stover, "CEE's Goal: Gain Control of Local School Boards," *School Board News*, 1 September 1992, pp. 1, 5.

26. Robert Simonds, *How to Elect Christians to Public Office* (Costa Mesa, Calif.: National Association of Christian Educators/Citizens for Excellence in Education, 1985).

27. Quoted in J. Charles Park, "The Religious Right and Public Education," *Educational Leadership*, May 1987, p. 9.

28. Kropp, p. 3.

29. Quoted in Viadero, p. 8.

30. See Adler and Tellez, op. cit.

31. McCarthy and Langdon, op. cit.

32. For example, teachers in school districts in Virginia and Oregon refused to air Channel One's student news program the day it included a picture of Michelangelo's *David*, because they feared negative reactions to the statue's nudity. See "Schools Face Disputes Over Religious Issues," *Executive Educator*, November 1991, p. 11.

33. Henry Reichman, *Censorship and Selection* (Chicago and Arlington, Va.: American Library Association and American Association of School Administrators, 1988), p. 13. See also "Censorship Strips Teachers of Faith in Textbooks, Survey Says," *Education Daily*, 3 January 1990, p. 5; and Sissy Kegley and Gene Guerrero, *Censorship in the South — A Report of Four States 1980-1985* (New York: American Civil Liberties Union, 1985).

34. See William Carnes, "The Effective Schools Model: Learning to Listen," *Contemporary Education*, vol. 63, 1992, pp. 128-29.

35. Michelle Marder Kamhi, "Censorship vs. Selection — Choosing the Books Our Children Shall Read," *Educational Leadership*, December 1981, p. 211.

36. See Reichman, p. 13.

37. Martha McCarthy, "Secular Humanism and Education," *Journal of Law and Education*, vol. 19, 1990, pp. 495-96.

Building School Communities: An Experience-Based Model

To foster community among students, teachers require training that gives them a positive community experience and equips them with experience-based pedagogical and curricular tools, these authors point out.

....

By Joel Westheimer
and Joseph Kahne

JOEL WESTHEIMER directs the Experiential Curricula Project at the School of Education, Stanford University, where he is also a teaching fellow and doctoral candidate. JOSEPH KAHNE, an assistant professor at the University of Illinois at Chicago, has been involved in the project's development and assessment. They wish to thank participants in the Experiential Curricula Project, as well as Milbrey McLaughlin, Myron Atkin, Gary Lichtenstein, and Pamela Burdman, who commented on drafts of this article.

Illustration by Susan Hunsberger

MANY schools showcased by reformers share a characteristic that a growing number of researchers and practitioners consider essential: students and teachers derive support, motivation, and direction from one another.[1] Students work collaboratively on active projects toward goals they find meaningful. Teachers meet during lunch, after school, and during preparatory periods to discuss curriculum, pedagogy, and individual students. All are engaged in what John Dewey calls a "social" mode of learning. Rather than the isolation and alienation that seem so common in many of today's schools, these students and

From *Phi Delta Kappan*, Vol. 75, No. 4, December 1993, pp. 324-328. © 1993 by Phi Delta Kappa, Inc. Reprinted by permission.

teachers experience a sense of membership. They are part of learning communities.

Influential reports in the mid-1980s, such as *Tomorrow's Teachers* and *A Nation Prepared*, spurred a series of reforms intended to enhance both teachers' and students' commitment to education by strengthening teacher and school communities.[2] Exactly what these communities would look like, however, and how to move toward them are questions too often left to the imagination and frustration of those who work in schools. As one teacher told us, "Yesterday, a staff development person came in and told us that our staff needs a sense of community — that we should work together toward a supportive school environment. I asked him, 'What exactly do you mean by a sense of community? Do we just sign on the dotted line and — presto — community?'" Do students working together on a set of math problems constitute a learning community? Will reducing school size or introducing team-teaching or school-based management automatically produce more personal, supportive settings for students? Will these conditions lead to professional bonds among teachers?

In this article, we argue that reformers' efforts to build school communities lack two essential components. First, they fail to provide teachers with experiences that will familiarize them with the nature and benefits of strong communities. Second, they do not equip teachers with the pedagogical techniques needed to foster and sustain school communities. We highlight the need for teacher education that responds to these shortcomings and illustrate our point by describing the Experiential Curricula Project, an experience-based teacher training and staff development program piloted at the Stanford University School of Education.

MISSING COMPONENTS OF CURRENT REFORM STRATEGIES

Such popular reform strategies as site-based management, house systems, and magnet programs aim to build school communities by creating smaller, more personal settings and by granting teachers greater control over their schools. These changes provide an organizational foundation from which to begin. However, by themselves they are not likely to engender the support, sense of shared mission, and strong personal ties that develop among

members of school communities. Communities cannot be mandated or concocted. Smaller schools may provide necessary conditions, but communities must ultimately be built from the interests and experiences of their members. When reformers expect organizational changes alone to result in strong school communities, they make two assumptions: 1) that teachers and administrators know how to turn organizational potential into truly communal relationships and 2) that teachers seek such communities. Voices from the field indicate otherwise.

Researchers have found that teacher behavior — even in settings that should accommodate community — often reflects the emphasis on individualism and autonomy so pervasive in our culture.[3] Some teachers welcome team-teaching and scheduling changes that allow them to watch their colleagues in the classroom; others prefer not to have their teaching observed. In some schools, teachers meet frequently to design school policies and to work together on interdisciplinary projects; in many schools, however, teachers shy away from such collective undertakings.

Current organizational reforms may "empower" teachers, but they will not necessarily foster strong bonds in hierarchical and isolating school environments — ones in which teachers value control of their own classroom and must often compete for scarce resources, prestige, and choice assignments. When teachers are granted greater decision-making authority, they often feel compelled to protect their autonomy rather than to pursue communal ties. Site-based management plans free teachers from bureaucracy but do not connect them to one another.[4]

To counter the tendency toward professional isolation and to give teachers a sense of what they want to create for students, firsthand experiences in communal settings are necessary. Just as members of a close-knit drama group or political campaign develop attachments to one another and commitment to the group, teachers working in schools need opportunities for interaction, mutual dependence, and identification with a group. They must experience the sense of connectedness, purpose, and direction that membership in a supportive community provides.

In addition, if teachers are to foster community among their students, they need training in community-building pedagogy and curriculum. "The educator,"

writes Dewey, "is responsible for [selecting activities] which lend themselves to social organization, an organization in which all individuals have an opportunity to contribute something."[5] How are teachers to develop these abilities? Considering the scope of reforms designed to build school communities, it is striking that little notice is given to the need to change classroom practices. Teachers need practice with pedagogical techniques as well as sensitivity to classroom norms that are consistent with community building.

WHAT IS COMMUNITY?

Before we describe a program of experience-based education that enables teachers to develop their capacity to build communities, we should clarify the vision of community that we hope to promote. Robert Pirsig notes that the more we point to beauty, the quicker it disappears.[6] Those struggling to describe the nature of communities face a similar challenge. This difficulty may help to explain why notions of community are commonly invoked but not spelled out in the literature of school reform. As a starting point, we offer a few guidelines.

We see community as a process marked by interaction and deliberation among individuals who share interests and commitment to common goals. They pursue these goals collectively, building on the distinct talents and capacities of members while valuing consensus and, at times, deferring to strongly held minority opinions. Acceptance of these opinions stems both from respect for members of the community and from a commitment to the belief that divergent ideas are often the engine of progress. Meaningful interactions among members lead to a sense of shared responsibility for both the process and its outcomes. Reflection is encouraged, and dissent is honored.

Such communities grow out of shared experiences. Indeed, communities both shape and are shaped by experience. The example of the traditional barn raising may help to clarify this point. Local residents work together to build a neighbor's barn. This event is often seen as testimony to the strength of 19th-century rural communities. While barn raising clearly requires strong bonds among neighbors, it is also itself a community-building experience. As local families engage in a common effort, their interdependence is made clear and their connections to one another are strengthened. The implications for educators are dramatic.

Students form bonds as they work together toward common goals. Richard Bowman tells us that it is "relationship which educates."[7] Communities are defined by those relationships. In short, teachers can use experience-based education to create settings in which bonds form and communities flourish.

THE EXPERIENTIAL CURRICULA PROJECT

The Experiential Curricula Project began in 1990 as an experimental course offered to prospective teachers attending the Stanford University School of Education. The program has grown to serve 20 prospective teachers, 80 middle and high school students, and five teachers each year. The prospective teachers work together designing, implementing, reflecting on, and redesigning experience-based curricula for students and teachers from local schools. Their work is informed by a solid grounding in the literature on experiential teaching and learning, as well as by the sharing and analysis of their own educational experiences.

Our involvement with the project has led us to identify five principles that seem to be particularly effective for fostering and sustaining community — both among the project participants (prospective teachers) and, later, among their own students.

• Move from students' experience to theory.

• Engage students in common projects.

• Break norms to create opportunities for new relationships.

• Motivate students within the context of community.

• Encourage reflection, and respect dissent.

1. *Move from students' experience to theory.* Students in the project participate in seminar classes that both draw from their prior experiences and provide them with new experiences in order to build community. During the first class, for example, groups of students discuss stories of their best and worst educational experiences. For much of the following three weeks, excerpts of these stories are categorized, analyzed, transcribed, and distributed. After considering one another's positive and negative educational experiences and reading the literature of Dewey and those who have built on his work, the students are able to construct a theoretical framework for developing

educational activities that build community.

Several students' stories, for example, led the class to identify "emotional engagement" as an important component of the framework. Janet,[8] a student teacher, wrote of a weeklong field research project for 10th-graders: "Karen and Doug and Tom and Marshall (students in my class) I now know in a different way than anyone else knows them. I have seen them fail, I have seen them succeed, I have seen them scared and jubilant. I have not just seen these events and emotions, however; I have been a part of them."

Among other positive components students included in their framework were "mutual learning," "leadership opportunities," "extended time together," "challenge," and "recognizing talents and abilities." These categories guided them as they developed curricula for high school students.

Using students' experiences as the basis of a theoretical framework transforms norms and expectations regarding viable and legitimate sources of knowledge. Most important, building on students' collective knowledge and experience strengthens the community. Students come to understand that the quality of the curricula they develop depends on their own sharing of ideas. In addition, as students share personal and often emotionally significant experiences, they become familiar with one another's ideas, values, and world views, and bonds are created.

2. *Engage students in common projects.* Today's schools stress autonomy and assess individual achievement. Even the value of cooperative learning is commonly measured by individual success. Promoting community requires significant shifts in practice. Collective projects can bring about such shifts.

For example, throughout the seminar, the students work together as they develop curricula for the local schools. One prospective teacher explained, "As we developed the curricula we got to know a lot about each other's talents, values, and temperaments." In addition, students assume collective responsibility even when one student is formally designated as being in charge of a particular event or activity.

The prospective teachers also devise group experiences to foster community among the high school students with whom they will be working. This year's seminar participants had the high school

students collaborating to draft political platforms, survey a plot of land, and grapple with the dilemma of access for the handicapped to national parks. Such activities teach students how to work collectively toward common ends at the same time that they demonstrate the degree to which our ability to pursue particular goals depends on social organization.

These collective projects do not downplay individual differences. At their best, they showcase student talents and model the use of these talents for social purposes. Rather than submerge the individual within the group, such projects provide an opportunity to develop an individual identity within the group.

3. *Break norms to create opportunities for new relationships.* The traditional norms of schools and classrooms often prevent the development of communities. We must acknowledge a long history of individuality and emphasis on autonomy and competition in schools. Experiences outside the classroom or norm-breaking experiences in the classroom can alter student expectations. One way to create the space needed to recast relationships is to have students and teachers spend time outdoors. As one prospective teacher put it, "The absence of four walls, a ceiling, a floor, and central heating forces the group to be held together by more than the physical confines of a classroom and raises in an immediate way the need for interdependence."

Prospective teachers design classroom curricula throughout the seminar. They implement many of the large-scale curricular activities over weekends and in outdoor settings in order to allow for the innovative use of time, space, and social interaction. Classrooms are created in tents, by lakes, on trails, and under trees. This is done not so that students might study trees or lakes or flowers, but rather so that they will re-create their own notion of schooling and of the relationships within the school community.

In addition to providing an environment in which students and teachers are more receptive to alternative approaches, such settings easily accommodate community-building educational projects that channel individuals' skills toward a common effort.[9] For example, students must work together in order to survey a land form, create a detailed map of a seashore, or simply make dinner. Norms can be broken within the classroom as well. As students work together producing a magazine or simulating a market economy, they rely on and interact with one another, altering expectations for classroom passivity and individualism.[10]

Though out-of-classroom and other norm-breaking experiences can clearly build community, this result is hardly inevitable. Field trips to museums, for example, may reinforce rather than alter classroom norms of passivity and unequal status.

4. *Motivate students within the context of community.* John Dewey observed that

the mere absorbing of facts and truths is so exclusively individual an affair that it tends very naturally to pass into selfishness. Indeed, almost the only measure for success is a competitive one, in the bad sense of that term. . . . [S]o thoroughly is this the prevailing atmosphere that for one child to help another in his task has become a school crime.[11]

When motivation stems from instructional arrangements in which one child's success depends on another's failure, bonds between students are undermined. At times the competition is overt. Students receive grades that have been "curved" explicitly to reflect their performance relative to that of others in the class. Students also engage in a more subtle form of competition as they vie for teachers' attention and praise. In either case, the competition weakens social bonds by promoting a narrow understanding of self-interest and a false split between individual and social needs.

Not all competition is detrimental. But competition directed toward extrinsic rewards can detract from students' natural curiosity, energy, and commitment to the group. Furthermore, reliance on extrinsic motivation often leads to narrow measures of school success and leaves little room to appreciate the diverse ways individuals can contribute to a group effort.

In contrast, when students work together toward goals they hold collectively, their motivation stems both from their ties to one another and from the importance they place on the task at hand. Whether critiquing seminar readings, planning and implementing curricula, or grappling with difficult ethical and practical issues, seminar participants supported and rewarded one another's efforts. One prospective teacher wrote that the tasks the group performed together did not feel like duties. Because "we were with our friends," she

observed, "commitment came from within."

This sentiment makes clear the need to adopt a broad understanding of intrinsic and extrinsic motivation. Educators who use these terms commonly view motivation as an individual affair. However, when members of a community are motivated as a group, it is useful to consider the way in which the community, rather than the individual, is motivated. From this standpoint, we might characterize extrinsic motivation as that which comes from outside the group: a businessman offers a prize to the class for accomplishing a task they would otherwise avoid. Similarly, when bonds among students are strong, it is more appropriate to describe intrinsic motivation as that which the group, rather than the individual, finds compelling: success on a project becomes important to individual members because it matters so much to the group as a whole.

5. *Encourage reflection, and respect dissent.* Members of a community, while sharing interests and commitments to one another, don't always agree. Individual differences, in fact, can foster growth within the community by providing opportunities for the exchange and consideration of alternative perspectives. When consensus cannot be reached, compromise often permits communities to remain cohesive while allowing for what John Gardner calls a "wholeness incorporating diversity."[12]

Consequently, as the group worked together developing curricula, we strove for consensus. Rather than simply defer to the majority, we adopted minority views when they were vitally important to a few class members.[13] We aimed to respect dissent and encourage critical review.

SOME DILEMMAS

Of the dilemmas that arose as we worked on this project, two stand out. The first is simply stated, if difficult to resolve: strong communities can become unnecessarily exclusionary. Should a thriving school community always be prepared to welcome new members? What are the consequences of excluding new members? Is this an inevitable problem, or can school communities be both strong and accessible?

Students were required to enroll in the seminar for two consecutive terms. However, two students who had not been pres-

ent during the first term wished to enroll for the second. One had taken the first term the previous year (when it was only a one-term course) and had therefore completed the prerequisite for the second term. The other was an undergraduate who had helped develop a segment of the course that deals with special populations. Linda is legally blind and had been invaluable as we prepared a program for students with learning and physical disabilities.

Some students had very strong feelings about letting new people into the class. We discussed the issue for 30 minutes or so, and several students went on to explain their personal positions outside of the class. Two of them wrote three-page notes saying that they felt bad about wanting to exclude other students from the class. This was an emotionally charged issue, and it raises a second, more subtle dilemma.

The students' negative reactions made it clear that they did not recognize the source of cohesion among seminar participants. Despite their experience (or perhaps because of it), these students did not trust the community-building process. They worried that newcomers would dilute what they believed was a lucky alliance of talented and spirited individuals. Though they recognized the power of many of the community-building techniques used in class (and we discussed many of them in detail), they continued to believe that good fortune was responsible for the compatibility of these particular people — that others coming in would not form similar bonds.

This outlook is particularly troubling. New members of a community provide opportunities for exposure to and reflection on new ideas. For some students in the class, however, newcomers represented a threat instead of an opportunity. This phenomenon underscores the need to demonstrate to participants that newcomers can strengthen rather than detract from the group. Experience is the best teacher in this regard. Within two or three weeks, the new students had been incorporated into the group, and the concerned students had seen that the social cohesion they valued was not threatened.

COMMUNITY AT THE SCHOOL SITE

How do the challenges confronting reformers who want to build communities in schools differ from those we faced when designing a program for prospective teachers? First, schools are frequently subject to significant student and teacher turnover. Sustaining a community from year to year therefore requires an institutional culture and a set of practices that are capable of regenerating community. Establishing such conditions is no easy task. Institutional history and resistance to change demand that those pursuing community do more than hope that new teachers will work well with seasoned veterans. Community is not self-winding.

Second, educators hoping to strengthen communities in schools must frequently confront long-standing divisions and lack of consensus on both educational goals and the appropriate means for their advancement. These tensions can easily undermine community-building efforts.

Third, the pursuit of community may seem at cross-purposes with many current policy reforms. "How," a teacher, principal, or school board member might ask, "can we hold students accountable and pursue standardized curriculum objectives when students are working collectively on projects that reflect their experiences and interests rather than state-mandated subject matter?" In some respects, this is a false choice. Many curricular goals are easily aligned with students' interests and experiences. Still, the concern is valid. When curricular frameworks are highly specified, they are likely to constrain practitioners from undertaking complex, experience-based projects that boast broad rather than narrow goals. Though experience-based projects can teach a variety of skills (writing, computation, critical thinking, and so

on), particular outcomes are difficult to specify in advance.

John Goodlad maintains the centrality of strong school communities in *A Place Called School*. He writes, "The most important thing about school for the children and youth who go there is the living out of their daily personal and social lives." Our own motivation stems from concern that we are losing a sense of connection between individuals and, with it, much that brings meaning to our lives.

The current emphasis on such organizational reforms as site-based management and schools-within-schools provides conditions that enable school communities to grow. Favorable conditions, however, are only the first step. If teachers are to provide a sense of community for students, then teacher educators need to provide it for teachers — in both preservice and inservice programs. To foster community among students, teachers require training that gives them a positive community experience and equips them with experience-based pedagogical and curricular tools.

1. See, for example, Theodore Sizer, *Horace's School: Redesigning the American High School* (Boston: Houghton Mifflin, 1992); and David K. Cohen, Milbrey W. McLaughlin, and Joan Talbert, *Teaching for Understanding: Challenges for Policy and Practice* (San Francisco: Jossey-Bass, 1993).

2. *Tomorrow's Teachers* (East Lansing, Mich.: Holmes Group, 1986); Carnegie Task Force on Teaching as a Profession, *A Nation Prepared: Teachers for the 21st Century* (New York: Carnegie Forum on Education and the Economy, 1986); Gary Wehlage et al., *Reducing the Risk: Schools as Communities of Support* (New York: Falmer Press, 1989); Judith Warren Little, "Norms of Collegiality and Experimentation: Workplace Conditions of School Success," *American Educational Research Journal*, vol. 19, 1982, pp. 325-40; Ann Lieberman, *Building a Professional Culture in Schools* (New York: Teachers College Press, 1988); and Milbrey W. McLaughlin, "Crafting Community in Secondary Schools," paper presented at the annual meeting of the American Educational Research Association, San Francisco, 1992.

3. Judith Warren Little, "The Persistence of Privacy: Autonomy and Initiative in Teachers' Professional Relations," *Teachers College Record*, vol. 91, 1990, pp. 509-36; and Susan Moore Johnson, "Teacher Unions in Schools: Authority and Accommodation," *Harvard Educational Review*, vol. 53, 1983, pp. 309-26.

4. Susan Rosenholtz, *Teachers' Workplace: The Social Organization of Schools* (New York: Longman, 1989); and Mark Smylie, "Teacher Participation in School Decision Making: Assessing Willingness to Participate," *Educational Evaluation and Policy Analysis*, vol. 14, 1992, pp. 53-67.

5. John Dewey, *Experience and Education* (New York: Collier Books, 1938), p. 56.

6. Robert Pirsig, *Zen and the Art of Motorcycle Maintenance* (New York: Morrow, 1974).

7. Richard Bowman, "Relationship Educates: An Interactive Instructional Strategy," *Contemporary Education*, vol. 56, 1984, pp. 101-3.

8. All names are pseudonyms.

9. For an in-depth discussion, see Joel Westheimer, Joseph Kahne, and Amy Gerstein, "School Reform for the Nineties: Opportunities and Obstacles for Experiential Educators," *Journal of Experiential Education*, vol. 15, 1992, pp. 44-49.

10. See, for example, Eliot Wigginton, *Sometimes a Shining Moment: The Foxfire Experience* (Garden City, N.Y.: Doubleday, 1985); and William Bigelow and Norman Diamond, *The Power in Our Hands* (New York: Monthly Review Press, 1988).

11. John Dewey, *The School and Society; the Child and the Curriculum* (1900; reprint, Chicago: University of Chicago Press, 1990), pp. 15-16.

12. John Gardner, "Building Community," prepared for Independent Sector, Leadership Studies Program, Palo Alto, Calif., 1990, p. 15.

13. For a discussion of applying this principle to faculty decision making, see Deborah Meier, "Retaining the Teacher's Perspective in the Principalship," *Education and Urban Society*, vol. 17, 1985, pp. 302-10.

Exploring the Thinking of Thoughtful Teachers

JOSEPH J. ONOSKO

Joseph J. Onosko is Assistant Professor, University of New Hampshire, Department of Education, Morrill Hall, Durham, NH 03824-3595.

The development of higher-order thinking has been and will continue to be a fundamental goal in education, despite persistent reports that it is hard to find in classrooms (Cuban 1984, Goodlad 1984, Sirotnik 1983). To remedy this situation, concerned educators have enhanced our conceptual understanding of higher-order thinking, proposed instructional practices to promote it, designed curriculum and instructional materials that emphasize it, and developed assessment techniques that attempt to measure it.

Other researchers have begun to explore how teachers think about their work. Questions that drive this research include: How do teachers think about problems and issues related to promoting students' higher-order thinking? Do outstanding teachers conceptualize their work differently from their less-than-outstanding colleagues? Do their thoughts and beliefs reveal a consistent perspective on how to promote thinking? Here I report findings from a research project that attempted to answer these questions.

Teachers who reflect about their own practices, value thinking, and emphasize depth over breadth of coverage tend to have classrooms with a measurable climate of thoughtfulness.

Background to the Study

The 20 social studies teachers selected for this study were drawn from a pool of 48 teachers from 16 secondary schools as part of the Higher Order Thinking in the Humanities Project at the National Center on Effective Secondary Schools (for details, see Newmann 1991). We identified 10 teachers as outstanding and 10 as less than outstanding through classroom observations using the following six dimensions of instructional practice related to promoting students' thinking:

1. *There is sustained examination of a few topics rather than superficial coverage of many.* As Newmann (1988) has stated, there is little to probe or analyze in a curriculum that is "a mile wide and an inch deep."

2. *The lesson displays substantive coherence and continuity.* Lessons that contain factual and conceptual inaccuracies, gaps in logic, inappropriate transitions, and so on are detrimental to the development of higher-order thinking.

3. *Students are given an appropriate amount of time to prepare responses to questions.* Research has shown that increased "wait time" results in longer, more sophisticated student responses (Tobin 1987). Wait time also suggests to students that reflection is valued.

4. *The teacher asks challenging questions and/or structures challenging tasks.* By definition, thinking is unnecessary unless there is a problem, question, or task that challenges the mind (Schrag 1988).

5. *The teacher is a model of thoughtfulness.* Higher-order thinking involves a set of attitudes or dispositions as much as it does a set of skills or content understanding (Dewey 1933, Passmore 1967, Schrag 1988, Siegel 1988). Collectively, these dispositions might be called "thoughtfulness." Teachers model thoughtfulness by showing appreciation for students' ideas and for alternative approaches if based on sound reasoning, by acknowledging the difficulty of acquiring knowledge, and by explaining how they think through problems.

6. *Students offer explanations and*

reasons for their conclusions. During lessons students must talk if teachers are to determine whether higher-order thinking is being promoted. Students must share not only their answers, ideas, and opinions, but also the reasons that support them.

The 10 teachers whose classroom practice most consistently reflected the six dimensions will hereafter be called the "high scorers." The 10 whose practice least consistently reflected the dimensions will hereafter be called the "low scorers." The remaining group of 28 "middle scorers" were not included in the study.

Incidentally, the research team did not know which teachers from the pool of 48 would eventually compose the two groups of teachers; that is, the analysis of teachers' instructional practice to identify high and low scorers occurred months after the interview data were gathered.

We examined four areas of teachers' beliefs and theories: instructional goals, depth vs. breadth of content coverage, perceptions of students, and conceptions of thinking.

Instructional Goals

Teachers are asked to pursue a vast number of instructional goals. We were curious to see whether outstanding teachers of thinking place greater emphasis on the goal of thinking than their less successful colleagues. Here's what we found.

On a written questionnaire, high scorers unanimously mentioned the development of students' thinking as a fundamental goal of instruction, com-pared to only half of the low scorers. When we asked the two groups what gave them satisfaction as teachers, all of the high scorers, but only one low scorer, cited activities readily associated with thinking (for example, "students wrestling with values and making links," "seeing kids think and express their thoughts," "students citing reasons for their position"). Low scorers, on the other hand, referred to activities that may or may not involve thinking ("when students show interest," "when they feel

good about themselves," "helping them to understand the information being imparted.").

Equally dramatic differences showed up during our interviews with teachers. High scorers offered more elaborate responses when discussing their goals and placed greater emphasis on developing students' thinking. For example, Harold, a high scorer, wants to cultivate attitudes and skills related to thinking. Consider his comment:

> I want them to be able to study the material in my class and when they are finished with that course to be able to take the analytic skills and think through for themselves problems and situations that otherwise they would have ignored. To give them some confidence in their own mental abilities and what they can achieve; to examine, analyze, and decide. . . . Kids need to be "crap detectors," and they have to be able to think in order to put it into motion. . . . You've got to be able to think to filter out what's garbage and what's not; what's meaningful and what's not. The mind is a wonderful thing students can learn to use. It's not something that happens automatically. I really have a motivation to want them to think. It bothers me if they don't use their minds.

Except for two members, low scorers' responses to the question about instructional goals were generally much shorter and lacked the articulate, impassioned elaboration of high scorers — regardless of the goal cited. In addition, they emphasized teacher transmission rather than student exploration and critique of ideas. For example, unlike Harold, who has kids filtering, analyzing, and deciding, low scorer Laura wants her students to "know," "understand," and "pick up" knowledge:

> I want to relate my lesson to students' own lives. My goal is to have them know economic concepts that can help them become productive members of society. This can be as basic as staying in high school! In government the goal is to have them understand that these laws are for them, that this democracy is for them, to know their rights. This applies mostly to the hu-

manities students. The economics and government students are at a higher level, so I expect them to pick up more content in addition to relating it to their own lives.

Depth vs. Breadth

Clear, effective thinking about topics and issues requires a certain degree of immersion or depth of study. Immersion often comes in conflict with efforts to expose students to a breadth of content. We were curious to see how teachers think about the coverage dilemma.

Though both groups of teachers unanimously acknowledged their conflict over the issue, high scorers were more likely to believe content coverage impedes students' thinking and in turn were more willing to reduce coverage to pursue the goal of thinking. Further, high scorers identified their pressure to cover material as externally imposed (by the department chair, colleagues, state guidelines, and tests), whereas low scorers identified themselves as their primary source of coverage pressure.

Harold's statement is representative of many high scorers' disdain for extensive content coverage:

> I do not preoccupy myself with finishing the curriculum. Instead, I attempt to teach whatever I teach well and select classroom topics and materials very carefully. . . . It's ludicrous to attempt to cover 100 years of history in a month or two. I focus on concepts and ideas. The problem with most courses is that they are survey courses that are homogenized.

Conversely, Laura's statement highlights low scorers' self-imposed breadth orientation and awareness of its negative effect on promoting students' thinking:

> I'm more survey oriented. There's a conflict in my head, but I go for coverage. The kids like it, I like it, exposure is important. If they know a little, they can go on to further understanding themselves or in college. . . . Often times I feel like I squeeze information in and am not able to cover it all. It becomes a survey course. . . . Often times this reduces the ability to use critical

Using six dimensions of classroom practice that appear to promote thinking, we identified 10 teachers as outstanding and 10 as less than outstanding.

thinking skills because you want to try to cover the material more quickly.

Perceptions of Students

Research has documented the powerful impact teachers' perceptions of students have on their instructional practices and student achievement. Our analysis of teachers' perceptions of students revealed a defeatist orientation among half of all low scorers compared to none among the high scorers. While high scorers often acknowledged the difficulty of getting students to think (especially low achievers or early in the school year), their statements did not indicate frustration toward students or resignation about trying to promote their thinking. Instead, most high scorers expressed optimism about the prospects of engaging students' minds.

Group differences in the perception of students can be observed in the statements of low scorer Leonard and high scorer Howard. Leonard complains of student disinterest and low motivation, implicitly exonerating himself from responsibility for students' less-than-adequate performance:

What is most disappointing is that the students aren't interested in learning. . . . They are just not willing to put much effort into school. Their attention span is short, and they are apathetic. . . . High

achievers can be just as apathetic as low achievers.

Howard, on the other hand, believes that students of all achievement levels are capable of "responding favorably" to challenging tasks and that teachers must persist in challenging them. For Howard, factors that have created student resistance to thinking tasks can be overcome:

I believe many or even most students find a thinking task challenging and interesting. Some see it as too difficult and too much trouble. If the task is presented to them reasonably well, they respond favorably. . . . To think requires a lot more time and a lot more effort. But it is possible to change their attitudes. . . . There are a lot of teachers who could do more of it. . . . A lot of kids with limitations have been told, "You can't do this or that," so they aren't too motivated. Thinking can be fun. Low achievers can show good, solid thinking.

Conceptions of Thinking

Many staff development and reform efforts have assumed that developing teachers' conceptual understanding of thinking will help improve teachers' instruction in this area. We found that compared to low scorers, high scorers manifested lengthier, more elaborate, and more precise perspectives on what thinking entails. In part, this involves a greater ability to indicate the kinds of behaviors students and teachers should exhibit in a thoughtful classroom (for example, "critique but also defend a position," "understand the relevance of data to a central theme," "determine points of view and identify their effects," "formulate hypotheses and subject some to criticism").

In addition, high scorers identified a greater number of intellectual dispositions (curiosity, confidence, a thirst for reasons, willingness to take risk) and intellectual skills (interpret information, generalize from data, formulate conclusions) that cognitive scientists and other researchers typically associate with good thinkers.

Finally, high scorers include in their

statements points of clarification and subtle but important distinctions between their own views and possible alternative conceptions. For example, high scorer Hans challenges the notion that Benjamin Bloom's taxonomy of cognitive processes should be viewed hierarchically, observing that a Level Two "comprehension" question may be of greater difficulty to students than a Level Six "evaluation" question. In addition, he takes aim at skill approaches to thinking by calling "mindless" any activities that are not tied to the goal of understanding subject matter. Harriet, in her discussion of thinking, disagreed with the view that students need direct instruction in logical fallacies to become good thinkers. A third high scorer, Hilary, argued that "intellectual curiosity" can be cultivated and therefore should be distinguished from

Our conclusion is that thoughtful classroom practice requires thoughtful reflection on practice.

"cognitive capacity," which is physiologically determined. Distinctions of this kind were not found in the conceptions of thinking offered by low scorers.

Thoughtful Reflection on Practice

We began our study to compare outstanding teachers of thinking with their less successful colleagues. We looked at teachers' instructional goals, whether they emphasized depth or breadth of content coverage, their perceptions of students, and their understanding of thinking. What we found is that there is a correlation between teachers' goals and perspectives and the climate of thoughtfulness we perceived in their classrooms.

Reform efforts in the area of thinking that focus primarily on "how to" instructional techniques and that minimize opportunities for teachers to reflect upon and reconceptualize facets of their teaching are unlikely to produce significant, long-term change. Our conclusion is that thoughtful classroom practice requires thoughtful reflection on practice.

References

Cuban, L. (1984). *How Teachers Taught: Constancy and Change in American Classrooms: 1890-1980.* New York: Longman.

Dewey, J. (1933). *How We Think.* Boston: D.C. Heath.

Goodlad, J. (1984). *A Place Called School: Prospects for the Future.* New York: McGraw-Hill.

Newmann, F. M. (1988). "Can Depth Replace Coverage in the High School Curriculum?" *Phi Delta Kappan* 68, 5: 345-348.

Newmann, F. M. (1991). "Promoting Higher Order Thinking in Social Studies: Overview of a Study of Sixteen High School Departments." *Theory and Research in Social Education* 19, 4: 323-339.

Passmore, J. (1967). "On Teaching To Be Critical." In *The Concept of Education,* edited by R. S. Peters. London: Routledge and Kegan Paul.

Schrag, F. (1988). *Thinking in School and Society.* New York: Routledge and Kegan Paul.

Siegel, H. (1988). *Educating Reason.* New York: Routledge and Kegan Paul.

Sirotnik, K. (1983). "What You See Is What You Get — Constancy, Persistency, and Mediocrity in Classrooms." *Harvard Educational Review* 53, 1: 16-31.

Tobin, K. (1987). "The Role of Wait Time in Higher Cognitive Level Learning." *Review of Educational Research* 57, 1:69-95.

Author's note: This paper was supported by the National Center on Effective Secondary Schools; the U.S. Department of Education, Office of Educational Research and Improvement (Grant No. G-008690007); and the Wisconsin Center for Education Research, School of Education, University of Wisconsin-Madison. Contributions to this work have been made by Fred Newmann, Dae-Dong Hahn, Bruce King, Jim Ladwig, Robert Stevenson, Cameron McCarthy, Francis Schrag, and the cooperative staff in 16 high schools. The opinions expressed in this publication are mine and do not necessarily reflect the views of the supporting agencies or the contributors.

Five Standards of Authentic Instruction

Fred M. Newmann and Gary G. Wehlage

Fred M. Newmann is Director of the Center on Organization and Restructuring of Schools and Professor of Curriculum and Instruction, University of Wisconsin-Madison, Wisconsin Center for Education Research, 1025 W. Johnson St., Madison, WI 53706. **Gary G. Wehlage** is Associate Director of the Center on Organization and Restructuring of Schools and Professor of Curriculum and Instruction, University of Wisconsin-Madison, same address.

What types of instruction engage students in using their minds well? A framework developed at Wisconsin's Center on Organization and Restructuring of Schools may be a valuable tool for teachers and researchers attempting to answer this complex question.

Why do many innovations fail to improve the quality of instruction or student achievement? In 1990, we began to explore this question by studying schools that have tried to restructure. Unfortunately, even the most innovative activities—from school councils and shared decision making to cooperative learning and assessment by portfolio—can be implemented in ways that undermine meaningful learning, unless they are guided by substantive, worthwhile educational ends. We contend that innovations should aim toward a vision of authentic student achievement, and we are examining the extent to which instruction in restructured schools is directed toward authentic forms of student achievement. We use the word *authentic* to distinguish between achievement that is significant and meaningful and that which is trivial and useless.

To define authentic achievement more precisely, we rely on three criteria that are consistent with major proposals in the restructuring movement:[1] (1) students construct meaning and produce knowledge, (2) students use disciplined inquiry to construct meaning, and (3) students aim their work toward production of discourse, products, and performances that have value or meaning beyond success in school.[2]

The Need for Standards for Instruction

While there has been much recent attention to standards for curriculum and for assessment,[3] public and professional discussion of standards for instruction tends to focus on procedural and technical aspects, with little attention to more fundamental standards of quality. Is achievement more likely to be authentic when the length of class periods varies, when teachers teach in teams, when students participate in hands-on activities, or when students spend time in cooperative groups, museums, or on-the-job apprenticeships?

We were cautious not to assume that technical processes or specific sites for learning, however innovative, necessarily produce experiences of high intellectual quality. Even activities that place students in the role of a more active, cooperative learner and that seem to respect student voices can be implemented in ways that do not produce authentic achievement. The challenge is not simply to adopt innovative teaching techniques or to find new locations for learning, but deliberately to counteract two persistent maladies that make conventional schooling inauthentic:

1. Often the work students do does not allow them to use their minds well.

2. The work has no intrinsic meaning or value to students beyond achieving success in school.

To face these problems head-on, we articulated standards for instruction that represented the quality of intellectual work but that were not tied to any specific learning activity (for example, lecture or small-group discussion). Indeed, the point was to assess the extent to which any given activity—traditional or innovative, in or out of school—engages students in using their minds well.

Instruction is complex, and quantification in education can often be as misleading as informative. To guard against oversimplification, we formulated several standards, rather than only one or two, and we conceptualized each standard as a continuous construct from "less" to "more" of a quality, rather than as a categorical (yes or no) variable. We expressed each standard as a dimensional construct on a five-point scale. Instructions for rating lessons include specific criteria for each score—1 to 5—on each standard. Space does not permit us to present criteria for every possible rating, but for each standard we first distinguish between high and low scoring lessons and then offer examples of criteria for some specific ratings. Raters consider both the number of students to which the criterion applies and the proportion of class time during which it applies.[4] The five standards are: higher-order thinking, depth of knowledge, connectedness to the world beyond the classroom, substantive conversation, and social support for student achievement (see fig. 1).

Higher-Order Thinking

The first scale measures the degree to which students use higher-order thinking.

Lower-order thinking (LOT) occurs when students are asked to receive or recite factual information or to employ rules and algorithms through repetitive routines. As information-receivers, students are given pre-specified knowledge ranging from simple facts and information to more complex concepts. Students are in this role when they recite previously acquired knowledge by responding to questions that require recall of pre-specified knowledge.

Higher-order thinking (HOT) requires students to manipulate information and ideas in ways that transform their meaning and implications, such as when students combine facts and ideas in order to synthesize, generalize, explain, hypothesize, or arrive at some conclusion or interpretation. Manipulating information and ideas through these processes allows students to solve problems and discover new (for them) meanings and understandings. When students engage in HOT, an element of uncertainty is introduced, and instructional outcomes are not always predictable.

Criteria for higher-order thinking:
3 = Students primarily engage in routine LOT operations a good share of the lesson. There is at least one significant question or activity in which some students perform some HOT operations.
4 = Students engage in an at least one major activity during the lesson in which they perform HOT operations. This activity occupies a substantial portion of the lesson, and many students perform HOT.

We wanted to assess the extent to which any given activity— traditional or innovative, in or out of school— engages students in using their minds well.

Depth of Knowledge

From "knowledge is shallow" (1) to "knowledge is deep" (5), the next scale assesses students' depth of knowledge and understanding. This term refers to the substantive character of the ideas in a lesson and to the level of understanding that students demonstrate as they consider these ideas.

Knowledge is thin or superficial when it does not deal with significant concepts of a topic or discipline—for example, when students have a trivial understanding of important concepts or when they have only a surface acquaintance with their meaning. Superficiality can be due, in part, to instructional strategies that emphasize coverage of large quantities of fragmented information.

Knowledge is deep or thick when it concerns the central ideas of a topic or discipline. For students, knowledge is deep when they make clear distinctions, develop arguments, solve problems, construct explanations, and otherwise work with relatively complex understandings. Depth is produced, in part, by covering fewer topics in systematic and connected ways.

Criteria for depth of knowledge:
2 = Knowledge remains superficial and fragmented; while some key concepts and ideas are mentioned or covered, only a superficial acquaintance or trivialized understanding of these complex ideas is evident.
3 = Knowledge is treated unevenly during instruction; that is, deep understanding of something is countered by superficial understanding of other ideas. At least one significant idea may be presented in depth and its significance grasped, but in general the focus is not sustained.

Connectedness to the World

The third scale measures the extent to which the class has value and meaning beyond the instructional context. In a class with little or no value beyond, activities are deemed important for success only in school (now or later). Students' work has no impact on others and serves only to certify their level of compliance with the norms of formal schooling.

A lesson gains in authenticity the more there is a connection to the larger social context within which students live. Instruction can exhibit some degree of connectedness when (1) students address real-world public problems (for example, clarifying a contemporary issue by applying statistical analysis in a report to the city council on the homeless); or (2) students use personal experiences as a context for applying knowledge (such as using conflict resolution techniques in their own school).

Criteria for connectedness:
1 = Lesson topic and activities have no clear connection to issues or experience beyond the classroom. The teacher offers no justification for the work beyond the need to perform well in class.
5 = Students work on a problem or issue that the teacher and students see as connected to their personal experiences or contemporary public situations. They explore these connections in ways that create personal meaning. Students are involved in an effort to influence an audience beyond their classroom; for example, by communicating knowledge to others, advocating solutions to social problems, providing assistance to people, or creating performances or products with utilitarian or aesthetic value.

Substantive Conversation

From "no substantive conversation" (1) to "high-level substantive conversation" (5), the fourth scale assesses the extent of talking to learn and understand the substance of a subject. In classes with little or no substantive conversation, interaction typically consists of a lecture with recitation in which the teacher deviates very little from delivering a preplanned body of information and set of questions; students routinely give very short answers. Teachers' list of questions, facts, and concepts tend to make the discourse choppy, rather than coherent; there is often little or no follow-up of student responses. Such discourse is the oral equivalent of fill-in-the-blank or short-answer study questions.

High levels of substantive conversation are indicated by three features:

1. There is considerable interaction about the ideas of a topic (the talk is about disciplined subject matter and includes indicators of higher-order thinking such as making distinctions, applying ideas, forming generalizations, raising questions, and not just reporting experiences, facts, definitions, or procedures).

2. Sharing of ideas is evident in exchanges that are not completely scripted or controlled (as in a teacher-led recitation). Sharing is best illustrated when participants explain themselves or ask questions in complete sentences and when they respond directly to comments of previous speakers.

3. The dialogue builds coherently on participants' ideas to promote improved collective understanding of a theme or topic.

Criteria for substantive conversation:
To score 2 or above, conversation must focus on subject matter as in feature (1) above.
2 = Sharing (2) and/or coherent promotion of collective understanding (3) occurs briefly and involves at least one example of two consecutive interchanges.
4 = All three features of substantive conversation occur, with at least one example of sustained conversation

Figure 1

Five Standards of Authentic Instruction

1. Higher-Order Thinking
lower-order thinking only 1...2...3...4...5 higher-order thinking is central

2. Depth of Knowledge
knowledge is shallow 1...2...3...4...5 knowledge is deep

3. Connectedness to the World Beyond the Classroom
no connection 1...2...3...4...5 connected

4. Substantive Conversation
no substantive conversation 1...2...3...4...5 high-level substantive conversation

5. Social Support for Student Achievement
negative social support 1...2...3...4...5 positive social support

(that is, at least three consecutive interchanges), and many students participate.

Social Support for Student Achievement

The social support scale involves high expectations, respect, and inclusion of all students in the learning process. Social support is low when teacher or student behavior, comments, and actions tend to discourage effort, participation, or willingness to express one's views. Support can also be low if no overt acts like the above occur, but when the overall atmosphere of the class is negative as a result of previous behavior. Token acknowledgments, even praise, by the teacher of student actions or responses do not necessarily constitute evidence of social support.

Social support is high in classes when the teacher conveys high expectations for all students, including that it is necessary to take risks and try hard to master challenging academic work, that all members of the class can learn important knowledge and skills, and that a climate of mutual respect among all members of the class contributes to achievement by all. "Mutual respect" means that students with less skill or proficiency in a subject are treated in ways that

encourage their efforts and value their contributions.

Criteria for social support:
2 = Social support is mixed. Both negative and positive behaviors or comments are observed.
5 = Social support is strong. The class is characterized by high expectations, challenging work, strong effort, mutual respect, and assistance in achievement for almost all students. Both teacher and students demonstrate a number of these attitudes by soliciting and welcoming contributions from all students. Broad student participation may indicate that low-achieving students receive social support for learning.

Using the Framework to Observe Instruction

We are now using the five standards to estimate levels of authentic instruction in social studies and mathematics in elementary, middle, and high schools that have restructured in various ways. Our purpose is not to evaluate schools or teachers, but to learn how authentic instruction and student achievement are facilitated or impeded by:

■ organizational features of schools (teacher workload, scheduling of instruction, governance structure);

■ the content of particular programs aimed at curriculum, assessment, or staff development;

- the quality of school leadership;
- school and community culture.

We are also examining how actions of districts, states, and regional or national reform projects influence instruction. The findings will describe the conditions under which "restructuring" improves instruction for students and suggest implications for policy and practice.

Apart from its value as a research tool, the framework should also help teachers reflect upon their teaching. The framework provides a set of standards through which to view assignments, instructional activities, and the dialogue between teacher and students and students with one another. Teachers, either alone or with peers, can use the framework to generate questions, clarify goals, and critique their teaching. For example, students may seem more engaged in activities such as cooperative learning or long-term projects, but heightened participation alone is not sufficient. The standards provide further criteria for examining the extent to which such activities actually put students' minds to work on authentic questions.

In using the framework, either for reflective critiques of teaching or for research, it is important to recognize its limitations. First, the framework does not try to capture in an exhaustive way all that teachers may be trying to accomplish with students. The standards attempt only to represent in a quantitative sense the degree of authentic instruction observed within discrete class periods. Numerical ratings alone cannot portray how lessons relate to one another or how multiple lessons might accumulate into experiences more complex than the sum of individual lessons. Second, the relative importance of the different standards remains open for discussion. Each suggests a distinct ideal, but it is probably not possible for most teachers to show high performance on all standards in most of their lessons. Instead, it may be important to ask, "Which standards should receive higher priority and under what circumstances?"[5]

Finally, although previous research indicates that teaching for thinking, problem solving, and understanding often has more positive effects on student achievement than traditional teaching, the effects of this specific framework for authentic instruction on student achievement have not been examined.[6] Many educators insist that there are appropriate times for traditional, less authentic instruction—emphasizing memorization, repetitive practice, silent study without conversation, and brief exposure—as well as teaching for in-depth understanding.

Rather than choosing rigidly and exclusively between traditional and authentic forms of instruction, it seems more reasonable to focus on how to move instruction toward more authentic accomplishments for students. Without promising to resolve all the dilemmas faced by thoughtful teachers, we hope the standards will offer some help in this venture.

---

[1] See Carnegie Corporation of New York (1989), Elmore and Associates (1990), and Murphy (1991).

[2] See Archbald and Newmann 1988, Newmann 1991, Newmann and Archbald 1992, Newmann et al. 1992, and Wehlage et al. 1989.

[3] For example, see the arguments for standards in National Council on Education Standards and Testing (1992), and Smith and O'Day (1991).

[4] In three semesters of data collection, correlations between raters were .7 or higher, and precise agreement between raters was about 60 percent or higher for each of the dimensions. A detailed scoring manual will be available to the public following completion of data collection in 1994.

[5] The standards may be conceptually distinct, but initial findings indicate that they cluster together statistically as a single construct. That is, lessons rated high or low on some dimensions tend to be rated in the same direction on others.

[6] Evidence for positive achievement effects of teaching for thinking is provided in diverse sources such as Brown and Palinscar (1989), Carpenter and Fennema (1992), Knapp et al. (1992), and Resnick (1987). However, no significant body of research to date has clarified key dimen-

sions of instruction that produce *authentic* forms of student achievement as defined here.

References

Archbald, D., and F.M. Newmann. (1988). *Beyond Standardized Testing: Assessing Authentic Academic Achievement in the Secondary School*. Reston, Va.: National Association of Secondary School Principals.

Brown, A., and A. Palinscar. (March 1989). "Coherence and Causality in Science Readings." Paper presented at the annual meeting of the American Educational Research Association, San Francisco.

Carnegie Corporation of New York. (1989). *Turning Points: Preparing American Youth for the 21st Century*. Report on the Carnegie Task Force on the Education of Young Adolescents. New York: Carnegie Council on Adolescent Development.

Carpenter, T. P., and E. Fennema. (1992). "Cognitively Guided Instruction: Building on the Knowledge of Students and Teachers." In *Curriculum Reform: The Case of Mathematics in the United States*. Special issue of *International Journal of Educational Research*, edited by W. Secada, pp. 457-470. Elmsford, N.Y.: Pergamon Press, Inc.

Elmore, R. F., and Associates. (1990). *Restructuring Schools: The Next Generation of Educational Reform*. San Francisco: Jossey-Bass.

Knapp, M. S., P.M. Shields, and B.J. Turnbull. (1992). *Academic Challenge for the Children of Poverty: Summary Report*. Washington, D.C.: U.S. Department of Education, Office of Policy and Planning.

Murphy, J. (1991). *Restructuring Schools: Capturing and Assessing the Phenomena*. Nashville, Tenn.: National Center for Educational Leadership, Vanderbilt University.

National Council on Education Standards and Testing. (1992). *Raising Standards for American Education*. A Report to Congress, the Secretary of Education, the National Education Goals Panel, and the American People. Washington, D.C.: U.S. Government Printing Office, Superintendent of Documents, Mail Stop SSOP.

Newmann, F. M. (1991). "Linking Restructuring to Authentic Student Achievement." *Phi Delta Kappan* 72, 6: 458-463.

Newmann, F.M., and D. Archbald. (1992).
"The Nature of Authentic Academic
Achievement." In *Toward a New Science
of Educational Testing and Assessment*,
edited by H. Berlak, F.M. Newmann,
E. Adams, D.A. Archbald, T. Burgess,
J. Raven, and T.A. Romberg, pp. 71-84.
Albany, N.Y.: SUNY Press.

Newmann, F. M., G.G. Wehlage, and S.D.
Lamborn. (1992). "The Significance and
Sources of Student Engagement." In
*Student Engagement and Achievement in
American Secondary Schools*, edited by
F.M. Newmann, pp. 11-30. New York:
Teachers College Press.

Resnick, L. (1987). *Education and
Learning to Think*. Washington, D.C.:
National Academy Press.

Smith, M. S., and J. O'Day. (1991).
"Systemic School Reform." In *The Politics of Curriculum and Testing: The
1990 Yearbook of the Politics of Education Association*, edited by S.H. Fuhrman
and B. Malen, pp. 233-267. Philadelphia:
Falmer Press.

Wehlage, G. G., R.A. Rutter, G.A. Smith,
N. Lesko, and R.R. Fernandez. (1989).
*Reducing the Risk: Schools as Communi-
ties of Support*. Philadelphia: Falmer
Press.

Authors' note: This paper was
prepared at the Center on Organization
and Restructuring of Schools, supported
by the U.S. Department of Education,
Office of Educational Research and
Improvement (Grant No. R117Q0005-92)
and by the Wisconsin Center for
Education Research, School of
Education, University of Wisconsin-
Madison. Major contributions to the
development of these standards have
been made by Center staff members.
The opinions expressed here are those of
the authors and do not necessarily reflect
the views of the supporting agencies.

A Look to the Future

The breakthroughs that are developing in new learning and communications technologies are really quite impressive. They will definitely affect how human beings learn in the very near-term future. Two new essays on this topic explore some of these new technologies. While we look forward with considerable optimism and confidence to these future educational developments, there are still presently many controversies that will still be debated in the early years of the twentieth century; the "school choice" issue is one. We will not attain all the goals that were set for us for the year 2000 by the governors of the states and former president George Bush in 1989; but we will make significant progress toward them. Some very interesting new proposals for new forms of schooling, both in public schools and private schools, are under development. We can expect to see at least a few of these proposals tried in practice in the next few years.

Some of the demographic changes and challenges involving young people in the United States are staggering. Ten percent of all American teenage girls will become pregnant each year, the highest rate in the developed world. At least 100,000 American elementary school children get drunk once a week. Incidence of venereal disease has tripled among adolescents in the United States since 1965. The actual school dropout rate in the United States stands at 30 percent.

On other fronts, the student populations of North America reflect vital social and cultural forces at work to destroy our progress. In the United States, a massive secondary school dropout problem has been developing steadily through the past decade. The 1990s will reveal how public school systems will address this and other unresolved problems brought about by dramatic upheavals in demographics. There is the issue, as well, of how great a shortfall in the supply of new teachers will be experienced in the 1990s. In the immediate future, we will be able to see if a massive teacher shortage is indeed beginning; if it is, how will emergency or alternative certification measures adopted by states affect achievement of the objectives of our reforms?

At any given moment in a people's history, several alternative future directions are open to them. Since 1970, North American educational systems have been subjected to one wave after another of recommendations for programmatic change. Is it any wonder that *change* is a sensitive watchword for persons in teacher education on this continent? What specific directions it will take in the immediate future depend on which recommendations of the reform agenda are implemented, which agencies of government (local, state/provincial, and federal) will pay for the very high costs of reform, and which shifts in perceived national educational priorities by the public will occur that will effect fundamental realignments of our educational goals.

Basic changes in society's career patterns should also be considered. It is estimated that in the United States the average nonagricultural worker now makes a major job change about five times in his or her career. The schools will surely be affected, indirectly or directly, by this major social phenomenon. Changes in the social structure due to divorce, unemployment, and job retraining efforts will also have an impact. Educational systems are integral parts of the broader social systems that created them; if the larger social system experiences fundamental change, this is reflected in the educational system.

In the area of information science and computer technologies applicable for use in educational systems, the development of new products is so rapid that we cannot predict what technological capacities may be available to schools 20 years from now. In addition, basic computer literacy is becoming more and more widespread in the population. We are entering—indeed we are in—a period of human history when knowledgeable people can control far greater information (and have immediate access to it) than at any previous time. As new information command systems evolve, this phenomenon will become more and more meaningful to all of us.

The future of education will be determined by the current debate concerning what constitutes a just, national response to human needs in a period of technological change. The history of technological change in all human societies since the beginning of industrial development clearly demonstrates that major advances in technology and breakthroughs in the basic sciences lead to more rapid rates of social change. Society is on the verge of discoveries that will lead to the creation of entirely new technologies in the dawning years of the twenty-first century. All of the social, economic, and educational institutions globally will be affected by these scientific breakthroughs. The basic issue is not whether schools can remain aloof from the needs of industry or the economic demands of society but how they can emphasize the nobelest ideals of free persons in the face of inevitable technological and economic changes. Another concern is how to let go of predetermined visions of the future that limit our possibilities as free people. The schools, of course, will be called upon to face these issues. We need the most enlightened, insightful, and compassionate teachers ever educated by North American universities to prepare the youth of the future in a manner that will humanize the high-tech world in which they live.

All of the articles included in this unit can be related to discussions on the goals of education, the future of

education, or curriculum development. They also reflect highly divergent perspectives in the philosophy of education.

Looking Ahead: Challenge Questions

What might be the shape of school curricula by the year 2020?

What changes in society are most likely to affect educational change?

Based on all of the commission reports of recent years, is it possible to identify any clear directions in which teacher education in North America is headed? How can we build a better future for teachers?

How can information about population demographics,

potential discoveries in the basic sciences, and the rate and direction of technological change assist in planning for our educational future?

How can schools prepare students to live and work in an uncertain future? What knowledge bases are most important? What skills are most important?

Will privatized schools represent an expansion of the educational opportunities for our children?

Should school "choice" proposals include the concept that tax dollars follow the student? Why, or why not?

What is made possible in the classroom by the new learning and communications technologies that have been developed?

—F. S.

SEARCHING FOR TERMS

Rick Wilber

Rick Wilber is a journalism professor at the School of Mass Communications at the University of South Florida.

Sit down at your computer keyboard, move that mouse around on its pad, click on an icon or two, and log onto a good data base. Now, type in a few search terms that have to do with education and its use of emerging technologies.

If that didn't make any sense to you, just ask your children for help. They'll know what it means. More than 97 percent of American elementary schools and high schools have computers for student use these days,[1] so you can bet your children will be comfortable–probably a lot more comfortable than you are–with the digital future. To them, a mouse is a device you use to move a cursor around on a computer screen, and the idea of using particular search terms to dive into a data base seems quite the ordinary way to do a little research for that high school term paper.

To research the new technologies and their impact on our children's education, try terms like *elementary* and *education* and *technology,* or *elementary* or *secondary* and *technology,* or if you want to narrow things down, add the words *future* and *quality* or the catch-phrase *multimedia.* Anything similar to those terms should jog the enormous memory of the data base.

Wait a few seconds, and watch what comes up on the screen. When I tried the first few terms recently on Nexis (a leading data base that collects full text from thousands of newspapers, magazines, and other sources), I confined the search to recent magazine articles and still had more than a thousand "hits," or stories where the terms were used. Limiting the search by adding the terms *quality* and *future* narrowed things down some, but there were still hundreds of hits.

THE INFORMATION AGE: A HOT TOPIC NOW

Not only does my little exercise in modern research show how quick and effective a data base search can be these days, but it also shows how hot this topic is. Educators nationwide are working hard to find the best ways to make use of the new technologies to improve the way we teach our children.

We all know the bad news—the horrific anecdotes and statistics of violence and fear in some schools, of illiterate high school graduates, of declining test scores and the subsequent dumbing down of America.

Some of this is media hyperbole. The percentage of high school graduates who enrolled in a college or university, after all, was at an all-time high of 63 percent in 1992. And the percentage of high school students who graduated was just over 71 percent. So the news is not all bad.[2]

But are those graduates ready for the work force or college? And what of the 29 percent who didn't graduate, some four hundred thousand young people who dropped out? What kind of future do they face?

1. World Almanac and Book of Facts, 1994.

2. World Almanac.

These are compelling worries. Something has to be done, or America's very future will be in doubt.

There must be a way to revive America's educational system, a way to raise the standards, do a better job of teaching, produce better students, better citizens.

Maybe the information age (coming right at you on the newly minted information highway) offers us that something, that answer. After all, many of the educational experts say, computer technology has the ability to lower costs while increasing educational quality. All we have to do is make the initial investment and wait for the educational and societal profits to roll in.

Elementary students, these experts promise us, will learn the basics better if only we use these new tools properly. And at the high school level, the information highway and its technological side streets will help today's students prepare better for the needs of the workplace of tomorrow.

As a longtime professor of journalism who has watched the writing skills of our entering students decline for some two decades, I certainly hope these experts are right. And as a writer of science fiction stories, I find these new technologies fascinating and full of promise. They are a kind of science fictional future rushing into reality so quickly that the futurists can barely stay ahead of the game.

But it is as the father of a three-year-old girl that I find the entire issue of education and technology of preeminent importance. Like most parents, my wife and I worry for little Samantha's educational future. Will her schooling be safe, interesting, useful, exciting, and worthwhile? Will it help us prepare her for what lies ahead in a world that promises to be very different from the one we are in now?

THESE TECHNOLOGIES IN ELEMENTARY AND SECONDARY EDUCATION

There are, it seems to me, several ways that these technologies promise to have a positive impact—perhaps a dramatic one—on elementary and secondary education.

But there are also several major roadblocks—some of them financial, some institutional, some just personal reluctance on the part of teachers and administrators—in the way of realizing this promise.

And one major issue that the information age brings to us seems to me, as a writer, a teacher, and a parent, to be so profound that it threatens to change one of the most basic tenets of education as we've known it for two hundred years. Article after article in magazines like *Technology Review*, *PC World*, *T.H.E.* (Technological Horizons in Education) *Journal*, and *CD-ROM World* point out that if today's students don't have the skills to navigate properly, they will be, literally and metaphorically, lost while driving down that information highway at breakneck speed.

A few of the "new" technologies having an impact in current education aren't really very new at all. There is a flurry of interest at the college level in televised (and videotaped) lectures, for instance. The relatively low cost of equipment combined with improvements in quality have prompted renewed interest in television during this era of tight budgets and demand for increased teacher productivity.

The televised lecture has some obvious advantages. Such classes are not necessarily time-or space-dependent, for one thing. On many campuses, a student can either watch the lecture live from a remote location or have access to a videotape of the class. The videotape means that the student can replay the lecture at his leisure, stopping and starting as needed to make note taking easier and to help understand particularly difficult information or concepts.

Also, using even low-cost television production techniques can provide appealing, if minimal (at most campuses), special effects to enhance the presentation of the material. It's quite possible, as a matter of fact, that a lecture as seen on the TV screen may be more effective than the live presentation in the lecture hall.

But there are significant drawbacks to the televised lecture, too, even at the college level.

When students watch a lecture on videotape, they can't interact with the lec-

PRÉCIS

With the recent arrival of video and new computer technologies, the opportunity is at hand for enormous change and dramatic improvement in the U.S. education system. The changes may be so profound, in fact, that the very need for literacy is eliminated.

On the college level, televised lectures are becoming a reality on many campuses. Instead of gathering at a central lecture hall, students may go to several satellite rooms to see the professor, or master teacher, on a video monitor as he delivers his lecture. The presentation becomes interactive through a video camera and microphones in each satellite room that are linked to the professor, who is able to answer the students' questions.

On the elementary and secondary school levels, the computer—with its ability to retrieve vast quantities of information through CD-ROMs and on-line databases—is beginning to assume the position of a master teacher, replacing the traditional classroom teacher. The computer's software is able to present information in an entertaining, informative way to the student, and the classroom teacher becomes an assistant to the electronic teacher, helping students understand the presented material, while occasionally expanding on it.

Ultimately, it may transpire that most entertainment and communication will be accomplished without the need for reading and writing, making literacy a less important social and professional value.

The problem of interaction is at least partially solved by requiring students to see the lecture live at their remote site, where graduate assistants or other teachers should be available to answer questions. In these cases the on-screen lecturer serves as a sort of master teacher, using available visuals to enhance the lecture and counting on the on-site teachers to explain or clarify as needed.

Indeed, at many universities the format uses the "teleconferencing" idea, in much the same way that corporate America does. A centrally televised presenter lectures, and microphones at each remote site allow for questions to be asked of the principal lecturer. A camera at each site, and some extra monitors at the central location, mean the lecturer can see the questioner as well as hear the request.

This method is effective, in terms of both communication and cost, at the college level, but even teleconferencing doesn't solve all the problems, especially from the students' perspective. Even with interaction, televised lectures can be both intimidating and distant for too many students. They don't have the courage to stand up in front of a camera and ask a question, and they miss the relative personal warmth of a real live person in the front of the lecture hall.

Another problem is that televised lectures are heavily dependent on the entertainment skills of the master teacher to communicate through this medium. The best informed teacher, unfortunately, is not always the best entertainer, and few things are as tedious as a poorly presented television lecture.

Still, the televised lecture works and is again in vogue on many campuses, perhaps primarily because administrators love it for its cost effectiveness, if nothing else.

At elementary and high school levels the televised lecture has a whole new set of problems, compounded by the relative immaturity of the audience and the inability of the teacher to have constant interaction with each student.

CD-ROM TECHNOLOGY

ther technologies, though, hold great promise for younger students. CD-ROMs, on-line services, and the data bases that

turer—they can't immediately ask questions or get clarification as they can in real time. It is ironic that video's lack of interaction should be such a stumbling block at exactly the same time as the newer multimedia technologies—CD-ROMs and computer networks, principally—gain a major part of their appeal from being interactive.

CD–ROMs, on-line services, and the data bases that come with both form the troika of new technology that is poised to lead our elementary and high school education system into dramatic change.

come with both form the troika of new technology that is poised, if we let it (or even if we don't), to lead our elementary and high school education system into dramatic change.

CD–ROMs (compact *d*isk, *r*ead *o*nly *m*emory) are disks that can store hundreds of millions of characters' worth of information that a special disk player (attached by cable to a computer) can read by laser. When you use a CD–ROM you may read text, hear music or other sounds, and see visual images, some of them in motion.

When the three-year-old in our home, for instance, wanted to learn something about elephants we might, in the past, have described one to her, drawn a picture, looked up a picture in a book, or, best case, have taken her to a zoo that has an elephant. But alas, our local zoo has no elephants, and the animals were surprisingly hard to find in the dozens of books lining the shelves in her room.

Enter the new family computer with its CD–ROM. We looked up "elephant" in the encyclopedia disk that slides into the CD–ROM with a gentle click and quickly found information in the form of text. Also on the screen were a number of other choices for other kinds of information. With a quick move of the mouse and a click or two, we saw a picture of an elephant, heard its bellow, and then watched it amble off into the thicket with the rest of the herd.

Now that sort of multimedia approach is undeniably an effective way to teach a child about elephants or electrons, government, geography, or anything else you can think of.

CD–ROM technology offers an incredible array of knowledge available at the touch of a keyboard or the slight movement of a mouse and a double click, and the number of CD–ROMs is rapidly increasing. But they aren't the only new thing out there.

COMPUTER NETWORKS

Many educators these days extol the benefits of teachers and students joining computer networks.

There are a number of cases now where students in one elementary or high school communicate regularly with students from another via computer. They can share information, work on projects together, or even gossip through e-mail (electronic mail).

Also, there are a number of on-line services, companies that offer access to a wide variety of data bases, computer bulletin boards, special on-line publications, and much more—the list of possibilities seems to grow daily.

These services range from the vast Internet through the growing, prosperous on-line services like Prodigy, America Online, Genie, CompuServe, and others all the way down to local bulletin boards, where relatively few people in one town can share information.

Computers interconnected in this way offer a powerful means of sharing information and knowledge. Using our computers, another writer and I are collaborating on a novel, sending chapters back and forth to each other through computers connected by telephone lines—a process that takes only a few minutes instead of the several days it would take by mail.

Such computerized collaboration has the added advantage of the chapters being instantly incorporated into our computer software (in our case, WordPerfect, a popular word-processing program), so that we already have them stored and can edit or print them out as needed.

Teachers, administrators, and students, of course, are already doing much the same thing with research, bureaucratic paperwork, term papers, and more.

Many educators these days extol the benefits of teachers and students joining computer networks.

From the computer networks you can also find access to the data bases, like Nexis/Lexis. There are a number of these, and they all offer quick access to information that would have taken days to uncover just a few years ago. Now it is the work of minutes.

IMPROVING QUALITY WHILE CUTTING COSTS

One example of the way that technology could be used to improve quality and cut cost is offered by Lohn O'Looney in an article in *Phi Delta Kappan* magazine.[3]

O'Looney suggests an alternative to the current heavily stratified, top-down educational structure, where one teacher routinely spends a relatively short time with a student and then passes him on to the next teacher, and where various administrative levels handle the paperwork associated with each student, rarely giving the teacher a look but amassing a lot of paperwork that has little educationally useful information.

His case management system, based on current trends in corporate America, depends heavily on generalist teachers who would stay with students for longer periods of time than the traditional semester or year.

"Shared data bases and expert systems, in combination with a redesigned work environment, could help generalist teachers educate children more effectively," he argues.

Using this computer-dependent approach, he says, "A single teacher could: (1) use data bases and computer networks both to enter and to extract information that would be of actual use to that teacher and to other teachers, as well as infor-

mation that is currently compiled and processed by administrators; (2) teach a group of children for as long a period of time as the bonds of teacher/student relationship appear to warrant; and (3) teach—or, perhaps more accurately, facilitate—lessons in a variety of subject-matter areas. This facilitation would make use of an assortment of computer-based instructional systems, individual diagnostic programs, and support from expert systems."

O'Looney believes the case management approach can eliminate numerous administrative positions, counter the "alienation of teachers who feel they have no control over their work environment or the outcome of their work, make creative and powerful use of information technologies" that are often poorly used, and finally, promote "more stable and more psychologically productive teacher/student/parent relationships."

It's a grand idea. As he points out, data bases, interactive CD–ROMs, on-line services, and the rest mean that students will have ready access to the factual information they need to progress through a body of knowledge at their own pace. So teachers, in effect, will spend most of their time helping students acquire the knowledge from the computer, not lecturing on the material. In this sense, the teacher becomes a kind of coach, a facilitator, for students, and if a solid teacher-student bond is formed, there is no reason why one teacher could not spend several years with a particular student or group of students.

THE ONE-ROOM SCHOOLHOUSE

This idea seems to be, in some ways, a return to the days of the rural one-room schoolhouse, and perhaps that's good. One hundred fifty years ago, a single teacher with a

3. Lohn O'Looney, "Redesigning the Work of Education," *Phi Delta Kappan*, January 1993, 375.

group of students ranging in ability and age from those just starting their education to those ready for high school or college could meet the needs of each one as long as the number of students wasn't overwhelming. After all, the body of knowledge was much smaller, the competitive pressures less acute on both students and teacher, and the bond between them often a productive one that encouraged learning.

But the one-room schoolhouse couldn't compete with mass production. The current school structure follows a pattern that has its roots in the Industrial Revolution, one based on mass production techniques. Anyone who has read Charles Dickens' *Hard Times* has seen what this system can be like carried to its extreme. Still, it served us well in its time, doing an average job for the average student and generally educating the masses to a level that society found useful. Most adults today went through an educational system based, for the most part, on these techniques.

O'Looney raises the argument that just as industry has had to retool and rethink how to produce products—abandoning, in many cases, the principles of assembly line mass production—the educational system must do the same, and computer-based case management techniques hold great promise.

PROBLEMS WITH INCORPORATING THESE TECHNOLOGIES INTO THE SCHOOL SYSTEM

There are, as you might suspect, some problems with incorporating case management style into the educational setting. The first is reluctance on the part of administrators, who see it not only as expensive and experimental (two words that do not make a typical administrator happy), but also as a threat. For if successful, the case

management approach would mean fewer administrators are needed and perhaps a smaller support staff all around. That sounds pretty menacing to current school administrators.

But an equally troublesome problem is reluctance on the part of teachers. This new system asks something very different of the typical elementary or high school teacher from what has been asked before. Under the new system, there is no need to pour information into the students—the computers do that. Instead, the teacher must learn new techniques to help the students learn.

These new techniques are interpersonal, and just learning how to work with students in this new way will be a challenge for many teachers. There are serious technological hurdles as well. Teachers will have to be on comfortable, even expert, terms with the computers themselves if they are to expect their students to use them daily as the major source of information.

Teachers who can't show students how to use the computer to find information, or can't help them work their way through a particularly demanding piece of educational software, will not be of much use as facilitators.

THE VIDEO-CLASS APPROACH

In a sense, this new approach is reflective of the video-class approach that has been around for some time. The computer and its software become the master teacher, presenting information in an entertaining, informative way to the student. And the classroom teacher becomes an assistant to the electronic master teacher, helping students understand the material presented, expanding on it from time to time but primarily helping the student to learn through the ongoing encounter with the software.

This new system asks something very different of the typical elementary or high school teacher from what has been asked before.

A number of such software packages already exist, and many more are in the works, though slow acceptance of the new technology by school systems has, in turn, slowed the software makers' progress. But the numbers suggest, as we'll see in a bit, that the interactive future is, for the most part, already here. The educational establishment, like it or not, is going to have to deal with an information age future.

If one looks a little further ahead, an even more ambitious variant of how we might use computers is possible, one where each student will have access to virtually any information he could need to learn almost anything.

Seymour Papert, Lego Professor of Learning Research at the MIT Media Laboratory, asserts that the new technologies make it possible at last for the educational establishment to undertake dramatic, effective change in the way we teach our children. "No technical obstacle stands in the way of making a machine—let's call it the Knowledge Machine—that would put the power to know what others know [into the hands of students]," he writes. Having this material readily available, he adds, means a typical elementary student, for instance, could,

> using speech, touch, or gestures, . . . steer the machine to the topic of interest, quickly navigating through a knowledge space much broader than the contents of any printed encyclopedia. Whether she is interested in giraffes or panthers or fleas, whether she wants to see them eating, sleeping, running, fighting, or birthing, she would be able to find her way to the relevant sounds and images. This availability will one day extend to experiencing the smell and touch of being with animals.[4]

Imagine its capacity to teach.

THE DECLINE OF READING?

But think of some of the implications, too. On the negative side, this near-future world of Knowledge Machines, or CD–ROMS, data bases, and on-line information, spells

danger to those who think that reading is the main route to learning. For the fact is that reading and writing, or at least some elements of both skills, are terribly threatened by this new technology.

With a CD–ROM, you can be informed and entertained at great depth, and yet you don't really have to read much and have little need to memorize. It's that simple. Reading and retention skills aren't really necessary.

Of course, some minimal skills are useful. But the idea of teaching a high school student to write a cogent three-page essay seems terribly irrelevant in an age where no one needs that approach to sharing information or entertaining. With multimedia computerized sources of information, the acquisition of knowledge becomes something that is entertaining, easy, and powerful—and it doesn't require that you read much.

One of the major difficulties in teaching reading and writing skills to current elementary and secondary students is that they have little need to apply those skills outside the classroom setting. For them, most forms of entertainment and communication are accomplished without reading and writing skills.

CD–ROMs, just now making their way into many homes, add a whole new level of difficulty for the teacher who wants to impart some reading and writing skills. For most students, reading is likely to become more and more of an academic activity, like geography or mathematics or history—something learned for its own sake, not for its actual utility in the lives of the students.

As Papert points out,

> Written language is not likely to be abandoned. But we need to think anew about the position assigned to it as the prerequisite to children's accumulation of knowledge. Children who grow up with the opportunity to explore the jungles and the cities and the deep oceans and ancient myths and outer space will be even less likely than the players of video games to sit quietly through anything even vaguely resembling the elementary school curriculum as we now know it. And why should they?[5]

4. "The Children's Machine," *Technology Review*, July 1993, 28. This article was adapted from Seymour Papert's book *The Children's Machine: Rethinking School in the Age of the Computer* (New York: Basic Books, 1993).

5. Seymour Papert, "The Children's Machine" *Technology Review*, July 1993, 28.

*In a few years, perhaps, someone putting together an article like this
will not need a keyboard at all, but instead will pull together a wide
variety of illustrations, sound bites, graphs, charts, and copy to get the
same information across to the reader, er, user.*

Clearly, what Papert and others are pointing out is that the opportunity is there for great change in the educational system. The new technologies offer the chance for dramatic improvements in the ways we teach, while also containing some very real threats to the methods we have thought most basic for some two centuries. Literacy, in effect, may no longer be necessary.

HOW SOON WILL ALL THIS HAPPEN?

One could argue that it won't happen all that fast, that teachers' reluctance and administrators' fear will slow the acceptance of this approach in schools. It might be said that it is all still too expensive, and that it discriminates between the more affluent students able to afford it at home and the less affluent, who will be forced to make do with the archaic idea of teachers lecturing them and then reading material in books or using the occasional computer found these days in even the most underfunded of school districts.

And there is some merit to that argument. After all, while 97 percent of schools nationwide have computers, only 20 percent of students have access to their own computer, and only a little over 10 percent of personal computers currently have a CD–ROM drive.[6]

6. Don Menn, "Multimedia in Education," *PC World*, October 1993, M52.

However, not only is the number of home CD–ROM units rising fast (there should be nearly 8.8 million by the end of 1994), but there is also the near-future possibility of CD–ROM-style interactive availability without even owning a personal computer.

The fiber-optic promise of 500-or 1,000-channel television (yes, the information highway's off-ramp right into the home) is one way that this material might be brought into every home.

When that happens—when Everyman's cable television hookup brings some form, at least, of interactive multimedia into the home—the change will be profound. And it won't be just the children who won't need to read very much or very well; it will be all of us.

Perhaps, of course, this isn't a problem—it may be merely a shift in our social paradigm. Mass literacy, after all, has been around for only a couple centuries, and maybe its time is now past.

In a few years, perhaps, someone putting together an article like this will not need a keyboard at all, but instead will pull together a wide variety of illustrations, sound bites, graphs, charts, and a few brief paragraphs of copy to get the same information across to the reader, er, user.

It will no doubt be much more informative and a lot more fun. And only some of us, the real dinosaurs, will miss all those words.

THE
Plug-In School

A LEARNING ENVIRONMENT FOR THE 21ST CENTURY

**New technologies make it possible for learning to take place anywhere.
The Plug-In School may show the way.**

*Text and Illustrations
By David Pesanelli*

David Pesanelli is an advanced planner and conceptual designer who develops communications, environments, and products. His address is David Pesanelli and Company, 14508 Barkwood Drive, Rockville, Maryland 20853, telephone 301/871-7355.

The Plug-In School concept was developed with his collaborator on education projects, Bill Raxsdale, who is an educator, author, and researcher based in Lafayette, Louisiana, telephone 318/232-5025.

I n the future, technologies will allow learning to take place virtually everywhere. School buildings as they now exist could even be eliminated, replaced with a ubiquitous array of stimulating, interactive, and flexible learning technologies embedded in all human habitats.

While eliminating the school is a revolutionary change in the distribution of education services that deserves serious consideration, it is also fruitful to examine ways in which the educational physical plant might shed its "factory school" format and emerge in new forms. We

can then begin to see how the classroom could become a precursor of

"The Morning Surprise" (Scenario One) awaits students in the "Plug-In School" of the twenty-first century. Transporters (left, rear) bring learning packages to an unloading dock. The modules are unpacked and checked in the preview area. Two students (right) assemble a robot, which guides them in the process. Others (center, rear) check out the portable planetarium. One student (far left) uses a touch-screen monitor to log in to a database to receive information on an upcoming careers class. A video screen suspended from the ceiling provides timely information on special events at the school.

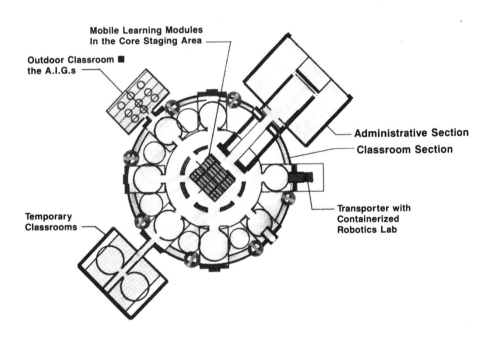

**Mobile Learning Modules
In the Core Staging Area**

**Outdoor Classroom ▪
the A.I.G.s**

Administrative Section

Classroom Section

**Temporary
Classrooms**

**Transporter with
Containerized
Robotics Lab**

**PLUG-IN SCHOOL
CONCEPTUAL PLAN**

In "Afternoon Career Class" (Scenario Two), students gather around a Mobile Learning Module. Video screens on the rear wall show close ups of the project they are working on. The elements in the room are all mobile, including work stations, project work benches, the learning modules, and the soft partitions connected to tracks in the ceiling. This allows the room to be reconfigured to meet the class's varying needs.

true twenty-first-century environments, a prototype for the evolving workplace and home.

New, integrated technologies enrich the learning experience by giving students access to encyclopedic amounts of information and data in any of their subject areas, integrated with rich images and animation. Curriculums enhanced by these exciting technologies could help teachers expose students to history and its meanings: Names and dates of historical events and actors come alive in full costumes of the times, embellished by period music.

The advanced physical learning environment would also teach students about life in the twenty-first century—at work, at home, and in places yet to be imagined.

Child sits at brightly colored work station when in class. The module can easily be moved and has an adjustable seat, a rear storage compartment, and a snap-in computer that the student can take home for assignments.

The school, the workplace, and the home are clearly integrating. Responsibilities, functions, activities, and tasks that once occurred exclusively within each domain are crossing over into the other environments. Corporate workers have home offices, students and older learners take cable-access university courses, and parents bring their toddlers to day-care learning centers at work sites. It may no longer be sensible to think about the school, the office, and the home as separate from one another. These three once-distinct entities are breaking apart, combining, and overlapping in new and unexpected ways. The next-generation school can lead this process of blending aspects of learning, living, and working.

The School as Change Agent

Dramatic and pervasive changes are occurring in the workplace, to which the advanced school environment can help orient students. Organization charts are flattening, team assignments are becoming prevalent, off-site work is increasing, and teleconferencing is expanding. Just beneath the surface of these visible transformations are powerful change-themes such as "fluidity," "mobil-ity," "flexibility," and "adaptability." These underlying qualities can guide the planning and design of advanced schools.

For example, children could easily rearrange colorful and mobile work stations in the classroom as they switch from teacher-led programs to individual assignments to team projects to distance-learning via satellite or cable broadcasts. These flexible learning situations have parallels in the ways that office and factory work are evolving.

The Plug-In School

The "Plug-In School" is a possibile first step toward the flexible learning environments of the twenty-first century. As now envisioned, this facility serves as a hub for receiving learning modules "injected" into its classrooms. The school has a physical structure that opens its walls to become part of the library, museum, science center, planetarium, laboratory, and corporation that is plugged in to it. Yet, the school never loses its own identity as the students' and teachers' environment.

The Plug-In School is conceived as a facility that, in addition to its traditional roles, functions at the center of a delivery and distribution system for education "packages." A key goal is to strengthen the school's relationships with informal learning centers and with employers to create both academic and career-oriented instructional programs.

Transporters deliver containerized modules to school facilities. These "packages" are planned, designed, and manufactured at science centers and museums. They might contain interactive exhibits or materials that will be used for pursuing creative problem-solving exercises. Corporations could create stimulating, career-oriented modules. An architectural firm might send models of buildings accompanied by optical discs showing computer-aided design. An industrial laboratory could provide a module that demonstrates state-of-the-art laser applications.

These education and career packages need not be exclusively high tech. A crafts company might send an entire section of a woodworking shop, complete with work benches and tools for the students to use in creating artistic and personal objects. Some containerized modules might literally plug in to openings in the school walls, and the craft shop or robotics lab or architectural studio would become a walk-in extension of the classroom.

At the center of the Plug-In School is a storage and staging core, where the school's own mobile learning modules are prepared for classroom use. Teachers request combinations of models, mockups, specimens, interactive devices, and media to enhance course experiences.

What might it be like to spend some time in this dynamic facility?

Scenario One: The Morning Surprise

The young children have been waiting impatiently for this morning's "surprises" to appear. And now their wait is over. Two sleek transporters have arrived, and their drivers unload containerized "packages" at one of the school's loading bays. One module is from Chicago's Adler Planetarium. Tina, Beverly, and Tom—a student teaching assistant—eagerly assemble the traveling planetarium. The projection instrument is a compact model designed to be transported easily. The inflatable dome will soon be in place and swept with galaxies, quasars, and galactic black holes.

The second vehicle brings a robotics lab from the National Institute of Science and Technology. Jimmy and Quan insert a program card into the instructor robot, which launches into a comedy routine while instructing the boys on assembling a mini-manufacturing plant to be used in the classroom this morning. A second section of the robotics lab, including microbots and videos depicting careers in the field, is loaded onto a mobile learning module and delivered to the school's storage core. Later, it will be sent to a physics class for a career-oriented program.

Scenario Two: Afternoon Career Class

The sun-drenched classroom is filled with bright, gregarious 15- to 17-year-old students, who chatter excitedly as they rearrange the room for the afternoon's career class. They reposition soft partitions and program the track lighting, then decide how to arrange their work stations for the two-hour session's rigorous agenda. The "stations" hold the snap-in computers that they will carry home in backpacks and use for their homework assignments.

As the session on robotics careers begins, a section of the classroom wall slides aside, and the students grow quiet. The teacher and a robotics expert enter the environment just ahead of a self-guided mobile unit. The "package" that it carries arrived earlier that day after being picked up at another school complex in the next county.

A teaching assistant slides back the cover of the mobile learning module. Inside are a laboratory's

Young student interacts with AIG (Artificial Intelligence Grounder), a personal learning environment that responds individually to each student. The personal environment could be integrated into the future "Plug-In School."

products—microbots. The module's video camera scans the array of electronic and mechanical marvels, and enlarged images appear on a suspended video screen. The lab expert explains how microbots are developed and manufactured, as well as what they can do.

After taking turns manipulating the microbots, the students watch a video on careers in the rapidly expanding robotics field and related disciplines. Interested students press a module section and receive a printout that identifies robotics labs and corporations in the region where interns are employed during vacation breaks.

The career-oriented session ends, and some of the class members eagerly rearrange their work stations for a team project. Others reconfigure the classroom area for a distance-learning course taught by a robotics engineer broadcasting via satellite from an upstate New York laboratory.

Everywhere Learning

Learning environments of the future should provide a context for technologies as well as a counterpoint to them. The "little red schoolhouse" of yore will disappear, re-

placed with a more futuristic design in which brilliant technologies seem natural and not overwhelming or intimidating. But at the same time, this high-tech environment should embrace its natural surroundings. The classrooms, for instance, might have large windows to give students a view of trees, meadows, and lakes, providing a serene visual respite for kids spending many hours with computer screens and electronic devices of one type or another.

The Plug-In School is but one potential concept for a twenty-first-century school. Students—and adult learners as well—will likely use several facilities of different sizes and complexity, including study environments in the home and workplace. In the twenty-first century, it will be possible for all of us to plug in to "schools"—wherever we may be.

American Schools: Good, Bad, or Indifferent?

As important as criticism is, it is only a call to arms, Mr. Doyle points out. It is necessary but not sufficient. Constructive critics know that the time has come for American education to move on — toward solutions.

DENIS P. DOYLE

DENIS P. DOYLE, a senior fellow with the Hudson Institute, Indianapolis, writes about education and human capital from his office in Washington, D.C.

ATTEMPTING to assess the temper of our times, historians of the next century will no doubt fall back on Dickens' memorable opening of *A Tale of Two Cities*: "It was the best of times, it was the worst of times." That at least captures the spirit of the fevered revisionism now unfolding. On the one hand, there are analysts such as *Kappan* contributor Gerald Bracey who argue that contemporary critics of education — myself included — are simply myopic naysayers who are attacking public schools for personal or ideological reasons. Luckily, there is nothing ideological about Bracey.

Then there is Jonathan Kozol. He believes that American education has gone to hell in a handcart (unlike Bracey, who appears to believe that reports of its decrepitude are greatly exaggerated). But Kozol's demonology turns out to be much the same as Bracey's: dread conservatives.

In Kozol's world, however, we are not just carping critics, misanthropes, and misguided methodologists; we are starving public schools into submission.

That the critics of the critics are themselves divided suggests the emergence of a modern scholasticism, in which fierce pleasure is taken in playing with the statement of the problem rather than with the problem itself. Numbers are marshaled to demonstrate that we critics have either over- or underreached: that is, things are not really as bad as they seem, or, as Kozol would have it, things are a lot worse. No matter, the critics are wrong. No doubt the next step will be to estimate the number of critics that can dance on the head of a pin. (In the case of angels, the scholastics contrived an appealing answer: an infinite number, because angels are immaterial. So too with critics?) One is reminded of Mark Twain's observation about Richard Wagner's music: "It is not as bad as it sounds."

Still, 10 years after the release of *A Nation at Risk*, it would be disingenuous not to admit that there is a powerful — and understandable — desire to assert that all is well. People do need a break. In particular, teachers and principals feel, with some justification, that they have been treated unkindly.

By and large, educators do not embrace the politicians' adage that the only thing worse than bad news is no news, and in fairness to educators it must be noted that the Eighties were not a pleasant decade in which to be an educator. But is it equally the case that educators have not, on balance, seized on the events of the Eighties as an opportunity to make things better? That, of course, was the reason for all the criticism to begin with.

As it happened, however, after the release of *A Nation at Risk* in 1983, most of the important books and reports of the Eighties did not dwell on a litany of complaint and criticism. We didn't need to. The projects with which I was associated — the Committee for Economic Development's 1985 report, *Investing in Our Children: Business and the Schools*; the book I co-authored with former Deputy Secretary of Education David Kearns, *Winning the Brain Race*; and the 175-page *Business Week* white paper, *Children of Promise* — deliberately steered away from the sorry state of public education, except for the briefest reprise to set the stage. My collaborators on these projects and I were convinced that a catalogue of horrors was not the way to stimulate change. Equally to the point, we believed that any description of how bad things are can only be justified if it is accompanied by constructive ideas about reform and renewal.

Not to put too fine a point on it, even in the best of times criticism serves only one legitimate function: to stimulate change. Without that objective it is both cynical and counterproductive. Yet the recent spate of revisionist arguments strikes me as equally cynical. Is it meant to suggest that we should leave well enough alone? Or that the only hope is a socialist workers' paradise? Attempting to unscramble the omelet is not only time-consuming, but it also diverts attention from real issues. We do have problems to solve.

And what might they be? The simple fact is that American education faces a productivity crisis. This assertion is neither name-calling nor carping criticism. It does not represent fantastical claims about either the problem or its solution. It

From *Phi Delta Kappan*, Vol. 74, No. 8, April 1993, pp. 626-631. © 1993 by Phi Delta Kappa, Inc. Reprinted by permission.

is both an analytic perspective and a simple statement of fact with powerful policy implications. To date, its absence as an analytic perspective has been a source of disappointment and great mischief because that absence makes it almost impossible to answer such sensible questions as, "How well are American schools doing in light of their expenditures?" or "What is the value added by schooling?" or "How great are the returns on human capital investment?"

THIS VIEW OF education, of course, owes a debt to the dismal science, economics — particularly political economics — which is preoccupied with questions concerning the allocation of scarce resources. We never have as much of many things as we might like: education, fine wine, medical care, inexpensive transportation, leisure — select your own list. This proposition is self-evident. On occasion, however, the issue of relative scarcity becomes more important than at other times. In the Sixties, before Vietnam at least, we enjoyed both guns and butter. This is not to be in the Nineties.

President Clinton and the Congress face deficits — current accounts, trade, and budget — so large that there is little room to maneuver. Without reciting the numbers in detail, suffice it to say that there is not enough room in local, state, and federal budgets to buy our way out of the educational impasse. There may be some new money for education — but not much. Schools will simply have to work smarter.

Let us agree to the following propositions: budgets for American education are necessarily limited, and American education is not as efficient — or as humane — as it must be if we are to face the next century with confidence. Does anyone really doubt these statements? It should be clear that this is not solely an economic argument, though it includes an economic component.

By "productivity crisis" I mean that schools must learn to do more with less — or, better yet, much more with a little bit more. I do not mean that schools as they once were failed; indeed, historically they have met their purposes reasonably well. So, too, did Detroit, at least through the era of "muscle cars." Remember the movie *A Man and a Woman*? The story line's centerpiece was a Mustang, the American car that was to

There is not enough room in local, state, and federal budgets to buy our way out of the educational impasse.

catapult Lee Iacocca to fame and fortune. Imagine the French glorifying an American car in the 1990s. How times have changed. The point is that Detroit's problem over the past few decades is not that it forgot how to make muscle cars or that someone else made them better or cheaper. Muscle cars are out. Period. Detroit didn't get it. Detroit couldn't figure out how to make the transition into the modern era. So too with schools.

But a problem remains. To most educators, no matter how the terms are defined or explained, such words as *efficiency* and *productivity* are verboten when talking about schools. They conjure up images of time-and-motion studies — of white-jacketed efficiency experts with stopwatches and clipboards, who understand the cost of everything and the value of nothing. But in the postindustrial world (or the postcapitalist world, as Peter Drucker now describes it), productivity has a very different meaning. It means the most efficient deployment of resources in the most effective work environment that can be designed.

Mine is not an argument for more or less spending on schools; it is an argument on behalf of better use of whatever we've got. The modern productivity model for schools is not Frederick Taylor's factory — but the symphony orchestra; Drucker's well-run, not-for-profit organization (e.g., the Red Cross or Girl Scouts); or the modern high-tech, high-performance firm. What do these modern organizational forms have in common with schools? In the days when the factory was king, when the gate clanged shut

at night, the capitalist's wealth was locked securely inside. At the end of the workday in these modern organizations, when the door swings closed behind the last worker, the organization's wealth, its capital (human in this case), has gone home for the evening.

Consider another analogy. Remember the days of the early mainframe computers? Not only did they produce great amounts of heat, but they were extremely sensitive to changes in temperature and humidity. As a consequence, the rooms that housed them were the first parts of an organization to be fully air-conditioned, 24 hours a day, 365 days a year. Workers should be so lucky. Yet in modern high-performance organizations, they are. Indeed, it is a matter not of luck but of good sense. Today's managers — at least those with their wits about them — recognize that their most valuable resource is their workers. And it is more often the case today that employees are not considered workers at all, but associates. The employer is the manager of production.

BEFORE I consider the implications of "productivity" as the central concern of the modern firm, however, let me turn briefly to the two questions that must be dealt with if we are to reform education rationally: What is good about American education? And what is bad about American education?

In important respects, the questions are not empirical but normative. True, test scores and other quantitative indicators can be marshaled in support of the schools' performance, but they are largely empty indicators, because they do not relate to an accepted metric. Such research can answer questions that ask, "How much?" But those that ask, "How much is enough?" can be answered only in the domains of philosophy and politics.

So how do I answer them? What is good about American education? What is bad? The two themes intertwine. American education is democratic, egalitarian, and meritocratic. It is robust, dynamic, and resilient. It is responsive — at least to fads of the moment — and it is well financed, by any measure. It is radically decentralized, at least by world standards, and each component of the education system, from humble rural school districts to great research universities, stands on its own bottom. Attempts to

> *American youngsters do not believe that their school performance will greatly affect their later life.*

centralize education have largely failed — save only the movement over the past 50 years to consolidate school districts. Yet even in this area the 15,700 that remain (of more than 100,000 before World War II) are largely "independent."

Indeed, the marked sameness that characterizes American education — the fact that most of our schools look alike and behave similarly — is a commentary on the power of the culture of education, rather than a reflection of statutes or administrative regulations. The similarity of statutes from state to state is as much a product as a cause of that uniformity.

The consequence of this decentralization (at least as it appears to foreigners) is a system that is a system in name only. In fact, American education is most accurately described as "measured anarchy." What does this mean to the participants? Enormous freedom, including the freedom to fail. As long as they observe the rituals of the school and respect the privacy of their office or classroom, teachers and principals are largely free to do as they like. So too are students. In fact, in no other aspect of American education is the anarchic tendency so strong as among students. As long as they observe the minimum conventions of civility and behavior, students may do pretty much what they like — to the chagrin of teachers, parents, administrators, and serious students alike, I might add. But this has always been so.

The upside of this set of arrangements is schooling without equal for those who are disciplined, energetic, motivated, and supported by family and friends. And in our anarchic system, these traits may surface at any time in a student's career, even though, as a practical matter, surfacing early is to be preferred to surfacing late. But surface late they do in the case of many students, in which event the American passion for "second chances" comes into full play. America, of course, is a nation of second chances; that is what we are all about. We are a nation of immigrants. As Octavio Paz notes in his marvelous account, *One Earth, Four or Five Worlds*, America is the quintessential second-chance society. A new people in a new world, freed of the baggage of hereditary class, Americans invent themselves anew with each generation.

Not surprisingly, these habits extend well beyond school. America is a global scandal in terms of the rate of small business failure; Europeans and Asians are simply aghast. But they are equally astonished and impressed by the rate of small business formation, which is the flip side of failure. It is not too much to assert that small business failure is the true school of hard knocks, in which entrepreneurs learn the ropes the hard way. So prevalent are such failures that, alone in the industrialized world, no stigma attaches to having failed in America — not as long as you get up and try again.

So too with school. The school dropout can, if sufficiently energetic, drop back in — if not to the school he left, then to another. Or he can earn an equivalency diploma or, on occasion, go straight to a community or four-year college. So "naturally" and so readily is this done that we take it for granted. Today, for example, the average age of postsecondary students hovers around 30, and it is the rare undergraduate who finishes a course of study in four consecutive years.

But if this fluid and dynamic system works well for some, it has a terrible downside for many. In particular, youngsters from disorganized backgrounds, broken homes, and poverty — and even more particularly, students who are members of microcultures that do not prize education — find themselves left out. Sadly, this lack of a support network too often characterizes poverty-stricken minority youths, students who need to capitalize on their first chance and who are unlikely to seek and find second chances.

As John Ogbu, a sociologist at the University of California, Berkeley, points out, profoundly disadvantaged Americans look like nothing so much as members of a lower caste: outcasts. This distinction helps explain why boat people — poor, dispossessed, speaking little or no English — can rise so rapidly and decisively in American public schools. They do not think of themselves as outcasts; they think of themselves as individuals who, through diligence and hard work, can significantly improve their life chances. And they are right. Ironically, it is they who best exemplify the American Dream.

This, then, is what is wrong with American education: it has no systematic and effective way to deal with youngsters who do not see themselves as part of the system — who, for whatever reason, are not *workers*. Neither American education nor the larger society motivates these youngsters. The enabling power that education confers is kept secret from them. Because they hate school, their lives become a cruel hoax. Unlike students in Japan and Europe — who know that their life chances will be decided by how well they do in school — American youngsters do not believe that their performance in school will have a great deal of impact on their later life. To many of these youngsters, education is not an opportunity but a burden, one to be tolerated at best or more frequently avoided altogether. When asked how he escaped Harlem's mean streets to become a Navy pilot, Drew Brown, son of boxing promoter Budini Brown, attributes his success to his devoted father's admonition: "College or death!"

HOWEVER, the views of American education I have set forth raise the risk of two unwelcome interpretations. First, it is possible to indulge in the popular sport of blaming the victim. As the late, unlamented Gov. Lester Maddox of Georgia observed, when asked about improving his state prison system, "It can't be done without a better class of prisoner."

The second possible unwelcome interpretation would lead us to ask the schools to bear more weight than they can carry. Because schools are first and foremost educational institutions, they are poorly suited to deliver noneducational services, popular impressions to the contrary notwithstanding.

The view that schools should somehow be social service providers has, of course, gained wide currency because of its superficial plausibility. Kids have problems; kids are in school; ergo, solve the problems in the school. There is a rough justice in this notion, and in theory it makes administrative sense. Inoculations, well-baby screening, feeding programs, Norplant implants, condom distribution, contacts with case workers, and similar activities can in fact take place in school buildings. And it is surely the case that schools are a convenient place to track down young people, at least as long as compulsory attendance is the law of the land. Moreover, hungry, sick, and disoriented children do not make good students, and ameliorating their problems is both a good thing to do in its own right and good for the schools.

But if the problems presented by youngsters from disorganized backgrounds make it difficult for schools to go about their business, it is not clear that schools should enter the business of providing social services. Put plainly, if schools can't teach a youngster to read, can they minister to his or her social needs? While the question is no doubt in part empirical, management theory provides some guidance. As Peter Drucker observes, effective organizations *optimize*; they do not *maximize*. They do what they are good at and let others do what they are good at.

What does this have to do with schools? They too should optimize. And what they are good at — one hopes — is educating youngsters. That some of their charges are poor and dispossessed does not lead ineluctably to the idea that schools should attempt to fill the social service breach. It is self-evidently true that a wealthy society that cares about its future must care for its children. But children's social needs are not necessarily best met in school.

I belabor this obvious point because so many defenders of the public schools have begun to assert that the problems of the public schools are the problems of their clients. Indeed, the assertion is so often made that schools cannot deal with "these" children that it is a commonplace. That it is usually offered as a rationale for school failure is too often overlooked. So close to "blaming the victim" is this assertion that one wonders if it is a distinction without a difference. Be that as it may, I am convinced that we must draw a distinction between the social and educational needs of children and not use the former as an excuse not to fulfill the latter.

To return to Drucker's distinction, the schools must optimize. They must ask themselves what their mission is, who their clients are, how they are to deliver the service called education, how they measure its quality, and how they know when they've met their goals. If schools try to be all things to all students — if they try to maximize — they will serve no one well. If they decide that they are social service institutions first and educational institutions second, they are not likely to meet either objective successfully. But if they decide that they are first and foremost educational institutions, charged with the responsibility of educating children, there is at least a chance that they may succeed.

The sorry fact is that most schools are not doing what they should be doing. And what they are doing, they are not doing well. They remind me of the Woody Allen routine in which a little old lady complains to her companion about airplane food. "Isn't it awful?" she asks. "Yes," her companion responds, "it certainly is, and the portions are so small!"

The one thing schools can and should do about the issue of social services is best illustrated by a program unfolding in Charlotte, North Carolina. No stranger to disadvantaged children, the schools in Charlotte are undertaking a comprehensive inventory of the needs of children; creating a catalogue of community resources, public and private; identifying the gaps in services; and bringing these gaps — deliberately, even provocatively — to the attention of the community as a whole. The superintendent, John Murphy, meets each month with representatives of the Charlotte Interfaith Council to coordinate a response. The Interfaith Council plans to build a countywide preschool network — the first facility opened in February 1993 — and the Charlotte schools are creating a pre-K parent/teacher organization to orient new parents. As evidence of how seriously it takes the issue, the school system will soon provide a brochure for mothers in the maternity ward. The objective: to welcome the newborns, but also to let parents know what their responsibilities are in helping their children get ready for school.

The strategy behind these programs stems from Charlotte's refusal to let its education budget hemorrhage in a futile attempt to *improvise* children's services. The school can sound the alarm, act as an honest broker, and make its facilities available. But responsibility for providing children's services lies with the community as a whole.

WHAT, THEN, is my vision of the future for education? First, debating the question of the quality of American schools — Are they as bad as the critics say? Are they better? — is a sterile and counterproductive exercise. Truly, it is the intellectual equivalent of rearranging the deck chairs on the *Titanic*. No good purpose is served by the exercise. The only legitimate reason to raise the question of school quality is to improve the schools. The question we must ask is, Are schools good enough for the future? Does anyone truly believe that they are?

The list of what might be done to improve our schools is understandably long, and I propose to treat only two examples here. Earlier I suggested that we need a coordinated children's policy; schools cannot go it alone. But at the same time, American schools face a productivity crisis. That is, they expect too little of teachers and students, and expecting little gets little. Few penalties — other than the remote possibility of failure as an adult, an incomprehensible idea for most adolescents — attach to a failure to perform, and few rewards attach to academic success.

As to the first part of the problem, the details of a children's policy are simply beyond the scope of this essay. I note only that such a policy is desirable, probably necessary, and possible *only if* President Clinton, working with his domestic policy council and relevant Cabinet members, can actually bring about real — I emphasize *real* — collaboration among the federal Departments of Education, Health and Human Services, and Labor (he could even encourage Commerce, Defense, and Energy to play a role). As an opponent of the creation of the Department of Education, I am fascinated that the interest groups that insisted that President Carter create it now lament the lack of connection between education and children's services. Might they ask Mr. Clinton to put the "E" back into HEW?

Whatever the interest groups do or fail to do, Washington is a major part of the problem. Consider employment, welfare, and health policies for starters. Washington must become part of the solution, and that means employment, welfare, and health policy reform on a massive scale if any lasting improvements in the condition of children are to be made. And it should be clear to all that education reform will not reach the poorest of the poor unless their social conditions are ameliorated.

Let me close by returning to my initial assertion that the real problem of American schools is a productivity crisis. Yet this problem is also an opportunity. Ironically, inefficiency — slack in the system — provides opportunities to save and invest and to improve dramatically. As an analogy, consider Americans' profligate use of energy. Wasting as much as we do, it is relatively easy, through conservation, to save a great deal of energy. In this light, we can see that there is one thing that schools can do for themselves that would make a difference: they can "benchmark."

Benchmarking, originally a topographical and nautical practice of defining permanent reference points against which measurements are made, has been appropriated by U.S. business, first by the Xerox Corporation, now by most high-tech, high-performance organizations. Not widely understood among educators, it is worth describing briefly. First, it is a form of self-measurement; it cannot be imposed from the outside. It is not a club with which to beat an organization over the head; it is a tool to permit members of the organization to improve their own performance by better understanding how other successful organizations achieve their success.

By way of illustration, Xerox seeks and finds the best performers in industry — not just other copier manufacturers, though Xerox looks at them closely, but the best performers, period. For copiers and office equipment, Xerox looks first at its direct competitors. When Xerox discovered that the Japanese were designing, manufacturing, assembling, shipping, and retailing high-quality copiers for less

than it took Xerox to manufacture them, the company recognized a clear message: restructure or collapse. Xerox chose the first course and remains one of the few American corporations to recapture market share from the Japanese.

In looking at generic processes, however, such as inventory control and management, the best performer Xerox could find was not Toyota or Kodak but L. L. Bean, the clothing and outdoor-wear catalogue house in Freeport, Maine. That's the standard of quality to which Xerox compares itself today. For customer response, in terms of both timeliness and courtesy, Xerox compares itself to Florida Light and Power.

Benchmarking is a form of accountability with special significance for public sector organizations — insulated as they are from the play of market forces — because, if it is to work, benchmarking must be self-imposed. It cannot be ordered up by a remote bureaucracy. Benchmarking forces organizations to rethink everything they do, from recruiting to compensation, from objectives to measurement, from assessment to management.

What kinds of things should benchmarking make schools think about? Outputs rather than inputs. The role of effort rather than innate ability. The importance of "mastery" as the appropriate measure of success in education. Making students workers and teachers managers of instruction. Using administrators as facilitators and superintendents as choreographers rather than autocrats. Using technology to increase output and not simply as glitz. These are only a few of the ideas that benchmarking will force schools to deal with.

That is precisely the challenge — and

the opportunity — American schools face. If they begin to benchmark seriously, they will compare themselves to the best of the best, not just in public elementary and secondary schools, but also in high-performance organizations. The power of benchmarking is that it does internally what competition is supposed to do externally: it holds organizations to high standards of performance, measurement, and reporting. It accepts no excuses. It is continuous. There is no finish line.

What's right with American education? There's much that's right. It has a proud history and an honorable tradition, it is generously funded, it is staffed by men and women of good will, and it is resilient. What's wrong with American education? It misconceives its own best interests in the Nineties; it tries to maximize when it should optimize; it comes perilously close to playing Lester Maddox with its clients, hoping for a "better class of student" as its salvation; and it sees problems where it should see opportunities.

What are the prospects for the future of American education? They are good. Criticism — constructive criticism — is the lifeblood of healthy organizations, just as it is the keystone of democracy. With it, conditions may be improved; without it, progress never occurs. It is for that reason that closed societies will not tolerate criticism; they fear it because they know it is the engine of change and renewal. But as important as criticism is, it is only a call to arms. It begins, but does not end, the dialogue. It is necessary but not sufficient. Constructive critics know that the time has come for American education to move on — toward solutions.

Credits/ Acknowledgments

Cover design by Charles Vitelli

1. How Others See Us and How We See Ourselves

Facing overview—The Dushkin Publishing Group, Inc., photo by Richard Pawlikowski of R. P. Photo. 7, 10-11—Illustrations by David Suter. 20—The New York Public Library Picture Collection photo.

2. Change and Rethinking of the Educative Effort

Facing overview—United Nations photo by John Isaac.

3. Striving for Excellence

Facing overview—Photo courtesy of Apple Computer, Inc.

4. Morality and Value in Education

Facing overview—United Nations photo by John Isaac.

5. Managing Life in Classrooms

Facing overview—Photo by Steve Takatsuno.

6. Equality of Educational Opportunity

Facing overview—Photo by Phil Degginger of Drew University. 140—Map by Angela Ulm of the *Christian Science Monitor.*

7. Serving Special Needs and Concerns

Facing overview—United Nations photo by Milton Grant.

8. The Profession of Teaching Today

Facing overview—The Dushkin Publishing Group, Inc., photo by Pamela Carley.

9. A Look to the Future

Facing overview—Photo courtesy of Apple Computer, Inc.

ANNUAL EDITIONS ARTICLE REVIEW FORM

■ NAME: _____ DATE: _____

■ TITLE AND NUMBER OF ARTICLE: _____

■ BRIEFLY STATE THE MAIN IDEA OF THIS ARTICLE: _____

_____

_____

_____

_____

■ LIST THREE IMPORTANT FACTS THAT THE AUTHOR USES TO SUPPORT THE MAIN IDEA:

_____

_____

_____

_____

_____

_____

■ WHAT INFORMATION OR IDEAS DISCUSSED IN THIS ARTICLE ARE ALSO DISCUSSED IN YOUR
TEXTBOOK OR OTHER READING YOU HAVE DONE? LIST THE TEXTBOOK CHAPTERS AND PAGE
NUMBERS:

_____

_____

_____

_____

_____

_____

■ LIST ANY EXAMPLES OF BIAS OR FAULTY REASONING THAT YOU FOUND IN THE ARTICLE:

_____

_____

_____

_____

■ LIST ANY NEW TERMS/CONCEPTS THAT WERE DISCUSSED IN THE ARTICLE AND WRITE A
SHORT DEFINITION:

_____

_____

_____

_____

_____

*Your instructor may require you to use this Annual Editions Article Review Form in any number of ways:
for articles that are assigned, for extra credit, as a tool to assist in developing assigned papers, or simply
for your own reference. Even if it is not required, we encourage you to photocopy and use this page;
you'll find that reflecting on the articles will greatly enhance the information from your text.

We Want Your Advice

ANNUAL EDITIONS: EDUCATION 95/96
Article Rating Form

Here is an opportunity for you to have direct input into the next revision of this volume. We would like you to rate each of the 46 articles listed below, using the following scale:

1. Excellent: should definitely be retained
2. Above average: should probably be retained
3. Below average: should probably be deleted
4. Poor: should definitely be deleted

Your ratings will play a vital part in the next revision. So please mail this prepaid form to us just as soon as you complete it.
Thanks for your help!

Annual Editions revisions depend on two major opinion sources: one is our Advisory Board, listed in the front of this volume, which works with us in scanning the thousands of articles published in the public press each year; the other is you—the person actually using the book. Please help us and the users of the next edition by completing the prepaid article rating form on this page and returning it to us. Thank you.

Rating	Article	Rating	Article
	1. America Skips School: Why We Talk So Much about Education and Do So Little		24. Investing in Our Children: A Struggle for America's Conscience and Future
	2. School Reform: What's Missing		25. Concerns about Teaching Culturally Diverse Students
	3. What's Behind the Decline of Public Schools?		26. School Guides Students to Goals and Self-Respect
	4. International Report Card Shows U.S. Schools Work		27. The Gender Machine
	5. The 26th Annual Phi Delta Kappa/Gallup Poll of the Public's Attitudes toward the Public Schools		28. The AAUW Report: How Schools Shortchange Girls
			29. The Case for Homeschooling
	6. On to the Past: Wrong-Headed School Reform		30. Violence as a Public Health Issue for Children
	7. European Schools Offer Contrasts and Similarities		31. Everyday School Violence: How Disorder Fuels It
	8. Selling the Schools: Is Private Enterprise the Future of Public Education in America?		32. Poverty, Rape, Adult/Teen Sex: Why 'Pregnancy Prevention' Programs Don't Work
	9. Myths & Facts about Private School Choice		33. Blowing up the Tracks
	10. The Precarious Politics Of Privatizing Schools		34. Everyone Is an Exception: Assumptions to Avoid in the Sex Education Classroom
	11. Redirecting Reform: Challenges to Popular Assumptions about Teachers and Students		35. Building a Smarter Work Force
			36. How to Recognize Good Teaching
	12. High Standards for All?		37. Needed: A New Literacy
	13. Blueprint for Renewal		38. Giving Their Best: Grading and Recognition Practices That Motivate Students to Work Hard
	14. Stop Expecting the Worst of Schools		
	15. The Return of Character Education		39. Educating for Understanding: An Interview with Howard Gardner
	16. Ethnic Studies and Ethics Studies: A Study in Contrasts?		40. Challenges to the Public School Curriculum: New Targets and Strategies
	17. Why Johnny Can't Tell Right from Wrong		41. Building School Communities: An Experience-Based Model
	18. Ethical Communication in the Classroom		
	19. Conflict Resolution and Peer Mediation: Pathways to Safer Schools		42. Exploring the Thinking of Thoughtful Teachers
	20. Middle-Schoolers "Do Justice" by Their Classmates		43. Five Standards of Authentic Instruction
			44. Searching for Terms
	21. How to Create Discipline Problems		45. The Plug-In School: A Learning Environment for the 21st Century
	22. A Lesson Plan Approach for Dealing with School Discipline		
	23. The Canon Debate, Knowledge Construction, and Multicultural Education		46. American Schools: Good, Bad, or Indifferent?

(Continued on next page)

ABOUT YOU

Name_____ Date_____

Are you a teacher? ☐ Or student? ☐

Your School Name _____

Department _____

Address _____

City _____ State _____ Zip _____

School Telephone # _____

YOUR COMMENTS ARE IMPORTANT TO US!

Please fill in the following information:

For which course did you use this book? _____

Did you use a text with this Annual Edition? ☐ yes ☐ no

The title of the text? _____

What are your general reactions to the Annual Editions concept?

Have you read any particular articles recently that you think should be included in the next edition?

Are there any articles you feel should be replaced in the next edition? Why?

Are there other areas that you feel would utilize an Annual Edition?

May we contact you for editorial input?

May we quote you from above?